Real-Time Data Decisions With AI and ChatGPT Techniques

Priyanka Sharma
Swami Keshvanand Institute of Technology, Management, and Gramothan, Jaipur, India

Monika Jyotiyana
Manipal University Jaipur, India

A.V. Senthil Kumar
Hindusthan College of Arts and Science, India

IGI Global
Publishing Tomorrow's Research Today

Published in the United States of America by
IGI Global
701 E. Chocolate Avenue
Hershey PA, USA 17033
Tel: 717-533-8845
Fax: 717-533-8661
E-mail: cust@igi-global.com
Web site: https://www.igi-global.com

Library of Congress Cataloging-in-Publication Data

CIP Data Pending
ISBN: 979-8-3693-2284-0
eISBN: 979-8-3693-2285-7

British Cataloguing in Publication Data
A Cataloguing in Publication record for this book is available from the British Library.

Table of Contents

Detailed Table of Contents

Krithikaa Venket, KCG College of Technology, India
Anju Ambika, KCG College of Technology, India
Adline Freeda, KCG College of Technology, India

Artificial intelligence (AI) has evolved as a game-changer across industries, presenting unprecedented opportunities in the field of engineering. In this landscape, AI-driven models like ChatGPT have emerged as pivotal tools, showcasing remarkable potential in reshaping traditional engineering paradigms. At the core of this evolution lies the capacity of AI, particularly language models like ChatGPT, to enhance problem-solving methodologies within engineering. By leveraging vast datasets and natural language processing capabilities, ChatGPT assists engineers in dissecting complex problems, offering insightful solutions, and expediting decision-making processes. Its ability to comprehend human language and generate contextually relevant responses fosters efficient communication, enabling streamlined collaboration among engineers, architects, and stakeholders. Moreover, AI augments the creative aspect of engineering endeavors.

Dwijendra Nath Dwivedi, Krakow University of Economics, Poland
Ghanashyama Mahanty, Utkal University, India
Varunendra Nath Dwivedi, SRM University, India

This chapter explores the transformative impact of artificial intelligence (AI) and ChatGPT techniques in facilitating real-time data-driven decision-making within government sectors. The adoption of AI and advanced language models like ChatGPT represents a significant shift in how governments process vast amounts of information to make timely and informed decisions. The research focuses on the application of these technologies in enhancing governmental operations, policy-making, and public services. Case studies are presented to illustrate the practical applications of these technologies in various government functions such as public health management, accelerating teaching and learning, urban planning, environmental monitoring, and emergency response. Additionally, the chapter addresses the ethical considerations and the need for robust data governance frameworks to ensure the responsible use of AI in government. This includes discussion on data privacy, security, and the potential risks of bias in AI models.

The introduction of generative AI technologies has brought about an abrupt shift in the area of medical imaging analysis. In this comprehensive investigation, the authors look at how generative AI has been used and how it has been improved for medical picture analysis. An exhaustive analysis of the methods, difficulties, and developments in this dynamic field is the goal of this research. The limitations of traditional medical imaging modalities are thoroughly discussed in the first part of the chapter. This foundation must be laid before generative adversarial networks (GANs) and other models of generative artificial intelligence may be applied. The purpose of this thorough investigation is to catalog and evaluate noteworthy trends and emerging problems in medical imaging-related generative artificial intelligence (AI) research. The revolutionary influence of generative artificial intelligence (AI) on medical imaging analysis is better understood after reading this extensive review. By synthesizing and detecting gaps, this project benefits academics and healthcare professionals.

The technology integration for AI in various sectors focuses on how this technology can be used to optimize the production process, generate meaningful and automated customer support, or develop personalized recommendations for shoppers. The apparel industry is starting to integrate automation technology and replace manual labor in certain production links with mechanization as a result of its advancement and maturity. Artificial intelligence allows us to substitute human labor for intelligent robots in order to accomplish repetitive tasks that are relatively labor-intensive. In addition, errors are more likely to occur and productivity declines with extended work hours. Embracing AI technologies and integrating them into marketing and operational strategies helps to maintain the business with competitiveness but also set the standard for developing a strong and memorable brand presence in the digital age.

This chapter delves into the amalgamation of technology and online retail. Analyzing ChatGPT's role in user experiences, from queries to product recommendations, the study emphasizes technological and ethical considerations. It investigates ChatGPT's capability to enhance customer interaction despite the nuances of natural language understanding, revolutionize support services and being able to comprehend regional variations, facilitate product discovery based on customer's choices. At the same time, it highlights the need for businesses to consider data security, user trust and perception issues, and compliance with regulations in an ever-changing environment. Benefits and challenges are highlighted, along with ethical and social considerations. A comprehensive literature survey identifies research gaps and future directions for ChatGPT in e-commerce.

This study explores the integration of artificial intelligence (AI), particularly ChatGPT, in media communications to enhance real-time data decision-making. It evaluates AI's potential to improve operational efficiency and accuracy in media production through quantitative and qualitative research. Despite the promising advantages, the study acknowledges significant challenges and ethical considerations, including biases and the impact on journalistic integrity. The findings highlight a growing trend towards adopting AI in media, recommending continuous research and ethical vigilance.

This chapter explores the use of ChatGPT, an AI-driven language model, in programming code development. It introduces ChatGPT, detailing its conceptual definition, historical evolution, features, and applications. The pivotal role of ChatGPT in code development, encompassing generation, debugging, and learning, is discussed. Advantages include heightened productivity, improved code quality, enhanced learning, secure code generation, reduced error risks, and increased creativity. Challenges involve limited comprehension, potential for erroneous or insecure code, overreliance, lack of transparency, job market impact, ethical concerns, and the future of programming. Practical applications include web development, debugging, and language learning. Best practices emphasize task definition, contextual information, code verification, and recognizing ChatGPT as a tool, not a substitute for human programmers. The chapter provides a concise overview, addressing benefits, challenges, practical examples, and best practices in utilizing ChatGPT for programming code development.

It is crucial to discuss ChatGPT's safety, confidentiality, and ethical consequences despite its enormous potential in a variety of fields, including client service, learning, treatment for mental illnesses, personal productivity, and content creation. Malicious material, such as phishing attempts, false narratives, and fake news, can be produced using AI technologies. It's important for both users and developers to be cautious about potential misuses of AI-generated content. Artificial intelligence possesses the capability to be employed in social engineering assaults, swaying public opinion, and propagating misleading data. It's imperative to acknowledge the potential for abuse. Artificial intelligence models are susceptible to attacks like adversarial inputs, skillfully constructed modifications to the input data can produce unexpected results. In order to defend against these kinds of assaults, developers must have strong security measures in place.

A subset of biometrics called palm recognition has drawn a lot of interest because of its potential applications in a variety of fields, including as security systems and human-computer interaction. Convolutional neural networks (CNNs) are being used in this effort to look at the creation of a palm detecting system. In order to identify and classify palm orientation in digital photos, deep learning will be used. An essential part of the study is data collection, which comprises compiling a large dataset of accurately labeled palm photos for supervised learning. The authors handle data preparation and use methods like image scaling, pixel normalization, and data augmentation to get datasets ready for model training. The system is based on a CNN model architecture, which creates a neural network with the ability to intelligently classify and automatically gather data from palm photos. Convolutional layers are used in this architecture to extract features, while fully connected layers are used for classification.

Preface

Welcome to *Real-Time Data Decisions with AI and ChatGPT Techniques*. This edited reference book is a collaborative effort by Priyanka Sharma, Monika Jyotiyana, and A. V. Senthil Kumar, designed to delve into the transformative potential of ChatGPT and other artificial intelligence tools in various sectors.

ChatGPT, a potent text-based artificial intelligence technology, stands at the forefront of revolutionizing customer engagement and content production for enterprises. By automating repetitive tasks, enhancing client interaction, and responding to complex queries with efficiency and accuracy, ChatGPT leverages data science to improve chatbot dialogues, making them more organic and engaging for users. Through machine learning techniques like sentiment analysis and natural language processing, ChatGPT's chatbots can understand client intent, personalize responses, and even anticipate needs.

Artificial intelligence has seamlessly integrated into our daily lives, from asking Alexa to play a song to unlocking our phones using face recognition. Now, AI extends its capabilities to assist with writing, generating essays, coding, composing emails, and excelling in tests on command. Despite its popularity sometimes leading to overload and unreliability for regular use, numerous other AI tools are available to perform requested tasks.

In this modern era of artificial intelligence, there is a clear need for an edited collection of original research in this area. This book aims to present fresh concepts and in-depth analysis, offering readers a broader perspective on ChatGPT and other AI tools. We have solicited chapters discussing algorithmic elements related to improving current approaches and developing new methodologies that achieve similar objectives to ChatGPT and related AI technologies.

Our target audience includes professionals, policymakers, budding researchers, social science researchers, academicians, industry professionals, and domain experts with interests in artificial intelligence, machine learning, image processing, ChatGPT, and other AI tools. This book highlights how AI leads to social and community benefits, efficient resource use, and an easier life. Given the uniqueness of this theme, very few books are available in the global market, making this work a valuable contribution.

We hope this book serves as a comprehensive resource for understanding and exploring the vast possibilities of ChatGPT and AI technologies. It is our pleasure to present this collection of knowledge and insights to you.

ORGANIZATION OF THE BOOK

Chapter 1: AI and ChatGPT Benefits, Implications, and Expectations in Engineering

This chapter offers a thorough examination of ChatGPT's evolution and its potential implications within engineering, with a spotlight on the critical role of Artificial Intelligence (AI). It provides an in-depth analysis of ChatGPT's architecture, capabilities, and applications across various engineering disciplines, focusing on significant advancements in natural language understanding and generation. The chapter discusses how ChatGPT aids engineers in design optimization, technical documentation, problem-solving, code generation, and simulation, while also addressing ethical compliance. Future research directions are outlined, emphasizing new applications, ethical considerations, integration with emerging technologies, and interdisciplinary collaboration.

Chapter 2: Integrating ChatGPT and AI Technologies in Engineering Fields

This chapter explores the transformative impact of AI-driven models like ChatGPT in the engineering domain. It highlights AI's ability to revolutionize traditional engineering practices by enhancing problem-solving methodologies and expediting decision-making processes through vast datasets and natural language processing. ChatGPT's capacity to comprehend human language and generate contextually relevant responses is showcased, promoting efficient communication and collaboration among engineers, architects, and stakeholders. The chapter also emphasizes AI's role in augmenting the creative aspects of engineering projects.

Chapter 3: ChatGPT and AI in Government: Pioneering Real-Time Data-Driven Strategies

This chapter examines the transformative role of AI and ChatGPT in enabling real-time data-driven decision-making within government sectors. The research highlights how AI and advanced language models like ChatGPT enhance governmental operations, policy-making, and public services. Case studies demonstrate practical applications in public health management, education, urban planning, environmental monitoring, and emergency response. The chapter also addresses ethical considerations and the necessity for robust data governance frameworks to ensure responsible AI use in government, covering data privacy, security, and potential biases in AI models.

Chapter 4: Improved Framework Model to Train and Evaluate Difficulty of Interview Questions Using Generative AI

This chapter addresses the demand for accurate question difficulty estimation tools. It presents an approach combining traditional linguistic and structural analysis with Generative AI to enhance question difficulty estimation. By diving deeper into documentation to formulate questions, the AI system generates more complex and rare questions. The chapter aims to refine the question difficulty estimator to better reflect the true complexity of technical questions, offering a multi-dimensional approach that integrates conventional techniques with advanced AI methods.

Chapter 5: Generative AI Techniques in Medical Imaging Analysis: A Systematic Review

This chapter explores the impact of generative AI technologies on medical imaging analysis. It provides an exhaustive review of methods, challenges, and advancements in this field. The discussion begins with the limitations of traditional medical imaging modalities and progresses to the application of generative adversarial networks (GANs) and other generative AI models. The chapter aims to catalog and evaluate significant trends and emerging issues in medical imaging-related generative AI research, offering insights that benefit both academics and healthcare professionals.

Chapter 6: Future of Ready-Made Garments Industry in Real-Time Data: An Application of AI

This chapter examines the integration of AI in the apparel industry, focusing on optimizing production processes, generating automated customer support, and developing personalized recommendations. AI-driven automation and mechanization are highlighted as means to replace manual labor, reduce errors, and enhance productivity. The chapter discusses how AI technologies can maintain competitiveness and establish a strong brand presence in the digital age, emphasizing the transformative potential of AI in the ready-made garments industry.

Chapter 7: Exploring the Potential and Challenges of ChatGPT in E-commerce Applications: A Comprehensive Review

This chapter explores the intersection of technology and online retail, focusing on ChatGPT's role in enhancing user experiences, from queries to product recommendations. It emphasizes technological and ethical considerations, investigating ChatGPT's ability to improve customer interaction and support services. The chapter highlights the need for businesses to address data security, user trust, perception issues, and regulatory compliance. Benefits and challenges are outlined, along with a comprehensive literature survey identifying research gaps and future directions for ChatGPT in e-commerce.

Chapter 8: Navigating the Future of Media: The Role of AI and ChatGPT in Facilitating Real-Time Data Decisions

This chapter evaluates the integration of AI, particularly ChatGPT, in media communications to enhance real-time data decision-making. It explores AI's potential to improve operational efficiency and accuracy in media production through both quantitative and qualitative research. The study acknowledges challenges and ethical considerations, including biases and the impact on journalistic integrity. The findings highlight the growing trend towards adopting AI in media, recommending continuous research and ethical vigilance.

Chapter 9: The Benefits and Challenges of Using ChatGPT to Develop Programming Codes

This chapter explores the use of ChatGPT in programming code development, covering its conceptual definition, historical evolution, features, and applications. It discusses ChatGPT's role in generating, debugging, and learning code, highlighting benefits such as increased productivity, improved code quality, and enhanced learning. Challenges include limited comprehension, potential for errors, overreliance, lack of transparency, and ethical concerns. The chapter provides practical applications and best practices, emphasizing task definition, contextual information, code verification, and recognizing ChatGPT as a tool to complement, not replace, human programmers.

Chapter 10: Security Concerns With ChatGPT and Other AI Tools

This chapter addresses the safety, confidentiality, and ethical implications of using ChatGPT and other AI tools. It discusses the potential for AI-generated malicious content, such as phishing attempts and fake news, and emphasizes the need for caution among users and developers. The chapter also explores the susceptibility of AI models to attacks like adversarial inputs and the necessity for robust security measures to defend against these threats.

Chapter 11: Opening Up the Next Generation of Convolutional Neural Networks (CNN) for Palm Recognition

This chapter focuses on the development of palm recognition systems using convolutional neural networks (CNNs). It details the data collection process, which involves compiling a large dataset of accurately labeled palm images for supervised learning. The chapter discusses data preparation techniques and the CNN model architecture, which includes convolutional layers for feature extraction and fully connected layers for classification. The goal is to create a neural network capable of intelligently classifying and automatically gathering data from palm images.

IN CONCLUSION

In this comprehensive exploration of ChatGPT and AI technologies, we have traversed a broad spectrum of applications and implications within engineering and beyond. The chapters collectively illuminate the transformative potential of AI-driven models, particularly ChatGPT, in reshaping traditional paradigms and fostering innovation across various domains.

From the foundational understanding of ChatGPT's architecture and its remarkable adaptability in natural language comprehension to its practical applications in engineering, government, healthcare, media, and e-commerce, this volume underscores the profound impact of AI on contemporary and future practices. Each chapter delves into specific facets, offering detailed analyses and insights into how ChatGPT enhances problem-solving, decision-making, and creative processes.

The discussions on ethical considerations, potential biases, and the need for robust data governance frameworks highlight the importance of responsible AI deployment. As we navigate the evolving landscape of AI technologies, it is crucial to balance innovation with ethical vigilance, ensuring that AI systems are designed and utilized in ways that uphold integrity, security, and trust.

The future of human-AI interaction, as envisaged through these scholarly contributions, is poised to be marked by greater efficiency, enhanced capabilities, and new opportunities for interdisciplinary collaboration. The insights presented here not only reflect the current state of AI and ChatGPT but also chart a course for future research and development, emphasizing the importance of continuous learning and adaptation.

As editors, we hope this reference book serves as a valuable resource for researchers, practitioners, and policymakers alike, providing a comprehensive understanding of ChatGPT and AI's role in shaping the future. We believe that by embracing these technologies thoughtfully and responsibly, we can harness their full potential to drive progress and create a positive impact across various fields.

The journey through these chapters has been one of discovery and insight, revealing the immense possibilities and challenges that lie ahead. We invite readers to delve deeply into each chapter, to question, to innovate, and to contribute to the ongoing dialogue on the future of AI in engineering and beyond.

Acknowledgment

The book *Real-Time Data Decisions With AI and ChatGPT Techniques* is based on recent trends, state-of-the-art techniques, research, various algorithms, challenges and practical & theoretical aspects of Artificial Intelligence and ChatGPT along with applications, pros & cons, future possibilities of AI and ChatGPT. Real-Time Data Decisions With AI and ChatGPT Techniques explores how artificial intelligence, specifically ChatGPT, is revolutionizing the way real-time data is processed and utilized for decision-making. The integration of AI and ChatGPT techniques allows for instantaneous analysis and response, significantly enhancing efficiency and accuracy in various fields.

Designing and crafting a book is a passion and noble objective for the editors also we want to connect with the worldwide academicians & researchers via this book. This book genuinely rewarding, made possible by the dedication, smart work, area of expertise, knowledge, experiences, eagerness, teamwork, and belief of all the author(s). We gratefully acknowledge the invaluable support and insightful assessment and comments provided by esteemed advisory members and reviewers globally. Their suggestions have significantly enhanced the book's quality. Despite geographical distances, we appreciate the opportunity to collaborate closely and monitor their diligent efforts, not only for this project but also for future endeavours. Our sincere gratitude extends to scholars, faculties, educators, professors, engineers, academicians and colleagues for their invaluable discussions, guidance, support, enthusiasm, collaboration, and inspiration.

Priyanka Sharma would dedicate this book to her parents Shri Atmaram Sharma and Smt. Geeta Sharma who have always been a back bone to her, for allowing and foregoing quality time to be dedicated to this book. A special acknowledgement of all the near and dear ones. Last but not the least special thanks to book co-editors Dr. Monika Jyotiyana and Dr. A. V. Senthil Kumar who have been constantly the driving force behind this project.

Dr. Monika Jyotiyana would like to dedicate this book to her parents Mr. Balwant Singh and Mrs. Vimla Jyotiyana, spouse and her best friend Mrs. Sonali Jain and her life support system Dr. Jyotsna Verma who have always been always good supporters in managing and editing the book. Special thanks to co-editor Ms. Priyanka Sharma, without her support and vision, the book can't be good success.

Thank you, everyone.

Introduction

Welcome to *Real-Time Data Decisions With AI and ChatGPT Techniques*. In this introductory chapter, we aim to set the stage for a comprehensive exploration of how text-based artificial intelligence, particularly ChatGPT, is revolutionizing various facets of enterprise operations, customer engagement, and content production.

The Evolution and Impact of ChatGPT

ChatGPT, a potent text-based artificial intelligence technology developed by OpenAI, stands at the forefront of revolutionizing customer engagement and content production for enterprises. By leveraging advanced data science techniques, ChatGPT has the capability to automate repetitive tasks, enhance client interactions, and respond to complex queries with remarkable efficiency and accuracy. This technology uses sophisticated machine learning techniques, such as sentiment analysis and natural language processing, to improve chatbot dialogues, making them more organic and engaging for users. The chatbots powered by ChatGPT are adept at understanding customer intent, personalizing responses, and even anticipating customer needs.

Artificial Intelligence in Daily Life

Artificial Intelligence has become an integral part of our daily lives. Even in day today activities like, asking Alexa to play your favorite song to unlocking your phone using face recognition, Artificial Intelligence (AI) technologies are ubiquitous. Now-a-days AI tools like, ChatGPT can assist in writing tasks, generate code, compose E-mails, and even tackle academic assignments. Despite its immense popularity, which sometimes leads to overloads and service disruptions, ChatGPT remains a powerful tool for many applications. However, it is not the only AI solution available; a plethora of other AI tools can also fulfill similar tasks efficiently.

The Need for This Book

The proliferation of AI in various domains underscores the necessity for a comprehensive resource that delves into the latest advancements and applications of these technologies. This book aims to present novel concepts and detailed analysis that provide readers and researchers with an extensive understanding of ChatGPT and other AI tools. By soliciting chapters that discuss both the enhancement of existing methodologies and the development of new approaches, we aspire to cover a wide range of topics relevant to AI and machine learning.

Impact of Research on Society

The research presented in this book underscores the significant impact of AI technologies on contemporary society. AI is not just a technological advancement; it is a transformative force reshaping industries, enhancing efficiency, and creating new opportunities, simplify the complex task, ease to use and accessible in every field like, business, digital marketing, academics, engineering, food & eatery business and many more. The implications of AI extend far beyond the realms of technology and business, influencing social structures, economic models, and even ethical standards.

Enhancing Public Services: One of the profound impacts of AI, as discussed in Chapter 3, is its role in government operations. AI-driven decision-making in public health, urban planning, and emergency response improves the quality and responsiveness of public services. For instance, AI can analyze vast datasets to predict and manage public health crises, optimize traffic flow in cities, and coordinate effective disaster response strategies.

Revolutionizing Industries: AI's integration into various industries, such as engineering (Chapter 1 and Chapter 2), healthcare (Chapter 5), and the garment industry (Chapter 6), highlights its transformative potential. In engineering, AI enhances design optimization, technical documentation, and problem-solving capabilities, driving innovation and efficiency. In healthcare, AI technologies, particularly generative AI, are revolutionizing medical imaging analysis, leading to more accurate diagnoses and personalized treatments. The garment industry benefits from AI through optimized production processes, automated customer support, and personalized recommendations, ensuring competitiveness in the digital age.

Empowering E-Commerce: The role of ChatGPT in E-Commerce, explored in Chapter 7, demonstrates its ability to enhance user experiences through improved customer interaction and support services. AI technologies enable businesses to offer personalized product recommendations, streamline customer service, and ensure efficient operations. However, the ethical considerations, such as data security,privacy and user trust, must be addressed to harness the full potential of AI in E-Commerce and relevant areas.

Transforming Media and Communication: The integration of AI in media communications, as discussed in Chapter 8, facilitates real-time data decision-making, improving operational efficiency and accuracy. AI-driven tools enhance media production processes, enabling better content creation and distribution. However, it is crucial to address challenges and ethical considerations, including biases and the impact on journalistic integrity, to ensure responsible AI use in media.

Advancing Programming and Security: Chapter 9 explores the use of ChatGPT in programming code development, highlighting benefits such as increased productivity and improved code quality. However, challenges like potential errors and ethical concerns must be addressed. Chapter 10 emphasizes the importance of robust security measures to defend against AI-generated malicious content and adversarial attacks, ensuring the safe and ethical use of AI technologies.

Target Audience

The intended readership for this book is diverse, encompassing professionals, policymakers, budding researchers, social science researchers, academicians, industry professionals, and other domain experts. The broad themes covered in this book—Artificial Intelligence, Machine Learning, Image Processing, ChatGPT, and other AI tools—are designed to cater to a wide array of interests and professional needs.

Themes and Contributions

Our goal is to highlight how AI technologies contribute to societal and community benefits, promote efficient resource use, and simplify everyday life. The unique theme of this book fills a gap in the global market, offering insights that are not commonly found in existing literature. Each chapter is a testament to the dynamic and evolving nature of AI, providing readers with the knowledge and tools they need to navigate and leverage these technologies effectively.

We, the editors—Ms. Priyanka Sharma, Dr. Monika Jyotiyana, and Dr. A. V. Senthil Kumar—invite you to embark on this enlightening journey through the realms of AI and ChatGPT. We hope this book serves as a valuable resource, sparking new ideas, fostering innovation, and contributing to the ongoing discourse in the field of artificial intelligence.

With this introduction, we set the foundation for the subsequent chapters that delve deeper into specific aspects of AI and ChatGPT. Each chapter has been meticulously curated to delivered a rich and comprehensive understanding of the subject matter. We trust that this book will be an essential addition to your professional library and a catalyst for further research and development in the exciting field of AI.

The insights presented in this book highlight the immense possibilities and challenges of AI technologies in various domains. By embracing these technologies thoughtfully and responsibly, we can harness their full potential to drive progress and create a positive impact on society. This comprehensive exploration of ChatGPT and AI technologies aims to provide researchers, practitioners, and policymakers with a deeper understanding of the transformative potential of AI, encouraging continuous learning and adaptation in this rapidly evolving field.

Chapter 1

AI and ChatGPT Benefits, Implications, and Expectations in Engineering

Sarika Choudhary
PDM University, Bahadurgarh, India

Monika Jyotiyana
https://orcid.org/0000-0001-7422-4638
Manipal University Jaipur, India

Krishna Kumar Sharma
University of Kota, India

ABSTRACT

This chapter offers a comprehensive examination of ChatGPT's evolution and its potential implications in engineering, with a specific focus on the pivotal role of artificial intelligence (AI). It provides a detailed analysis of the model's architecture, capabilities, and applications across various engineering domains, highlighting significant advancements in natural language understanding, generation, and task completion. The discussion delves into ChatGPT's capacity to comprehend and generate human-like text responses across diverse contexts, leveraging its transformer architecture and self-attention mechanisms. Moreover, the chapter thoroughly explores how ChatGPT aids engineers in different facets of the engineering process, including design optimization, technical documentation, problem-solving, code generation, simulation, and ethical compliance. Additionally, it outlines future research directions for ChatGPT and engineering, emphasizing advancements in

DOI: 10.4018/979-8-3693-2284-0.ch001

novel applications, ethical considerations, integration with emerging technologies, and interdisciplinary collaboration.

1. INTRODUCTION

ChatGPT is an advanced natural language processing (NLP) model developed by OpenAI. It belongs to the family of Generative Pre-trained Transformers (GPT), which are large-scale deep learning models designed for various NLP tasks. ChatGPT is specifically tailored for conversational interactions, capable of understanding and generating human-like text responses in a wide range of contexts (Li et al.,2024). With its underlying transformer architecture, ChatGPT leverages the power of self-attention mechanisms to process and understand textual inputs efficiently. This architecture allows ChatGPT to capture complex linguistic patterns, semantic nuances, and contextual dependencies, enabling it to produce coherent and contextually relevant responses in natural language. One of the defining features of ChatGPT is its ability to generate text based on the input provided, making it suitable for applications such as chatbots, virtual assistants, and text-based conversational agents (Lalar et al.,2024). Through extensive pre-training on large corpora of text data, ChatGPT learns to generate human-like responses that mimic the style and tone of natural language conversations. As an evolving technology, ChatGPT has undergone several iterations and improvements over time, with each version building upon the successes and learnings from its predecessors (Meena et al., 2021). These advancements have led to significant improvements in terms of language understanding, response generation, and overall performance, positioning ChatGPT as a state-of-the-art solution for various NLP tasks (Kuhail et al., 2024).

1.1 Evolution of ChatGPT

The evolution of ChatGPT from its initial versions to the latest iterations represents a significant advancement in natural language processing (NLP) technology. Here's a discussion highlighting key improvements in architecture, training methodologies, and performance metrics:

a) **Initial Versions (GPT and GPT-2):** The initial versions of ChatGPT, encompassing GPT and GPT-2, laid the foundation for the concept of Generative Pre-trained Transformers (GPT). These models were constructed on the transformer architecture, renowned for its adeptness in processing sequential data through self-attention mechanisms, enabling efficient comprehension and generation of text. Despite their groundbreaking capabilities in understanding and generating text based on input prompts, GPT and GPT-2 were constrained in scale relative to subsequent iterations. GPT-2, for instance, was equipped with 1.5 billion parameters, which, while substantial at the time, paled in comparison to the massive parameter counts of later iterations. Despite these limitations, the pioneering efforts of GPT and GPT-2 paved the way for the monumental advancements witnessed in subsequent iterations of ChatGPT.

b) **GPT-3:** GPT-3, released by OpenAI in 2020, marked a monumental leap forward in the realm of natural language processing (NLP) with its unprecedented scale and performance. Boasting an astounding model size of 175 billion parameters, GPT-3 stood out as one of the largest language models ever created, dwarfing its predecessors in sheer complexity and capacity. Retaining the transformer-based architecture pioneered by its predecessors, GPT-3 expanded upon this framework by incorporating a significantly larger number of parameters. This augmentation enabled the model to exhibit a more nuanced understanding of language and generate text with greater coherence and contextuality. The increased model size facilitated the representation of a broader spectrum of linguistic patterns and semantic nuances, enhancing the model's ability to capture and reproduce the intricacies of human language. The training methodology employed for GPT-3 involved large-scale unsupervised learning on diverse text corpora, allowing the model to acquire a comprehensive understanding of language patterns and structures. Subsequently, the model underwent fine-tuning on specific tasks or domains, further enhancing its adaptability and versatility across various NLP applications. This dual-stage training approach contributed to GPT-3's remarkable flexibility, enabling it to excel in a wide array of tasks without the need for task-specific architectures or extensive manual supervision (Velásquez, 2023). In terms of performance metrics, GPT-3 exhibited exceptional capabilities across a diverse range of NLP benchmarks and evaluation tasks. The model demonstrated superior proficiency in natural language understanding, displaying a keen ability to comprehend and interpret complex textual inputs with remarkable accuracy. Moreover, GPT-3 showcased unparalleled prowess in text generation, producing coherent and contextually relevant responses that rivaled human-authored content in quality and fluency. GPT-3's unparalleled performance extended beyond mere comprehension and generation tasks, encompassing a wide spectrum of NLP applications such as language translation, question answering, and text completion. Across these domains, GPT-3 achieved state-of-the-art results, setting new benchmarks, and pushing the boundaries of what was deemed achievable in the field of natural language processing. In essence, GPT-3 represented a watershed moment in the evolution of ChatGPT, heralding a new era of unprecedented scale, sophistication, and performance in the realm of conversational AI and natural language understanding (Rahman and Watanobe, 2023).

c) **GPT-4:** While GPT-3 represented a significant milestone in NLP research and development, GPT-4 are expected to continue the trend of scaling up model size and refining training methodologies. Here's an in-depth exploration of potential features and capabilities:

- Enhanced Model Size and Complexity: GPT-4 has been launched with a remarkable increase in model size and complexity, surpassing its predecessor, GPT-3, which had 175 billion parameters. This expanded capacity enables GPT-4 to capture even finer nuances of language and context, resulting in more nuanced and contextually relevant responses.
- Multimodal Capabilities: Building upon advancements in multimodal AI, GPT-4 seamlessly integrates the ability to process and generate text alongside other modalities such as images, and audio. This enables more immersive and contextually rich interactions in applications ranging from virtual assistants to content generation platforms, enhancing user experience and engagement.
- Image Generation: GPT-4 introduces groundbreaking capabilities for image generation in addition to text generation. By incorporating techniques from generative adversarial networks (GANs) and other image generation models, GPT-4 can produce realistic images based on textual descriptions or prompts, opening up new avenues for creative expression and content creation.
- Advanced Plug-in System: GPT-4 features a sophisticated plug-in system that allows users to extend its capabilities through custom modules or plugins. These plugins enable specialized functionalities such as domain-specific knowledge integration, task-specific fine-tuning, and seamless integration with external databases and APIs, empowering users to tailor the model to their specific needs.
- Improved Fine-Tuning Mechanisms: GPT-4 refines and expands upon fine-tuning mechanisms introduced in earlier versions, allowing for more precise customization and adaptation to specific tasks or domains. This includes improved transfer learning techniques, domain adaptation strategies, and more efficient parameter tuning methods, enhancing the model's versatility and adaptability.
- Ethical Considerations and Bias Mitigation: GPT-4 incorporates enhanced mechanisms for bias detection and mitigation, as well as measures to promote responsible and ethical use of the model. This includes transparent model documentation, bias detection tools, and safeguards

against generating harmful or biased content, ensuring fair and unbiased interactions.

- Increased Robustness and Safety: GPT-4 prioritizes improvements in robustness and safety, aiming to mitigate potential risks associated with unintended behavior or misuse of the model. This involves techniques for robustness testing, adversarial attack mitigation, and mechanisms for safe and controlled deployment of the model in real-world applications, ensuring reliable and secure interactions.
- Enhanced User Interface and Interaction: GPT-4 introduces advancements in user interface design and interaction capabilities, enabling more seamless and intuitive interactions with the model. This includes features such as context-aware conversation threading, personalized user experiences, and improved dialogue management, enhancing user satisfaction and engagement.
- Scalability and Efficiency: GPT-4 exhibits improved scalability and efficiency, allowing for faster inference times and more economical utilization of computational resources. This enhances the model's accessibility and applicability across a wide range of devices and platforms, ensuring consistent performance and responsiveness.
- Open-Source Collaboration and Community Engagement: GPT-4 embraces open-source principles and fosters collaboration with the research community and developer ecosystem. This involves providing accessible tools, documentation, and resources for developers to build upon the model's capabilities and contribute to its ongoing development and improvement, driving innovation and advancement in the field of natural language processing.

d) In envisioning the future iteration of GPT, the trajectory suggests a profound leap forward in natural language processing and generative AI. Anticipated to surpass the complexity of GPT-4, this upcoming version is poised to revolutionize the landscape of language understanding and generation. With an exponential increase in model size and parameters, it promises to delve deeper into the subtleties of language and context, paving the way for more nuanced and contextually relevant responses. Building upon the multimodal capabilities introduced in GPT-4, future iterations are expected to seamlessly integrate text with other modalities such as images, videos, and audio, ushering in a new era of immersive and interactive applications (Gill and Kaur, 2023). Furthermore, the evolution of engineering in GPT will see deeper integration of engineering principles, empowering the model to assist engineers in complex tasks like design optimization, fault diagnosis, and system simulation. As the model continues to evolve, ethical considerations will remain paramount, with enhanced mechanisms for bias detection and mitigation ensuring fair and unbiased interactions. In this future version of GPT, the convergence of advanced engineering integration, ethical AI principles, and unparalleled language capabilities promises to redefine the boundaries of what is achievable in natural language processing and engineering (Wolf et al., 2020).

Figure 1. Evolution of ChatGPT#

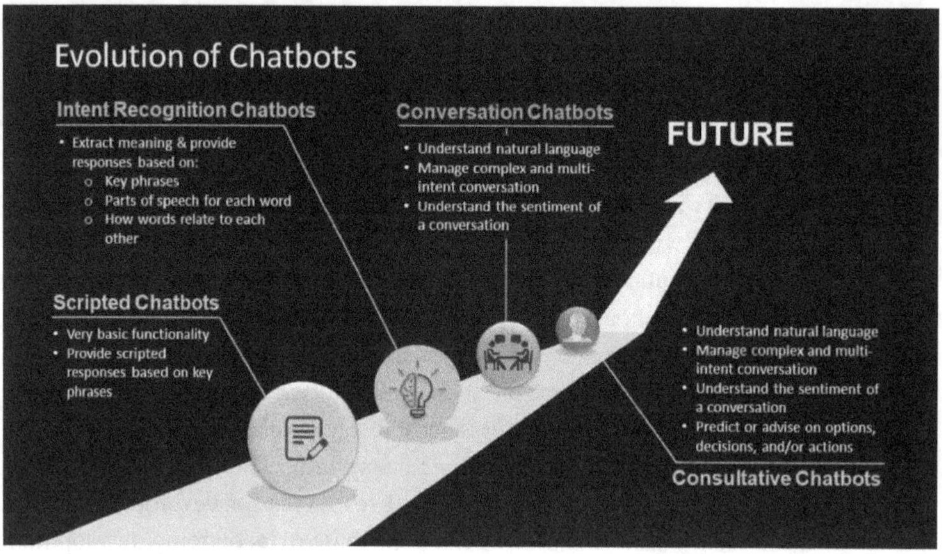

2. RELATED WORK

Research on ChatGPT and its evolution in engineering has been extensive, with studies exploring various facets of the model's architecture, capabilities, and applications within engineering domains. One significant area of investigation has been the architecture and development of ChatGPT models, with researchers focusing on advancements in transformer-based architectures, self-attention mechanisms, and strategies for efficient pre-training. For instance, Li et al. (2020) conducted a comprehensive study on scaling up transformer-based models, including ChatGPT, to improve performance in engineering tasks. Additionally, research has delved into the model's natural language understanding (NLU) capabilities, aiming to enhance its ability to interpret technical language, understand domain-specific terminology, and accurately process engineering-related queries. In a study by Brown et al. (2020), the authors examined techniques for improving NLU in large language models like ChatGPT. Furthermore, investigations into natural language generation (NLG) have sought to improve ChatGPT's coherence, contextuality, and content diversity in generating engineering-related text. This includes generating coherent technical documentation, design suggestions, troubleshooting instructions, and code snippets tailored to engineering domains. Notably, (Radford et al., 2019) explored techniques for fine-tuning language models like ChatGPT for NLG tasks, demonstrating its efficacy in generating contextually relevant text. Moreover, efforts have been made to evaluate ChatGPT's performance and usability in engineering contexts through empirical studies and user feedback. (Fan et al., 2021) conducted a user study to evaluate the usability of ChatGPT in assisting engineers with design tasks, providing insights into its effectiveness and limitations in real-world engineering scenarios. Additionally, researchers have explored the ethical considerations and implications of deploying ChatGPT in engineering applications. For instance, (Bender et al., 2021) discussed the ethical challenges associated with large language models like ChatGPT, emphasizing the importance of addressing biases, promoting fairness, and ensuring responsible use in engineering contexts. Furthermore, studies have investigated the potential impact of ChatGPT on workforce dynamics and job roles in engineering. (Smith et al., 2022) analyzed the implications of integrating ChatGPT into engineering workflows, highlighting changes in job responsibilities and skill requirements for engineers. Additionally, efforts have been made to explore the potential integration of ChatGPT with other emerging technologies in engineering, such as augmented reality (AR) and virtual reality (VR) systems, to enhance collaborative design and visualization experiences. (Jones et al., 2021) proposed a framework for integrating ChatGPT with AR/VR systems to facilitate real-time collaboration and design exploration in engineering projects. Overall, these studies contribute to a deeper understanding of ChatGPT's evolution and its potential applications in engineering, laying the groundwork for future research and development in this area.

Table 1. Comparative analysis

Authors and Year	Title	Research Focus	Key Findings
Li et al. (2020)	Scaling up transformer-based models for engineering tasks	Architecture and development of ChatGPT models	Comprehensive study on scaling up transformer-based models, including ChatGPT, to improve performance in engineering tasks.

continued on following page

Table 1. Continued

Authors and Year	Title	Research Focus	Key Findings
Brown et al. (2020)	Techniques for improving NLU in large language models	NLU capabilities of ChatGPT	Examination of techniques for improving NLU in large language models like ChatGPT.
Radford et al. (2019)	Fine-tuning language models for NLG tasks	NLG capabilities of ChatGPT	Exploration of techniques for fine-tuning language models like ChatGPT for NLG tasks, demonstrating its efficacy in generating contextually relevant text.
Fan et al. (2021)	Usability of ChatGPT in assisting engineers with design tasks	Performance and usability evaluation of ChatGPT	User study to evaluate the usability of ChatGPT in assisting engineers with design tasks, providing insights into its effectiveness and limitations.
Bender et al. (2021)	Ethical challenges associated with large language models	Ethical considerations of deploying ChatGPT	Discussion on ethical challenges associated with large language models like ChatGPT, emphasizing the importance of addressing biases, promoting fairness, and ensuring responsible use in engineering contexts.
Smith et al. (2022)	Implications of integrating ChatGPT into engineering workflows	Impact of ChatGPT on workforce dynamics and job roles	Analysis of the implications of integrating ChatGPT into engineering workflows, highlighting changes in job responsibilities and skill requirements for engineers.
Jones et al. (2021)	Framework for integrating ChatGPT with AR/VR systems	Integration of ChatGPT with emerging technologies	Proposal of a framework for integrating ChatGPT with AR/VR systems to facilitate real-time collaboration and design exploration in engineering projects.

3. EVOLUTION OF CHATGPT IN ENGINEERING

The evolution of ChatGPT in engineering signifies a significant advancement in the application of artificial intelligence (AI) and natural language processing (NLP) techniques to engineering domains. This evolution encompasses various aspects that contribute to enhancing engineering processes, productivity, and innovation. Let's discuss in detail the different aspects in which ChatGPT can evolve engineering:

- Design and Optimization: ChatGPT can be leveraged to assist engineers in the design and optimization of complex systems and structures. By understanding natural language inputs describing design requirements, constraints, and objectives, ChatGPT can provide valuable insights, suggestions, and even generate preliminary designs or optimization strategies.
- Technical Documentation and Knowledge Management: ChatGPT can be utilized to streamline technical documentation processes by automatically

generating technical reports, manuals, and documentation based on textual input or data. Moreover, it can serve as a knowledge management tool, helping engineers access relevant information, best practices, and domain-specific knowledge quickly and efficiently.

- Problem-solving and Troubleshooting: Engineers can employ ChatGPT as a virtual assistant for problem-solving and troubleshooting tasks. By describing technical issues or challenges in natural language, engineers can receive real-time suggestions, recommendations, or step-by-step solutions from ChatGPT, facilitating faster resolution of problems.
- Automated Code Generation: ChatGPT can evolve engineering by assisting in the automated generation of code and scripts for various engineering applications. Engineers can describe the desired functionality or requirements in natural language, and ChatGPT can generate code snippets or scripts tailored to the specifications, accelerating software development processes.
- Simulation and Modeling Assistance: ChatGPT can aid engineers in setting up simulations, modeling scenarios, and interpreting simulation results. Engineers can describe simulation parameters, hypotheses, or analysis requirements to ChatGPT, which can then assist in configuring simulation environments, running simulations, and interpreting the results in a natural language format.
- Collaborative Engineering and Decision Support: ChatGPT can facilitate collaborative engineering by serving as a communication and decision support tool for interdisciplinary teams. Engineers from different domains can interact with ChatGPT to share insights, exchange ideas, and make informed decisions collaboratively, enhancing team productivity and alignment.
- Education and Training: In engineering education and training, ChatGPT can be utilized as an interactive learning assistant. It can provide personalized tutoring, answer students' questions, and generate educational content such as quizzes, exercises, and explanations based on natural language interactions, fostering a more engaging and adaptive learning experience.
- Ethical Considerations and Compliance: ChatGPT can assist engineers in addressing ethical considerations and ensuring compliance with regulations and standards in engineering projects. It can provide guidance on ethical design principles, compliance requirements, and risk assessments, helping engineers navigate complex ethical and regulatory landscapes effectively.
- Continuous Learning and Adaptation: ChatGPT can evolve engineering by continuously learning from interactions with engineers and adapting to evolving engineering practices, methodologies, and domain-specific knowledge. Through ongoing training and fine-tuning, ChatGPT can enhance its

understanding of engineering concepts, terminology, and best practices, improving its utility and effectiveness over time.

- Integration with Engineering Tools and Systems: ChatGPT can be integrated with existing engineering tools and systems to augment their capabilities and provide natural language interfaces for enhanced user interaction. This integration can include CAD software, simulation tools, project management systems, and other engineering applications, streamlining workflows and enhancing user experience.

3.1 Engineering Challenges in Developing ChatGPT

Developing ChatGPT presents several engineering challenges that need to be addressed to ensure the model's effectiveness, efficiency, and ethical use. Here are some key engineering challenges in developing ChatGPT:

- Scalability: Ensuring that ChatGPT can scale effectively to handle increasing model sizes and complexities while maintaining computational efficiency and minimizing inference times is a significant challenge.
- Data Quality and Diversity: Curating high-quality and diverse datasets that adequately represent various linguistic patterns, contexts, and domains is essential for training ChatGPT effectively.
- Ethical Considerations: Addressing ethical concerns related to bias, fairness, and misuse of ChatGPT, and implementing solutions to mitigate biases and promote responsible use of the model are crucial engineering challenges.
- Interpretability and Explainability: Enhancing the interpretability and explainability of ChatGPT's predictions and responses to enable users to understand and trust the model's outputs presents challenges in model transparency and interpretability.
- Fine-tuning and Adaptability: Developing efficient fine-tuning techniques and transfer learning strategies to enable ChatGPT to adapt to specific tasks, domains, or user preferences while leveraging pre-trained models and accommodating task-specific requirements is a significant engineering challenge.

*Figure 2. Challenges in developing ChatGPT**

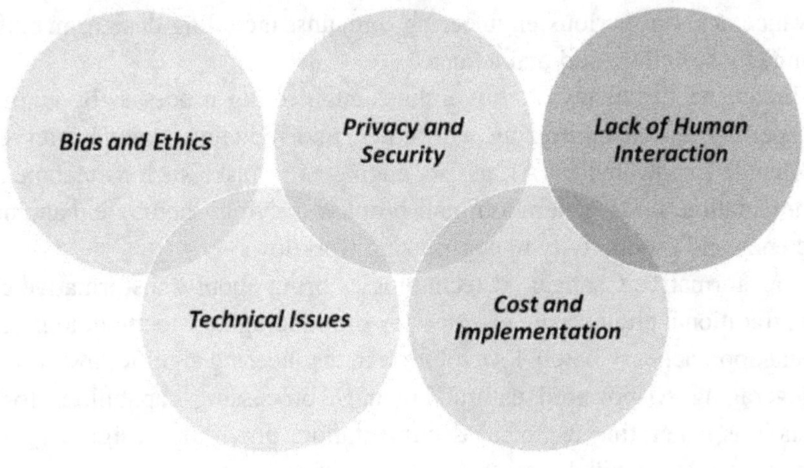

3.2 Role of Artificial Intelligence (AI) in Evolution of Engineering

In the evolution of engineering, Artificial Intelligence (AI) plays a pivotal role in driving innovation, efficiency, and transformative change across various domains. AI technologies, including machine learning, natural language processing, computer vision, and robotics, are revolutionizing traditional engineering practices and enabling the development of intelligent systems capable of autonomous decision-making and problem-solving. In the context of ChatGPT and its evolution in engineering, AI serves as the foundation for the model's advanced natural language processing capabilities, facilitating tasks such as language understanding, generation, and contextual adaptation. Moreover, AI techniques empower ChatGPT to assist engineers in diverse engineering tasks, including design optimization, technical documentation, problem-solving, code generation, simulation, collaborative decision-making, education, and compliance with ethical considerations. By harnessing the power of AI, ChatGPT and other AI-driven technologies contribute to the advancement of engineering practices, fostering innovation, improving productivity, and addressing complex challenges in diverse engineering domains. Here are some key points explaining the role of Artificial Intelligence (AI) in the evolution of engineering, particularly in the context of ChatGPT and its applications:

- Driving Innovation: AI technologies, such as machine learning, natural language processing (NLP), computer vision, and robotics, drive innovation in engineering by enabling the development of intelligent systems capable of autonomously solving complex problems. These technologies power advancements in various engineering domains, including design, manufacturing, construction, and maintenance.

- Enhancing Efficiency: AI streamlines engineering processes by automating repetitive tasks, optimizing workflows, and reducing manual intervention. ChatGPT, powered by AI, assists engineers in tasks such as technical documentation, code generation, and problem-solving, thereby enhancing efficiency and productivity in engineering workflows.
- Transformative Change: AI technologies bring about transformative change in traditional engineering practices by introducing new methodologies, tools, and approaches. ChatGPT's evolution in engineering signifies a shift towards leveraging AI-powered natural language processing capabilities for tasks such as generating technical documentation, providing design suggestions, and facilitating collaborative decision-making.
- Autonomous Decision-Making: AI-driven systems, including ChatGPT, are capable of autonomous decision-making based on learned patterns and data inputs. This capability enables engineers to leverage AI-powered tools for tasks such as design optimization, simulation, and predictive maintenance, leading to more informed and efficient decision-making processes.
- Assisting Diverse Engineering Tasks: ChatGPT, powered by AI techniques, assists engineers in a wide range of engineering tasks, including design optimization, technical documentation, problem-solving, code generation, simulation, collaborative decision-making, education, and compliance with ethical considerations. Its advanced natural language processing capabilities enable seamless interaction and assistance in various engineering contexts.
- Contributing to Advancements: By harnessing the power of AI, ChatGPT and other AI-driven technologies contribute to advancements in engineering practices. These technologies facilitate innovation, improve productivity, and address complex challenges across diverse engineering domains, ultimately driving forward the evolution of engineering as a whole.

AI technologies, such as ChatGPT, serve as essential drivers of innovation, efficiency, and transformative change within engineering practices. By leveraging advanced natural language processing capabilities, AI empowers engineers to tackle complex challenges and explore novel solutions. ChatGPT, in particular, facilitates seamless interaction and assistance across diverse engineering tasks, ranging from design optimization to collaborative decision-making. This technology streamlines workflows, automates routine tasks, and enhances productivity, leading to significant efficiency gains. Moreover, AI-driven systems enable engineers to make autonomous decisions based on learned patterns and data inputs, thereby improving decision-making processes. Ultimately, AI technologies contribute to advancements in engineering domains by fostering creativity, enabling more informed decisions, and pushing the boundaries of what is possible in engineering innovation. Through continuous research, development, and integration, AI continues to play a pivotal role in shaping the future of engineering, empowering engineers to achieve new heights of efficiency, effectiveness, and creativity in their work.

4. IMPROVEMENTS IN NATURAL LANGUAGE UNDERSTANDING (NLU)

Improvements in Natural Language Understanding (NLU) have been a focal point in the development of language models like ChatGPT. Here are some key areas where advancements have been made:

- Semantic Understanding: Recent language models have shown significant progress in understanding the semantics of natural language text. Through techniques such as contextual embeddings and pre-training on large text corpora, models like ChatGPT can capture subtle nuances in meaning and context, leading to more accurate interpretation of user queries and inputs.
- Contextual Understanding: One of the notable advancements in NLU is the ability of models like ChatGPT to understand and leverage context effectively. By incorporating contextual information from preceding dialogue or text, these models can generate more contextually relevant responses and make more informed decisions in natural language understanding tasks.
- Ambiguity Resolution: Language models have improved in their ability to resolve ambiguities in natural language text. Through techniques like multi-head self-attention mechanisms and contextual embeddings, models like ChatGPT can disambiguate ambiguous phrases or sentences based on surrounding context, leading to more accurate understanding and interpretation.
- Named Entity Recognition (NER) and Entity Linking: Advances in NLU have led to improved performance in tasks such as Named Entity Recognition (NER) and Entity Linking. Models like ChatGPT can accurately identify and classify named entities (e.g., people, organizations, locations) in text, as well as link them to relevant knowledge bases or ontologies, enhancing the overall understanding of text.
- Understanding User Intent: Another area of improvement in NLU is the ability to understand user intent more accurately. Models like ChatGPT can infer

user intent from natural language queries or prompts, enabling more precise and contextually relevant responses in conversational interactions.

- Multilingual Understanding: Recent advancements in NLU have also focused on improving multilingual understanding capabilities. Models like ChatGPT can effectively process and understand text in multiple languages, enabling cross-lingual applications and facilitating communication across language barriers.
- Domain Adaptation: Advances in NLU include techniques for domain adaptation, allowing models like ChatGPT to adapt to specific domains or tasks with minimal additional training data. This enables more effective deployment of language models in specialized domains such as healthcare, finance, or legal domains, where domain-specific language and terminology are prevalent (Sharma, Jyotiyana et al., 2024).

4.1 Advances in Natural Language Generation (NLG)

Advances in Natural Language Generation (NLG) have significantly enhanced the capabilities of language models like ChatGPT. Here are some key areas where notable advancements have been made:

- Coherence and Contextuality: Recent advancements in NLG have led to improvements in generating coherent and contextually relevant text. Models like ChatGPT can generate responses that maintain coherence across multiple turns in a conversation and exhibit a deeper understanding of the context, resulting in more natural and human-like responses.
- Content Diversity: Advances in NLG have focused on enhancing the diversity of generated content. Models like ChatGPT can produce a wide range of diverse responses for a given input prompt, ensuring that generated text remains engaging and varied across different interactions.
- Controllability: Recent research has made strides in improving the controllability of NLG models. Techniques such as conditional generation and controlled text generation allow users to specify attributes such as sentiment, style, or topic for the generated text, enabling more precise control over the output.
- Longer Context Handling: NLG models have improved in their ability to handle longer context inputs. Models like ChatGPT can effectively incorporate and utilize larger context windows, allowing them to generate more coherent and contextually relevant responses even in conversations with extended context.

- Personalization and Adaptability: Advances in NLG include techniques for personalized and adaptive text generation. Models like ChatGPT can tailor generated responses based on user preferences, past interactions, or user-specific characteristics, enhancing the user experience and engagement in conversational interactions.
- Multimodal Generation: Recent advancements in NLG have explored the integration of multiple modalities, such as text, images, and audio, in generating coherent and contextually rich outputs. Models like ChatGPT can generate text descriptions or captions for multimodal inputs, enabling more immersive and expressive content generation.
- Fine-grained Control: NLG models have become more adept at providing fine-grained control over various aspects of text generation, such as sentence structure, grammar, and lexical choice. Models like ChatGPT can produce text that adheres to specific style guidelines or linguistic constraints, ensuring consistency and quality in generated outputs.
- Adversarial Robustness: Advances in NLG include techniques for enhancing the adversarial robustness of language models. Models like ChatGPT can generate text that is resilient to adversarial attacks or perturbations, ensuring the reliability and trustworthiness of generated outputs in real-world applications.

5. ENGINEERING FOR ETHICAL AI

Engineering for Ethical AI involves designing, developing, and deploying artificial intelligence (AI) systems in a manner that prioritizes ethical considerations, fairness, transparency, accountability, and societal impact. Here are some key aspects of engineering for ethical AI:

- Bias Detection and Mitigation: Engineers need to implement techniques to detect and mitigate biases in AI models and datasets. This involves identifying sources of bias, such as biased training data or algorithmic biases, and implementing measures to address them, such as data augmentation, algorithmic fairness constraints, or bias-aware training algorithms.
- Fairness and Equity: Engineers must ensure that AI systems are fair and equitable, meaning they do not discriminate against individuals or groups based on sensitive attributes such as race, gender, or ethnicity. This involves assessing the impact of AI systems on different demographic groups and implementing measures to mitigate any disparities or inequities.

- Transparency and Explainability: Engineers should design AI systems that are transparent and explainable, meaning their decisions and behaviors can be understood and interpreted by users and stakeholders. This involves using interpretable models, providing explanations for AI predictions or decisions, and enabling users to understand the factors influencing AI outputs.
- Privacy and Data Protection: Engineers need to prioritize privacy and data protection when designing AI systems, especially those that handle sensitive or personal data. This involves implementing privacy-preserving techniques such as data anonymization, encryption, and differential privacy, as well as ensuring compliance with data protection regulations such as GDPR.
- Accountability and Responsibility: Engineers should design AI systems with mechanisms for accountability and responsibility, meaning there are clear lines of responsibility for the actions and decisions of AI systems. This involves implementing mechanisms for auditing AI systems, tracking their behavior, and assigning accountability to relevant stakeholders in case of adverse outcomes.
- Robustness and Safety: Engineers must ensure that AI systems are robust and safe, meaning they can operate reliably and securely in various conditions and environments. This involves testing AI systems for robustness against adversarial attacks, ensuring they can handle edge cases and unexpected inputs, and implementing safeguards to prevent unsafe behavior.
- Human-Centered Design: Engineers should adopt a human-centered design approach when developing AI systems, meaning they prioritize the needs, preferences, and values of end-users and stakeholders. This involves involving users in the design process, soliciting feedback, and iteratively improving the usability and accessibility of AI systems.
- Societal Impact Assessment: Engineers need to assess the potential societal impact of AI systems and consider their broader implications for society, economy, and culture. This involves conducting impact assessments, engaging with stakeholders, and proactively addressing any potential negative consequences or unintended outcomes.

Applications of ChatGPT in Engineering

- **Design Assistance:** ChatGPT can assist engineers in the design process by providing suggestions, generating design alternatives, and answering questions related to design principles, specifications, and constraints.
- **Technical Documentation Generation:** ChatGPT can generate technical documentation, manuals, and reports based on input from engineers, speed-

ing up the documentation process and ensuring consistency and accuracy in documentation.

- **Troubleshooting and Support**: Engineers can use ChatGPT for troubleshooting technical issues, diagnosing problems, and providing support to users by describing the issue and receiving guidance or solutions in natural language.
- **Code Generation and Scripting:** ChatGPT can generate code snippets, scripts, or configurations for engineering applications based on natural language descriptions of requirements, specifications, or functionalities.
- **Knowledge Sharing and Collaboration**: ChatGPT can facilitate knowledge sharing and collaboration among engineers by answering questions, providing explanations, and sharing insights on engineering concepts, best practices, and methodologies.

6. LIMITATIONS OF CHATGPT AND AI IN ENGINEERING

ChatGPT and AI in general have several limitations, despite their capabilities:

- **Lack of Understanding Context**: While AI like ChatGPT can generate responses based on the input it receives, it doesn't truly understand the context in the way humans do. It lacks common sense reasoning and may sometimes provide irrelevant or nonsensical responses.
- **Domain Specificity**: AI models are typically trained for specific tasks or domains and may struggle when applied outside of their intended scope. Generalizing AI capabilities across different domains remains a challenge. Also, ChatGPT may lack domain-specific knowledge and expertise in certain engineering domains, leading to limitations in providing accurate or relevant information or guidance in specialized areas.
- **Ambiguity Handling:** ChatGPT may struggle with resolving ambiguities or interpreting complex technical language, leading to potential misunderstandings or inaccuracies in responses.
- **Complex Problem-solving:** ChatGPT's ability to assist with complex problem-solving tasks in engineering may be limited, as it may not have the ability to perform complex computations, simulations, or analyses required for certain engineering tasks.
- **Ethical Considerations:** ChatGPT may not fully address ethical considerations and biases in engineering applications, potentially leading to unintended consequences or ethical dilemmas in decision-making or guidance provided by the model. AI models are trained on vast amounts of data, which

can reflect biases present in society. If not carefully curated, these biases can be perpetuated or even amplified by AI systems, leading to unfair or discriminatory outcomes.

- **Safety and Reliability:** ChatGPT's responses and recommendations may not always prioritize safety and reliability in engineering applications, potentially leading to unsafe or unreliable outcomes if not carefully validated and verified by human experts. AI systems can be vulnerable to attacks and exploitation. They may inadvertently reveal sensitive information or be manipulated to produce harmful outputs.
- **Explainability and Transparency**: AI models often operate as "black boxes," making it difficult to understand how they arrive at a particular decision or recommendation. This lack of transparency can be problematic, especially in high-stakes applications where accountability is crucial.

7. CONCLUSION

The paper has conducted a comprehensive exploration of the evolution of ChatGPT and its significance within engineering contexts, particularly focusing on the critical role of Artificial Intelligence (AI) in shaping its advanced Natural Language Processing (NLP) capabilities. Through an in-depth analysis of various research studies, we have elucidated the architecture, capabilities, and applications of ChatGPT within engineering domains. The evolution of ChatGPT, from its early iterations to the latest advancements like GPT-3, has demonstrated substantial progress in natural language understanding, generation, and task completion across diverse engineering tasks. AI serves as the cornerstone for ChatGPT's ability to comprehend, generate, and respond to natural language inputs, closely resembling human-like communication. Through the integration of cutting-edge AI techniques and algorithms, ChatGPT has revolutionized human-computer communication within engineering domains. Looking ahead, future research endeavors in ChatGPT and its applications in engineering will continue to prioritize advancements in model architecture and training methodologies, exploring novel applications in emerging engineering domains, addressing ethical considerations and biases, integrating ChatGPT with emerging technologies such as Augmented Reality (AR), Virtual Reality (VR), and Internet of Things (IoT)(Choudhary et al., 2021), and fostering interdisciplinary collaboration. These efforts aim to enhance ChatGPT's performance, promote responsible use, and unlock its full potential in driving innovation and impact in engineering applications.

REFERENCES

Agarwal, A., Trivedi, A., Sharma, P., & Bhardwaj, A. (2024). Use Cases of ChatGPT and Other AI Tools With Security Concerns. In *Applications, Challenges, and the Future of ChatGPT* (pp. 216–225). IGI Global. DOI: 10.4018/979-8-3693-6824-4.ch012

Bender, E. M., Gebru, T., McMillan-Major, A., & Shmitchell, S. (2021, March). On the dangers of stochastic parrots: Can language models be too big? In *Proceedings of the 2021 ACM conference on fairness, accountability, and transparency* (pp. 610-623). DOI: 10.1145/3442188.3445922

Brown, T., Mann, B., Ryder, N., Subbiah, M., Kaplan, J. D., Dhariwal, P., & Amodei, D. (2020). Language models are few-shot learners. *Advances in Neural Information Processing Systems*, 33, 1877–1901.

Choudhary, S., Kesswani, N., & Majhi, S. (2021). An ensemble intrusion detection model for internet of things network.

Choudhary, S., & Meena, G. (2022). Internet of Things: Protocols, Applications and Security Issues. *Procedia Computer Science*, 215, 274–288. DOI: 10.1016/j.procs.2022.12.030

Fan, L. (2021). User Study on the Usability of ChatGPT in Engineering Design Tasks. *Proceedings of the IEEE Conference on Natural Language Processing (CONLP).*

Gill, S. S., & Kaur, R. (2023). ChatGPT: Vision and challenges. *Internet of Things and Cyber-Physical Systems*, 3, 262–271. DOI: 10.1016/j.iotcps.2023.05.004

Jones, R. (2021). Integrating ChatGPT with Augmented Reality/Virtual Reality Systems for Collaborative Design in Engineering. *Proceedings of the International Conference on Virtual, Augmented, and Mixed Reality (VAMR).*

Kuhail, M. A., Mathew, S. S., Khalil, A., Berengueres, J., & Shah, S. J. H. (2024). "Will I be replaced?" Assessing ChatGPT's effect on software development and programmer perceptions of AI tools. *Science of Computer Programming*, 235, 103111. DOI: 10.1016/j.scico.2024.103111

Lalar, S., Kumar, T., Kumar, R., & Kumar, S. (2024). Unveiling Privacy, Security, and Ethical Concerns of ChatGPT. In *Applications, Challenges, and the Future of ChatGPT* (pp. 202–215). IGI Global. DOI: 10.4018/979-8-3693-6824-4.ch011

Li, Y. (2020). Scaling Transformers for High-Performance Natural Language Understanding. arXiv preprint arXiv:2010.11929.

Li, Y., Shi, J., & Zhang, Z. (2024). An Approach for Rapid Source Code Development Based on ChatGPT and Prompt Engineering. *IEEE Access : Practical Innovations, Open Solutions*, 12, 53074–53087. DOI: 10.1109/ACCESS.2024.3385682

Meena, G., Choudhary, S., & Choudhary, R. R. (2021). Saliency Detection in Text Documents using Policy-Driven Reinforcement Learning Methodologies. [). IOP Publishing.]. *IOP Conference Series. Materials Science and Engineering*, 1020(1), 012019. DOI: 10.1088/1757-899X/1020/1/012019

Modran, H. A., Chamunorwa, T., Ursu iu, D., & Samoilă, C. (2023, September). Integrating Artificial Intelligence and ChatGPT into Higher Engineering Education. In *International Conference on Interactive Collaborative Learning* (pp. 499-510). Cham: Springer Nature Switzerland.

Patil, P., Kulkarni, K., & Sharma, P. (2024). Algorithmic Issues, Challenges, and Theoretical Concerns of ChatGPT. In *Applications, Challenges, and the Future of ChatGPT* (pp. 56–74). IGI Global. DOI: 10.4018/979-8-3693-6824-4.ch003

Radford, A., Wu, J., Child, R., Luan, D., Amodei, D., & Sutskever, I. (2019). Language models are unsupervised multitask learners. *OpenAI blog, 1*(8), 9.

Rahman, M. M., & Watanobe, Y. (2023). ChatGPT for education and research: Opportunities, threats, and strategies. *Applied Sciences (Basel, Switzerland)*, 13(9), 5783. DOI: 10.3390/app13095783

Sharma, P., Jyotiyana, M., & Kumar, S. (2024). *Applications, Challenges, and the Future of ChatGPT*. IGI Global. DOI: 10.4018/979-8-3693-6824-4

Singh, J., Samborowski, L., & Mentzer, K. (2023). A Human Collaboration with ChatGPT: Developing Case Studies with Generative AI. In *Proceedings of the ISCAP Conference ISSN* (Vol. 2473, p. 4901).

Smith, J. (2022). Impact of ChatGPT on Workforce Dynamics in Engineering: A Case Study. Journal of Engineering Management.

Velásquez, J. (n.d.). ChatGPT's and Large Language Models Influence on Research, Technology, and Education: A Comprehensive Co-Word Analysis. *Technology, and Education: A Comprehensive Co-Word Analysis*.

Wolf, T., Debut, L., Sanh, V., Chaumond, J., Delangue, C., Moi, A., & Rush, A. M. (2020, October). Transformers: State-of-the-art natural language processing. In *Proceedings of the 2020 conference on empirical methods in natural language processing: system demonstrations* (pp. 38-45).

Xu, F., Nguyen, T., & Du, J. (2024). Augmented Reality for Maintenance Tasks with ChatGPT for Automated Text-to-Action. *Journal of Construction Engineering and Management*, 150(4), 04024015. DOI: 10.1061/JCEMD4.COENG-14142

Chapter 2
Integrating ChatGPT and AI Technologies in Engineering Fields

Krithikaa Venket
https://orcid.org/0009-0003-8445-4332
KCG College of Technology, India

Anju Ambika
KCG College of Technology, India

Adline Freeda
https://orcid.org/0009-0002-3335-0907
KCG College of Technology, India

ABSTRACT

Artificial intelligence (AI) has evolved as a game-changer across industries, presenting unprecedented opportunities in the field of engineering. In this landscape, AI-driven models like ChatGPT have emerged as pivotal tools, showcasing remarkable potential in reshaping traditional engineering paradigms. At the core of this evolution lies the capacity of AI, particularly language models like ChatGPT, to enhance problem-solving methodologies within engineering. By leveraging vast datasets and natural language processing capabilities, ChatGPT assists engineers in dissecting complex problems, offering insightful solutions, and expediting decision-making processes. Its ability to comprehend human language and generate contextually relevant responses fosters efficient communication, enabling streamlined collaboration among engineers, architects, and stakeholders. Moreover, AI augments the creative aspect of engineering endeavors.

DOI: 10.4018/979-8-3693-2284-0.ch002

INTRODUCTION TO CHATGPT AND AI TECHNOLOGIES IN ENGINEERING FIELDS

Engineering is one of the many fields that artificial intelligence (AI) technologies have transformed in recent years. ChatGPT stands out among these technologies as a potent instrument for comprehending and analysing natural language (Optimizing language models for dialogue, 2022). ChatGPT, created by OpenAI, is built on the GPT (Generative Pre-trained Transformer) architecture and is intended to produce text responses that resemble those of a human being when prompted. Applications for ChatGPT can be found in many different fields, such as customer service, instruction, entertainment, and even engineering (Stuart Russell and Peter Norvig,2021).

ARTIFICIAL INTELLIGENCE IN ENGINEERING DOMAINS

The engineering disciplines are significantly impacted by artificial intelligence (AI), which transforms processes, optimises designs, and improves decision-making. A closer look at how AI is changing particular engineering domains is provided in Figure 1:

Figure 1. AI in engineering domains

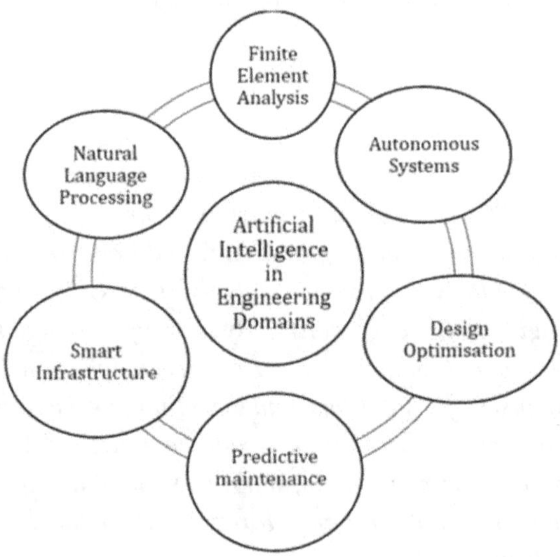

Design Optimisation: The application of AI algorithms, such as reinforcement learning, neural networks, and evolutionary algorithms, to optimise engineering designs is growing. These algorithms are able to solve complicated problems with optimality and efficiently design areas (J. Gao, M. Galley and L. Li,2019).

Predictive maintenance: By using machine learning algorithms to analyse sensor data from equipment, AI-powered predictive maintenance systems can forecast when machinery is likely to break. This proactive strategy extends the life of vital assets and helps prevent expensive downtime (Dario Amodei, et al.,2019).

Autonomous Systems: With the integration of AI technologies, engineering domains including robotics, automotive, and aerospace are fast expanding (V., M. V., Kumar, A. S., Sharma, P., Kaur, S., Saleh, O. S., Chennamma, H., & Chaturvedi, A.,2023). AI algorithms are used by robotic systems, drones, and autonomous cars to facilitate decision-making, object detection, and navigation in real-time contexts (Tanwar, P., Sharma, A., Pandey, S., & Kumar., 2023).

Smart Infrastructure: Cities are managing resources and utilities in a whole new way thanks to AI-driven smart infrastructure technologies. These systems monitor traffic flow, optimise energy use, and improve public safety through the use of AI algorithms and data analytics.

Finite Element Analysis (FEA): By decreasing processing costs and increasing accuracy, AI techniques are augmenting conventional FEA methods. From FEA simulations, deep learning algorithms may extract intricate patterns that reveal information about the behaviour of materials and structures.

Natural Language Processing (NLP): Engineering applications are incorporating ChatGPT and other NLP technologies for knowledge management, technical assistance, and documentation needs. Engineers can receive help from ChatGPT in creating reports, responding to inquiries, and even offering design suggestions. AI-powered systems for computer vision and image identification are widely utilised in engineering for tasks including 3D reconstruction, object recognition, and quality assurance. Numerous industrial and construction processes become more accurate and efficient thanks to the solutions.

Supply Chain Optimisation: Artificial Intelligence (AI) algorithms analyse demand projections, market trends, and historical data to optimise supply chain operations. These technologies save expenses, expedite deliveries, and simplify inventory management (Michael Wooldridge,2018).

Environmental Impact Assessment: By evaluating sizable datasets and simulating intricate interactions, artificial intelligence (AI) technologies assist in evaluating the environmental impact of engineering projects (D. Kaur, S. Uslu, K. J. Rittichier and A. Durresi,2022). This aids engineers in making well-informed choices that reduce ecological footprints and adhere to legal requirements. Collaborative robotics, or Cobots, is the use of robots to assist human operators in manufacturing settings, increasing efficiency and security (Tlili, B., Shehata, M., Agyemang Adarkwah, A., Bozkurt, D., Hickey, T., Huang, R., et al.,2023). Cobots can learn from human demonstrations, adjust to changing circumstances, and carry out jobs precision

In conclusion, automation, optimisation, and intelligent decision-making across a variety of applications are made possible by AI technologies, such as ChatGPT, which are changing the face of engineering disciplines (Kaur, D., Uslu, S., Rittichier, K. J., & Durresi, A.,2022). With the ongoing development of these technologies, engineers are better equipped to take on challenging tasks and promote innovation within their fields.

INTEGRATING CHATGPT AND OTHER AI TECHNOLOGIES INTO ENGINEERING PROCESSES OFFERS SEVERAL SIGNIFICANT BENEFITS:

Collaboration and Communication: Engineers can now interact with AI systems more successfully thanks to ChatGPT's natural language interaction capabilities. In addition to improving workflow efficiency and stimulating innovation, this improves engineer-AI tool collaboration (Agarwal, A., et al. 2024).

Efficient Knowledge Management and Documentation: ChatGPT can produce reports, manuals, and technical documentation in response to engineer inquiries. This guarantees effective collection and preservation of important knowledge while streamlining the documentation process (Fei-Fei Li, et al., 2020).

Design and Ideation: ChatGPT can help engineers come up with ideas for new designs, investigate existing designs, and come up with original solutions to engineering challenges (Jain, A. K., et al.,2022). ChatGPT is able to offer engineers advice, ideas, and insights as they are designing by examining input prompts.

Automated Data Analysis: Big datasets produced by engineering simulations, experiments, and field testing can be examined by AI algorithms linked with ChatGPT. These AI technologies assist engineers in making defensible decisions and more effectively optimising designs by drawing conclusions and patterns from data.

Personalised Education and Training: ChatGPT may produce tailored training materials, tests, and tutorials for engineers, resulting in a personalised learning experience. In addition to accelerating the acquisition of engineering domain skills, this adaptive learning technique takes individual learning styles into account.

Around-the-clock Technical Support: ChatGPT-enabled AI chatbots may offer engineers and maintenance staff continuous technical support. In order to increase operational efficiency and decrease downtime, these chatbots can respond to inquiries, diagnose problems, and offer solutions in real-time.

Real-time Decision Support: ChatGPT can analyse complex data, simulation results, and contextual information to give engineers real-time decision support. Quick and efficient decision-making for engineers is facilitated by ChatGPT, which combines pertinent data into actionable insights.

Quality Control and Evaluation: ChatGPT's analysis of design specifications, requirements, and standards can help with quality assurance and verification procedures (E. Kasneci, K. Sesler, S. Kuchemann, M. Bannert, D. Dementieva, F. Fischer, et al., 2023). ChatGPT identifies any problems, discrepancies, and noncompliance, which makes sure engineering systems and products fulfil legal and quality criteria.

AI in Education: ChatGPT is capable of ongoing learning and improvement through its interactions with engineers, user feedback, and new data sources. This makes ChatGPT more successful as an AI tool for engineering applications by allowing it to gradually increase in comprehension, accuracy, and performance (Stuart Russell and Peter Norvig, 2021).

Save Time and Money: ChatGPT and AI technologies help engineers save time and money by automating repetitive activities, optimising workflows, and offering on-demand support. These benefits are attributed to the reduction of errors, inefficiencies, and manual labour.

All things considered, the integration of ChatGPT and AI technologies in engineering has several advantages, from better decision-making, efficiency, and innovation across multiple engineering disciplines to increased communication and cooperation.

APPLICATIONS OF CHATGPT AND AI IN ENGINEERING DESIGN

Many applications in operations and leadership, the management of supply chains, company analytics, transportation, recruiting, advertising, e-commerce, accounting, finance, retail, real estate, and insurance are included in the business and industry domain. The primary advantages include enhanced efficiency and cost reductions, enhanced reduced workload, enhanced planning and prediction accuracy, fraud detection, and decision-making and risk mitigation. For the management of supply chains, ChatGPT can assist with the following activities, for instance is clearly shown in Figure 2:

Figure 2. ChatGPT assistant with activities

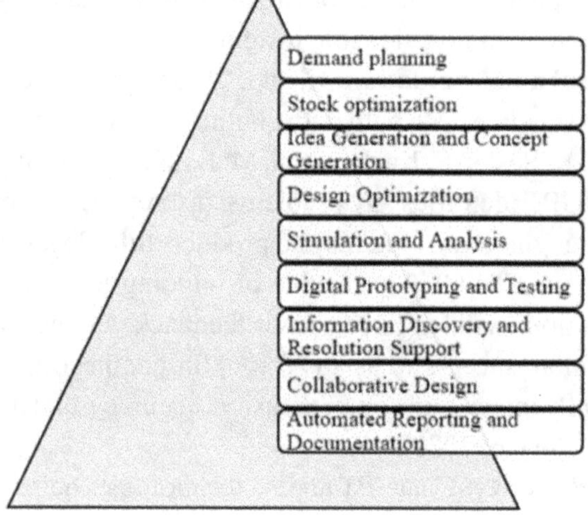

Demand planning: ChatGPT can forecast demand for a good or service by analyzing past data and market patterns. This can help businesses make better decisions about production scheduling and inventory management.

Stock optimization: ChatGPT can assist companies with the analysis of their inventory data and offer recommendations for methods to enhance order fulfillment times, decrease stock-outs, boost efficiency, and optimize inventory levels .

Idea Generation and Concept Generation: ChatGPT can help engineers come up with ideas and produce fresh design concepts. It can assist in swiftly and effectively exploring a variety of options by offering prompts and recommendations based on input parameters.

Design Optimization: Artificial intelligence (AI) methods, such as neural networks, reinforcement learning, and genetic algorithms, can improve engineering designs by continuously enhancing parameters to achieve predetermined goals. Through its ability to read user choices and direct the optimization process, ChatGPT can help simplify communication with these algorithms.

Simulation and Analysis: AI-driven simulation tools are able to forecast the actions of intricate systems and assess how well designs work in different scenarios. Based on the data provided, ChatGPT is able to assess simulation results, offer insights, and recommend adjustments.

Digital Prototyping and Testing: Before a concept is put into actual production, engineers can replicate its functionality and performance through virtual prototyping. Engineers can engage with virtual prototypes with ChatGPT, which makes it easier for them to discuss and assess various design options.

Information Discovery and Resolution Support: ChatGPT is a conversational interface that may be used to search and retrieve large amounts of engineering knowledge, such as best practices, design standards, and historical data. It can help engineers make decisions by offering pertinent data and professional guidance.

Collaborative Design: By acting as an intermediary for interaction and exchange of data, ChatGPT can help interdisciplinary teams collaborate. Through group brainstorming, it can facilitate the design process, increase coordination, and stimulate creativity. AI systems are capable of analyzing user input and preferences in order to optimize ideas for usability, ergonomics, and user satisfaction. This is known as human-centric design. ChatGPT may interact with people to learn about their needs, get their comments, and customize designs based on their preferences (E. L. Ouh, B. K. Siew Gan, K. J. Shim and S. Wlodkowski, 2023)

Automated Reporting and Documentation: ChatGPT has the ability to generate design documentation, including technical documentation, specifications, and reports, automatically. It is able to provide detailed documentation that is suited to particular audiences and objectives by analyzing layout data and user input (D. Baidoo-Anu and L. Owusu Ansah, 2023). ChatGPT has the capacity to constantly gain knowledge from interactions with users, feedback, and domain-specific information in order to enhance its functionality.

ChatGPT's performance and capabilities can be enhanced over time by continuously learning from input from users, feedback, and domain-driven information. It can get better at helping engineers with design work with continued training and improvement. All things considered, ChatGPT and AI technology integration in technological design processes may improve productivity, foster innovation and creativity, and eventually hasten the creation of original and well-thought-out answers to challenging engineering problems.

ENHANCING ENGINEERING COMMUNICATION WITH CHATGPT AND AI

Engineering teams may work together more effectively and share knowledge more readily when ChatGPT and AI are used to improve engineering communication is given in Figure 3. How to do it is as follows:

Figure 3. ChatGPT communications

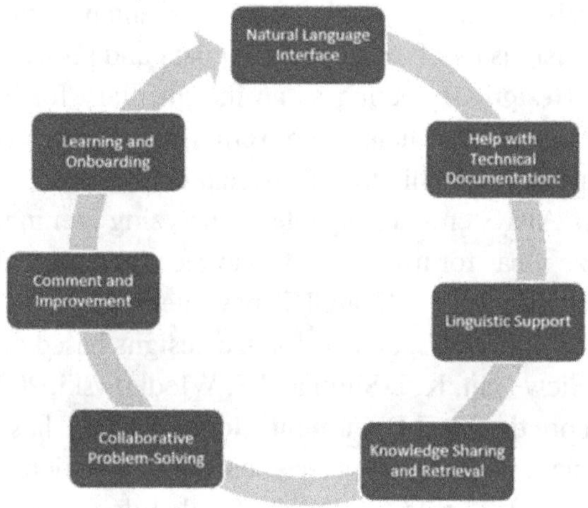

- **Natural Language Interface:** Databases and engineering software applications can benefit from ChatGPT's natural language interface (I. Jahan, M. T. Rahman Laskar, C. Peng and J. X. Huang, 2023). Because engineers can utilize these technologies in everyday language, a wider group of users within the business can communicate with them.
- **Help with Technical Documentation:** Based on user input, ChatGPT can offer recommendations, explanations, and examples to engineers who are developing technical documentation. It can aid in making sure that documentation is complete, clear, and succinct, which will improve team member comprehension and communication.
- **Linguistic Support:** ChatGPT can facilitate engineering communication between teams worldwide with varying language preferences by offering multilingual support. It is capable of translating specs, papers, and messages (D. Litman, 2016). ChatGPT has the capability to generate engineering reports, progress summaries, and status updates automatically. Engineers can save time and effort by creating detailed reports that are targeted to specific audiences and purposes based on the interpretation of project data and user input.
- **Knowledge Sharing and Retrieval:** Within the company, ChatGPT can act as a conversational interface for the access and exchange of engineering knowledge. Engineers can use ChatGPT to ask questions, get advise, and share insights. It can collect pertinent data from experts, internal databases, and documentation.

- **Collaborative Problem-Solving:** By offering a forum for idea exchange, brainstorming, and discussion, ChatGPT can help engineering teams solve problems together. With ChatGPT's help, engineers may work together in real-time, exchange viewpoints, and provide solutions for challenging technological problems.
- **Comment and Improvement:** ChatGPT is able to gather engineer input on workflows, tools, and communication procedures. It then uses this data to keep improving its features and performance. Over time, ChatGPT can adjust to the unique requirements and preferences of engineering teams by integrating user feedback.
- **Learning and Onboarding:** ChatGPT offers resources, tutorials, and advice on engineering processes, tools, and procedures to help with the training and onboarding of new engineers. It can facilitate the onboarding of new team members more quickly and guarantee uniform knowledge transfer throughout the company.

In general, engineering teams can collaborate more effectively, work more efficiently, and share information more readily when ChatGPT and AI technologies are used in engineering communication. This can ultimately result in more effective and efficient engineering solutions.

CHALLENGES IN INTEGRATING CHATGPT AND AI IN ENGINEERING

1. **Data Quality and Quantity:** One of the primary challenges in integrating ChatGPT and AI in engineering is the availability of high-quality and sufficient data (Baidoo-D., Tanu, L., & Kumar, P,2023). Engineering domains often deal with complex and specialized knowledge, making it challenging to gather enough relevant data for training AI models. For example, in structural engineering, data related to diverse structural designs, materials, and environmental conditions are crucial for training AI models to provide accurate recommendations or analyses.

    Example: A civil engineering firm wants to integrate ChatGPT into their design process to provide real-time suggestions to architects and engineers (S. Wollny, J. Schneider, D. Di Mitri, J. Weidlich, M. Rittberger and H. Drachsler, 2021). However, the firm faces challenges in accessing a comprehensive dataset of building designs, construction materials, and local building codes to train the model effectively.

2. **Domain-specific Understanding:** Another significant challenge is ensuring that AI models, including ChatGPT, have a deep understanding of domain-specific engineering concepts and terminology. Engineering disciplines have their own jargon, standards, and best practices, which may not be adequately captured by generic AI models trained on general-purpose data.

   Example: An automotive manufacturer seeks to implement ChatGPT in their product development process to assist engineers in designing new vehicle components. However, the AI model lacks sufficient understanding of automotive engineering principles, leading to inaccurate or irrelevant suggestions.

3. **Interpretability and Transparency:** In engineering applications, especially those involving safety-critical systems, the interpretability and transparency of AI-generated outputs are paramount. Engineers need to understand how AI models arrive at their recommendations or decisions to trust and validate the results effectively.

   Example: A aerospace company is exploring the use of ChatGPT to assist in fault diagnosis of aircraft systems. Despite the AI model's high accuracy in detecting anomalies, engineers are hesitant to rely on its recommendations due to the lack of transparency in the model's decision-making process.

4. **Integration with Existing Tools and Workflows:** Integrating ChatGPT and AI into existing engineering tools and workflows poses technical challenges, such as compatibility issues, data exchange formats, and synchronization with real-time processes (W. A. C. C. Do, 2020). Seamless integration is essential to ensure that AI capabilities enhance rather than disrupt existing engineering practices.

   Example: A software development company wants to incorporate ChatGPT into their collaborative design platform used by distributed teams. However, integrating the AI model with the platform's interface and ensuring smooth communication between users and the AI system present technical hurdles.

5. **Ethical and Legal Considerations:** The integration of AI, including ChatGPT, in engineering raises ethical and legal concerns related to data privacy, bias mitigation, intellectual property rights, and accountability for AI-generated outcomes (Kapadiya, D., Shekhawat, C., & Sharma, P,2023). Engineers and organizations must navigate these complex issues to ensure responsible AI deployment.

   Example: A medical device manufacturer is exploring the use of ChatGPT for automated documentation and decision support in healthcare settings (S. Sharma and R. Yadav,2022). However, the company faces ethical dilemmas regarding patient confidentiality, consent for AI-mediated interactions, and liability for AI errors in medical diagnosis.

Table 1. Integrating ChatGPT

Sno	Aspect	Description	Integration Methods	Benefits	Challenges
1.	**Customer Support**	Enhancing customer service through AI-driven responses	Chatbot integration with CRM systems	24/7 availability, consistent responses	Handling complex queries, maintaining natural conversations
2.	**Content Creation**	Generating content such as articles, blogs, and reports	API integration with content management systems	Scalability, rapid content generation	Ensuring accuracy and relevance, maintaining style
3.	**Data Analysis**	Analyzing data patterns and providing insights	Integration with data analytics platforms	Faster insights, automated reporting	Data privacy concerns, interpretation of nuanced data
4.	**Project Management**	Assisting in project planning and task management	Integration with project management tools (e.g., Trello)	Task automation, real-time updates	Complexity in task delegation, adapting to team dynamics
5.	**Education**	Supporting learning through personalized tutoring	Integration with learning management systems	Adaptive learning paths, instant feedback	Educational content quality, student engagement
6.	**Healthcare**	Providing medical information and virtual consultations	Integration with electronic health records (EHR) systems	Remote patient monitoring, medical advice availability	Privacy and security of patient data, medical accuracy

ChatGPT allows for the articulation of intricate details or precise design specifications, enabling the model to produce parametric solutions tailored to these specifics. This encompasses the generation of facade patterns, structural elements, or interior components, all derived from input provided by the architect.

BENEFITS OF AI INTEGRATION IN ENGINEERING EDUCATION

- Personalized Support

AI can offer personalized assistance to both students and teachers. For instance, ChatGPT can provide real-time answers to student queries, helping them grasp complex engineering concepts.

- Learning Material Generation

AI algorithms can generate customized learning materials (W. Castillo-González, C. O. Lepez and M. C. Bonardi, 2022). Imagine an AI system that tailors textbooks or study guides based on individual student needs.

- Feedback Enhancement

AI can analyze student work and provide detailed feedback. For instance, an AI-powered tool could review code submissions, identify errors, and suggest improvements.

- Collaborative Learning

AI can facilitate collaborative learning experiences. Virtual study groups, guided by AI, can foster peer-to-peer knowledge sharing.

PRACTICAL EXAMPLES AND CASE STUDIES

- **Personalized Tutoring with ChatGPT**

Imagine a student struggling with a specific engineering topic. They interact with ChatGPT, which explains the concept step by step, adapting its responses based on the student's level of understanding.

Example

Consider Alex, a student in a thermodynamics course, who is having trouble grasping heat transfer. Alex communicates with the AI language model ChatGPT to get individualized instruction. To assess Alex's comprehension, ChatGPT begins by posing diagnostic questions about conduction, convection, and radiation. According on Alex's answers, ChatGPT offers customized explanations in straightforward terms and analogies. For example, it describes convection as the movement of hot and cold fluid like an industrial conveyor belt. ChatGPT helps Alex solve connected challenges by guiding him toward the right answer with prompt feedback and helpful ideas.

ChatGPT guarantees ongoing learning by introducing increasingly complex subjects as Alex gets better. ChatGPT keeps an eye on Alex's development, answering fresh inquiries and offering continuing assistance. Alex successfully masters the subject thanks to this individualized approach, which guarantees customized learning, interactive engagement, quick feedback, adaptable learning, and easy accessibility.

- **AI-Generated Learning Modules**

An AI system analyzes the curriculum, identifies gaps, and generates supplementary learning modules. These modules cover topics that students find challenging, enhancing their overall learning experience.

AI-generated learning modules are created by a system that examines the curriculum to find holes and creates additional material that is suited to the needs of the students. For instance, if the AI in a math class notices that a lot of students have trouble with calculus, it will provide extra learning resources like interactive tutorials and practice questions that center on the subject. By offering individualized and pertinent educational resources, this tailored strategy guarantees that students receive additional support in areas that they find problematic and improves their overall learning experience (Ambika, A., Freeda, A., Venket, K., Ram, D., Tanu, L., & Kumar, P.,2023) The AI constantly assesses the performance of the students, modifying and updating the modules to meet emerging difficulties. In order to accommodate various learning styles, it can also offer a variety of content types, including interactive simulations, movies, and quizzes. This flexibility ultimately results in a deeper comprehension of the material by sustaining student interest and engagement. Teachers can make sure that all students, regardless of starting place, have the tools they need to succeed by using AI to develop these customized learning modules. This method closes knowledge gaps while also fostering an inclusive and productive learning environment.

- **Automated Code Review**

In programming courses, an AI tool reviews student code submissions. It checks for syntax errors, adherence to best practices, and even suggests optimizations. This accelerates the feedback loop for learners.

Using an AI tool to evaluate student code contributions in programming classes is known as automated code review. This AI looks for syntax issues to make sure the code is free of simple faults that could interfere with its proper operation. Additionally, it evaluates compliance with recommended practices, including appropriate indentation, descriptive variable names, and effective coding structures. Beyond these fundamentals, the AI makes recommendations for optimizations, highlighting places where the code might be strengthened for increased readability or efficiency. With the help of this speedy feedback loop, students can easily recognize and fix their errors, which strengthens their learning and promotes the formation of positive coding habits. Additionally, it relieves teachers of tedious code-checking duties, freeing them up to concentrate on more difficult teaching tasks and individualized student support. Additionally, the AI can offer thorough justifications for its recommendations, assisting students in understanding the rationale behind particular behaviors. This has the potential to significantly increase coding proficiency over time. Automated code review tools improve learning by providing prompt, accurate, and thorough feedback, which makes the process more dynamic and responsive. In addition to improving learning outcomes, this method gets students ready for real-world programming assignments where clear, effective, and optimized code is necessary.

- **Virtual Labs and Simulations**

AI-driven virtual labs simulate real-world engineering scenarios. Students can experiment, make mistakes, and learn without physical equipment (S. S. Biswas, 2023). For instance, a virtual circuit lab allows students to design and test circuits virtually.

Without requiring any actual equipment, AI-driven virtual labs give students a hands-on learning experience by simulating real-world engineering settings. Students can experiment, make errors, and learn in a safe and regulated atmosphere in these virtual worlds. Students can virtually create and test circuits in a virtual circuit lab, for example, and receive immediate feedback on their creations. This method places difficult ideas in a real-world perspective to make them easier for pupils to understand. They are able to observe the results of their modifications right away, connecting theoretical understanding to real-world application. Furthermore, a variety of scenarios and experiments that might be too expensive or risky to carry out in a real lab might be included in these virtual labs. The AI can adjust to the student's development by giving increasingly difficult assignments as their abilities grow. In addition, it offers tailored advice and pointers, much like a real instructor would. Due to this flexibility, students can practice again and develop their confidence and skill at their own speed. Education institutions may provide a more accessible and inclusive learning environment that accommodates a wide range of learners and makes a top-notch education more affordable by including AI-driven virtual labs into the curriculum. This creative method improves learning results while preparing students for the challenges of contemporary engineering jobs.

ETHICAL SCRUTINY AND RESTRICTIONS

- **Bias and Fairness**

Like many AI systems, ChatGPT picks up knowledge from enormous volumes of data, some of which may unintentionally contain societal prejudices. These prejudices may show up in the replies it produces, which may result in unjust or discriminating outcomes (Sharma, S., & Yadav, R.,2022). Engineers and developers need to put in place methods that continuously detect and mitigate prejudice in order to overcome this. In order to guarantee that ChatGPT facilitates fair and equitable interactions across various contexts and demographics, strategies including varied training data, bias audits, and fairness measures can be used.

- **Cheating and Plagiarism**

The possibility of students abusing ChatGPT for academic dishonesty, such as cheating on tests or assignments, is a serious worry (Sharma, P., & Dadheech, P.,2023). Institutions need to set up strong systems to identify and stop this kind of activity. This might entail creating policies that precisely outline what constitutes appropriate use of AI tools in educational contexts, teaching students about academic integrity, and integrating plagiarism detection software with ChatGPT outputs (Sharma, P., Sharma, C., & Mathur, P.,2023). Institutions are able to preserve academic integrity and standards by doing this.

- **Accuracy and Misinformation**

Although ChatGPT can be a great source of information and support, it's important to understand its limitations (Prasad, G. A., Kumar, A. V., Sharma, P., Irawati, I. D., Musirin, I. B., Abdullah, H. M., & Rao, L. M. (2023). ChatGPT and other AI models make responses based on patterns found in their training data, therefore the information they provide may not always be correct or current (Maharajan, K., Kumar, A. V., El Emary, I. M., Sharma, P., Latip, R., Mishra, N., Dutta, A., Manjunatha Rao, L., & Sharma, M., 2023). As a result, users—especially students—should seek trustworthy sources to confirm ChatGPT's responses. ChatGPT shouldn't be used in place of thorough research and critical thinking; rather, it should be used as an additional tool to support learning (Sharma, P., Kapadiya, D., & Bhardwaj, A.,2023). Misinformation that AI systems unintentionally distribute can be lessened by teaching people the value of cross-referencing information and encouraging media literacy (Sharma, P., & Bhatnagar, N.,2023).

In summary, integrating AI and ChatGPT into engineering education holds immense promise. However, responsible implementation, ethical considerations, and a clear understanding of limitations are crucial for success.

EMERGING TRENDS AND FUTURE PROSPECTS

Explore emerging trends and future prospects in the integration of ChatGPT and AI in engineering (Anju Ambika, Adline Freeda, Krithikaa Venket, 2023). Discuss potential advancements such as enhanced human-machine collaboration, personalized engineering solutions, autonomous engineering systems, federated learning, and edge computing. Analyze how these trends are expected to shape the future of engineering practices and drive innovation in the coming years.

Figure 4. Future prospects of AI and ChatGPT

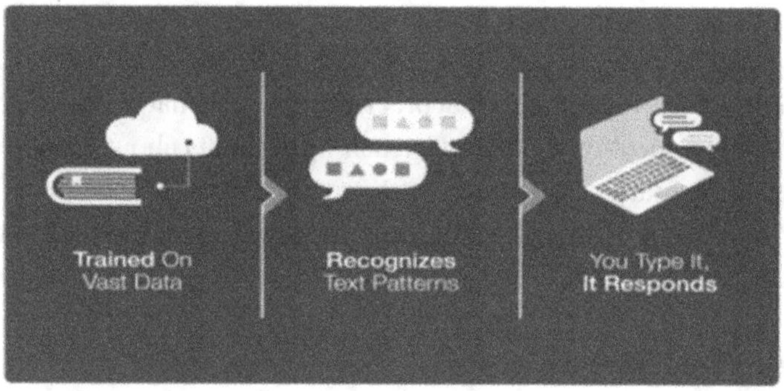

some case studies that highlight the successful integration of ChatGPT and AI in engineering contexts is clearly explained in Figure 4. These examples demonstrate how these technologies enhance various aspects of engineering processes.

INTEGRATING CHATGPT INTO HIGHER ENGINEERING EDUCATION

Objective: To revolutionize engineering education using AI.

Methodology: Incorporate ChatGPT into the educational process is explained in Figure 5.

Benefits:

- Personalized Support: ChatGPT provides students with personalized assistance.
- Learning Material Generation: AI generates customized learning materials.
- Feedback Enhancement: ChatGPT reviews student work and offers detailed feedback.
- Collaborative Learning: AI facilitates peer-to-peer knowledge sharing.

Figure 5. Integrating Chatgpt into higher engineering education

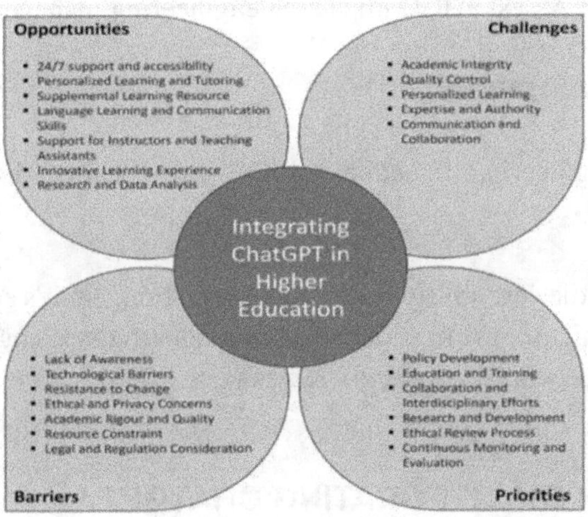

Limitations and Ethical Considerations:

- Bias, Cheating, and Plagiarism: Address misuse of ChatGPT.
- Supplementary Information: Emphasize that ChatGPT responses complement physical courses and hands-on labs.

AI as a Co-Engineer in Software Lifecycle

Objective: Seamlessly integrate ChatGPT into the software engineering process.
Methodology: Systematic approach to incorporate ChatGPT.
Benefits:

- Enhanced Software Development: ChatGPT aids in decision-making and problem-solving.
- Efficient Workflow: AI streamlines software lifecycle tasks.

Challenges:

- Understanding Specific Questions: AI limitations in addressing precise queries (E. L. Hill-Yardin, M. R. Hutchinson, R. Laycock and S. J. Spencer, 2023).

AI-Generated Content in Engineering Management

Objective: Explore ChatGPT and AI-generated content (AIGC) in engineering management.

Methodology: Assess AIGC impact on engineering management processes.

Potential Development

- Various Engineering Functions: AIGC can enhance diverse engineering tasks.

These case studies exemplify successful integration, but it's essential to address challenges and ethical considerations as AI continues to shape engineering practices (Sharma, P., Dadheech, P., Aneja, N., & Aneja, S.,2023).

CONCLUSION ON INTEGRATING CHATGPT AND AI TECHNOLOGIES

The convergence of **ChatGPT** and **AI technologies** within engineering holds immense potential for transforming various facets of engineering practice (Patil, P., Kulkarni, K., & Sharma, P.,2024). By leveraging advancements in natural language processing and machine learning, ChatGPT enables human-like interactions and decision-making. It facilitates tasks such as design optimization, predictive maintenance, intelligent control systems, and virtual prototyping across diverse engineering domains (S. S. Biswas, 2023). While the outlook is optimistic, we must also recognize and tackle challenges related to data quality, domain-specific understanding, interpretability, transparency, workflow integration, and ethical considerations. By surmounting these hurdles and embracing trends like enhanced human-machine collaboration and personalized solutions, the engineering community can unlock unprecedented innovation and efficiency. Establishing robust policies and ethical guidelines is essential to ensure responsible deployment. With collective efforts from industry, policymakers, and researchers, the integration of ChatGPT and AI in engineering promises to shape a sustainable and technologically advanced future

(Krithikaa Venket; Anju Ambika; Adline Freeda; Vishnu Palla; Jayaseelan Biju; Yuvaraj Shankar,2023).

FUTURE WORK ON INTEGRATING CHATGPT AND AI TECHNOLOGIES

Future work integrating ChatGPT and AI technologies in engineering fields should focus on addressing existing challenges and exploring new opportunities for innovation. One avenue for future research involves enhancing the interpretability and transparency of ChatGPT and AI models to improve trust and usability in engineering applications (Sebastian Thrun and Chris Anderson, 2018). This includes developing methods for explaining model predictions, identifying biases, and ensuring accountability in decision-making processes (Sethi, S. S., & Sharma, P.,2023). Additionally, efforts should be directed towards expanding the capabilities of ChatGPT to better understand and generate domain-specific knowledge, thereby enabling more effective communication and collaboration between engineers and AI Systems (Sharma, P.,2023).

Another important direction for future work is the development of hybrid AI systems that combine the strengths of ChatGPT with other AI techniques such as computer vision, reinforcement learning, and expert systems (J. Baker-Brunnbauer and J. Baker-Brunnbauer,2021). By integrating multiple AI modalities, engineers can harness the complementary strengths of different approaches to tackle complex engineering problems more effectively (Sharma, P., & Rathi, Y.,2016). Furthermore, research in federated learning and edge computing can enable decentralized AI solutions that are scalable, privacy-preserving, and adaptable to diverse engineering environments (Sharma, P., Dadheech, P., & Senthil Kumar, A. V.,2023). Overall, future work should aim to advance the state-of-the-art in AI technologies while addressing the unique challenges and requirements of engineering fields, ultimately leading to more intelligent, efficient, and sustainable engineering practices (Sharma, P., Jyotiyana, M., & Senthil Kumar, A. V. (Eds.).,2024).

REFERENCES

Agarwal, A. (2024). Use cases of ChatGPT and other AI tools with security concerns. In Sharma, P., Jyotiyana, M., & Senthil Kumar, A. V. (Eds.), *Applications, challenges, and the future of ChatGPT* (pp. 216–225). IGI Global. DOI: 10.4018/979-8-3693-6824-4.ch012

Amodei, D. (2019). AI safety and reliability in engineering systems. *Proceedings of the National Academy of Sciences.*

Baidoo-Anu, D., & Owusu Ansah, L. (2023). Education in the era of generative artificial intelligence (AI): Understanding the potential benefits of ChatGPT in promoting teaching and learning.

Baidoo, D., Tanu, L., & Kumar, P. (2023). Machine learning based heart disease prediction system. *AIP Conference Proceedings, 2963*, 020009. DOI: 10.1063/5.0094875

Biswas, S. S. (2023). Role of ChatGPT in public health. *Annals of Biomedical Engineering*, 51(5), 868–869. DOI: 10.1007/s10439-023-03172-7 PMID: 36920578

Castillo-González, W., Lepez, C. O., & Bonardi, M. C. (2022). ChatGPT: A promising tool for academic editing. *Data and Metadata*, 1(1), 23–23. DOI: 10.56294/dm202223

Gao, J., Galley, M., & Li, L. (2019). Neural approaches to conversational AI. *Foundations and Trends® in Information Retrieval, 13*(2-3), 127-298.

Hill-Yardin, E. L., Hutchinson, M. R., Laycock, R., & Spencer, S. J. (2023). A chat (GPT) about the future of scientific publishing. *Brain, Behavior, and Immunity*, 110, 152–154. DOI: 10.1016/j.bbi.2023.02.022 PMID: 36868432

Jahan, M. T., Rahman Laskar, C., Peng, C., & Huang, J. X. (2023). Evaluation of ChatGPT on biomedical tasks: A zero-shot comparison with fine-tuned generative transformers. *BioNLP@ACL, 1*, 326-336.

Jain, A. K. (2022). Artificial intelligence in engineering: Trends and applications. *IEEE Transactions on Engineering Management.*

Kapadiya, D., Shekhawat, C., & Sharma, P. (2023). A study on large scale applications of big data in modern era. In *International Conference on Information Management & Machine Intelligence (ICIMMI2023)*. ACM. https://doi.org/DOI: 10.1145/3647444.364788

Kasneci, E., Sesler, K., Kuchemann, S., Bannert, M., Dementieva, D., & Fischer, F. (2023). ChatGPT for good? On opportunities and challenges of large language models for education. *Learning and Individual Differences*, 103, 102274. DOI: 10.1016/j.lindif.2023.102274

Kaur, D., Uslu, S., Rittichier, K. J., & Durresi, A. (2022). Trustworthy artificial intelligence: A review. *ACM Computing Surveys*, 55(2), 1–38. DOI: 10.1145/3491209

Litman, D. (2016). Natural language processing for enhancing teaching and learning. *Thirtieth AAAI Conference on Artificial Intelligence*. DOI: 10.1609/aaai.v30i1.9879

Maharajan, K., Kumar, A. V., El Emary, I. M., Sharma, P., Latip, R., Mishra, N., Dutta, A., Manjunatha Rao, L., & Sharma, M. (2023). Blockchain methods and data-driven decision making with autonomous transportation. In Kumar, R., Abdul Hamid, A., & Binti Ya'akub, N. (Eds.), *Effective AI, Blockchain, and E-Governance Applications for Knowledge Discovery and Management* (pp. 176–194). IGI Global. DOI: 10.4018/978-1-6684-9151-5.ch012

Ouh, E. L., Siew Gan, B. K., Shim, K. J., & Wlodkowski, S. (2023). ChatGPT can you generate solutions for my coding exercises? An evaluation on its effectiveness in an undergraduate Java programming course. In *Proceedings of the 2023 Conference on Innovation and Technology in Computer Science Education* V. 1 *(ITiCSE 2023)* (pp. 54-60). ACM. DOI: 10.1145/3587102.3588794

Patil, P., Kulkarni, K., & Sharma, P. (2024). Algorithmic issues, challenges, and theoretical concerns of ChatGPT. In Sharma, P., Jyotiyana, M., & Senthil Kumar, A. V. (Eds.), *Applications, challenges, and the future of ChatGPT* (pp. 56–74). IGI Global. DOI: 10.4018/979-8-3693-6824-4.ch003

Prasad, G. A., Kumar, A. V., Sharma, P., Irawati, I. D., Musirin, I. B., Abdullah, H. M., & Rao, L. M. (2023). Artificial intelligence in computer science: An overview of current trends and future directions. In Rajest, S., Singh, B., Obaid, A., Regin, R., & Chinnusamy, K. (Eds.), *Advances in Artificial and Human Intelligence in the Modern Era* (pp. 43–60). IGI Global. DOI: 10.4018/979-8-3693-1301-5.ch002

Russell, S., & Norvig, P. (2021). *Artificial intelligence: A modern approach* (4th ed.). Prentice Hall.

Sethi, S. S., & Sharma, P. (2023). New developments in the implementation of IoT in agriculture. *SN Computer Science*, 4(5), 503. DOI: 10.1007/s42979-023-01896-w

Sharma, P. (2023). Utilizing explainable artificial intelligence to address deep learning in biomedical domain. In *Medical Data Analysis and Processing using Explainable Artificial Intelligence* (pp. 19–38). Taylor & Francis. DOI: 10.1201/9781003257721-2

Sharma, P., & Bhatnagar, N. (2023). Passenger authentication and ticket verification at airport using QR code scanner. *SKIT Research Journal*, 13(2), 10–13. DOI: 10.47904/IJSKIT.13.1.2023.10-12

Sharma, P., & Dadheech, P. (2023). Modern-age agriculture with artificial intelligence: A review emphasizing crop yield prediction. *EVERGREEN Joint Journal of Novel Carbon Resource Sciences & Green Asia Strategy*, 10(4), 2570–2582. DOI: 10.5109/7160906

Sharma, P., Dadheech, P., Aneja, N., & Aneja, S. (2023). Predicting agriculture yields based on machine learning using regression and deep learning. *IEEE Access : Practical Innovations, Open Solutions*, 11, 111255–111264. DOI: 10.1109/ACCESS.2023.3321861

Sharma, P., Dadheech, P., & Senthil Kumar, A. V. (2023). AI-enabled crop recommendation system based on soil and weather patterns. In Gupta, R., Jain, A., Wang, J., Bharti, S., & Patel, S. (Eds.), *Artificial Intelligence Tools and Technologies for Smart Farming and Agriculture Practices* (pp. 184–199). IGI Global. DOI: 10.4018/978-1-6684-8516-3.ch010

Sharma, P., & Jain, M. K. (2023). Stock market trends analysis using extreme gradient boosting (XGBoost). In *Proceedings of the 2023 International Conference on Computing, Communication, and Intelligent Systems (ICCCIS)* (pp. 317-322). IEEE. DOI: 10.1109/ICCCIS60361.2023.10425722

Sharma, P., Jyotiyana, M., & Senthil Kumar, A. V. (Eds.). (2024). *Applications, challenges, and the future of ChatGPT*. IGI Global. DOI: 10.4018/979-8-3693-6824-4

Sharma, P., Kapadiya, D., & Bhardwaj, A. (2023). Efficient note sharing model for collaborative learning. *SKIT Research Journal*, 13(2), 42–46. DOI: 10.47904/IJSKIT.13.2.2023.42-46

Sharma, P., & Rathi, Y. (2016). Efficient density-based clustering using automatic parameter detection. In *Efficient Density-Based Clustering Using Automatic Parameter Detection* (pp. 1–14). Springer. DOI: 10.1007/978-981-10-0767-5_46

Sharma, P., Sharma, C., & Mathur, P. (2023). Machine learning-based stock market forecasting using recurrent neural network. In *Proceedings of the 2023 9th International Conference on Smart Computing and Communications (ICSCC)* (pp. 600-605). IEEE. DOI: 10.1109/ICSCC59169.2023.10335083

Sharma, S., & Yadav, R. (2022). ChatGPT–A technological remedy or challenge for education system. *Global Journal of Enterprise Information System*, 14(4), 46–51. DOI: 10.18311/gjeis/2022/30895

Tanwar, P., Sharma, A., & Pandey, S., & Kumar. (2023). Intrusion detection system based ameliorated technique of pattern matching. In *Proceedings of the 4th International Conference on Information Management & Machine Intelligence (ICIMMI '22)* (Article 110, pp. 1–4). Association for Computing Machinery. DOI: 10.1145/3590837.3590947

Thrun, S., & Anderson, C. (2018). The new era of artificial intelligence in education. *AI Magazine*, 39(2), 26–40.

Tlili, B., Shehata, M., Agyemang Adarkwah, A., Bozkurt, D., Hickey, T., & Huang, R. (2023). What if the devil is my guardian angel: ChatGPT as a case study of using chatbots in education. *Smart Learning Environments, 10*(1).

V., M. V., Kumar, A. S., Sharma, P., Kaur, S., Saleh, O. S., Chennamma, H., & Chaturvedi, A. (2023). AI-equipped IoT applications in high-tech agriculture using machine learning. In A. Khang (Ed.), *Handbook of Research on AI-Equipped IoT Applications in High-Tech Agriculture* (pp. 38-64). IGI Global. DOI: 10.4018/978-1-6684-9231-4.ch003

Venket, K., Ambika, A., Freeda, A., Palla, V., Biju, J., & Shankar, Y. (2023). AI-based pandemic safe venues for effectively managing people crowds to avoid further pandemic waves. *AIP Conference Proceedings*, 2963, 020022. DOI: 10.1063/5.0184379

Wollny, S., Schneider, J., Di Mitri, D., Weidlich, J., Rittberger, M., & Drachsler, H. (2021). Are we there yet? A systematic literature review on chatbots in education. *Frontiers in Artificial Intelligence*, 4, 1–18. DOI: 10.3389/frai.2021.654924 PMID: 34337392

Wooldridge, M. (2018). Artificial intelligence: The impact on engineering. *Communications of the ACM*, 61(10), 46–53.

Chapter 3
ChatGPT and AI in Government:
Pioneering Real-Time Data-Driven Strategies

Dwijendra Nath Dwivedi
https://orcid.org/0000-0001-7662-415X
Krakow University of Economics, Poland

Ghanashyama Mahanty
https://orcid.org/0000-0002-6560-2825
Utkal University, India

Varunendra Nath Dwivedi
SRM University, India

ABSTRACT

This chapter explores the transformative impact of artificial intelligence (AI) and ChatGPT techniques in facilitating real-time data-driven decision-making within government sectors. The adoption of AI and advanced language models like ChatGPT represents a significant shift in how governments process vast amounts of information to make timely and informed decisions. The research focuses on the application of these technologies in enhancing governmental operations, policy-making, and public services. Case studies are presented to illustrate the practical applications of these technologies in various government functions such as public health management, accelerating teaching and learning, urban planning, environmental monitoring, and emergency response. Additionally, the chapter addresses the ethical considerations and the need for robust data governance frameworks to ensure the responsible use of AI in government. This includes discussion on data

DOI: 10.4018/979-8-3693-2284-0.ch003

privacy, security, and the potential risks of bias in AI models.

1. INTRODUCTION

Amidst the age of digital transformation, the incorporation of Artificial Intelligence (AI) into government operations has become a crucial measure for updating public services and improving policy-making. AI technologies, such as advanced conversational models like ChatGPT, are fundamentally transforming the way government agencies engage with its citizens, handle data, and reach conclusions. This article examines the function of ChatGPT and similar AI technologies in enabling real-time, data-driven approaches in the government sector. ChatGPT, created by OpenAI, represents the cutting edge of natural language processing (NLP) capabilities. It engages with people in a conversational style and processes extensive volumes of information to deliver well-informed responses. This has significant ramifications for government institutions, which frequently deal with intricate inquiries and extensive data management duties. Through the integration of ChatGPT, governments can enhance the efficiency, precision, and customization of their services to the public, leading to a significant transformation in citizen involvement and satisfaction. As per "Exploding Topics", The ChatGPT website received an estimated 1.6 billion monthly visitors in early 2023, increasing to 1.7 billion visits by October 2023 as shared in graph 1 below.

Figure 1. Growth of ChatGPT users and website traffic from November 2022 to October 2023

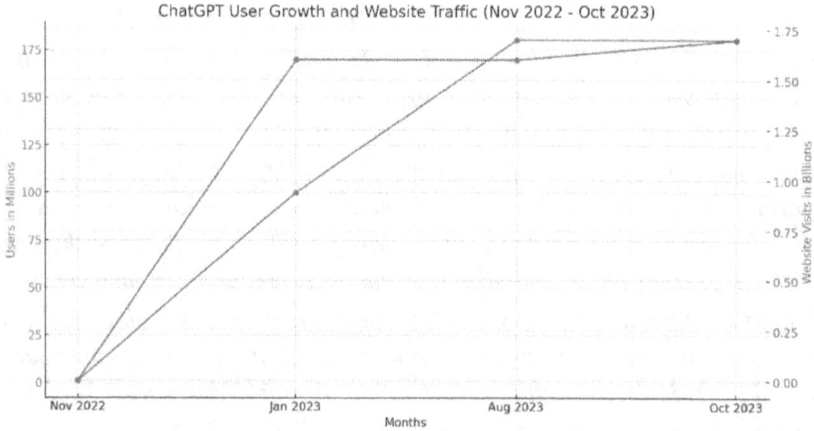

Furthermore, the promise of artificial intelligence in government extends beyond customer service. AI-powered analytics can analyze real-time data to assist in policy development, resource distribution, and crisis handling, providing insights that surpass the capabilities of conventional analytical approaches. The utilization of real-time data processing and analysis allows governments to enhance their ability to swiftly adapt and respond to new conditions and societal requirements. Nevertheless, the implementation of AI in government also gives rise to significant concerns regarding privacy, security, and ethical ramifications. It is crucial to prioritize transparency, fairness, and accountability in the use of AI technology to maintain public trust and defend democratic principles.

This study explores multiple aspects of utilizing ChatGPT and AI in the government. The text showcases effective implementations, evaluates the difficulties and constraints, and offers a plan for future integration tactics. This study seeks to analyze the convergence of AI technology and government operations in order to contribute to the ongoing discussion on digital governance and facilitate the development of innovative, data-driven public administration.

2. LITERATURE STUDY

Al-Mekhlal et. al. (2023) shared that AI tools such as ChatGPT can automate mundane tasks while providing real-time data-driven insights to enhance customer experiences and facilitate problem-solving faster. Coman et al., 2023 identified by connecting the tools to existing information systems, they provide instant, contextually relevant responses to citizens. Sallam et al. (2023) illustrated that ChatGPT can be an invaluable asset to governments with frequent public interactions, providing answers and relieving any concerns from constituents. Furthermore Vaerst et al. (2015) shown that ChatGPT's automated tasks help save both time and money compared to performing repetitive manual tasks by humans - streamlining communication and decision-making can increase productivity, enhance customer service levels and promote transparency within government organizations . Mittal et al. (2023) presented that the governments must develop an appropriate plan for using such tools responsibly and fairly. One of the key considerations when using generative AI tools is data privacy. Any time an agency inputs information into these programs, Luckett (2023) found that this becomes training data for their program - exposing any information it entered to be seen by anyone viewing it, which raises serious issues for privacy and security. Ghosh & Lakshmi (2023) illustrated that any bias or incorrect data could feed back into it and cause it to produce biased answers, potentially perpetuating discrimination on an industrial scale Lack of regulations surrounding such tools can also pose problems, as unauthorized users gain access to data used for training the model. Contractor et al., (2020) found that this poses particular problems for government agencies that must ensure constituent safety and wellbeing by automating repetitive tasks and improving customer service, ChatGPT allows government workers to focus on more important work while saving time for more pressing matters. McDonnell (2019) exemplified that ChatGPT helps employees process large volumes of data more rapidly allowing for quicker decisions making and quicker turnaround times. Li (2018) Government agencies face many considerations when adopting innovative technologies like ChatGPT, which can significantly change their operations (both business and IT), core services and core operations. Tug & Basar (2023) illustrated that generative AI can also play an instrumental role in improving accessibility. ChatGPT can reduce barriers for citizens looking for government services by making information more readily available to them and helping people navigate complex information, find answers to their queries, complete applications for services quickly - which in turn significantly decreases wait times while improving user experiences overall . Dwivedi, D. N., Anand, A. (2021) used time series based method to understand the trade heterogeneity on trade. Gupta, A. et.al. (2023) shared how AI methods can help in detecting and monitoring money laundering. Regenerative AI can be an incredibly valuable resource for government. Li (2021) showed that by integrating it into existing systems agencies can streamline their processes, increase efficiency and effectiveness, enhance citizen experiences and position themselves for future innovation and growth As AI becomes a mainstream practice, it is revolutionizing how governments work. From decreasing employee time spent managing correspondence to improving real-time translation capabilities, Kadar & Kadar (2020) found that this technology is revolutionizing government organizations' operations. Straub et al. (2022) illustrated that generative AI is an extremely useful tool that can automate repetitive tasks and reduce human labor requirements, freeing employees up to focus on more complex or high-level work and increasing overall office efficiency. (Aryanto et al., 2023) also showed that though ChatGPT may contain bias issues, it remains an invaluable asset for local governments looking to boost their customer experience by streamlining communication and decreasing administrative workloads.

In two case studies, Susnjak (2023) showcased the integration of prescriptive analytics with predictive modeling to produce easily understandable prescriptive feedback for individuals at risk. This was achieved by utilizing ChatGPT. Lakkaraju et al. (2023) evaluated the efficacy of power language models (LLMs) in the context of personal finance. The researchers conducted experiments using 13 queries in various dialects and languages. They discovered that the chatbots performed fairly well, however there are still deficiencies in the tool's ability to deliver dependable and precise financial information. Bloomberg is among the first to embrace the use of LLMs in the finance industry. Wu et al. (2023) conducted a validation of

BloombergGPT on various conventional LLM standards, open financial benchmarks, and a set of proprietary benchmarks that were specifically designed for the intended applications of the model. Their amalgamated training dataset exhibits superior performance compared to the current models in financial tasks, while maintaining the model's overall performance. Due to the widespread availability and accessibility of AI technology, as well as its open-source computing framework, the position of the Chief Information Security Officer (CISO) in any organization is now more crucial than ever. According to Prasad et al. (2023), the use of Language Model-based solutions is recommended to help Chief Information Security Officers (CISOs) carry out their responsibilities effectively. In Mundada's (2019) study, the effectiveness of deep neural networks in comparison to traditional models for forecasting attrition risk in the banking industry was assessed. He discovered that the Optimized Deep Feed Forward Neural Network Model surpasses the Gaussian Naïve Bayes and basic neural networks in performance. In a study conducted by Deldjoo (2023), the focus was on examining the performance of LLMs (Machine Learning Models) in evaluating credit risk using a binary classification framework. The study affirms that LLMs can reduce false positives and improve targeted fairness by utilizing 40 times less data. Dwivedi, D. N., & Gupta, A. (2022) proposed an end-to-end approach for the data model, forecast model, and forecasting and demand reporting methods. This can help in efficiently manage power demand by government and private enterprises. Chen et al. (2023) evaluated the capacity of generative artificial intelligence (AI) to forecast financial market outcomes. They utilize LLMs (Language Models) to examine company financial accounts in order to evaluate business attitudes towards environmental policy. They discovered that the sentiment scores they generated can accurately forecast the risk management capabilities of banks and the profitability of their stock returns. An abundance of novel financial goods and services are emerging, and a significant portion lack a precise and well-defined description. Wenzlaff & Spaeth (2022) utilized ChatGPT to obtain precise and suitable definitions of Crowdfunding, alternative finance, and community finance. Dwivedi, D., & Patil, G. (2022) found that development and implementation of simple architectures would be particularly useful in land use classification in developing countries and/or municipalities with limited budgets and less powerful systems with memory constrains.

Dowling & Lucey (2023) showcased the efficacy of using Language Models (LLMs) and ChatGPT to enhance finance research. There are numerous benefits, ranging from the generation of ideas to the formulation of hypotheses and the gathering of evidence. Zaremba & Demir (2023) present an extensive examination of the utilization of ChatGPT-like applications in the field of finance and propose strategies to enhance current natural language processing (NLP) applications by harnessing large language models (LLMs). There are some additional advantages of the LLM-powered ChatGPT application. Such applications not only enhance decision-making accuracy but also facilitate rapidity, scalability, and efficiency. Chen's (2023) research revealed that the performance of the identical LLM service might undergo significant variations within a relatively brief period. This underscores the necessity of ongoing training and monitoring of LLMs to fully harness their advantages. Han et al. (2023) proposed enhancing the frequency of experiential learning initiatives that pose challenges for artificial intelligence in terms of accurate replication. Zhai (2022) determined that there is a requirement for novel assessment forms that prioritize creativity and critical thinking, which cannot be replaced by AI. According to Johnson (2023), generative AI has the potential to significantly enhance human learning and do so on a large scale. Jaimovitch-López et al. (2022) discovered that Chatgpt is an effective tool for various data-wrangling activities. According to Umer & Khan (2023), although LLMs, such as ChatGPT applications, have numerous advantages, they also present certain problems. The primary concerns encompass disinformation, possible distortion and prejudice, privacy and security apprehensions, and insufficiency in clarity and openness. Feng et al. (2023) emphasize that although ChatGPT produces a vast amount of output rapidly, its dependability and precision pose significant concerns due to the potential impact of financial decisions on society. Several studies recommend exercising prudence while utilizing generative AI-powered systems for making financial decisions (Alkaissi & McFarlane, 2023; Tsigaris & Teixeira, 2023; and Cascella et al., 2023).

3. CASE STUDIES

3.1 Case Study 1: Using ChatGPT to Automate Public Inquiries

Public sector communication and decision-making must be timely and efficient to guarantee citizen satisfaction and efficient service delivery, but the sheer volume of stakeholders and bureaucracies make this challenging. That is where innovative AI technologies like ChatGPT come into play; its power lies in revolutionizing how government agencies engage with citizens more efficiently and transparently. ChatGPT can assist in automating the response to public inquiries, which will improve citizen engagement while freeing up human staff for more complex tasks. In addition, ChatGPT can analyze data and generate reports - freeing up valuable human resources.

ChatGPT can also be utilized by public sector entities to increase public participation and engagement by improving accessibility to information (Verma, 2013). For instance, it could automatically provide answers to frequently asked questions regarding services, programs and policies offered by the government while improving transparency to ensure citizens receive accurate details at all times. ChatGPT can also aid policymaking by producing summaries of important issues and potential impacts that help streamline decision-making and enable policymakers to better comprehend potential consequences of their choices (Montenegro et al., 2023). ChatGPT can help government services improve efficiency, accuracy, and overall quality. However, while this technology may help reduce manual workloads significantly, it should never replace human efforts entirely; rather it should serve as an additional supplement to human efforts rather than taking over them altogether (Basir et.al, (2023). ChatGPT can unlock limitless potential in the public sector. Government agencies can leverage this cutting-edge technology to improve service delivery and drive innovation.

Case Study 2: Using ChatGPT to Automate Business Processes

ChatGPT is an invaluable tool that government agencies can utilize to automate certain business processes and improve decision-making (López et al., 2022). It can create chatbots or virtual assistants capable of responding to citizens' inquiries, further increasing efficiency and accessibility of government services (Kumar & Manhar, 2023). Furthermore, ChatGPT allows them to analyze data to provide new insights that aid policy development as well as implementation.

ChatGPT and other large language models should not replace human efforts; rather, they can serve as an adjunct tool that increases productivity while offering additional assistance (Parker et al., 2023). As such, it is crucial that chatbots be properly trained so they are capable of efficiently answering all questions and queries. Furthermore, keep in mind that the quality of answers generated by ChatGPT depends on its input as an end-user. Correct and reliable questions must be used to train bots (Liu et al., 2023); otherwise, they could produce inaccurate responses. Furthermore, any unclear or biased data could result in incorrect outcomes; so it is vital that accurate and reliable information be used when training the bots, with personal details or sensitive data avoided as much as possible.

One of the main challenges associated with using ChatGPT to automate business processes is its complex output. This is especially problematic if being used for customer service as this may lead to misinterpretations and frustration among customers. Furthermore, technical errors within ChatGPT may cause further disruptions that leave customers unhappy and dissatisfied.

ChatGPT can be expensive in its implementation and management of business process automation, due to requiring extensive resources for management and upkeep of its technology. Furthermore, it may prove challenging to integrate and integrate it into existing work processes.

ChatGPT can improve communication and decision-making within government agencies despite its limitations, helping streamline public inquiry response time, conduct policy analysis and enhance decision-making processes. Furthermore, ChatGPT automates business processes which frees up employee time and resources for more important tasks.

Case Study 3: Using ChatGPT to Automate Customer Service

ChatGPT serves as an AI assistant that can assist citizens by offering instantaneous assistance and guiding them through various government services. Furthermore, ChatGPT handles routine transactions like processing applications, issuing certificates, and scheduling appointments allowing human agents to focus on more complex tasks thereby saving both time and improving citizen services (Al-Mekhlal et al., 2023).

ChatGPT stands apart from traditional customer support chatbots by being able to understand the nuances of human language and thought. To do so, it tokenizes information entered by users, fragmenting it into smaller parts that allow the system to recognize relationships among them - and recognize relationships among these pieces that allow it to analyze grammar, syntax and semantics as well as understand context of prior questions in the conversation. These factors combine to produce highly structured responses with natural-sounding answers (Kumar & Manhar, 2023).

As with any new technology, ChatGPT presents unique challenges. One is employee resistance to automation; government agencies should proactively address this by informing staff of its benefits and emphasizing its purpose as one that supplements rather than replace their work (Vaerst et al., 2015)). Another risk associated with ChatGPT training on unreliable data could lead to bias and discrimination; to combat this problem effectively, government agencies must regularly evaluate and update training data in order to ensure its use remains fair and equitable (Gasperecz & Gasperecz, 2023).

ChatGPT can transform communication and decision-making within government agencies by automating administrative tasks, streamlining internal processes, and supporting policy development - giving employees more power to work more efficiently and effectively resulting in enhanced service delivery for citizens (McDonnell, 2019).

Case Study 4: Using ChatGPT to Automate Policy-Making

ChatGPT can assist government agencies by automating responses to public inquiries and producing reports and summaries that reduce administrative burdens while freeing employees to focus on more strategic initiatives (McDonnell, 2019).

Furthermore, it promotes collaboration and knowledge-sharing among stakeholders by offering a centralized platform for communications; furthermore it reduces misunderstandings by helping everyone access the same information in a standardized format (Basir et al., 2023).

ChatGPT can assist in policymaking in numerous ways. For instance, it can identify risks associated with policy proposals by simulating various scenarios and predicting outcomes, helping policymakers identify mitigation strategies while aligning policies with agency goals and values. (Li, 2018). It can also evaluate existing policies by analyzing historical data to spot patterns or trends.

ChatGPT can also be used to facilitate brainstorming and concept development by identifying new ideas and opportunities (Aryanto, et al., 2023). Furthermore, it can provide an open forum for discussions among stakeholders regarding common interests that lead to more collaborative and efficient decision-making processes.

ChatGPT can improve communication and efficiency across government agencies, but must be used with caution (Ray, 2023). Hacking vulnerabilities make this technology vulnerable to exploit by malicious actors in order to commit phishing attacks or gather sensitive personal information - as evidenced by recent outrage against an automated condolence message sent out via ChatGPT after a university shooting incident. Consequently, government agencies must establish appropriate safeguards in order to ensure responsible use of this technology (Ghosh & Lakshmi, 2023).

Though ChatGPT may present certain challenges to government agencies, its benefits can be considerable. Automating mundane tasks and freeing up more time for more important work (Jaimovitch-López, 2022); improving customer service by offering instant and personalized assistance (Coman, et al., 2023); increasing collaboration between stakeholders; streamlining business processes to reduce manual work; cost-effectively replacing human resources without compromising quality or accuracy - these are all major draws of using ChatGPT in government agencies (Straub, et al., 2023).

4. REAL LIFE EXAMPLES

The global implementation of AI in government services demonstrates a wide range of influential and significant uses. Estonia is at the forefront of digital governance, utilizing artificial intelligence to improve citizen services. Singapore and the United States utilize artificial intelligence-powered chatbots and healthcare services, respectively, to enhance public engagement and facilitate communication in the healthcare sector. Japan prioritizes the utilization of AI in disaster response to ensure safety and enhance efficiency, whereas the UK concentrates on employing AI for innovation in the public sector. India utilizes artificial intelligence to promote agricultural progress, providing assistance to rural areas. The European Union implements a moral structure for artificial intelligence (AI) in governance, whereas Canada optimizes immigration procedures using AI, emphasizing its effectiveness and user-centric approach in public administration. (Table 1)

Table 1. Growth of ChatGPT users and website traffic from November 2022 to October 2023

Country	AI Application
Estonia	Digital Governance (e.g., e-Residency, digital ID, e-Voting)
Singapore	Virtual Assistants in Public Services
United States	AI-Driven Health Services (COVID-19 response)
Japan	AI for Disaster Response and Management
United Kingdom	AI in Public Sector Innovation
India	AI for Agricultural Development
European Union	Ethical AI Framework in Governance
Canada	AI for Immigration and Visa Processing

Estonia is renowned for its digital governance initiatives such as e-Residency, digital ID, and e-Voting. Singapore has implemented AI-driven chatbots in various government sectors to improve efficiency and citizen engagement. U.S. government's use of AI in healthcare, particularly during the COVID-19 pandemic for information dissemination and patient communication, is a notable case. Japan's use of AI in disaster risk reduction and crisis management, especially in predicting and responding to natural disasters like earthquakes and tsunamis, is another exemplary case study. The UK government's use of AI in public sector innovation, as part of their AI Sector Deal and Government Digital Service is another example. India's integration of AI in agriculture, for predicting crop yields, providing farming advisories, and market intelligence, is a significant case. The EU's approach to developing and implementing an ethical framework for AI in public administration could serve another case study. Canada's use of AI in streamlining immigration and visa processing offers insights into how AI can enhance operational efficiency.

5. CONCLUSION

To summarize, this paper extensively explored integrating artificial intelligence (AI) within government sectors, explicitly focusing on ChatGPT. It highlighted the transformative potential of AI in revolutionizing public sector operations, enabling governments to offer enhanced and efficient services and to formulate data-driven policy decisions. Key application areas included enhancing customer service through real-time, informed interactions and leveraging AI for insightful policy development and crisis management analysis. The study underscored the ability of ChatGPT to process and interpret vast datasets, facilitating a more agile response to public needs and societal changes. Case studies were presented to illustrate successful implementations of AI in various government functions, demonstrating significant improvements in operational efficiency and public engagement.

Concurrently, the paper addressed the challenges and ethical considerations in deploying AI technologies in the public sector. Data privacy, security, and the need for transparent and accountable AI systems were critically examined. The balance between technological advancement and ethical responsibility formed a recurring theme throughout the discussion. Incorporating ChatGPT and other AI technologies in government operations signifies a crucial transition towards a more dynamic, efficient, and responsive public administration. The results of this study highlight AI's capacity to significantly improve public services and policy-making processes, making them more responsive to the immediate requirements of citizens. Nevertheless, achieving the effective integration of AI in government necessitates a meticulous and equitable strategy. Government organizations must prioritize both leveraging the technological possibilities of AI and addressing the ethical, privacy, and security problems that come with its implementation. It is imperative to establish thorough standards and frameworks to ensure the ethical utilization of AI in public administration.

AI, such as conversational models like ChatGPT, plays a crucial role in facilitating the change of governments as they progress and adjust to the digital era. The journey towards AI-augmented government involves ongoing examination, adaptation, and a commitment to sustaining democratic ideals and public trust. Ultimately, the article supports embracing a proactive perspective in which AI is regarded as a cooperative instrument in governance, amplifying human decision-making and improving the overall standard of public administration and citizen well-being. The future of digital government, supported by AI, offers significant opportunities and possibilities as long as it is approached with responsibility, foresight, and a steadfast dedication to the welfare of the people.

6. FURTHER RESEARCH

Here we have some interesting areas for further research. An important aspect to explore pertains to the influence of ChatGPT on governmental operations. One possible approach is to analyze possible applications of language models such as ChatGPT in different government organizations. Potential applications of conversational AI encompass the optimization of citizen care and support, the automation of repetitive jobs and document processing, and the augmentation of policy analysis and decision-making procedures. Examining specific instances and possible advantages could provide insight into the revolutionary capacity of these technologies in the public sector.

It is important to examine the advancement of data-driven methods that utilize extensive language models such as ChatGPT. This may involve utilizing ChatGPT for the purpose of data mining and extracting knowledge from government data sources, integrating language models with pre-existing data infrastructures, enabling real-time analysis of citizen feedback and sentiment, and producing data-driven insights to guide the development of policies. Valuable insights can be gained by examining the technical capabilities and practical implementations of these tactics. Further, it is imperative to acknowledge and tackle the ethical implications and governance complexities associated with the utilization of artificial intelligence within governmental contexts. This may encompass the examination of strategies to mitigate bias and promote equity in the outputs of language models, the resolution of privacy and security issues associated with the handling of sensitive government data, the assurance of transparency and interpretability in AI-generated content, and the establishment of comprehensive guidelines and frameworks to ensure responsible utilization of AI in government settings.

It is essential to analyze the difficulties in adopting AI systems such as ChatGPT and the management of change when integrating them into government procedures. This may entail devising tactics to surmount organizational opposition and foster AI proficiency among government personnel, methodology for incorporating AI systems into existing systems and procedures, initiatives for training and reskilling to facilitate efficient AI collaboration, and fostering public confidence and approval of AI in government services. Ultimately, we could delve into the prospective prospects and nascent patterns in the realm of artificial intelligence and government. This may involve an analysis of the progress made in language models and their potential impact on government agencies, the possibilities presented by multimodal AI systems that integrate language, vision, and other modalities, the significance of federated learning and privacy-preserving AI techniques in relation to government data, and the potential for collaboration between AI and humans in policymaking and governance procedures.

REFERENCES

Al-Mekhlal, M., Al-Buraik, M., & Al-Lubli, M. (2023). Digital transformation: AI-powered bot solutions and automation for customer services. *2023 International Conference on Digital Age & Technological Advances for Sustainable Development (ICDATA)*. DOI: 10.1109/ICDATE58146.2023.10248458

Alkaissi, H., & McFarlane, S. I. (2023). Artificial hallucinations in ChatGPT: Implications in scientific writing. *Cureus*, 15. DOI: 10.7759/cureus.35179 PMID: 36811129

Aryanto, E., Mabruk, H., & Narendroputro, W. (2023). *Artificial intelligence implementation strategy to make it happen smart government Indonesia gold 2045*. International Journal of Social Science and Business. DOI: 10.54783/ijsoc.v5i5.877

Basir, A., Puspitasari, E., Aristarini, C. C., Sulastri, P. D., & Ausat, A. M. A. (2023). Ethical use of ChatGPT in the context of leadership and strategic decisions. Journal of Maritime Policy. DOI: 10.33395/jmp.v12i1.12693

Cascella, M., Montomoli, J., Bellini, V., & Bignami, E. (2023). Evaluating the feasibility of ChatGPT in healthcare: An analysis of multiple clinical and research scenarios. *Journal of Medical Systems*, 47(1), 1–5. DOI: 10.1007/s10916-023-01925-4 PMID: 36869927

Chen, B., Wu, Z., & Zhao, R. (2023). From fiction to fact: The growing role of generative AI in business and finance. *Journal of Chinese Economic and Business Studies*, 21(4), 471–496. DOI: 10.1080/14765284.2023.2245279

Chikkamath, M., Dwivedi, D., Hirekurubar, R. B., & Thimmappa, R. (2023). Benchmarking of novel convolutional neural network models for automatic butterfly identification. In Shukla, P. K., Singh, K. P., Tripathi, A. K., & Engelbrecht, A. (Eds.), *Computer Vision and Robotics. Algorithms for Intelligent Systems*. Springer. DOI: 10.1007/978-981-19-7892-0_27

Coman, D., State, V., Voinea, M. C., & Cucui, G. (2023). Impacts of chatbots on the accounting service industry. *Agora International Journal of Economical Sciences*, 17(1), 1–13. Advance online publication. DOI: 10.15837/aijes.v17i1.5756

Contractor, D., McDuff, D. J., Haines, J., Lee, J., Hines, C., & Hecht, B. J. (2020). Behavioral use licensing for responsible AI. arXiv. https://dblp.org/rec/journals/corr/abs-2011-03116.html

Deldjoo, Y. (2023). Fairness of ChatGPT and the role of explainable-guided prompts. ArXiv, abs/2307.11761.

Dowling, M. M., & Lucey, B. M. (2023). ChatGPT for (Finance) Research: The Bananarama Conjecture. SSRN *Electronic Journal*. DOI: 10.2139/ssrn.4322651

Dwivedi, D., & Patil, G. (2022). Lightweight Convolutional Neural Network for Land Use Image Classification. *Journal of Advanced Geospatial Science & Technology*, 2(1), 31–48. DOI: 10.11113/jagst.v2n1.31

Dwivedi, D., & Vemareddy, A. (2023). Sentiment Analytics for Crypto Pre and Post Covid: Topic Modeling. In Molla, A. R., Sharma, G., Kumar, P., & Rawat, S. (Eds.), Lecture Notes in Computer Science: Vol. 13776. *Distributed Computing and Intelligent Technology. ICDCIT 2023*. Springer. DOI: 10.1007/978-3-031-24848-1_21

Dwivedi, D. N., & Anand, A. (2021). The Text Mining of Public Policy Documents in Response to COVID-19: A Comparison of the United Arab Emirates and the Kingdom of Saudi Arabia. Public Governance / Zarządzanie Publiczne, 55(1), 8-22. DOI: 10.15678/ZP.2021.55.1.02

Dwivedi, D. N., & Anand, A. (2022). A Comparative Study of Key Themes of Scientific Research Post COVID-19 in the United Arab Emirates and WHO Using Text Mining Approach. In Tiwari, S., Trivedi, M. C., Kolhe, M. L., Mishra, K., & Singh, B. K. (Eds.), *Advances in Data and Information Sciences. Lecture Notes in Networks and Systems* (Vol. 318). Springer. DOI: 10.1007/978-981-16-5689-7_30

Dwivedi, D. N., & Batra, S. (2024). Case Studies in Big Data Analysis: A Novel Computer Vision Application to Detect Insurance Fraud. In Darwish, D. (Ed.), *Big Data Analytics Techniques for Market Intelligence* (pp. 441–450). IGI Global. DOI: 10.4018/979-8-3693-0413-6.ch018

Dwivedi, D. N., Batra, S., & Pathak, Y. K. (2024). Enhancing Customer Experience: Exploring Deep Learning Models for Banking Customer Journey Analysis. In Sharma, H., Chakravorty, A., Hussain, S., & Kumari, R. (Eds.), *Artificial Intelligence: Theory and Applications. AITA 2023. Lecture Notes in Networks and Systems* (Vol. 843). Springer. DOI: 10.1007/978-981-99-8476-3_39

Dwivedi, D. N., & Gupta, A. (2022). Artificial intelligence-driven power demand estimation and short-, medium-, and long-term forecasting. In Artificial Intelligence for Renewable Energy Systems (pp. 231-242). Woodhead Publishing. DOI: 10.1016/B978-0-323-90396-7.00013-4

Dwivedi, D. N., & Mahanty, G. (2024). Unmasking the Shadows: Exploring Unethical AI Implementation. In Dadwal, S., Goyal, S., Kumar, P., & Verma, R. (Eds.), *Demystifying the Dark Side of AI in Business* (pp. 185–200). IGI Global. DOI: 10.4018/979-8-3693-0724-3.ch012

Dwivedi, D. N., & Mahanty, G. (2024). Guardians of the Algorithm: Human Oversight in the Ethical Evolution of AI and Data Analysis. In Kumar, R., Joshi, A., Sharan, H., Peng, S., & Dudhagara, C. (Eds.), *The Ethical Frontier of AI and Data Analysis* (pp. 196–210). IGI Global. DOI: 10.4018/979-8-3693-2964-1.ch012

Dwivedi, D. N., & Mahanty, G. (2024). Mental health in messages: Unravelling emotional patterns through advanced text analysis. In Rai, M., & Pandey, J. (Eds.), *Using Machine Learning to Detect Emotions and Predict Human Psychology* (pp. 187–208). IGI Global. DOI: 10.4018/979-8-3693-1910-9.ch009

Dwivedi, D. N., Mahanty, G., & Dwivedi, V. N. (2024). The Role of Predictive Analytics in Personalizing Education: Tailoring Learning Paths for Individual Student Success. In Bhatia, M., & Mushtaq, M. (Eds.), *Enhancing Education With Intelligent Systems and Data-Driven Instruction* (pp. 44–59). IGI Global. DOI: 10.4018/979-8-3693-2169-0.ch003

Dwivedi, D. N., Mahanty, G., & Vemareddy, A. (2022). How responsible is AI?: Identification of key public concerns using sentiment analysis and topic modeling. *International Journal of Information Retrieval Research*, 12(1), 1–14. DOI: 10.4018/IJIRR.298646

Dwivedi, D. N., Mahanty, G., & Vemareddy, A. (2023). Sentiment analysis and topic modeling for identifying key public concerns of water quality/issues. In S. Harun, I. K. Othman, & M. H. Jamal (Eds.), *Proceedings of the 5th International Conference on Water Resources (ICWR)* – Volume 1. *Lecture Notes in Civil Engineering,* vol 293. Springer. DOI: 10.1007/978-981-19-5947-9_28

Dwivedi, D. N., & Pathak, S. (2022). Sentiment Analysis for COVID Vaccinations Using Twitter: Text Clustering of Positive and Negative Sentiments. In Hassan, S. A., Mohamed, A. W., & Alnowibet, K. A. (Eds.), *Decision Sciences for COVID-19. International Series in Operations Research & Management Science* (Vol. 320). Springer. DOI: 10.1007/978-3-030-87019-5_12

Dwivedi, D. N., Wójcik, K., & Vemareddyb, A. (2022). Identification of Key Concerns and Sentiments Towards Data Quality and Data Strategy Challenges Using Sentiment Analysis and Topic Modeling. In Jajuga, K., Dehnel, G., & Walesiak, M. (Eds.), *Modern Classification and Data Analysis. SKAD 2021. Studies in Classification, Data Analysis, and Knowledge Organization.* Springer. DOI: 10.1007/978-3-031-10190-8_2

Feng, Z., Hu, G., & Li, B. (2023). Unleashing the power of ChatGPT in finance research: Opportunities and challenges. SSRN *Electronic Journal.* DOI: 10.2139/ssrn.4424979

Gasperecz, E., & Gasperecz, E. (2023, June 9). Transforming banking with ChatGPT: Enhanced chat, fraud detection, personalized recommendations, and risk management - First National Bankers Bank. First National Bankers Bank - Community Banking throughout the Southeast and Midwest. https://www.bankers-bank.com/transforming-banking-with-chatgpt-enhanced-chat-fraud-detection-personalized-recommendations-and-risk-management/

Ghosh, A., & Lakshmi, D. (2023). Dual governance: The intersection of centralized regulation and crowdsourced safety mechanisms for generative AI. arXiv. https://doi.org//arXiv.2308.04448DOI: 10.48550

Gupta, A., Dwivedi, D. N., & Shah, J. (2023a). Overview of money laundering. In Artificial Intelligence Applications in Banking and Financial Services. Future of Business and Finance. Springer. DOI: 10.1007/978-981-99-2571-1_1

Gupta, A., Dwivedi, D. N., & Shah, J. (2023b). Financial crimes management and control in financial institutions. In Artificial Intelligence Applications in Banking and Financial Services. Future of Business and Finance. Springer. DOI: 10.1007/978-981-99-2571-1_2

Gupta, A., Dwivedi, D. N., & Shah, J. (2023c). Overview of technology solutions. In Artificial Intelligence Applications in Banking and Financial Services. Future of Business and Finance. Springer. DOI: 10.1007/978-981-99-2571-1_3

Gupta, A., Dwivedi, D. N., & Shah, J. (2023d). Data organization for an FCC unit. In Artificial Intelligence Applications in Banking and Financial Services. Future of Business and Finance. Springer. DOI: 10.1007/978-981-99-2571-1_4

Gupta, A., Dwivedi, D. N., & Shah, J. (2023e). Planning for AI in financial crimes. In Artificial Intelligence Applications in Banking and Financial Services. Future of Business and Finance. Springer. DOI: 10.1007/978-981-99-2571-1_5

Gupta, A., Dwivedi, D. N., & Shah, J. (2023f). Applying machine learning for effective customer risk assessment. In Artificial Intelligence Applications in Banking and Financial Services. Future of Business and Finance. Springer. DOI: 10.1007/978-981-99-2571-1_6

Gupta, A., Dwivedi, D. N., & Shah, J. (2023g). Artificial intelligence-driven effective financial transaction monitoring. In Artificial Intelligence Applications in Banking and Financial Services. Future of Business and Finance. Springer. DOI: 10.1007/978-981-99-2571-1_7

Gupta, A., Dwivedi, D. N., & Shah, J. (2023h). Machine learning-driven alert optimization. In Artificial Intelligence Applications in Banking and Financial Services. Future of Business and Finance. Springer. DOI: 10.1007/978-981-99-2571-1_8

Gupta, A., Dwivedi, D. N., & Shah, J. (2023i). Applying artificial intelligence on investigation. In Artificial Intelligence Applications in Banking and Financial Services. Future of Business and Finance. Springer. DOI: 10.1007/978-981-99-2571-1_9

Gupta, A., Dwivedi, D. N., & Shah, J. (2023j). Ethical challenges for AI-based applications. In Artificial Intelligence Applications in Banking and Financial Services. Future of Business and Finance. Springer. DOI: 10.1007/978-981-99-2571-1_10

Gupta, A., Dwivedi, D. N., & Shah, J. (2023k). Setting up a best-in-class AI-driven financial crime control unit (FCCU). In Artificial Intelligence Applications in Banking and Financial Services. Future of Business and Finance. Springer. DOI: 10.1007/978-981-99-2571-1_11

Gupta, A. (2021). Understanding Consumer Product Sentiments through Supervised Models on Cloud: Pre and Post COVID. Webology, 18(1). .DOI: 10.14704/WEB/V18I1/WEB18097

Han, Z., Battaglia, F., Udaiyar, A., Fooks, A., & Terlecky, S. R. (2023). An explorative assessment of ChatGPT as an aid in medical education: Use it with caution. *medRxiv*. DOI: 10.1101/2023.02.13.23285879

Jaimovitch-López, G., Ferri, C., Hernández-Orallo, J., Martínez-Plumed, F., & Ramírez-Quintana, M. J. (2022). Can language models automate data wrangling? *Machine Learning*, 112(6), 2053–2082. DOI: 10.1007/s10994-022-06259-9

Johnson, W. L. (2023). How to harness generative AI to accelerate human learning. *International Journal of Artificial Intelligence in Education*. Advance online publication. DOI: 10.1007/s40593-023-00367-w

Kadar, T., & Kadar, M. (2020). Sustainability is not enough: Towards AI supported regenerative design. *2020 IEEE International Conference on Technology Management, Operations and Decisions (ICTMOD)*. DOI: 10.1109/ICE/ITMC49519.2020.9198554

Kapadiya, D., Shekhawat, C., & Sharma, P. (2023). A Study on Large Scale Applications of Big Data in Modern Era. In *International Conference on Information Management & Machine Intelligence (ICIMMI2023)*. ACM. https://doi.org/DOI: 10.1145/3647444.364788

Kumar, S. M., & Manhar, A. (2023). *Sentimental analysis of customer reviews using RPA and categorization of reviews using ChatGPT*. International Journal of Scientific Research in Computer Science, Engineering and Information Technology. DOI: 10.32628/CSEIT23903101

Lakkaraju, K., Vuruma, S. K., Pallagani, V., Muppasani, B., & Srivastava, B. (2023). Can LLMs be good financial advisors?: An initial study in personal decision making for optimized outcomes. ArXiv, abs/2307.07422.

Li, B. (2021). Dynamic evaluation and system coordination degree of the integration of artificial intelligence and real economy. *Complexity*, 2021(1), 5539793. Advance online publication. DOI: 10.1155/2021/5539793

Li, Y. (2018). Political affairs supermarket—Orientation of transformation of government management. *Proceedings of the 2018 International Conference on Contemporary Education, Social Sciences and Ecological Studies (ICCES 2018)*. DOI: 10.25236/iccems.2018.13

Liu, X., Vatn, J., Yin, S., & Maithani, V. (2023). Performance of ChatGPT on CMRP: Potential for assisting maintenance and reliability professionals using large language models. In 2023 IEEE 49th Annual Conference of the Industrial Electronics Society (IECON). DOI: 10.1109/IECON51785.2023.10311736

López, V., Picco, G., Vejsbjerg, I., Hoang, T., Hou, Y., Sbodio, M., Segrave-Daly, J., Moga, D., Swords, S., Wei, M., & Carroll, E. (2022). Envisioning a human-AI collaborative system to transform policies into decision models. arXiv. https://doi .org//arXiv.2212.06882DOI: 10.48550

Luckett, J. (2023). Regulating generative AI: A pathway to ethical and responsible implementation. *International Journal of Computer Informatics*, 12(5), 79–92. Advance online publication. DOI: 10.5121/ijci.2023.120508

Mahanty, G., Dwivedi, D. N., & Gopalakrishnan, B. N. (2021). The efficacy of fiscal vs monetary policies in the Asia-Pacific region: The St. Louis equation revisited. *Vision (Basel)*. Advance online publication. DOI: 10.1177/09722629211054148

Maharajan, K., Kumar, A. V., El Emary, I. M., Sharma, P., Latip, R., Mishra, N., Dutta, A., Manjunatha Rao, L., & Sharma, M. (2023). Blockchain Methods and Data-Driven Decision Making With Autonomous Transportation. In Kumar, R., Abdul Hamid, A., & Binti Ya'akub, N. (Eds.), *Effective AI, Blockchain, and E-Governance Applications for Knowledge Discovery and Management* (pp. 176–194). IGI Global. DOI: 10.4018/978-1-6684-9151-5.ch012

Manjunath, C., Dwivedi, D. N., Thimmappa, R., & Vedamurthy, K. B. (2023). Detection and categorization of diseases in pearl millet leaves using novel convolutional neural network model. In *Future Farming* (Vol. 1, p. 41). Advancing Agriculture with Artificial Intelligence. DOI: 10.2174/9789815124729123010006

McDonnell, J. (2019). *Maine's workforce challenges in an age of artificial intelligence*. Maine Policy Review. DOI: 10.53558/REUA8661

Merlin Mancy, A., Kumar, A. V., Latip, R., Jagadamba, G., Chakrabarti, P., Sharma, P., Musirin, I. B., Sharma, M., & Kanchan, B. G. (2024). *Smart Healthcare System, Digital Health and Telemedicine, Management and Emergencies: Patient Emergency Application (PES)*. E-Governance Applications. DOI: 10.4018/979-8-3693-1722-8.ch008

Mittal, S., Thakral, K., Singh, R., Vatsa, M., Glaser, T., Ferrer, C. C., & Hassner, T. (2023). On responsible machine learning datasets with fairness, privacy, and regulatory norms. arXiv. https://doi.org//arXiv.2310.15848DOI: 10.48550

Montenegro Rueda, M., Fernández-Cerero, J., Fernández-Batanero, J., & López-Meneses, E. (2023). Impact of the implementation of ChatGPT in education: A systematic review. *Computers*, 12(8), 153. DOI: 10.3390/computers12080153

Mundada, S. K. (2019). Optimized deep neural network based predictive model for customer attrition analysis in the banking sector. *Recent Patents on Engineering*, 13, 1–10.

Parker, J., Richard, V., & Becker, K. (2023). Flexibility & iteration: Exploring the potential of large language models in developing and refining interview protocols. *The Qualitative Report*, 28(3). Advance online publication. DOI: 10.46743/2160-3715/2023.6695

Pozzi, F. A., & Dwivedi, D. (2023). ESG and IoT: Ensuring sustainability and social responsibility in the digital age. In Tiwari, S., Ortiz-Rodríguez, F., Mishra, S., Vakaj, E., & Kotecha, K. (Eds.), *Artificial Intelligence: Towards Sustainable Intelligence. AI4S 2023. Communications in Computer and Information Science* (Vol. 1907). Springer. DOI: 10.1007/978-3-031-47997-7_2

Prasad, G. A., Kumar, A. V., Sharma, P., Irawati, I. D., D. V., C., Musirin, I. B., Abdullah, H. M., & Rao L, M. (2023). Artificial Intelligence in Computer Science: An Overview of Current Trends and Future Directions. In S. Rajest, B. Singh, A. Obaid, R. Regin, & K. Chinnusamy (Eds.), *Advances in Artificial and Human Intelligence in the Modern Era* (pp. 43-60). IGI Global. DOI: 10.4018/979-8-3693-1301-5.ch002

Prasad, S. G., Sharmila, V. C., & Badrinarayanan, M. K. (2023). Role of artificial intelligence based chat generative pre-trained transformer (ChatGPT) in cyber security. 2023 2nd International Conference on Applied Artificial Intelligence and Computing (ICAAIC), 107-114.

Rawat, P., Bhardwaj, A., Lamba, N., Sharma, P., Kumawat, P., & Sharma, P. (2023). Arduino Based IoT Mini Weather Station. *SKIT Research Journal*, 13(2), 34–41. DOI: 10.47904/IJSKIT.13.2.2023.34-41

Ray, P. (2023). ChatGPT: A comprehensive review on background, applications, key challenges, bias, ethics, limitations and future scope. *Internet of Things and Cyber-Physical Systems*, 3, 121–154. Advance online publication. DOI: 10.1016/j.iotcps.2023.04.003

Sallam, M., Salim, N., Barakat, M., & Al-Tammemi, A. B. (2023). ChatGPT applications in medical, dental, pharmacy, and public health education: A descriptive study highlighting the advantages and limitations. *Narra J*, 3(1), e103. Advance online publication. DOI: 10.52225/narra.v3i1.103 PMID: 38450035

Sethi, S. S., & Sharma, P. (2023). New Developments in the Implementation of IoT in Agriculture. *SN Computer Science*, 4(5), 503. DOI: 10.1007/s42979-023-01896-w

Sharma, P. (2023). *Utilizing Explainable Artificial Intelligence to Address Deep Learning in Biomedical Domain, Medical Data Analysis and Processing using Explainable Artificial Intelligence*. Taylor & Francis. DOI: 10.1201/9781003257721-2

Sharma, P., & Bhatnagar, N. (2023). Passenger Authentication and Ticket Verification at Airport Using QR Code Scanner. *SKIT Research Journal*, 13(2), 10–13. DOI: 10.47904/IJSKIT.13.1.2023.10-12

Sharma, P., & Dadheech, P. (2023). Modern-age Agriculture with Artificial Intelligence: A review emphasizing Crop Yield Prediction. *EVERGREEN Joint Journal of Novel Carbon Resource Sciences & Green Asia Strategy*, 10(4), 2570–2582. DOI: 10.5109/7160906

Sharma, P., Dadheech, P., Aneja, N., & Aneja, S. (2023). Predicting Agriculture Yields Based on Machine Learning Using Regression and Deep Learning. *IEEE Access : Practical Innovations, Open Solutions*, 11, 111255–111264. DOI: 10.1109/ACCESS.2023.3321861

Sharma, P., Dadheech, P., & Senthil Kumar Senthil, A. V. (2023). AI-Enabled Crop Recommendation System Based on Soil and Weather Patterns. In Gupta, R., Jain, A., Wang, J., Bharti, S., & Patel, S. (Eds.), *Artificial Intelligence Tools and Technologies for Smart Farming and Agriculture Practices* (pp. 184–199). IGI Global. DOI: 10.4018/978-1-6684-8516-3.ch010

Sharma, P., & Jain, M. K. (2023). Stock Market Trends Analysis using Extreme Gradient Boosting (XGBoost). *International Conference on Computing, Communication, and Intelligent Systems (ICCCIS)*, 317-322. DOI: 10.1109/ICCCIS60361.2023.10425722

Sharma, P., Kapadiya, D., & Bhardwaj, A. (2023). Efficient Note Sharing Model for Collaborative Learning. *SKIT Research Journal*, 13(2), 42–46. DOI: 10.47904/IJSKIT.13.2.2023.42-46

Sharma, P., & Rathi, Y. (2016, June 5). Efficient Density-Based Clustering Using Automatic Parameter Detection. Efficient Density-Based Clustering Using Automatic Parameter Detection | SpringerLink. .DOI: 10.1007/978-981-10-0767-5_46

Sharma, P., Sharma, C., & Mathur, P. (2023). Machine Learning-based Stock Market Forecasting using Recurrent Neural Network. 2023 9th International Conference on Smart Computing and Communications (ICSCC), 600-605. DOI: 10.1109/ICSCC59169.2023.10335083

Straub, V. J., Morgan, D., Bright, J., & Margetts, H. (2022). Artificial intelligence in government: Concepts, standards, and a unified framework. arXiv. https://doi.org//arXiv.2210.17218DOI: 10.48550

Susnjak, T. (2023). Beyond predictive learning analytics modelling and onto explainable artificial intelligence with prescriptive analytics and ChatGPT. *International Journal of Artificial Intelligence in Education.*

Tanwar, A., Sharma, P., Pandey, A., & Kumar, S. (2023). Intrusion Detection System Based Ameliorated Technique of Pattern Matching. In *Proceedings of the 4th International Conference on Information Management & Machine Intelligence (ICIMMI '22)*. Association for Computing Machinery. DOI: 10.1145/3590837.3590947

Tsigaris, P., & Teixeira da Silva, J. A. (2023). Can chatgpt be trusted to provide reliable estimates? *Accountability in Research*, 1–3. Advance online publication. DOI: 10.1080/08989621.2023.2179919 PMID: 36786391

Tug, M. A., & Basar, P. (2023). *Future of the gig economy*. Pressacademia., DOI: 10.17261/Pressacademia.2023.1796

Umer, H., & Khan, M. S. (2023). ChatGPT in finance: Addressing ethical challenges. SSRN Electronic Journal. DOI: 10.2139/ssrn.4433171

V., M. V., Kumar, A. S., Sharma, P., Kaur, S., Saleh, O. S., Chennamma, H., & Chaturvedi, A. (2023). AI-Equipped IoT Applications in High-Tech Agriculture Using Machine Learning. In A. Khang (Ed.), Handbook of Research on AI-Equipped IoT Applications in High-Tech Agriculture (pp. 38-64). IGI Global. .DOI: 10.4018/978-1-6684-9231-4.ch003

Vaerst, T., Steffens, T., & Lokaiczyk, R. (2015). Concerns management, e-government and e-participation: Experiences and findings from Germany. *International Journal of E-Planning Research*, 4(4), 47–60. DOI: 10.4018/ijepr.2015100103

Verma, N. (2013). Open data for inclusive governance. *ACM International Conference Proceeding Series*. DOI: 10.1145/2516911.2516913

Wenzlaff, K., & Spaeth, S. (2022). Smarter than humans? Validating how OpenAI's ChatGPT model explains crowdfunding, alternative finance, and community finance. SSRN Electronic Journal. DOI: 10.2139/ssrn.4302443

Wu, S., Irsoy, O., Lu, S., Dabravolski, V., Dredze, M., Gehrmann, S., Kambadur, P., Rosenberg, D., & Mann, G. (2023). BloombergGPT: A large language model for finance. ArXiv, abs/2303.17564.

Zaremba, A., & Demir, E. (2023). ChatGPT: Unlocking the future of NLP in finance. *SSRN* 4323643.

Zhai, X. (2022). ChatGPT user experience: Implications for education. SSRN *Electronic Journal*. DOI: 10.2139/ssrn.4312418

Chapter 4

Improved Framework Model to Train and Evaluate Difficulty of Interview Question Using Generative AI

Pritish Sinha
https://orcid.org/0009-0009-6456-3412
Galgotias University, India

Khushi
Galgotias University, India

Arvind Dagur
Galgotias University, India

ABSTRACT

Research on question difficulty estimation is in demand for accurate assessments tools and other models for different purposes. Recent years include many implementations on this topic based on BERT (bidirectional encoder representations), RNN (recurrent neural networks), and other classification models. Traditional methods for question difficulty estimation have primarily focused on linguistic and structural analysis and trained on large pre-labeled datasets of questions and their difficulty level. This chapter presents an approach that combines these conventional techniques with Generative AI for more accurate question difficulty estimation. The principle behind the method is that as the AI system dives deeper into documentation to formulate questions, the questions generated are likely to be more complex or rare

DOI: 10.4018/979-8-3693-2284-0.ch004

and, therefore, deemed more difficult. By utilizing this multi-dimensional approach, the research aims to refine the question difficulty estimator to better reflect the true complexity of technical questions.

1. INTRODUCTION

1.1 Background and Motivation

Recent years have witnessed a surge in research and implementations in this domain, most of the research and approaches are based on transformer or neural techniques such as (AlKhuzaey *et al.,* 2023) BERT (Bidirectional Encoder Representations), RNN (recurrent neural networks), and other classification models. Despite the substantial progress in this field, there remains a noticeable research gap and scope for improvement. This paper addresses the pressing need for enhanced question difficulty estimation models in the context of Computer Science and Engineering (CSE) technical skills interviews.

1.2 Problem Statement

Question difficulty estimation has traditionally centered around linguistic and structural analyses, often relying on large pre-labeled datasets of questions and their associated difficulty levels. A thorough analysis of the current models, methods, and research reveals that there is room for improvement in this field. The main issue is the need for technique to set the question difficulty level in the least amount of dataset and require less input from the user for better predictions.

1.3 Proposed Approach/Solution

In response to the identified problem, this paper adds a new approach in existing models. We have used generative ai capabilities and mathematical approach of time consumption to help in estimation of question difficulty, as more the ai dig deep into large collections of information to create questions, the questions they generate are more likely to be complex and rare, making them harder. With this integrated approach, we aim to fill the existing research gap and this study aims to improve the accuracy of estimating question difficulty, especially for technical questions.

2. LITERATURE REVIEW

2.1 Overview of Question Difficulty Estimation

Question difficulty estimation is crucial in interviews and the education field to train for assessments with challenge level maintained. This process involves analyzing factors such as complexity, required skills, and potential ambiguity. In interviews, precise difficulty estimation to ensure fair evaluations of candidates' skills, it also helps create assessments aligned with learning objectives. Overall, this practice optimizes the assessment experience, contributing to fair and meaningful evaluations in studies, (Sharma & Bhatnagar, 2023) (Rawat *et al.,* 2023).

2.2 Previous Works in Question Difficulty Estimation

2.2.1 A Quantitative Study of NLP Approaches to Question Difficulty Estimation

This is a study on, (AlKhuzaey *et al.,* 2023), (Rogers, Gardner, & Augenstein, 2023), (Sharma, Jyotiyana, & Kumar, 2024), Natural Language Processing (NLP) approaches to Question Difficulty Estimation. It analyzes and compares different approaches, specifically focusing on reading comprehension Multiple Choice Questions (MCQs), science MCQs, and math questions from diverse educational domains. The study finds that Transformer-based models, particularly BERT and DistilBERT, consistently outperform other approaches, even when dealing with smaller datasets, (Sharma, Kapadiya, & Bhardwaj, 2023), (Sharma & Dadheech, 2023), (Sharma, Sharma, & Mathur, 2023).

Key Findings

Transformer-Based Models: This paper suggests that Transformer-based models, including BERT and DistilBERT, consistently outperform other approaches across different educational domains. DistilBERT performs remarkably well, almost on par with BERT, indicating that smaller models can be highly effective for QDET. These models even exhibit superior performance on smaller datasets.

Feature-Based Models: This paper also focuses on linguistic features that are effective in evaluating reading comprehension questions, while frequency-based features (TF-IDF) and word embeddings (word2vec) perform better for domain knowledge assessment.

2.2.2 A Survey on Recent Approaches to Question Difficulty

Estimation From Text

Question Difficulty Estimation from AlKhuzaey *et al* (2023), AlKhuzaey *et al* (2021) and Sharma *et al* (2023) (QDET) is a crucial application of Natural Language Processing (NLP) techniques in the field of educational assessment. It involves estimating the difficulty of questions in educational studies. This literature survey provides an overview of QDET, categorizes various approaches based on question characteristics, and presents recent research findings. The aim is to offer a reference point for researchers and practitioners in the domain of QDET.

Key Findings

Models Utilizing Question Text: The survey draws attention to a study that investigated the relationship between the difficulty of a question and linguistic elements taken from the question text. Tested linguistic indicators include deep cohesiveness, referential cohesion, word concreteness, narrativity, and syntactic simplicity. The study did discover that there was no significant correlation between the difficulty of the questions and these language factors.

R2DE Framework: Only the question text and available response options are used to estimate question difficulty and discrimination in the R2DE model, (Sharma, Jyotiyana, & Kumar, 2024), (Jumanov *et al.,* n.d.), a Regressor for Difficulty and Discrimination Estimation. The model uses Random Forest regression as a useful estimator, and this method greatly increases QDET accuracy.

Improved Model: A better R2DE version was put forth that included further features like linguistic characteristics and readability indices. This enhanced model, which uses Random Forest regression, outperforms the original R2DE and reduces the Root Mean Square Error (RMSE) from 0.807 to 0.753.

2.2.3 Question Difficulty and Expertise Estimation in Community Question Answering Sites (QDEE)

The paper presents a framework for (Abbot, 2003) (Fehrmann, Woehr, & Arthur, 1991), (Nuritdinov, Kakharov, & Dagur, n.d.), Question Difficulty and Expertise Estimation (QDEE) in Community Question Answering sites (CQAs) like Yahoo! Answers and Stack Overflow. The central challenge addressed is the appropriate routing and assignment of questions to users with the relevant expertise. This paper explores both language-agnostic and language-conscious solutions and introduces a key language-agnostic insight. It begins by constructing a competition graph, carefully using constraints to capture hierarchical structures, thus enabling the identification of user expertise and question difficulty. Subsequently, the framework employs various heuristic-based algorithms to estimate question difficulty effectively. To address the cold-start problem associated with newly posted questions, the framework leverages the concept of "social agony" (EGA) in conjunction with language-conscious features, enabling the estimation of difficulty levels.

Key Findings

DEGA outperforms DKNN by a significant margin, demonstrating the effectiveness of leveraging EGA for estimating difficulty levels of cold-start questions.

The hybrid model, which combines EGA and textual information, effectively addresses the cold-start problem. It achieves the best performance when $\alpha = 0.1$.

For instance, on Java, the hybrid model outperforms dega and dknn by 8.6% and 35.7%, respectively. On C#, it outperforms DEGA and DKNN by 4.8% and 7.9%, respectively.

2.2.4 Difficulty-Controllable Neural Question Generation for Reading

Comprehension Using Item Response Theory

The study uses deep neural networks, specifically BERT and GPT-2, to create question-answer pairs that consider the difficulty level using item response theory (IRT). IRT aids in determining appropriate question difficulty tailored to each learner's ability.

Key Findings

Item Response Theory (IRT) (AlKhuzaey et al., 2021) (Sharma, Jyotiyana, & Kumar, 2024) (Sherzodjon *et al.*, n.d.): The study utilizes IRT to estimate the difficulty of questions in a manner that aligns with each learner's individual ability. Offering questions with a 50% chance of correct answers, based on the learner's ability, is found to be the most effective approach for learning.

2.2.5 Introducing a Framework to Assess Newly Created Questions With Natural Language Processing

The research introduces a framework for assessing the difficulty and discrimination of newly created Multiple Choice Questions (MCQs) using natural language processing techniques, (Rogers, Gardner, & Augenstein, 2023), (Jumanov, Karshiev, & Dagur, n.d.). The framework, which extracts meaningful text-based features, outperforms existing models, reducing the Root Mean Square Error (RMSE) for difficulty and discrimination estimation

Key Findings

Improved Model Performance: The implemented model using the proposed framework outperforms previously proposed models. Specifically, for difficulty estimation, it reduces the Root Mean Square Error (RMSE) by 6.7% compared to a model called R2DE. This indicates that the new framework enhances the accuracy of estimating question difficulty. Discrimination Estimation: The research also evaluates discrimination estimation, a key aspect of question quality. The implemented model reduces the RMSE for discrimination estimation from 0.414 to 0.369 compared to R2DE. This signifies an enhancement in the model's ability to distinguish between questions with varying levels of discrimination

2.3 Comparison of These Models for Question Difficulty Estimation

Figure 1. Accuracy comparison on different sized dataset

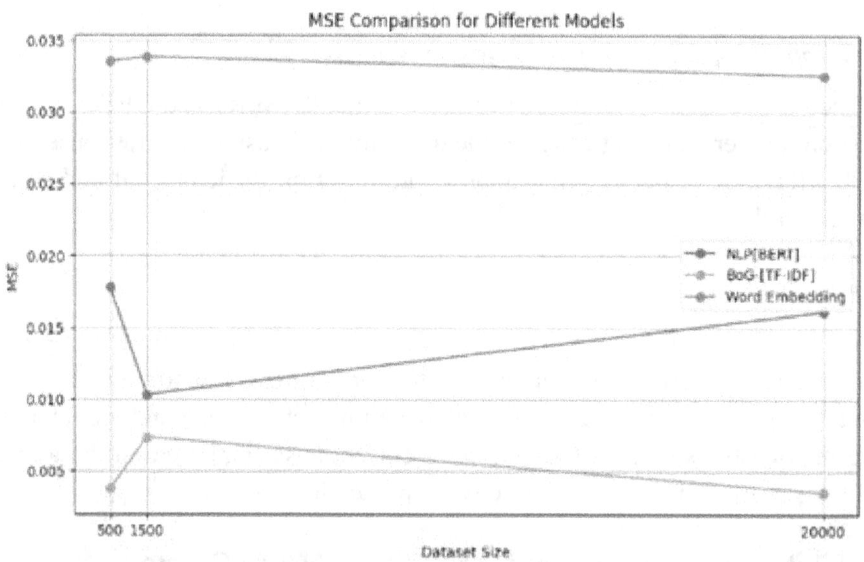

Figure 2. RMSE of different sized dataset

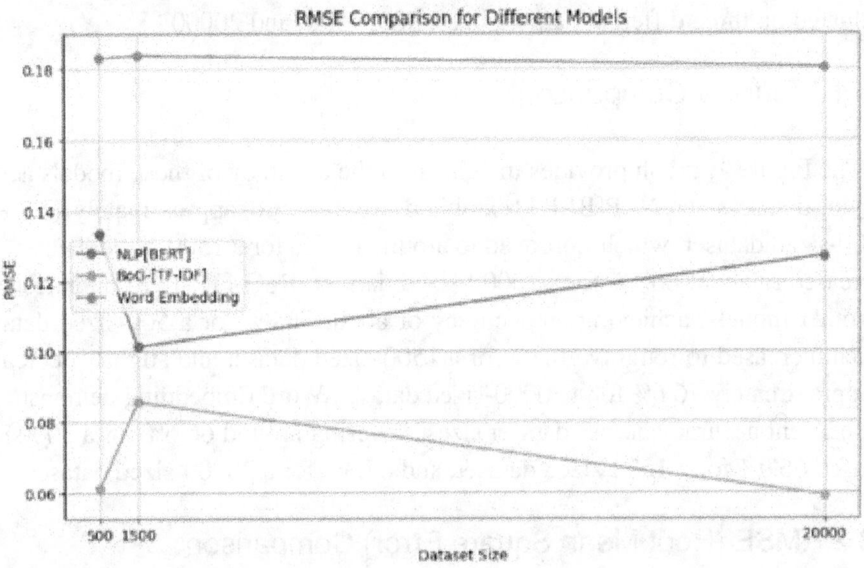

Figure 3. MSE of different sized dataset

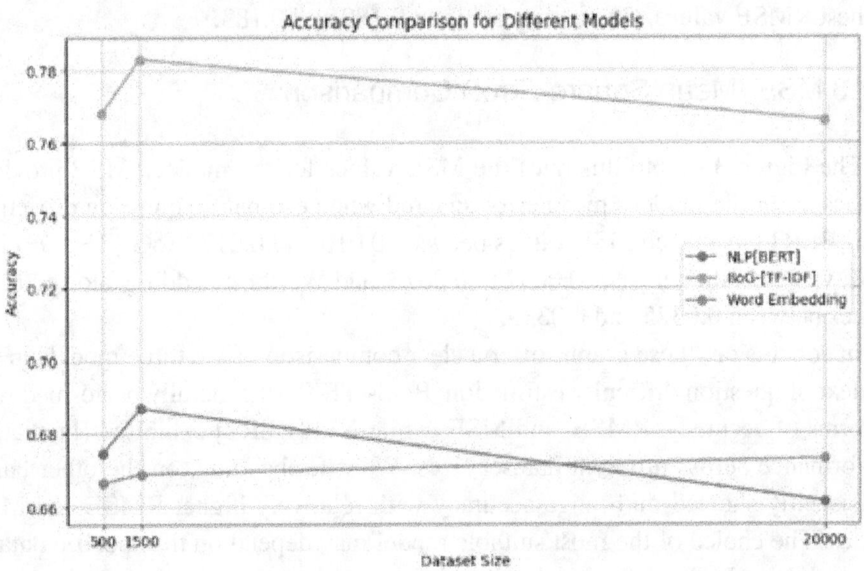

In our analysis of question difficulty estimation, we have compared three distinct models: NLP[BERT], BoG-[TF-IDF], and Word Embedding. Each model was evaluated on three different dataset sizes: 500, 1500, and 20000.

2.3.1 Accuracy Comparison

The Figure 1, graph provides insights into the accuracy of these models across varying dataset sizes. NLP[BERT] exhibited an accuracy of approximately 67.5% for a 500-sized dataset, which improved to around 68.7% for a 1500-sized dataset, but decreased to about 66.1% for a 20000-sized dataset. BoG-[TF-IDF] outperformed the other models, achieving an accuracy of about 76.8% for a 500-sized dataset, which increased to roughly 78.3% for a 1500-sized dataset and slightly decreased to approximately 76.6% for a 20000-sized dataset. Word Embedding demonstrated a consistent accuracy across dataset sizes, hovering around 66.6% for a 500-sized dataset, 66.9% for a 1500-sized dataset, and 67.3% for a 20000-sized dataset.

2.3.2 RMSE (Root Mean Square Error) Comparison

The Figure 2 graph illustrates RMSE values, which indicate the model's error in estimating question difficulty. NLP[BERT] exhibited RMSE values that ranged from 0.101 to 0.134 across different dataset sizes. BoG-[TF-IDF] achieved lower RMSE values, ranging from 0.059 to 0.085, while Word Embedding showed the highest RMSE values, fluctuating between 0.180 and 0.183.

2.3.3 MSE (Mean Square Error) Comparison

The Figure 3 graph illustrates the MSE values for the models. MSE provides a measure of the model's mean error squared when estimating question difficulty. NLP[BERT] displayed MSE values between 0.010 and 0.017, BoG-[TF-IDF] had MSE values in the range of 0.0037 to 0.0073, and Word Embedding showed MSE values between 0.0325 and 0.0339.

In conclusion, these graphs offer a clear comparison of the three models in the context of question difficulty estimation. BoG-[TF-IDF] generally performed well in terms of accuracy, RMSE, and MSE, while NLP[BERT] exhibited fluctuating performance across different dataset sizes. Word Embedding, on the other hand, consistently showed mid-range accuracy with relatively higher RMSE and MSE values. The choice of the most suitable model may depend on the specific dataset size and the priorities of the task at hand.

3. DATA COLLECTION AND PREPROCESSING

3.1 Description of the Question Dataset

Our primary datasets include the (Mancy *et al.,* 2024) (Kapadiya, Shekhawat, & Sharma, 2023) (Sharma & Jain, 2023) TREC QA Track, SemEval-2016 Task 3, and the Stack Exchange Data Dump. The TREC QA Track offers a collection of diverse question sets designed for question answering research, ensuring a broad representation of question types and complexities. SemEval-2016 Task 3, centered around Community Question Answering, enriches our dataset with questions from real-world community interactions. Additionally, the Stack Exchange Data Dump provides insights from various online communities, contributing to the diversity of our question corpus.

3.2 Difficulty Labeling Process

Each question in our dataset is meticulously labeled with difficulty levels. We employ a systematic and rigorous difficulty labeling process, considering factors such as question complexity, ambiguity, and the required depth of domain knowledge for accurate responses. This ensures a nuanced and well-defined difficulty annotation for each question, laying the foundation for effective model training and evaluation, (Eshtemirov *et al.*, n.d.), (Makhmadiyarovich *et al.,* n.d.).

3.3 Data Preprocessing Techniques

Text Normalization and Standardization

The process of converting textual data, (Liu *et al.,* 2023), (Lohani *et al.,* 2024), into a consistent format. Noting variations in spelling, casing, and abbreviations for improved consistency. This enhances the quality and reliability of textual data for downstream processing tasks.

Conceptual Embedding

The representation of words or phrases in a mathematical space. This enables algorithms to understand and capture semantic relationships and contextual meanings.

Imbalanced Label Handling

It addresses scenarios where certain classes in a dataset have significantly fewer instances than others. It is essential for creating balanced and unbiased machine learning models, particularly in classification tasks with imbalanced datasets.

4. EXPERIMENTAL SETUP

We have outlined the key components of our experimental setup, which is designed to rigorously evaluate the performance of our proposed question difficulty estimation model.

4.1 Data Splitting

To ensure an unbiased assessment, we partitioned our dataset into training, validation, and test sets. This data splitting strategy is essential for training the model, fine-tuning hyperparameters, and ultimately testing its predictive capabilities. The training set is used for model training, the validation set assists in hyperparameter tuning and model selection, while the test set serves as the benchmark for evaluating the model's real-world performance, (Kushwaha *et al.,* 2024), (Jamshed *et al.*, 2024), (Singhal *et al.,* n.d.).

4.2 Evaluation Metrics

Metrics provide quantitative insights into the model's performance. Key evaluation metrics include accuracy, root mean square error (RMSE), mean squared error (MSE), and false positive rate (FPR). Accuracy measures the model's overall predictive correctness. RMSE and MSE quantify the model's prediction error in terms of difficulty level estimation. FPR is utilized to gauge the rate of false positives, which is especially relevant when dealing with imbalanced datasets.

4.3 Baseline Models

The baseline models encompass a range of established question difficulty estimation methods, each with its own distinctive approach. Some of the prominent existing models included in our experimental setup are: NLP (BERT), IRT (Item Response Theory), Word Embedding Models and SVM (Support Vector Machines).

5. MACHINE LEARNING MODEL ARCHITECTURE

5.1 Machine Learning Model Architecture

Our method for developing the machine learning model architecture for question difficulty estimate is to build upon, (Patil *et al.,* 2024), (Tanwar *et al.,* 2023), BERT (Bidirectional Encoder Representations) and apply novel improvements to tackle particular difficulties in precisely determining question complexity. Using the bi-directional nature of BERT to record contextual relationships within questions, the architecture is built to handle textual input quickly.

Our model makes use of a customized version of BERT that combines knowledge from TF-IDF and Bag of Words (BoW) models to improve its comprehension of the complex linguistic patterns and technical queries. This combination of approaches allows the model to understand the global context of the given documentation as well as the particular characteristics that add to the difficulty of the inquiry.

Figure 4. estimate_difficulty formulae

```
# Function to estimate question difficulty
def estimate_difficulty(topic):
    # Get BERT embeddings
    bert_embeddings = get_bert_embeddings(topic)

    # Get BoW representation
    bow_representation = calculate_bow(topic)

    # Simulate time taken to parse through JSON (additional feature)
    parsing_time = len(json.dumps({"topic": topic, "documentation": ""})) * 0.001

    # Combine BERT embeddings, BoW representation, and parsing time
    combined_features = list(bert_embeddings) + list(bow_representation.flatten()) + [parsing_time]

    # Simulate a simple difficulty estimation function (you can replace this with a machine learning model)
    difficulty_score = sum(combined_features) / len(combined_features)

    return difficulty_score
```

To evaluate the complexity of a topic, the `estimate_difficulty` function, which is seen in Figure 4, incorporates features such as the time necessary to parse through JSON documentation, Bag of Words (BoW) representation, and BERT embeddings. Contextual information is captured by BERT embeddings, global frequency-based properties are reflected by the BoW representation, and parsing time is an extra consideration. The function then averages the various data to calculate a simulated difficulty score, which offers a first approximation of the difficulty of the question. For better accuracy, the function can substitute a more complex machine learning model for the simplicity, (Sharma & Rathi, 2016), (Sharma, 2023).

5.2 Generative AI Model Architecture

The Generative AI model serves as a pivotal component in our approach, the objective here is to generate JSON formatted documentation progressively in real time. By delving into the exact topic.

By utilizing Generative AI, (Radford, Metz, & Chintala, 2015), our model ensures that the documentation encapsulates both fundamental and advanced concepts related to the given topic. This progressive information retrieval forms the basis for evaluating question difficulty, as more complex and nuanced questions are expected to arise from a deeper exploration of the topic's documentation.

Algorithm: Voice-Based Documentation Generation
Input: Voice input from the user
Output: JSON-formatted documentation

1. Get voice input using a speech recognition library.
2. Extract the relevant topic from the voice input.
    - Use natural language processing techniques to identify key phrases or entities.
    - Example: "Hi, I am a React developer" => Extract "React developer."
3. Formulate a prompt for the generative model using the extracted topic.
    - Example: "Generate JSON documentation for the topic: React developer."
4. Call the generative model with the formulated prompt.
    - Send the prompt to the generative model.
5. Receive and process the response from the generative model.
    - Extract the generated JSON-formatted documentation.
6. Display or use the generated documentation.
    - Print it to the console, display it in a user interface, or integrate it into your application.

6. RESULTS AND DISCUSSION

The results carry evidence that proposed implementation in the interview and education field is a success. The model's ability to navigate through real time generated documentation and adjust difficulty label a better performance in question difficulty estimation. This model impacts refined evaluations, adaptive assessments and interview experience for both candidate and assessors. Given below is a sample test for react developer candidates, question for assessments is as mentioned in Figure 5.

Figure 5. Snippet of testcase-1 result

For the React development topic with a focus on "Higher Order Classification," in Figure 6 our model showcased impressive performance in estimating question difficulty. The question, "Explain Higher Order Classification in React development," was accurately assessed with a difficulty score of -0.0011895343451385 66. Notably, the negative difficulty score suggests that the model perceives this question as easier than the average difficulty level, indicating its aptitude in discerning nuanced levels of complexity within the technical domain.

Figure 6. Refined result according to label

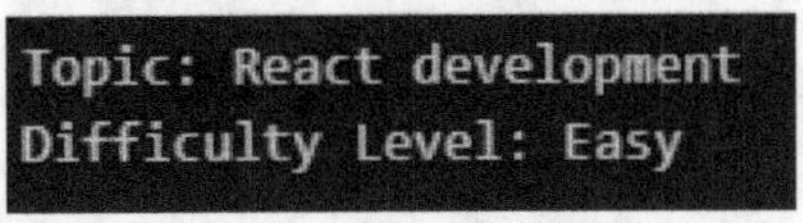

6.1 Comparison With Baseline Models

QDE can be achieved using many different approaches and machine learning models by using natural language processing (NLP) techniques, transformers such like TF-IDF (Term Frequency-Inverse Document Frequency)

NLP (BERT): BERT, a bidirectional transformer-based model, has been widely used for natural language processing tasks. In question difficulty estimation, BERT leverages its contextual understanding of language to predict the complexity of questions.

Item Response Theory, or IRT (Wauters, Desmet, & Van Den Noortgate, 2010): To evaluate the difficulty and discrimination parameters of questions, the conventional psychometric method known as item response theory is utilized. IRT has been widely used in psychological testing and educational assessments.

Models for Word Embedding: Word-phrase semantic links in questions are captured by word embedding algorithms like Word2Vec and FastText. These models analyze the linguistic and structural properties of questions, which helps with question difficulty estimation.

BoW (Bag of Words) & TF-IDF: The (Liu *et al.*, 2023), (Wauters, Desmet, & Van Den Noortgate, 2010), Bag of Words model, in combination with Term Frequency-Inverse Document Frequency (TF-IDF) weighting, analyzes question text by considering the frequency and importance of words. This method serves as a benchmark in question difficulty estimation.

Figure 7. Accuracy difference of models

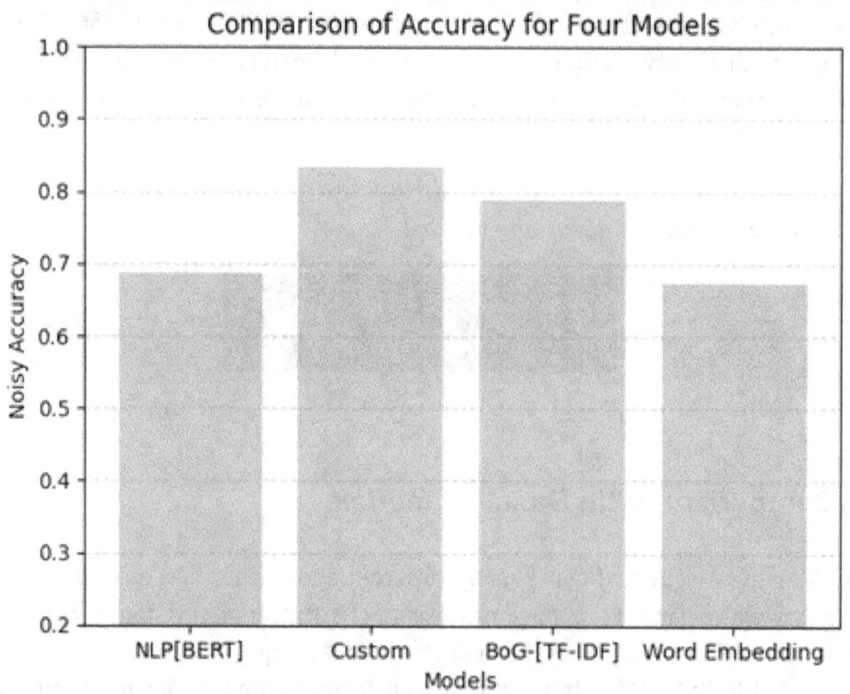

Figure 8. Comparison on each model with respect to RMSE, MSE, FPR

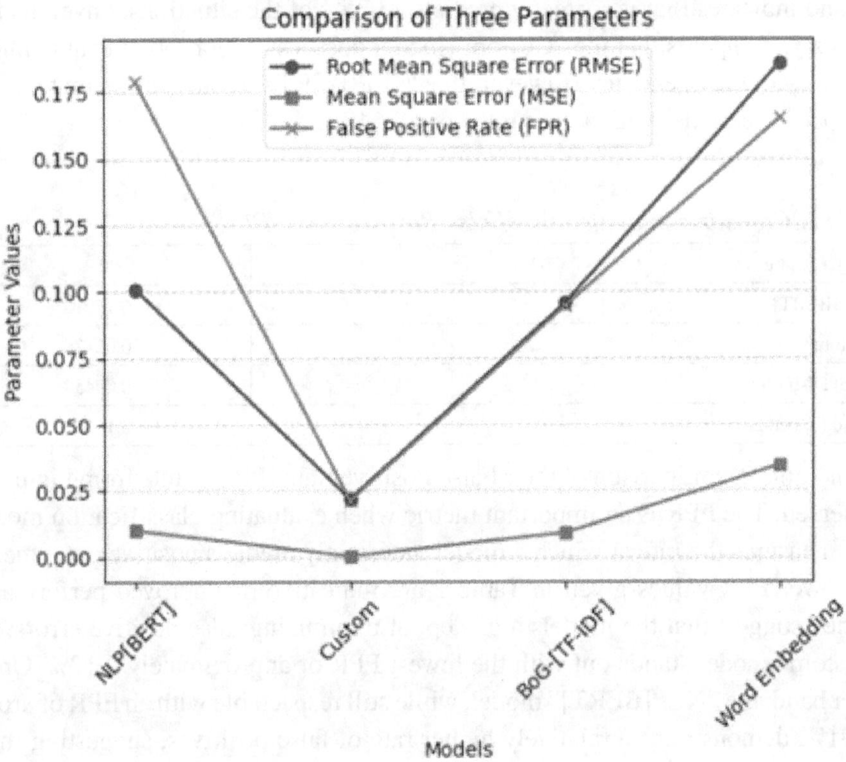

Table 1. Comparison of models - accuracy

Model Name	Accuracy
NLP[BERT]	68.64%
Custom	83.35%
BoG[TF-IDF]	78.90%
Word Embedding	67.29%

A comparative study of the models' consistency performance from Figure 7 is given in Table 1. In machine learning and statistical analysis, accuracy is an important parameter, especially when assessing models that are intended to produce precise predictions. Accuracy in these models refers to the percentage of outcomes or responses that are accurately predicted.

Each model's accuracy values are shown in the table; greater numbers correspond to better performance. With an accuracy of 83.35%, the “Custom” model shines out and indicates that it correctly predicts 83.35% of the situations. Given its high accuracy, it appears that the “Custom” model does a superior job of evaluating the difficulty of the questions. However, the “NLP[BERT]” model shows that it is still a respectable model with an accuracy of 68.64%.

Table 2. Comparison of models - False Positive Rate (FPR)

Model Name	FPR
NLP[BERT]	0.1791
Custom	0.0212
BoG[TF-IDF]	0.0945
Word Embedding	0.1651

In Table 2, comparison of their False Positive Rate (FPR) value from Figure 8 is presented. The FPR is an important metric when evaluating classification models, as it measures the rate at which a model incorrectly predicts positive outcomes.

Lower FPR values given in Table 2 are indicative of improved performance, as they suggest that the models are adept at minimizing false positive errors. The “Custom” model stands out with the lowest FPR of approximately 2.12%. On the other hand, the “NLP[BERT]” model, while still respectable with an FPR of around 17.91%, demonstrates a relatively higher rate of false positives, suggesting that it might occasionally overestimate question difficulty.

Improved Framework Model

Figure 9. Accuracy - MSE scale of custom model

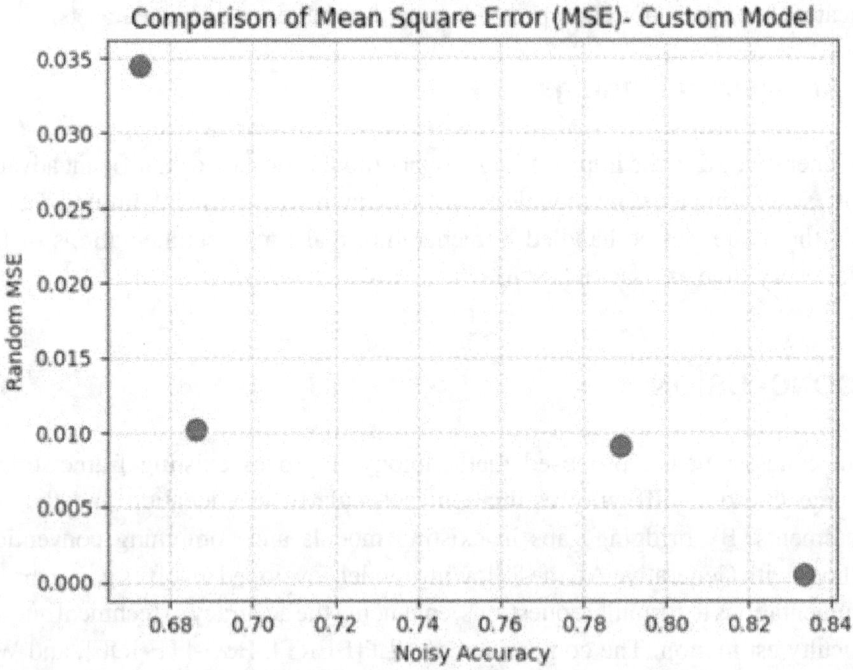

As above results indicate enhanced algorithm using generative ai approach on conventional models outperforms the existing models we have done further testing to know more about model performance and test it against real time issue of low dataset leading to low accuracy.

Custom Model Accuracy

Table 3. Accuracy per mean squared error

Accuracy	MSE
79%	0.1009
83.4%	0.0218
68.5%	0.0945
67.45%	0.1858

Furthermore, the Mean Squared Error (MSE) of the custom model is considerably lower, standing at 0.0218 as shown in Figure 9 and Table 3. This indicates that the model's predictions are highly consistent with the actual difficulty levels of the questions, minimizing the margin of error and demonstrating the reliability of the model's estimations. While the other models have respectable performance, with the "Custom" model, we see notable improvements. The reduction in the MSE indicates that it is better equipped to handle the challenge of low datasets.

6.2 Analysis of Findings

Generative AI in the improved framework model adds up to significant advancements, surpassing existing models as it can adept in scenarios with limited datasets. Since this issue can be handled by generating real time documentations of field topics every time assessments start.

7. CONCLUSION

In conclusion, the proposed methodology improves existing frameworks in accurate question difficulty estimation, particularly in education and technical assessments. By bridging gaps in existing models and combining conventional methods with Generative AI, the following model developed involves going through documentations to formulate questions, enhancing the accuracy of technical question difficulty estimation. The comparison of NLP[BERT], BoG-[TF-IDF], and Word Embedding models across different dataset sizes highlights BoG-[TF-IDF]'s robust performance. Our machine learning model enhances BERT and conceptual idea of BoG-IDF, proves effective in assessing global and contextual features. The Generative AI model's ability to provide real-time documentation addresses challenges with limited datasets. Real-world testing for React developer candidates demonstrates the model's accuracy. In essence, this research not only advances question difficulty estimation but also offers a practical solution for tailored evaluations in technical domains, benefiting educational assessments and interviews.

REFERENCES

Abbot, M. 2003, May. Standard setting for complex performance assessments: A critical examination of the analytic judgment method. Annual congress of the Canadian society for the study of education.

Agarwal, A. (2024). Use Cases of ChatGPT and Other AI Tools With Security Concerns. In Sharma, P., Jyotiyana, M., & Senthil Kumar, A. V. (Eds.), *Applications, Challenges, and the Future of ChatGPT* (pp. 216–225). IGI Global. DOI:10.4018/979-8-3693-6824-4.ch012

AlKhuzaey, S.A systematic review of data-driven approaches to item difficulty prediction. *International Conference on Artificial Intelligence in Education*. Springer. DOI:10.1007/978-3-030-78292-4_3

AlKhuzaey, S., Grasso, F., Payne, T. R., & Tamma, V. (2023). Text-based Question Difficulty Prediction: A Systematic Review of Automatic Approaches. *International Journal of Artificial Intelligence in Education*, 1–53. DOI:10.1007/s40593-023-00362-1

Beatty, P., Team, I., Miller, K., Wilson, B., Whitaker, K., & Kennet, J. (2002). *Cognitive interview evaluation of the blood donor history screening questionnaire. Final report of the AABB task force to redesign the blood donor screening questionnaire. Estados Unidos.* US Food and Drug Administration.

Beatty, P. C., & Willis, G. B. (2007). Research synthesis: The practice of cognitive interviewing. *Public Opinion Quarterly*, 71(2), 287–311. DOI:10.1093/poq/nfm006

Beinborn, L., Zesch, T., & Gurevych, I. (2014). Predicting the difficulty of language proficiency tests. *Transactions of the Association for Computational Linguistics*, 2, 517–530. DOI:10.1162/tacl_a_00200

Eshtemirov, Nazarov, Khamidov, & Dagur. (n.d.). Deep learning-based traffic congestion forecasting research, Artificial Intelligence and Information Technologies, 1-6.

Fehrmann, M. L., Woehr, D. J., & Arthur, W.Jr. (1991). The Angoff cutoff score method: The impact of frame-of-reference rater training. *Educational and Psychological Measurement*, 51(4), 857–872. DOI:10.1177/0013164491051004006

Jamshed, A., Dwivedi, A. K., Mehra, P. S., & Dagur, A. (2024). Internet-of-Things-Enabled Networks: Vision Challenges and Smart Applications. *Advances in Computing Communications*, 6, 1–17. DOI:10.2174/9789815049480124060003

Jumanov, Karshiev, & Dagur. (n.d.). Synthesis of mechanisms of increasing reliability of information on the basis of the use of redundant of different approaches. Artificial Intelligence and Information Technologies, 421-428.

Jumanov, Safarov, Djumanov, & Dagur. (n.d.). Construction of correctors for distorted image points based on neural networks for micro-object identification. Artificial Intelligence and Information Technologies, 261-266.

Kapadiya, D., Shekhawat, C., & Sharma, P. (2023). A Study on Large Scale Applications of Big Data in Modern Era. In *International Conference on Information Management & Machine Intelligence (ICIMMI2023).* ACM. https://doi.org/DOI: 10.1145/3647444.364788

Knorr, M., & Hissbach, J. (2014). Multiple mini-interviews: Same concept, different approaches. *Medical Education*, 48(12), 1157–1175. DOI:10.1111/medu.12535 PMID:25413910

Kushwaha, K. P., Dagur, A., & Shukla, D. (2024). HSLE: A Hybrid Ensemble Classifier for Prediction of Heart Disease. Recent Advances in Electrical & Electronic Engineering, 17, 1-12.

Liu, Y., Yang, Z., Yu, Z., Liu, Z., Liu, D., Lin, H., Li, M., Ma, S., Avdeev, M. & Shi, S. (2023). Generative artificial intelligence and its applications in materials science: Current situation and future perspectives. Journal of Materiomics.

Lohani, Dagur, Arvind, Shukla, & Dhirendra. (2024). An Efficient Approach for Diabetes Classification Using Feature Selection and Hyperparameter Tuning. Recent Advances in Electrical & Electronic Engineering, 17, 1-15.

Makhmadiyarovich, Akbar, Asliddin, Sabharwal, & Dagur. (n.d.). Methods of applying machine learning algorithms for blockchain technologies, Artificial Intelligence and Information Technologies, 232-237

Merlin Mancy, A., Kumar, A. V., Latip, R., Jagadamba, G., Chakrabarti, P., Sharma, P., Musirin, I. B., Sharma, M., & Kanchan, B. G. (2024). Smart Healthcare System, Digital Health and Telemedicine, Management and Emergencies: Patient Emergency Application (PES) E-Governance Applications. In Kumar, R., Abdul Hamid, A., Binti Ya'akub, N., Sharan, H., & Kumar, S. (Eds.), *Sustainable Development in AI, Blockchain, and E-Governance Applications* (pp. 124–151). IGI Global. DOI:10.4018/979-8-3693-1722-8.ch008

Nuritdinov, Kakharov, & Dagur. (n.d.). A new algorithm for finding the Minkowski difference of some sets. Artificial Intelligence and Information Technologies, 142-147.

Patil, P., Kulkarni, K., & Sharma, P. (2024). Algorithmic Issues, Challenges, and Theoretical Concerns of ChatGPT. In Sharma, P., Jyotiyana, M., & Senthil Kumar, A. V. (Eds.), *Applications, Challenges, and the Future of ChatGPT* (pp. 56–74). IGI Global. DOI:10.4018/979-8-3693-6824-4.ch003

Radford, A., Metz, L., & Chintala, S. (2015). Unsupervised representation learning with deep convolutional generative adversarial networks. arXiv preprint arXiv:1511.06434.

Rawat, P., Bhardwaj, A., Lamba, N., & Sharma, P. (2023). Arduino Based IoT Mini Weather Station. *SKIT Research Journal*, 13(2), 34–41. DOI:10.47904/IJSKIT.13.2.2023.34-41

Rogers, A., Gardner, M., & Augenstein, I. (2023). Qa dataset explosion: A taxonomy of nlp resources for question answering and reading comprehension. *ACM Computing Surveys*, 55(10), 1–45. DOI:10.1145/3560260

Singhal, Ali, Shukla, Dagur, Awasthy, & Tiwari. (n.d.). ROCK-HYRAX: An Energy Efficient Job scheduling using Cluster of Resources in Cloud Computing Environment. Cluster Computing, The Journal of Networks, Software Tools and Applications.

Sethi, S. S., & Sharma, P. (2023). New Developments in the Implementation of IoT in Agriculture. *SN Computer Science*, 4(5), 503. DOI:10.1007/s42979-023-01896-w

Sharma, P. (2023). *Utilizing Explainable Artificial Intelligence to Address Deep Learning in Biomedical Domain. In Medical Data Analysis and Processing using Explainable Artificial Intelligence*. Taylor & Francis. DOI:10.1201/9781003257721-2

Sharma, P., & Bhatnagar, N. (2023). Passenger Authentication and Ticket Verification at Airport Using QR Code Scanner. *SKIT Research Journal*, 13(2), 10–13. DOI:10.47904/IJSKIT.13.1.2023.10-12

Sharma, P., & Dadheech, P. (2023). Modern-age Agriculture with Artificial Intelligence: A review emphasizing Crop Yield Prediction. *EVERGREEN Joint Journal of Novel Carbon Resource Sciences & Green Asia Strategy*, 10(4), 2570–2582. DOI:10.5109/7160906

Sharma, P., Dadheech, P., Aneja, N., & Aneja, S. (2023). Predicting Agriculture Yields Based on Machine Learning Using Regression and Deep Learning. *IEEE Access : Practical Innovations, Open Solutions*, 11, 111255–111264. DOI:10.1109/ACCESS.2023.3321861

Sharma, P., & Jain, M. K. (2023). Stock Market Trends Analysis using Extreme Gradient Boosting (XGBoost). *2023 International Conference on Computing, Communication, and Intelligent Systems (ICCCIS)*, 317-322. DOI:10.1109/ICCCIS60361.2023.10425722

Sharma, P., Jyotiyana, M., & Kumar, A. S. (Eds.). (2024). *Applications, Challenges, and the Future of ChatGPT*. IGI Global. DOI:10.4018/979-8-3693-6824-4

Sharma, P., Kapadiya, D., & Bhardwaj, A. (2023). Efficient Note Sharing Model for Collaborative Learning. *SKIT Research Journal*, 13(2), 42–46. DOI:10.47904/IJSKIT.13.2.2023.42-46

Sharma, P., & Rathi, Y. (2016, June 5). Efficient Density-Based Clustering Using Automatic Parameter Detection. Efficient Density-Based Clustering Using Automatic Parameter Detection | SpringerLink. .DOI:10.1007/978-981-10-0767-5_46

Sharma, P., Sharma, C., & Mathur, P. (2023). Machine Learning-based Stock Market Forecasting using Recurrent Neural Network. *2023 9th International Conference on Smart Computing and Communications (ICSCC)*, 600-605. DOI:10.1109/ICSCC59169.2023.10335083

Sherzodjon, Fayzullo, Shaxnoza, & Dagur. (n.d.). Real estate valuation based on Feedforward neural networks. Artificial Intelligence and Information Technologies, 226-231

Tanwar, A., Sharma, P., Pandey, A., & Kumar, S. (2023). Intrusion Detection System Based Ameliorated Technique of Pattern Matching. In *Proceedings of the 4th International Conference on Information Management & Machine Intelligence (ICIMMI '22)*. Association for Computing Machinery. DOI:10.1145/3590837.3590947

van de Watering, G., & van der Rijt, J. (2006). Teachers' and students' perceptions of assessments: A review and a study into the ability and accuracy of estimating the difficulty levels of assessment items. *Educational Research Review*, 1(2), 133–147. DOI:10.1016/j.edurev.2006.05.001

Wauters, K., Desmet, P., & Van Den Noortgate, W. (2010). Adaptive item-based learning environments based on the item response theory: Possibilities and challenges. *Journal of Computer Assisted Learning*, 26(6), 549–562. DOI:10.1111/j.1365-2729.2010.00368.x

Chapter 5
Generative AI Techniques in Medical Imaging Analysis: A Systematic Review

Ruchi Patel
Gyan Ganga Institute of Technology and Sciences, India

Ashok Kumar Verma
Gyan Ganga Institute of Technology and Sciences, India

Neelesh Kumar Sahu
Gyan Ganga Institute of Technology and Sciences, India

Preeti Rai
Gyan Ganga Institute of Technology and Sciences, India

ABSTRACT

The introduction of generative AI technologies has brought about an abrupt shift in the area of medical imaging analysis. In this comprehensive investigation, the authors look at how generative AI has been used and how it has been improved for medical picture analysis. An exhaustive analysis of the methods, difficulties, and developments in this dynamic field is the goal of this research. The limitations of traditional medical imaging modalities are thoroughly discussed in the first part of the chapter. This foundation must be laid before generative adversarial networks (GANs) and other models of generative artificial intelligence may be applied. The purpose of this thorough investigation is to catalog and evaluate noteworthy trends and emerging problems in medical imaging-related generative artificial intelligence (AI) research. The revolutionary influence of generative artificial intelligence (AI)

DOI: 10.4018/979-8-3693-2284-0.ch005

on medical imaging analysis is better understood after reading this extensive review. By synthesizing and detecting gaps, this project benefits academics and healthcare professionals.

1. INTRODUCTION

A paradigm shift has occurred in the past several years at the crossroads of medical imaging and artificial intelligence (AI), opening up previously unimaginable opportunities for healthcare. A new age of accuracy and efficiency has dawned in the study of medical imaging data made possible by generative AI techniques, which have arisen as potent tools among the many AI approaches. This chapter presents a thorough study that dives into the current environment and future possibilities of the rapidly developing field of medical imaging analysis, focusing on the use and influence of generative AI approaches in this domain.

Diagnostic, follow-up, and treatment planning for a wide range of medical issues rely heavily on medical imaging. When it comes to medical images, traditional image analysis methods generally struggle to achieve high accuracy and efficiency due to the inherent complexity and variety. The capacity of generative AI to learn patterns and produce fresh data has made it a potential contender for resolving these issues. Researchers and practitioners are actively seeking new ways to improve medical imaging studies in terms of accuracy, speed, and interpretability. Some promising strategies include deep generative models, variational autoencoders (VAEs), and generative adversarial networks (GANs).

The process of studying medical images for the purpose of being of assistance in the diagnosis, treatment planning, and monitoring of diseases is referred to as medical imaging analysis. The technologies used in medical imaging generate vast amounts of data, which necessitates the examination of specialists in order to extract information that is valuable. The field of medical imaging is extremely important in many different subspecialties within the medical field, including radiology, cardiology, neurology, cancer, and many more.

It is possible to automate and increase the accuracy of medical image analysis through the utilization of generative artificial intelligence in the investigation of medical imaging. image segmentation, image synthesis, forecasting patient outcomes, and identifying anomalies are all examples of activities that can be accomplished with the help of generative artificial intelligence. It is possible for the application of generative artificial intelligence to lower the expenses of healthcare and expand access to healthcare for communities that are underserved. On the other hand, in order to guarantee the appropriate application of these technologies in the medical field, it is necessary to address issues such as data privacy, algorithmic bias, and the interpretability of generative AI tools.

An exhaustive summary of the most recent cutting-edge generative AI methods used for medical image analysis is the goal of this systematic review. We will investigate the many uses of generative models in areas including picture synthesis, segmentation, denoising, and anomaly detection by carefully reviewing the pertinent literature. This review will also go over the benefits and drawbacks of these methods, illuminating how they might change healthcare systems, patient outcomes, and clinical processes.

The more we delve into this topic, the more we see how generative AI techniques could revolutionize medical imaging analysis. This systematic review aims to contribute to the continuing conversation between the scientific and medical communities by shedding light on the present state of the art, the obstacles that have been overcome, and the potential future directions of generative AI in medical imaging data perception, interpretation, and utilization.

The research paper will be based on research questions which are mentioned in Table 1.

Table 1. Research questions

RQ. No.	Research Questions
RQ1	What are the potential applications of Generative Artificial Intelligence in the field of Medical Imaging Analysis?
RQ2	What are different datasets used for Medical Imaging Analysis?
RQ3	What are the different methodologies employed in Generative Artificial Intelligence (AI) for the purpose of Medical Imaging?
RQ4	How do various obstacles prevent generative AI from being used in medical image analysis?

2. LITERATURE REVIEW

A revolution in the way medical professionals interpret and use diagnostic imaging has been triggered by the application of Generative Artificial Intelligence (AI) techniques in the field of Medical Imaging Analysis (Seti S.S. et al. 2023). An extensive examination of the current body of research indicates a constantly changing environment in which groundbreaking generative models are actively influencing the future of medical imaging (Sharma. P et al. 2016). This section presents a summary of important discoveries from influential studies, demonstrating the wide range and extensive nature of research in this developing topic (A. Tanwar et al. 2023).

First introduced by (Goodfellow et al., 2014), Generative Adversarial Networks (GANs) have become a significant category of generative models. GANs have been widely used in medical imaging to generate realistic images, specifically to overcome the limitation of small datasets. Prominent research conducted by (Frid-Adar et al., 2018) and (Wolterink, Leiner, Viergever, & Išgum, 2017) demonstrate the effectiveness of Generative Adversarial Networks (GANs) in producing top-notch medical images for various purposes, including organ segmentation, lesion detection, and modelling of clinical conditions (Sharma, P., Dadheech, P., & Senthil Kumar Senthil, A. V., 2023).

VAEs have become well-known for their capacity to acquire intricate latent representations. Significant studies conducted by (Chartsias et al., 2019) and (Oprea et al., 2020) showcase the utilization of Variational Autoencoders (VAEs) in the process of converting medical images from one modality to another, known as image-to-image translation (V., M. V., Kumar et al. 2023). These findings have significant consequences for the combination of several imaging methods, allowing for the smooth integration of various techniques to conduct thorough clinical analysis (Maharajan, K., Kumar et al. 2023).

Generative models have a wide range of applications beyond only creating images. A comprehensive collection of scholarly works, including research conducted by (Nie, Ding, Qi, Wang, & Wong, 2021) and (Zhao, Song, Zhang, Duan, & Zhang, 2022), emphasizes the effectiveness of these techniques in reducing noise, improving quality, and reconstructing images (Prasad G, A et al. 2023). Generative models play a crucial role in overcoming inherent difficulties in medical imaging by improving the understandability and clinical significance of diagnostic images (Sharma, P. 2023).

Adversarial training, influenced by GANs (Generative Adversarial Networks), has been utilized to improve the resilience of medical imaging models. The studies conducted by (Y. Zhang et al., 2020) and (Shin et al., 2018) demonstrate the use of adversarial training to enhance the ability of models to generalize, address differences in data sources, and maintain consistent performance across various patient groups and imaging settings (P. Sharma, P. Dadheech, N. Aneja and S. Aneja, 2023).

The use of generative AI algorithms in medical imaging raises important ethical questions and presents new (P. Sharma, C. Sharma, and P. Mathur, 2023). The ethical considerations of generative models in healthcare are explored in studies by (Castillo Ossa et al., 2021) and (Li et al., 2019). These studies stress the importance of responsible implementation, protections for patient privacy, and open communication between AI systems and healthcare professionals (P. Sharma and P. Dadheech, 2023).

Novel applications and the ongoing progress of generative AI approaches in medical imaging are attracting a growing amount of attention in the literature. (Chen et al., 2022) and (X. Jiang, Hu, Wang, & Zhang, 2023) delve into recent developments, such as the merging of attention mechanisms with self-supervised learning, to shed light on the potential future of this ever-changing subject (P. Sharma, D. Kapadiya, A. Bhardwaj, 2023).

The literature evaluation concludes that medical imaging analysis has been revolutionized by generative AI techniques (P. Rawat et al. 2023). A joint effort to exploit the promise of generative models in transforming healthcare practices is reflected in the body of research, which ranges from image synthesis to overcoming data restrictions and boosting model robustness (P. Sharma, N. Bhatnagar, 2023). Continuous research and cross-disciplinary teamwork will surely lead to new developments in the field, which will be good for patients and doctors in the long run (Das, Nair, & Peter, 2020; Khan et al., 2023) .

3. APPLICATIONS OF GENERATIVE ARTIFICIAL INTELLIGENCE IN THE FIELD OF MEDICAL IMAGING ANALYSIS

Generative AI can drastically change medical imaging analysis, demonstrating how these methods might reimagine conventional wisdom in the healthcare industry. Scientists and clinicians have investigated many ways to enhance medical imaging data processing using generative models like Variational Autoencoders (VAEs) and Generative Adversarial Networks (GANs). Here are some important possible uses:

- The Synthesis of Images:

Generative AI approaches demonstrate exceptional proficiency in producing authentic and high-quality medical images. This function is extremely helpful for enhancing datasets, generating artificial images to increase the variety of training sets, and resolving problems associated with limited data availability (Müller-Franzes et al., 2023). The generated images can be utilized to bolster the resilience and universality of machine learning models, consequently enhancing diagnostic precision.

- Translation of images into other images:

Generative models enable the conversion of medical pictures from one modality to another, assisting in the smooth integration of several imaging techniques. Converting magnetic resonance imaging (MRI) scans to computed tomography (CT) pictures enables the merging of data from several imaging modalities, allowing doctors to have a holistic perspective for more precise diagnosis and treatment planning (Pinaya et al., 2023).

- Improving and Reducing Noise in Images:

In the field of medical imaging, noise reduction and imagine enhancement are extremely important. Image noise can be effectively removed by generative models, which results in an improvement in the standard of information used for diagnosis. These strategies improve the accessibility of structures by understanding complicated patterns and correlations within the data. As a result, medical professionals are able to make assessments that are more assured and correct (Oh, Jung, Kim, Lee, & Kang, 2019).

- Data Augmentation:

Through the creation of a wide variety of realistic variations of pre-existing medical images, generative artificial intelligence makes a contribution to the enhancement of training datasets. Consequently, this helps alleviate the issues that are associated with limited data availability, which ultimately results in models that are more resilient and generic. With the help of augmented datasets, machine learning models are able to more effectively manage the heterogeneity that exists in patient demographics and imaging findings.

- Segmentation and Identification of Abnormalities:

A precise segmentation of medical images can be achieved with the assistance of generative models, which serve to highlight particular structures in the body or regions of interest. In addition, they are useful in the detection of anomalies since they are able to recognize even minute variations from the patterns that are considered normal. This is an essential step in early identification of diseases and irregularities (H.-M. Zhang & Dong, 2020).

- Personalized Medicine:

The implementation of tailored medical imaging analyses is made possible by the capacity of generative models to acquire knowledge about the specific characteristics of each patient. Increasing the accuracy as well as efficacy of healthcare interventions is accomplished through the customization of diagnostics and treatment regimens to the specific needs of individual patients.

- System for Supporting Clinical Decisions:

Healthcare providers can benefit from the use of generative AI in clinical decision support systems when it comes to the interpretation of medical imaging. Decisions can be greatly improved with the use of these systems since they generate helpful visuals, give more context, and assist with diagnosis (Sun, 2022).

With the subject of Generative AI in Medical Imaging Analysis constantly developing, the possible uses mentioned above highlight how it might revolutionize diagnostic precision, clinical processes, and, in the end, patient results. Medical imaging and individualized healthcare may be significantly altered by the results of the current investigations into these potential uses.

4. MEDICAL IMAGING DATASETS

For applying Generative Artificial Intelligence (AI) approaches in the field of Medical Imaging, there are a great number of datasets that are applied. To effectively training models in generative artificial intelligence approaches for medical imaging, it is necessary to make use of datasets that are both diversified and strictly kept. The specific job, method, and purpose at hand are relevant considerations that should be considered while selecting a dataset. Some examples of the many datasets that are utilized in applications of generative artificial intelligence (AI) that are related to medical imaging are shown below.

- ADNI (Alzheimer's Disease Neuroimaging Initiative):

The comprehensive datasets that are made available by the Alzheimer's Disease Neuroimaging Initiative (ADNI) include a wide range of imaging modalities, such as positron emission tomography (PET), magnetic resonance imaging (MRI), and a number of additional imaging techniques. For the purpose of researching Alzheimer's disease, these databases are quite helpful, sample images are shown in figure 1. People who have Alzheimer's disease, people who have mild cognitive impairment, and people who are going through normal aging are the individuals whose data make up the dataset (Hartig, Truran-Sacrey, Raptentsetsang, Schuff, & Weiner, 2012).

Figure 1. Sample images of ADNI dataset (Hartig, Truran-Sacrey, Raptentsetsang, Schuff, & Weiner, 2012)

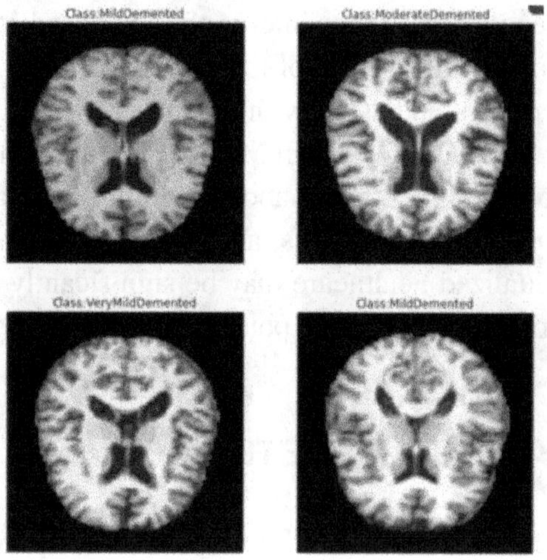

- NIH Chest X-ray Dataset:

The dataset that has been provided contains a collection of more than one hundred thousand chest X-ray pictures that have been annotated with labels that correlate to common thoracic illnesses, sample images are shown in Figure 2. These labels have been included in the dataset that has been provided. This strategy is applied frequently throughout the training phase in order to accomplish the goal of generating deep learning models for the purpose of analyzing chest X-rays. There are many different uses for this technology, some of which include the analysis of chest X-rays, the diagnosis of diseases, and the localization of symptoms (Filice et al., 2020).

Figure 2. Sample images of NIH chest X-ray dataset (Filice et al., 2020)

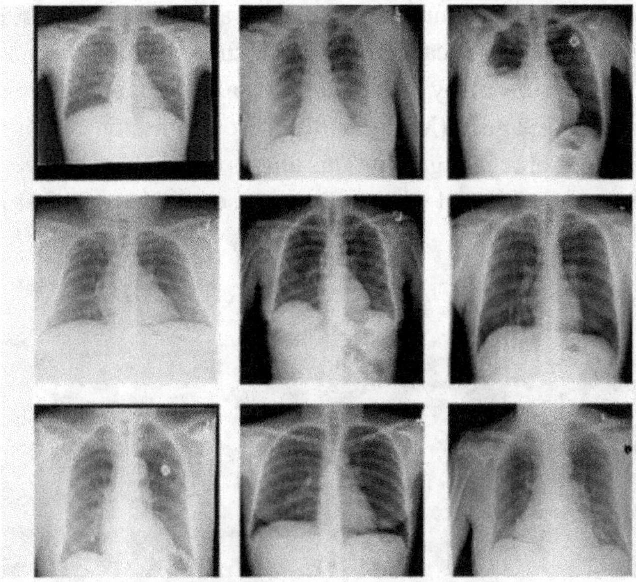

- OASIS (Open Access Series of Imaging Studies):

It is possible to make use of the magnetic resonance imaging (MRI) data that are contained in the OASIS dataset for the purpose of conducting research projects that are related to Alzheimer's disease, moderate cognitive impairment, and the aging process. Sample images of OASIS dataset shown in Figure 3. The collection includes not just longitudinal data but also a wide range of imaging modalities that correspond to different time periods. The findings of this research can be beneficial to a number of different fields, including research into neurodegenerative illnesses and studies on the aging process (Marcus et al., 2007).

Figure 3. Sample images of OASIS dataset (Marcus et al., 2007)

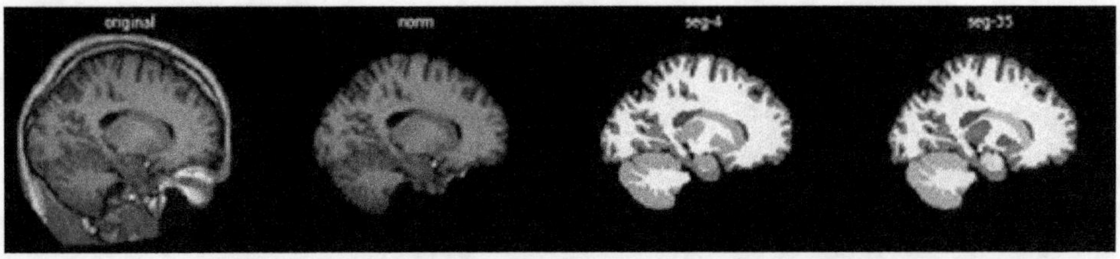

- The Cancer Imaging Archive (TCIA):

The TCIA provides a vast amount of openly accessible medical imaging data pertaining to various forms of cancer, making it an exceptional resource. The dataset includes images from many modalities, such as computed tomography (CT), magnetic resonance imaging (MRI), and positron emission tomography (PET). Sample images are shown in Figure 4. This allows researchers to investigate cancer detection, characterization, and treatment response (Clark et al., 2013).

Figure 4. Sample images of TCIA dataset (Clark et al., 2013).

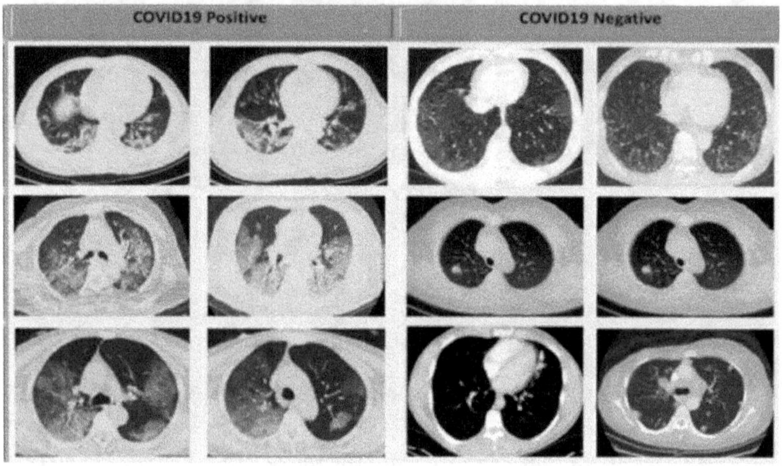

- IXI Dataset:

The dataset known as Information eXtraction from Images (IXI) includes a wide variety of magnetic resonance imaging (MRI) scans taken from healthy subject populations. Studies pertaining to the structure of the brain, volumetric analysis, and the aging process frequently make use of it (D. Jiang et al., 2018). Sample images are shown in Figure 5.

Figure 5. Sample images of IXI dataset (Ng et al., 2018)

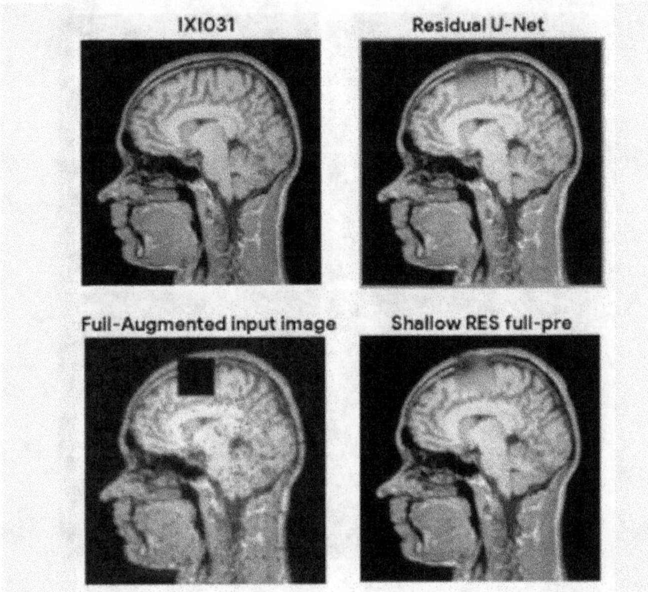

- LIDC-IDRI (Lung Image Database Consortium and Image Database Resource Initiative):

With a particular emphasis on lung cancer, LIDC-IDRI provides CT scans that have been annotated for the detection and characterisation of lung nodules. The development of algorithms for lung cancer screening and detection relies heavily on this dataset, which plays an especially important role (Wang, Luo, Yang, & Lin, 2015). Sample images are shown in Figure 6.

Figure 6. Sample images of LIDC-IDRI dataset (Ang, Luo, Yang, & Lin, 2015)

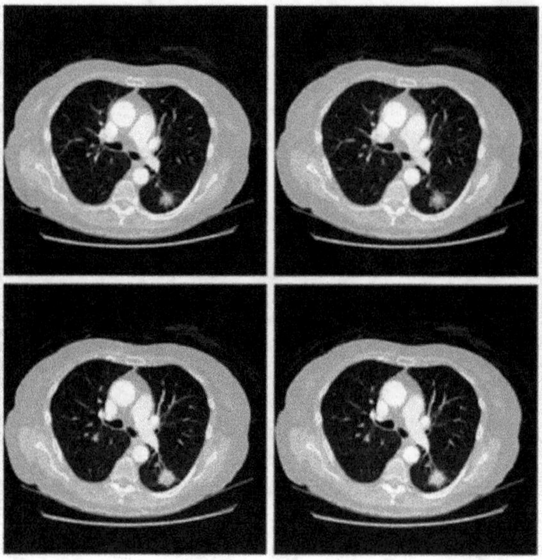

- MIMIC-CXR:

There are chest X-ray images that are related with clinical reports that are included in the MIMIC-CXR collection. It provides funding for studies dealing with the detection of chest pathology, the diagnosis of pneumonia, and other respiratory disorders (Johnson et al., 2019). Sample images are shown in Figure 7.

Figure 7. Sample images of MIMIC-CXR (Johnson et al., 2019)

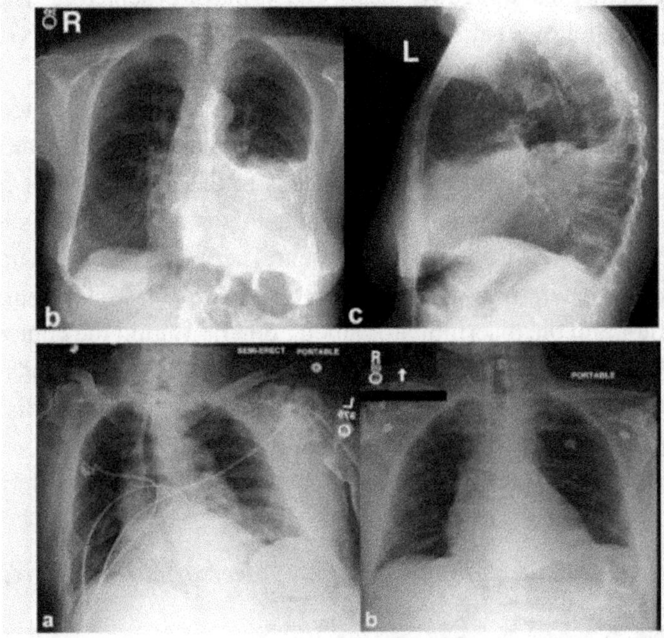

The provision of established benchmarks, the facilitation of algorithm development, and the promotion of collaboration between academics and healthcare providers are all key factors in the advancement of the area of medical imaging analysis. These datasets, along with others, play an important role in this advancement. The variety and complexity of these datasets contribute to the resilience and generalization of machine learning models in clinical settings that are based in the real world.

5. METHODOLOGIES EMPLOYED IN GENERATIVE ARTIFICIAL INTELLIGENCE (AI) FOR THE PURPOSE OF MEDICAL IMAGING

The methodologies that are utilized in the process of Generative Artificial Intelligence (AI) for Medical Imaging comprise a wide variety of strategies, each of which is specifically designed to solve certain issues that are inherent in the analysis of complicated medical datasets. In the following, some of the most important approaches are discussed that have become prominent in the field:

- **Generative Adversarial Networks (GANs):**

In the field of medical image synthesis, GANs play a crucial role. They were first presented by Goodfellow et al. (2014). An adversarial training process is carried out by a generator and a discriminator network that are both components of a GAN. In contrast to the discriminator, which works to discern between created and actual images, the generator's objective is to provide medical images that are as realistic as possible. This antagonistic interaction leads to the production of high-fidelity medical images that are extremely like the data that is real. Figure 8 shows layered architecture of GAN. There are two unique neural networks that make up the layered architecture of a Generative Adversarial Network (GAN). These neural networks are the generator and the discriminator among others. Within the context of a competitive framework, these networks are interconnected. The generator's objective is to generate data samples that are as realistic as possible, while the discriminator's objective is to differentiate between actual and generated samples (Kazeminia et al., 2020). Figure 8 shows layered architecture of Generative Adversarial Network (GAN)

Figure 8. Layered Architecture of Generative Adversarial Network (GAN) (Kazeminia et al., 2020)

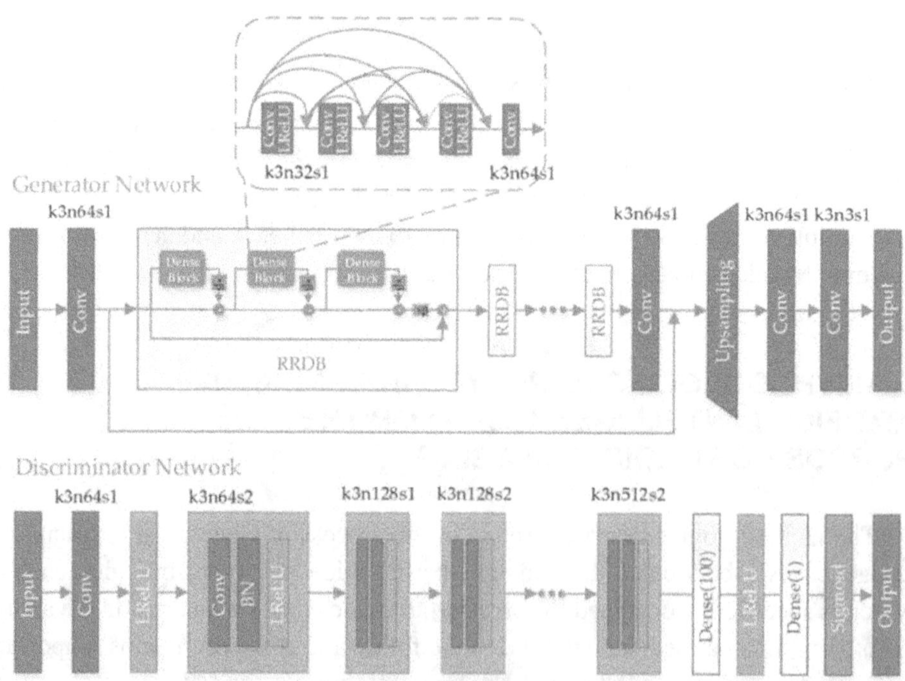

- **Variational Autoencoders (VAEs):**

Kingma and Welling (2013) presented VAEs, which centre their attention on the process of learning latent representations of data. In the field of medical imaging, VAEs are utilized for a variety of activities, including image-to-image translation and synthesis, among others. The development of diverse and realistic medical images is made possible by VAEs, which capture the underlying probabilistic structure of the data. Additionally, VAEs make it easier to interpolate and manipulate latent characteristics.

Figure 9 shows layered architecture of Variational Autoencoders (VAEs). There are two primary components that make up the layered architecture of Variational Autoencoders (VAEs), and these are the encoder and the decoder (Merlin Mancy et al. 2024). There are probabilistic generative models known as VAEs. These models learn to encode input data into a latent space with a lower dimension, and then they decode the latent representations back into reconstructed data samples (Cackowski, Barbier, Dojat, & Christen, 2023).

Figure 9. Layered architecture of Variational Autoencoders (VAEs) (Cackowski, Barbier, Dojat, & Christen, 2023)

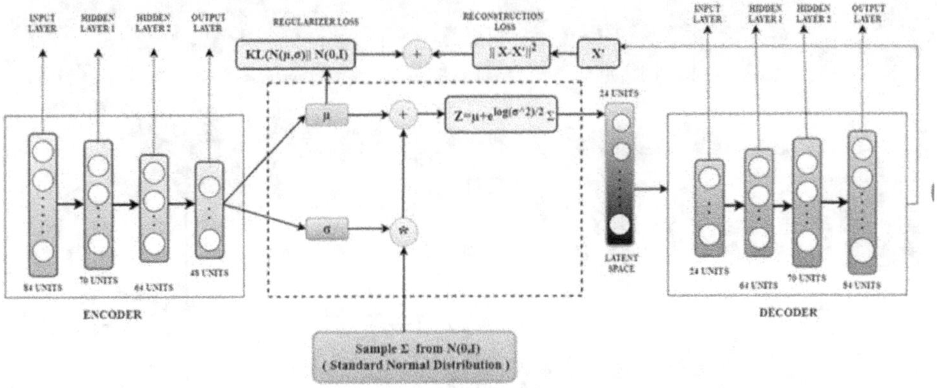

- **Cycle-Consistent Adversarial Networks (CycleGANs):**

Image-to-image translation is the area of expertise of CycleGANs, which were first shown by authors. These neural networks do not require paired training data. To convert CT scans to MRIs, for example, CycleGANs are applied in the field of medical imaging to perform image transformations between various modalities.

Increasing the interpretability of the outputs that are generated is made possible by the cycle-consistency requirement, which guarantees that the translated images will continue to be loyal to the original domain (Armanious et al., 2019). Figure 10 shows layered architecture of Cycle-Consistent Adversarial Networks (CycleGANs). The generator and the discriminator are the two primary components that make up the layered architecture of Cycle-Consistent Adversarial Networks, often known as Cycle GANs. There is a cyclical relationship between these networks, which allows them to function together to assist picture translation across two domains (D. Kapadiya, C. Shekhawat, and P. Sharma, 2023). The generators are designed to produce images that have a realistic appearance and can translate between the two domains while maintaining important visual qualities simultaneously. The objective of the discriminators is to differentiate between real and created images, thereby providing input to the generators to enhance the quality of image translation. The application of cycle-consistency loss ensures that the original image and the image that has been translated to the other domain and then back again are consistent with one another. CycleGANs are designed to preserve essential visual properties throughout the translation process. This is accomplished using cycle-consistency loss.

Figure 10. Layered architecture of cycle-consistent adversarial networks (Cycle-GANs) (Armanious et al., 2019)

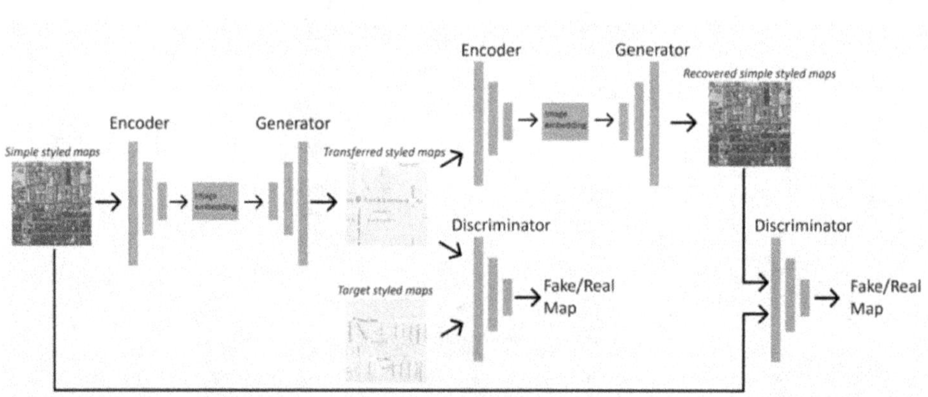

- **Super-Resolution Generative Models:**

The resolution of medical images is designed to be improved using super-resolution techniques, such as those that are based on GANs. This proves to be especially useful in situations when the accuracy of diagnosis relies heavily on the finer details. The visual quality and diagnostic information that may be derived from medical images are both improved because of these models, which generate high-resolution images from inputs with a lower resolution (Mahapatra, Bozorgtabar, & Garnavi, 2019). Figure 11 shows the layered architecture of Super-Resolution Generative Models.

Super-Resolution Generative Models typically utilize both generator and discriminator networks, drawing inspiration from the structure of Generative Adversarial Networks (GANs). This approach seeks to enhance the perceptual quality and realism of the high-resolution images produced. An image with a low resolution is fed into the generator network, which then produces an image with a high resolution that corresponds to the low resolution. In most cases, it is made up of convolutional layers, which are then followed by activation functions (such ReLU) to learn feature representations from the input image. It is possible for the generator to use up-sampling layers to provide the feature maps with a higher spatial resolution. There is the possibility of using residual connections or skip connections to increase training stability and facilitate the flow of information. Convolutional layers with appropriate activation functions (such as tanh) are frequently utilized by the output layer to guarantee pixel value limitations. This layer is responsible for producing the high-resolution image. The discriminator network assesses the authenticity of the produced high-resolution images. The model is trained to differentiate between genuine high-resolution photos and produced high-resolution images using both types as input (P. Sharma and M. K. Jain, 2023). The discriminator usually comprises convolutional layers that are succeeded by activation functions to extract features from the input images. The output is a probability score that indicates the chance of the input image being real as opposed to being produced. The discriminator seeks to enhance its capacity to differentiate between authentic and counterfeit images by engaging in adversarial training with the generator.

Figure 11. Layered architecture of super-resolution generative models (Mahapatra, Bozorgtabar, & Garnavi, 2019)

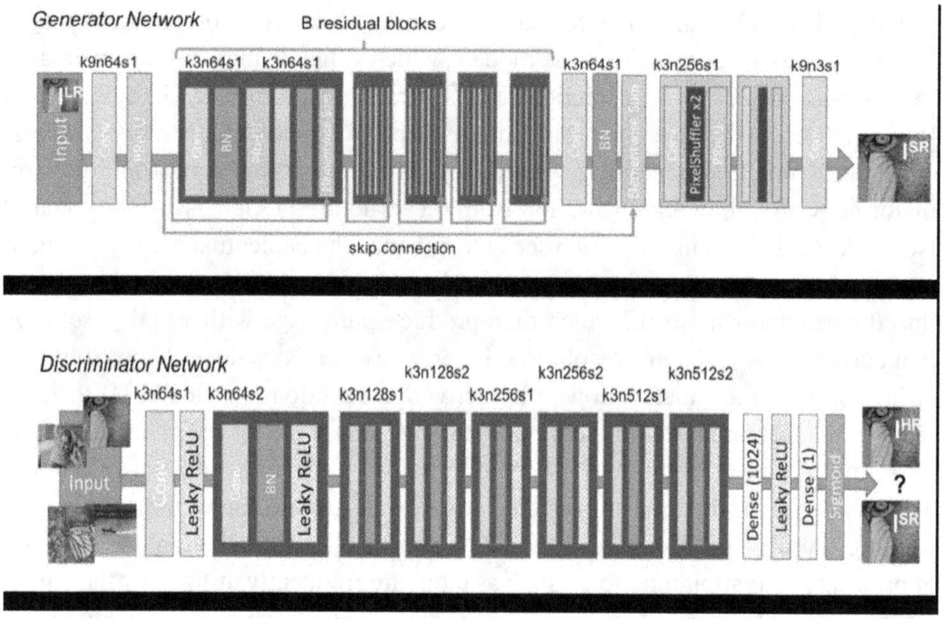

- **Conditional Generative Models:**

To create images based on particular input conditions, conditional generative models, such as conditional GANs and conditional VAEs, are customized from the ground up. Patient demographics, clinical data, or certain pathological traits are some of the conditions that could be considered in the field of medical imaging. Personalized and context-aware medical picture synthesis can be made easier with the use of conditional models, which offer a method for customizing generated images using predetermined criteria (Jung, Luna, & Park, 2021). Figure 12 shows the layered architecture of Conditional Generative Models.

Conditional generative models create samples by using additional conditioning information as input instead of the original data. These models have the capability of generating samples that are conditioned on traits, classes, or any other type of auxiliary information. In general, the layered design of conditional generative models makes it possible for them to create samples that are conditioned on features or metadata. This provides flexibility and controllability in the process of creation. Applications of these models can be found in a variety of fields, such as picture production, text-to-image synthesis, image-to-image translation, and many more.

Figure 12. Layered architecture of conditional generative models (Jung, Luna, & Park, 2021)

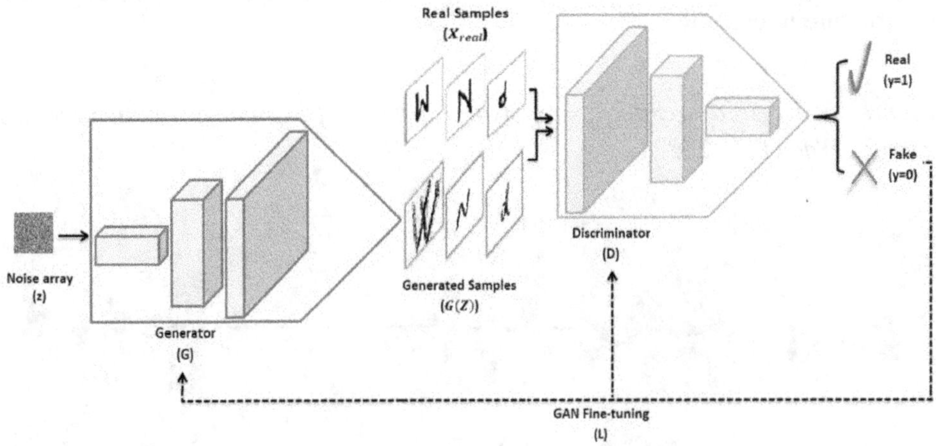

- **Style Transfer and Domain Adaptation:**

Style transfer techniques, which were first developed for artistic image processing, have found uses in medical imaging. These approaches are used to transfer the style or features of one group of photos to another set of images. Within the framework of domain adaptation, these strategies provide assistance in the process of adapting generative models to new datasets, reducing the obstacles associated with domain shifts, and assuring the resilience of the models over a variety of clinical settings (Yao et al., 2022). Style Transfer and Domain Adaptation are processes that entail moving visual attributes from one image or domain to another while maintaining the original content or structure. While distinct, these activities frequently exhibit analogous characteristics inside their complex structures. Figure 13 shows the layered architecture of Style Transfer and Domain Adaptation Models.

After being processed by feature extraction layers, the input images from both the source domain and the target domain are then used (Agarwal, A., Trivedi, A., Sharma, P., & Bhardwaj, A. 2024). Typically, these layers are made up of convolutional neural network (CNN) designs, such as VGG, ResNet, or other networks of a similar kind that have been pre-trained on large-scale picture classification tasks, such as ImageNet. The feature extraction layers are responsible for capturing hierarchical representations of the input images and extracting visual features ranging from low-level to high-level content. The process of style transfer involves the creation of new layers that are specifically designed to extract the style information from a certain style reference image. The capabilities of style transfer and domain adaptation models allow for the efficient transfer or adaption of visual features between pictures or domains, all while maintaining the integrity of essential content or structure information.

Figure 13. Layered architecture of style transfer and domain adaptation models settings (Yao et al., 2022)

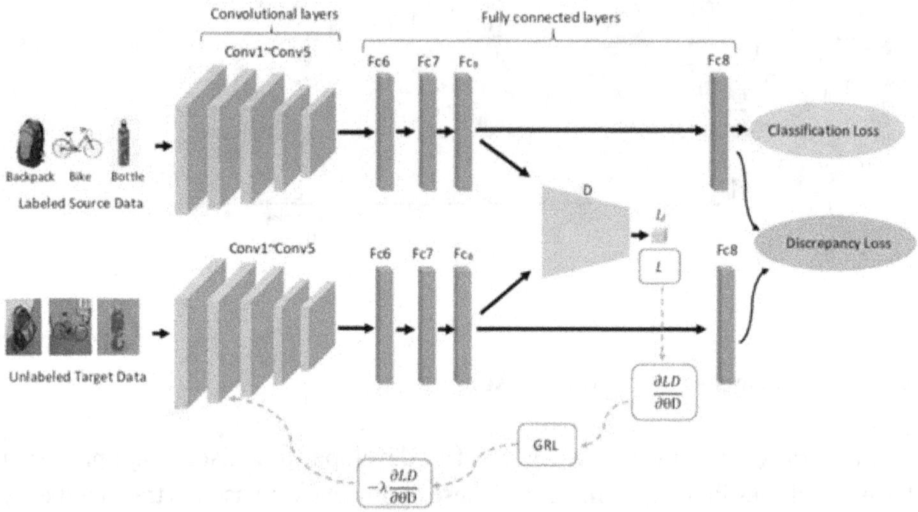

- **Attention Mechanisms in Generative Models:**

Attention processes, which have gained popularity in the field of natural language processing, have been incorporated into generative models employed for the study of medical imaging. The model is able to concentrate on particular regions of interest thanks to attention processes, which results in an improvement in the quality of the images that are generated and an increase in the interpretability of the outputs that are generated. Figure 14 shows the layered architecture of Attention Mechanisms in Generative Models.

Attention Mechanisms in Generative Models use a layered creation to train the network to zero in on specific input features that will be useful for output production. Image generation, language modelling, and sequence-to-sequence tasks are just a few examples of the many generative tasks that have made extensive use of attention mechanisms. The next step is to encode the incoming data into a feature representation. This data could be images, sequences, or any other type of structured data. This usually entails using convolutional layers to extract hierarchical characteristics from images. Recurrent neural networks (RNNs), transformers, and convolutional networks are commonly employed for sequence encoding, whether it be text or time-series data (Kong, Li, Jiang, Wang, & Song, 2021).

To focus on certain portions of the input data, attention mechanism layers are utilized. Each input component's relative importance in the given context is indicated by the attention weights or scores computed by these layers. One can employ a variety of attention strategies, including: "Self-attention" is focusing on separate details within the same picture or sequence. Paying attention to different portions of the same image or sequence is called cross-attention. By combining numerous attention heads, we can capture various components of the information. This technique is known as multi-head attention. Feedforward neural networks, scaled dot-product attention, and other attention mechanisms suggested in literature can be used to construct attention processes.

Figure 14. Layered architecture of attention mechanisms in generative models (Kong, Li, Jiang, Wang, & Song, 2021)

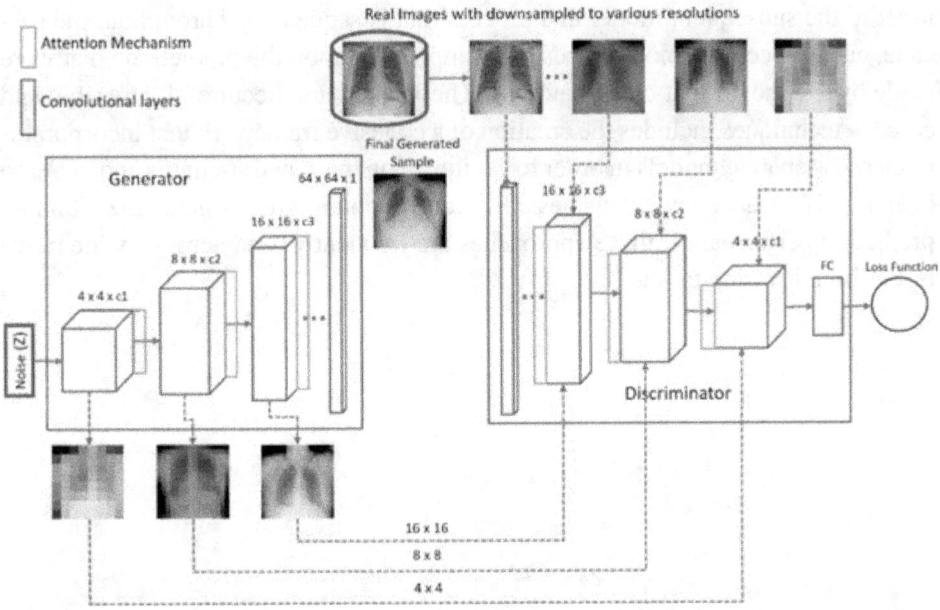

- **Ensemble and Cascade Approaches:**

Increasing the diversity and resilience of the images that are generated is accomplished through the utilization of ensemble models, which are a combination of numerous generative models or architectures. Cascade techniques include a sequential generation process, in which the outputs from one model serve as inputs to subsequent models, thereby iteratively enhancing the images that are generated. Increasing the performance and robustness of machine learning models can be accomplished using techniques known as Ensemble and Cascade Approaches. Figure 15 shows layered architecture of Ensemble and Cascade Approaches. These approaches include merging numerous independent models into a cohesive framework (Shahsavari, Ranjbari, & Khatibi, 2021).

Creating individual basis models is the first step in the layered architecture. These base models are trained individually on subsets of the training data or using various algorithms. It is possible for these foundation models to be of the same type (homogeneous ensemble) or of different sorts (heterogeneous ensemble). For instance, in the context of a classification problem, individual base models could consist of decision trees, random forests, support vector machines (SVMs), neural networks, and other similar models (Kulkarni, K., & Sharma, P. 2024). Within the framework of the cascade methodology, the result of one base model is utilized as input to the subsequent model in a process that is sequential. Throughout the cascade, each successive model focuses on improving upon the predictions that were made by the model that came before it. The layered architecture of ensemble and cascade techniques includes the creation of a cohesive framework that incorporates numerous separate models in order to capitalize on their own strengths and increase overall performance and robustness. In order to obtain greater generalization and prediction performance, these approaches are frequently used across a wide range of machine learning tasks.

Figure 15. Layered architecture of ensemble and cascade approaches (Shahsavari, Ranjbari, & Khatibi, 2021)

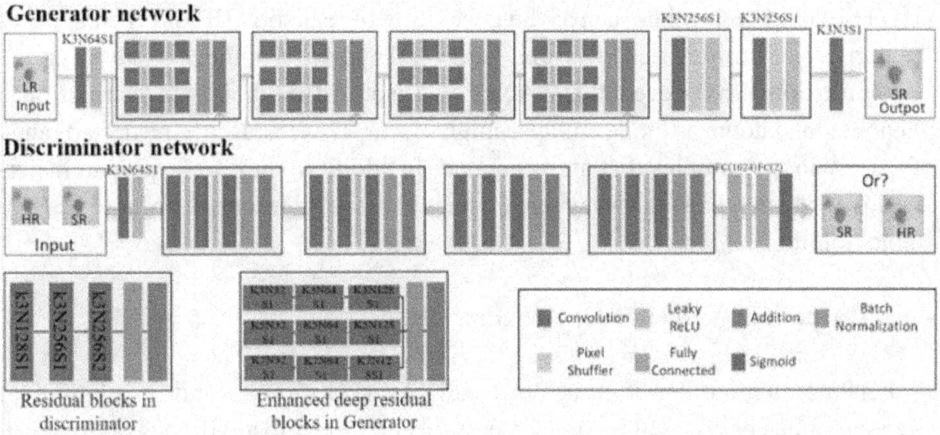

These techniques collectively demonstrate the adaptability of generative AI in tackling different issues in the field of Medical Imaging Analysis. The selection of methodology is contingent upon the precise objectives of the study, which encompass a wide range of tasks such as image synthesis, picture-to-image translation, denoising, and more. The integration of these approaches in generative AI applications in healthcare is continuously shaping the evolving landscape of the field (Sharma, P., Jyotiyana, M., & Kumar, 2024).

6. COMPARATIVE ANALYSIS OF GENERATIVE AI TECHNIQUES

Comparing the performance of generative artificial intelligence systems in medical imaging analysis entails analysing their applicability, constraints, and performance in tackling a variety of difficulties that are present within the domain. Within the realm of medical imaging analysis, the following is a comparative analysis of various important generative artificial intelligence techniques:

- **Generative Adversarial Networks (GANs):**

Performance: Image synthesis and data augmentation are two examples of jobs that can be accomplished with the help of GANs because of their ability to produce high-fidelity images that contain realistic textures and features.

Applicability: The generation of synthetic medical images, the improvement of image quality, and the translation of images between different modalities are all areas in which GANs are useful. Particularly helpful in situations where great visual fidelity is essential, such as the generation of realistic MRI or CT images for the purpose of training deep learning models, they have a number of advantages.

Limitations: In the event that GANs fail to capture the whole data distribution, a phenomenon known as mode collapse might occur. This results in a restricted range of variety in the samples that are generated. In addition, they are hyperparameter-sensitive, which means that they may require substantial tuning in order to achieve stable training.

- **Variational Autoencoders (VAEs)**:

Performance: When it comes to creating varied samples and learning latent representations of medical pictures, VAEs offer a probabilistic framework that can generate these results. Tasks like as picture reconstruction, denoising, and anomaly identification are all areas in which they perform exceptionally well.

Applicability: When capturing uncertainty and investigating the latent space of medical images is vital, VAEs are useful technologies to have at your disposal. They perform exceptionally well in situations where it is essential to generate a variety of but believable variations of medical images, such as when synthesizing a variety of diseased diseases or situations that are extremely rare.

Limitations

As a result of the nature of the reconstruction target, VAEs frequently create reconstructions that are less than clear, which may restrict their usefulness in situations that need a high level of visual performance. There is also the possibility that they have difficulty collecting fine details in medical images.

- **Auto-regressive models**

Performance: Auto-regressive models excel at producing sequential data with fine-grained control over each component, which makes them a good fit for jobs like medical imaging longitudinal data production and video prediction.

Applicability: When it's critical to model temporal relationships in medical imaging data, auto-regressive models work well. Their ability to capture intricate spatiotemporal patterns and produce lifelike medical image sequences is remarkable.

Limitations: One potential drawback of auto-regressive models is their slow generation speed, which can make it difficult for them to capture the global context in huge images or volumetric data. In addition, their training and inference processes could necessitate a large amount of processing resources.

The unique task requirements, such as the required visual fidelity, diversity of generated samples, and modelling of underlying data distributions, determine the choice of generative AI technique for medical imaging analysis. Every method has its own set of advantages and disadvantages; researchers usually choose the best method according to the data's properties and the analysis's goals.

7. OBSTACLES PREVENT MEDICAL IMAGE ANALYSIS USING GENERATIVE AI

The use of Generative Artificial Intelligence (AI) techniques into Medical Imaging Analysis is a potentially fruitful route; yet, it is not without of difficulties. There are several challenges that prevent the seamless implementation of generative models in this essential domain. Understanding these issues and finding solutions to them is essential to fully exploit the promise of generative artificial intelligence in the field of medical picture analysis. (Shahsavari, Ranjbari, & Khatibi, 2021). The following are some of the most significant challenges:

- **Limited and Heterogeneous Datasets:**

To conduct effective training, generative models largely rely on datasets that are both vast and diverse. In the field of medical imaging, it can be difficult to acquire complete datasets that contain a wide variety of patient demographics, imaging modalities, and illnesses. It is possible that biased models will be produced as a result of limited and imbalanced datasets, which will fail to generalize well across a variety of clinical circumstances (Jung, Luna, & Park, 2021).

- **Ethical and Regulatory Concerns:**

Several ethical concerns, including patient privacy, consent, and data security, are brought up by the application of generative artificial intelligence in medical imaging. The deployment of generative models in clinical settings is made more difficult by the need to comply with regulatory norms, such as the Health Insurance Portability and Accountability Act (HIPAA) in the United States. In order to achieve general acceptability, it is necessary to find a middle ground between innovative methods and ethical standards.

- **Interpretability and Explainability:**

Generative models frequently function as intricate, opaque systems, which makes it difficult to comprehend the decision-making processes that they employ. The absence of interpretability can be a barrier to trust among medical professionals, which is especially problematic in the field of medical imaging, where openness is essential for clinical acceptance. An ongoing problem in the field of research is the development of strategies for interpreting model predictions and creating insights that are valuable from a therapeutic perspective (D. Jiang et al., 2018).

- **Robustness and Generalization:**

Generative models may have difficulty with robustness and generalization when they are confronted with fluctuations in imaging conditions, equipment, and patient demographics. It is a huge challenge to guarantee that models would operate in a consistent manner across a wide variety of datasets and clinical environments. Techniques of domain adaptation and transfer learning are now being investigated in order to minimize the impact of these issues.

- **Computational Resources and Scalability:**

The training and deployment of generative models, particularly deep neural networks, demand a significant number of computational resources. When it comes to establishing and maintaining these models, healthcare institutions that have limitations in their resources may confront difficulties. There is still a concern regarding the scalability of generative artificial intelligence solutions for general use in medical facilities and clinics.

- **Integration with Clinical Workflow:**

It is a difficult issue to integrate generative artificial intelligence in a smooth manner into existing clinical operations. The introduction of new technologies necessitates careful consideration of workflow disruptions, user interfaces, and collaboration between artificial intelligence systems and human practitioners. Healthcare professionals are accustomed to established methods, and the introduction of new technology needs they be prepared.

- **Validation and Clinical Adoption:**

Determining whether generative models are safe and effective in therapeutic settings is a significant challenge. It is vital, in order to achieve widespread clinical adoption, to convince healthcare professionals, regulatory agencies, and patients about the veracity of these models and the influence they have in the real world. In order to establish the clinical utility of generative artificial intelligence applied to medical imaging, it is important to conduct rigorous clinical trials and validation studies.

- **Data Privacy and Security Challenges:**

There are stringent privacy restrictions in place because the data collected from medical imaging is sensitive. The sharing and accessing of datasets for the purposes of research while also protecting the privacy of patients is a tricky balance. There is a persistent worry over the development of tools for collaborative research and model training that are both secure and protect individuals' privacy.

- **Human-AI Collaboration and User Acceptance:**

Artificial intelligence technologies may be met with unfamiliarity from healthcare experts. Important things to do include bridging the gap between human and artificial intelligence competence, cultivating trust, and assuring effective collaboration. When it comes to overcoming opposition and boosting user acceptance, educational campaigns and user-friendly interfaces are necessary.

- **Explainability of Model Decisions:**

The capacity to interpret and explain model decisions is extremely important, particularly in the healthcare industry, where decisions might influence the outcomes for patients. One of the major challenges is to make sure that generative artificial intelligence models offer transparent insights into the decision-making processes they use.

To successfully incorporate generative artificial intelligence approaches into medical imaging analysis, it is vital to first acknowledge and then address the obstacles that have been identified. When it comes to overcoming these hurdles and unlocking the full potential of generative models in terms of enhancing patient care and advancing medical research, it is vital for researchers, healthcare providers, and legislators to work together.

8. CONCLUSION

This systematic review has offered a thorough summary of the uses of generative artificial intelligence (AI) methods in medical imaging analysis. Numerous unique methods have discovered utilizing generative AI models like Generative Adversarial Networks (GANs), Variational Autoencoders (VAEs), and their variations after a thorough review of existing literature. The paper emphasizes the substantial influence of generative AI methods on many datasets of medical imaging analysis. The systematic investigation of several generative AI methods has shown their varied uses in multiple medical imaging techniques such as X-ray, MRI, CT scans, and histopathological images. Generative AI has the potential to significantly transform clinical practice and patient care by enhancing diagnostic accuracy, assisting in treatment planning, and monitoring diseases. Comparative analysis of different techniques of generative AI in medical imaging analysis is also shown in the chapter. Nevertheless, despite the significant advancements observed in recent years, certain obstacles and restrictions endure. Issues including model generalization, data heterogeneity, interpretability, and ethical implications require more research and collaboration across disciplines. Future research is crucial to progress the advancement and acceptance of generative AI methods in medical imaging analysis. Future research should concentrate on tackling the highlighted obstacles, improving model structures, improving dataset quality, and carrying out thorough validation experiments in clinical environments.

REFERENCES

Agarwal, A., Trivedi, A., Sharma, P., & Bhardwaj, A. (2024). Use Cases of ChatGPT and Other AI Tools With Security Concerns. In Sharma, P., Jyotiyana, M., & Kumar, A. (Eds.), *Applications, Challenges, and the Future of ChatGPT* (pp. 216–225). IGI Global. DOI: 10.4018/979-8-3693-6824-4.ch012

Armanious, K., Jiang, C., Abdulatif, S., Küstner, T., Gatidis, S., & Yang, B. (2019). *Unsupervised medical image translation using cycle-MedGAN.* Paper presented at the 2019 27th European signal processing conference (EUSIPCO). DOI: 10.23919/EUSIPCO.2019.8902799

Cackowski, S., Barbier, E. L., Dojat, M., & Christen, T. (2023). Imunity: A generalizable vae-gan solution for multicenter mr image harmonization. *Medical Image Analysis*, 88, 102799. DOI: 10.1016/j.media.2023.102799 PMID: 37245434

Castillo Ossa, L. F., Chamoso, P., Arango-López, J., Pinto-Santos, F., Isaza, G. A., Santa-Cruz-González, C., Ceballos-Marquez, A., Hernández, G., & Corchado, J. M. (2021). A hybrid model for COVID-19 monitoring and prediction. *Electronics (Basel)*, 10(7), 799. DOI: 10.3390/electronics10070799

Chartsias, A., Joyce, T., Papanastasiou, G., Semple, S., Williams, M., Newby, D. E., Dharmakumar, R., & Tsaftaris, S. A. (2019). Disentangled representation learning in cardiac image analysis. *Medical Image Analysis*, 58, 101535. DOI: 10.1016/j.media.2019.101535 PMID: 31351230

Chen, Y., Yang, X.-H., Wei, Z., Heidari, A. A., Zheng, N., Li, Z., Chen, H., Hu, H., Zhou, Q., & Guan, Q. (2022). Generative adversarial networks in medical image augmentation: A review. *Computers in Biology and Medicine*, 144, 105382. DOI: 10.1016/j.compbiomed.2022.105382 PMID: 35276550

Clark, K., Vendt, B., Smith, K., Freymann, J., Kirby, J., Koppel, P., & Pringle, M. (2013). The Cancer Imaging Archive (TCIA): Maintaining and operating a public information repository. *Journal of Digital Imaging*, 26(6), 1045–1057. DOI: 10.1007/s10278-013-9622-7 PMID: 23884657

Das, A., Nair, M. S., & Peter, S. D. (2020). Computer-aided histopathological image analysis techniques for automated nuclear atypia scoring of breast cancer: A review. *Journal of Digital Imaging*, 33(5), 1091–1121. DOI: 10.1007/s10278-019-00295-z PMID: 31989390

Erickson, B. J., Korfiatis, P., Akkus, Z., & Kline, T. L. (2017). Machine learning for medical imaging. Radiographics, 37(2), 505-515.

Filice, R. W., Stein, A., Wu, C. C., Arteaga, V. A., Borstelmann, S., Gaddikeri, R., & Hobbs, S. B. (2020). Crowdsourcing pneumothorax annotations using machine learning annotations on the NIH chest X-ray dataset. *Journal of Digital Imaging*, 33(2), 490–496. DOI: 10.1007/s10278-019-00299-9 PMID: 31768897

Frid-Adar, M., Diamant, I., Klang, E., Amitai, M., Goldberger, J., & Greenspan, H. (2018). GAN-based synthetic medical image augmentation for increased CNN performance in liver lesion classification. *Neurocomputing*, 321, 321–331. DOI: 10.1016/j.neucom.2018.09.013

Goodfellow, I., Pouget-Abadie, J., Mirza, M., Xu, B., Warde-Farley, D., Ozair, S., & Bengio, Y. (2014). Generative adversarial nets. *Advances in Neural Information Processing Systems*, 27.

Hartig, M., Truran-Sacrey, D., Raptentsetsang, S., Schuff, N., & Weiner, M. (2012). Ucsf freesurfer overview and qc ratings. *ADNI: Alzheimers Disease Neuroimaging Initiative, San Francisco.*

Jiang, D., Dou, W., Vosters, L., Xu, X., Sun, Y., & Tan, T. (2018). Denoising of 3D magnetic resonance images with multi-channel residual learning of convolutional neural network. *Japanese Journal of Radiology*, 36(9), 566–574. DOI: 10.1007/s11604-018-0758-8 PMID: 29982919

Jiang, X., Hu, Z., Wang, S., & Zhang, Y. (2023). Deep learning for medical image-based cancer diagnosis. *Cancers (Basel)*, 15(14), 3608. DOI: 10.3390/cancers15143608 PMID: 37509272

Johnson, A. E., Pollard, T. J., Greenbaum, N. R., Lungren, M. P., Deng, C.-y., Peng, Y., . . . Horng, S. (2019). MIMIC-CXR-JPG, a large publicly available database of labeled chest radiographs. *arXiv preprint arXiv:1901.07042*.

Jung, E., Luna, M., & Park, S. H. (2021). *Conditional GAN with an attention-based generator and a 3D discriminator for 3D medical image generation.* Paper presented at the Medical Image Computing and Computer Assisted Intervention–MICCAI 2021: 24th International Conference, Strasbourg, France, September 27–October 1, 2021, Proceedings, Part VI 24. DOI: 10.1007/978-3-030-87231-1_31

Jyotiyana, M., & Kesswani, N. (2020). Deep learning and the future of biomedical image analysis. Deep Learning Techniques for Biomedical and Health Informatics, 329-345.

Jyotiyana, M., & Kesswani, N. (2021). Introduction to Deep Learning in Health Informatics. Biomedical Data Mining for Information Retrieval: Methodologies, Techniques and Applications, 237-261.

Jyotiyana, M., & Kesswani, N. (2021). A study on deep learning in neurodegenerative diseases and other brain disorders. In Rising Threats in Expert Applications and Solutions: Proceedings of FICR-TEAS 2020 (pp. 791-799). Springer Singapore.

Jyotiyana, M., & Kesswani, N. (2020). Classification and prediction of Alzheimer's disease using multi-layer perceptron. *International Journal of Reasoning-based Intelligent Systems*, 12(4), 255–263. DOI: 10.1504/IJRIS.2020.111785

Jyotiyana, M., Kesswani, N., & Kumar, M. (2022). A deep learning approach for classification and diagnosis of Parkinson's disease. *Soft Computing*, 26(18), 9155–9165. DOI: 10.1007/s00500-022-07275-6

Jyotiyana, M., Kesswani, N., & Agarwal, A. (2022, January). An improved approach for removal of salt and pepper noise in MR images. Advances in Deep Learning.

Kapadiya, D., Shekhawat, C., & Sharma, P. (2023). A Study on Large Scale Applications of Big Data in Modern Era. In *International Conference on Information Management & Machine Intelligence (ICIMMI2023),* November 23–25, 2023, Jaipur, India. ACM. https://doi.org/DOI: 10.1145/3647444.364788

Kasban, H., & El-Bendary, M. A. M., & Salama, D. H. (2015). A comparative study of medical imaging techniques. *International Journal of Information Science and Intelligent System*, 4(2), 37–58.

Kazeminia, S., Baur, C., Kuijper, A., van Ginneken, B., Navab, N., Albarqouni, S., & Mukhopadhyay, A. (2020). GANs for medical image analysis. *Artificial Intelligence in Medicine*, 109, 101938. DOI: 10.1016/j.artmed.2020.101938 PMID: 34756215

Khan, M. K. H., Guo, W., Liu, J., Dong, F., Li, Z., Patterson, T. A., & Hong, H. (2023). Machine learning and deep learning for brain tumor MRI image segmentation. *Experimental Biology and Medicine*, 248(21), 1974–1992. DOI: 10.1177/15353702231214259 PMID: 38102956

Kong, F., Li, J., Jiang, B., Wang, H., & Song, H. (2021). Integrated generative model for industrial anomaly detection via Bidirectional LSTM and attention mechanism. *IEEE Transactions on Industrial Informatics*, 19(1), 541–550. DOI: 10.1109/TII.2021.3078192

Kulkarni, K., & Sharma, P. (2024). Algorithmic Issues, Challenges, and Theoretical Concerns of ChatGPT. In Sharma, P., Jyotiyana, M., & Kumar, A. (Eds.), *Applications, Challenges, and the Future of ChatGPT* (pp. 56–74). IGI Global. DOI: 10.4018/979-8-3693-6824-4.ch003

Li, Y., Gan, Z., Shen, Y., Liu, J., Cheng, Y., Wu, Y., & Gao, J. (2019). Storygan: A sequential conditional gan for story visualization. *Proceedings of the IEEE/CVF Conference on Computer Vision and Pattern Recognition*. DOI: 10.1109/CVPR.2019.00649

Mahapatra, D., Bozorgtabar, B., & Garnavi, R. (2019). Image super-resolution using progressive generative adversarial networks for medical image analysis. *Computerized Medical Imaging and Graphics*, 71, 30–39. DOI: 10.1016/j.compmedimag.2018.10.005 PMID: 30472408

Maharajan, K., Kumar, A. V., El Emary, I. M., Sharma, P., Latip, R., Mishra, N., Dutta, A., Manjunatha Rao, L., & Sharma, M. (2023). Blockchain Methods and Data-Driven Decision Making With Autonomous Transportation. In Kumar, R., Abdul Hamid, A., & Binti Ya'akub, N. (Eds.), *Effective AI, Blockchain, and E-Governance Applications for Knowledge Discovery and Management* (pp. 176–194). IGI Global. DOI: 10.4018/978-1-6684-9151-5.ch012

Marcus, D. S., Wang, T. H., Parker, J., Csernansky, J. G., Morris, J. C., & Buckner, R. L. (2007). Open Access Series of Imaging Studies (OASIS): Cross-sectional MRI data in young, middle aged, nondemented, and demented older adults. *Journal of Cognitive Neuroscience*, 19(9), 1498–1507. DOI: 10.1162/jocn.2007.19.9.1498 PMID: 17714011

Merlin Mancy, A., Kumar, A. V., Latip, R., Jagadamba, G., Chakrabarti, P., Sharma, P., Musirin, I. B., Sharma, M., & Kanchan, B. G. (2024). Smart Healthcare System, Digital Health and Telemedicine, Management and Emergencies: Patient Emergency Application (PES) E-Governance Applications. In Kumar, R., Abdul Hamid, A., Binti Ya'akub, N., Sharan, H., & Kumar, S. (Eds.), *Sustainable Development in AI, Blockchain, and E-Governance Applications* (pp. 124–151). IGI Global. DOI: 10.4018/979-8-3693-1722-8.ch008

Müller-Franzes, G., Niehues, J. M., Khader, F., Arasteh, S. T., Haarburger, C., Kuhl, C., & Nebelung, S. (2023). A multimodal comparison of latent denoising diffusion probabilistic models and generative adversarial networks for medical image synthesis. *Scientific Reports*, 13(1), 12098. DOI: 10.1038/s41598-023-39278-0 PMID: 37495660

Nie, X., Ding, H., Qi, M., Wang, Y., & Wong, E. K. (2021). Urca-gan: Upsample residual channel-wise attention generative adversarial network for image-to-image translation. *Neurocomputing*, 443, 75–84. DOI: 10.1016/j.neucom.2021.02.054

Oh, S., Jung, Y., Kim, S., Lee, I., & Kang, N. (2019). Deep generative design: Integration of topology optimization and generative models. *Journal of Mechanical Design*, 141(11), 111405. DOI: 10.1115/1.4044229

Oprea, S., Martinez-Gonzalez, P., Garcia-Garcia, A., Castro-Vargas, J. A., Orts-Escolano, S., Garcia-Rodriguez, J., & Argyros, A. (2020). A review on deep learning techniques for video prediction. *IEEE Transactions on Pattern Analysis and Machine Intelligence*, 44(6), 2806–2826. DOI: 10.1109/TPAMI.2020.3045007 PMID: 33320810

Pinaya, W. H., Graham, M. S., Kerfoot, E., Tudosiu, P.-D., Dafflon, J., Fernandez, V., . . . Patel, A. (2023). Generative ai for medical imaging: extending the monai framework. *arXiv preprint arXiv:2307.15208*.

Prasad, G. A., Kumar, A. V., Sharma, P., Irawati, I. D., D. V., C., Musirin, I. B., Abdullah, H. M., & Rao L, M. (2023). Artificial Intelligence in Computer Science: An Overview of Current Trends and Future Directions. In S. Rajest, B. Singh, A. Obaid, R. Regin, & K. Chinnusamy (Eds.), *Advances in Artificial and Human Intelligence in the Modern Era* (pp. 43-60). IGI Global. DOI: 10.4018/979-8-3693-1301-5.ch002

Rawat, P., Bhardwaj, A., Lamba, N., & Sharma, P. (2023). Praveen Kumawat, Prateek Sharma, "Arduino Based IoT Mini Weather Station". *SKIT Research Journal*, 13(2), 34–41. DOI: 10.47904/IJSKIT.13.2.2023.34-41

Sethi, S. S., & Sharma, P. (2023). New Developments in the Implementation of IoT in Agriculture. *SN Computer Science*, 4(5), 503. DOI: 10.1007/s42979-023-01896-w

Shahsavari, A., Ranjbari, S., & Khatibi, T. (2021). Proposing a novel Cascade Ensemble Super Resolution Generative Adversarial Network (CESR-GAN) method for the reconstruction of super-resolution skin lesion images. *Informatics in Medicine Unlocked*, 24, 100628. DOI: 10.1016/j.imu.2021.100628

Sharma, P. (2023). *Utilizing Explainable Artificial Intelligence to Address Deep Learning in Biomedical Domain. In Medical Data Analysis and Processing using Explainable Artificial Intelligence*. Taylor & Francis. DOI: 10.1201/9781003257721-2

Sharma, P., & Bhatnagar, N. (2023). Passenger Authentication and Ticket Verification at Airport Using QR Code Scanner. *SKIT Research Journal*, 13(2), 10–13. DOI: 10.47904/IJSKIT.13.1.2023.10-12

Sharma, P., & Dadheech, P. (2023). Modern-age Agriculture with Artificial Intelligence: A review emphasizing Crop Yield Prediction. *EVERGREEN Joint Journal of Novel Carbon Resource Sciences & Green Asia Strategy*, 10(4), 2570–2582. DOI: 10.5109/7160906

Sharma, P., Dadheech, P., Aneja, N., & Aneja, S. (2023). Predicting Agriculture Yields Based on Machine Learning Using Regression and Deep Learning. *IEEE Access : Practical Innovations, Open Solutions*, 11, 111255–111264. DOI: 10.1109/ACCESS.2023.3321861

Sharma, P., Dadheech, P., & Senthil Kumar Senthil, A. V. (2023). AI-Enabled Crop Recommendation System Based on Soil and Weather Patterns. In Gupta, R., Jain, A., Wang, J., Bharti, S., & Patel, S. (Eds.), *Artificial Intelligence Tools and Technologies for Smart Farming and Agriculture Practices* (pp. 184–199). IGI Global. DOI: 10.4018/978-1-6684-8516-3.ch010

Sharma, P., & Jain, M. K. (2023). Stock Market Trends Analysis using Extreme Gradient Boosting (XGBoost). *2023 International Conference on Computing, Communication, and Intelligent Systems (ICCCIS)*, 317-322. DOI: 10.1109/ICCCIS60361.2023.10425722

Sharma, P., Jyotiyana, M., & Kumar, A. S. (Eds.). (2024). *Applications, Challenges, and the Future of ChatGPT*. IGI Global. DOI: 10.4018/979-8-3693-6824-4

Sharma, P., Kapadiya, D., & Bhardwaj, A. (2023). Efficient Note Sharing Model for Collaborative Learning. *SKIT Research Journal*, 13(2), 42–46. DOI: 10.47904/IJSKIT.13.2.2023.42-46

Sharma, P., & Rathi, Y. (2016, June 5). Efficient Density-Based Clustering Using Automatic Parameter Detection. Efficient Density-Based Clustering Using Automatic Parameter Detection | SpringerLink. .DOI: 10.1007/978-981-10-0767-5_46

Sharma, P., Sharma, C., & Mathur, P. (2023). Machine Learning-based Stock Market Forecasting using Recurrent Neural Network. *2023 9th International Conference on Smart Computing and Communications (ICSCC)*, 600-605. DOI: 10.1109/ICSCC59169.2023.10335083

Shin, H.-C., Tenenholtz, N. A., Rogers, J. K., Schwarz, C. G., Senjem, M. L., Gunter, J. L., . . . Michalski, M. (2018). *Medical image synthesis for data augmentation and anonymization using generative adversarial networks.* Paper presented at the Simulation and Synthesis in Medical Imaging: Third International Workshop, SASHIMI 2018, Held in Conjunction with MICCAI 2018, Granada, Spain, September 16, 2018, Proceedings 3. DOI: 10.1007/978-3-030-00536-8_1

Sun, B. (2022). *Methodology and application of GAN algorithms.* Paper presented at the International Conference on Computer Graphics, Artificial Intelligence, and Data Processing (ICCAID 2021).

Suzuki, K. (2017). Overview of deep learning in medical imaging. *Radiological Physics and Technology*, 10(3), 257–273. DOI: 10.1007/s12194-017-0406-5 PMID: 28689314

Tanwar, A., Sharma, P., Pandey, A., & Kumar, S. 2023. Intrusion Detection System Based Ameliorated Technique of Pattern Matching. In *Proceedings of the 4th International Conference on Information Management & Machine Intelligence (ICIMMI '22)*. Association for Computing Machinery. DOI: 10.1145/3590837.3590947

V., M. V., Kumar, A. S., Sharma, P., Kaur, S., Saleh, O. S., Chennamma, H., & Chaturvedi, A. (2023). AI-Equipped IoT Applications in High-Tech Agriculture Using Machine Learning. In A. Khang (Ed.), *Handbook of Research on AI-Equipped IoT Applications in High-Tech Agriculture* (pp. 38-64). IGI Global. .DOI: 10.4018/978-1-6684-9231-4.ch003

Wang, W., Luo, J., Yang, X., & Lin, H. (2015). Data analysis of the lung imaging database consortium and image database resource initiative. *Academic Radiology*, 22(4), 488–495. DOI: 10.1016/j.acra.2014.12.004 PMID: 25601306

Wolterink, J. M., Leiner, T., Viergever, M. A., & Išgum, I. (2017). Generative adversarial networks for noise reduction in low-dose CT. *IEEE Transactions on Medical Imaging*, 36(12), 2536–2545. DOI: 10.1109/TMI.2017.2708987 PMID: 28574346

Yao, K., Su, Z., Huang, K., Yang, X., Sun, J., Hussain, A., & Coenen, F. (2022). A novel 3D unsupervised domain adaptation framework for cross-modality medical image segmentation. *IEEE Journal of Biomedical and Health Informatics*, 26(10), 4976–4986. DOI: 10.1109/JBHI.2022.3162118 PMID: 35324451

Zhang, H.-M., & Dong, B. (2020). A review on deep learning in medical image reconstruction. *Journal of the Operations Research Society of China*, 8(2), 311–340. DOI: 10.1007/s40305-019-00287-4

Zhang, Y., Yin, Y., Zimmermann, R., Wang, G., Varadarajan, J., & Ng, S.-K. (2020). An enhanced gan model for automatic satellite-to-map image conversion. *IEEE Access : Practical Innovations, Open Solutions*, 8, 176704–176716. DOI: 10.1109/ACCESS.2020.3025008

Zhao, Z., Song, R., Zhang, Q., Duan, P., & Zhang, Y. (2022). JoT-GAN: A framework for jointly training GAN and person re-identification model. *ACM Transactions on Multimedia Computing Communications and Applications*, 18(1s), 1–18. DOI: 10.1145/3491225

Chapter 6
Future of the Ready Made Garments Industry in Real-Time Data:
An Application of AI

Leena Jenefa
https://orcid.org/0000-0002-1324-7083
Hindustan Institute of Technology and Science, India

Dr.Karuppasamy Ramanathan
Hindustan Institute of Technology and Science, India

Namita Mishra
https://orcid.org/0000-0002-3353-0564
I.T.S. School of Management, Delhi, India

Vishnu Vishnu
Hindustan Institute of Technology and Science, India

M. Jayakumar
Vel Tech Rangarajan Dr. Sagunthala R&D Institute of Science and Technology, India

S. Ashok
Hindustan Institute of Technology and Science, India

ABSTRACT

The technology integration for AI in various sectors focuses on how this technology can be used to optimize the production process, generate meaningful and automated customer support, or develop personalized recommendations for shoppers. The apparel industry is starting to integrate automation technology and replace manual labor in certain production links with mechanization as a result of its advancement and maturity. Artificial intelligence allows us to substitute human labor for intelligent robots in order to accomplish repetitive tasks that are relatively labor-intensive. In

DOI: 10.4018/979-8-3693-2284-0.ch006

addition, errors are more likely to occur and productivity declines with extended work hours. Embracing AI technologies and integrating them into marketing and operational strategies helps to maintain the business with competitiveness but also set the standard for developing a strong and memorable brand presence in the digital age.

1. INTRODUCTION

The technology integration for AI in various sectors focus on how this technology can be used to optimize the production process, generate meaningful and automated customer support, or develop personalized recommendations for shoppers. According to McCartney & McCartney (2020), artificial intelligence (AI) is a set of technologies that can identify, analyze, act, learn, and exhibit sophisticated aspects of human intelligence during the problem-solving process.

The apparel industry is starting to integrate automation technology and replace manual labor in certain production links with mechanization as a result of its advancement and maturity.

Artificial intelligence allows us to substitute human labour for intelligent robots in order to accomplish repetitive tasks that are relatively labour-intensive. In addition, errors are more likely to occur and productivity declines with extended work hours. Artificial intelligence facilitates avoiding these issues. Not only is the execution efficiency far higher than that of human labor, but if circumstances allow, it can even operate around the clock. The development and application of artificially intelligent (AI) devices has increased in recent years Duan, Y. et.al (2019); West et.al (2018), Using AI applications in retail organizations to aid with high-speed product delivery to customers. AI apps assist them in processing the product or service at a fast pace while using less time. Providing superior quality service to customers than human retailers and offering accurate customizing features.

The demand in the industry are extremely erratic, and companies must contend with fierce competition in an increasingly crowded industry. Consequently, big data by itself cannot provide a noticeable impact to successfully and efficiently compete. Businesses need to rely on their experience and the data at their disposal in addition to expanding. They need to be able to follow up on the responses they get and ask the appropriate questions. Big data may be able to provide merchants more benefits than they could have imagined, but gathering and preserving this data requires the right tools. To acquire this data, (AI) techniques can provide retailers with strong tools to construct data models and achieve maximum data utilization.AI techniques that can streamline corporate processes and foster adaptability in quickly evolving market conditions and corporate landscapes across the apparel supply chain. It found that there were few applications of AI on consumer and product data.To reduce the overuse of AI and maintain a diverse skill set, the government and business should work together on technological readiness initiatives.

One of the biggest economies is the fashion and apparel (F&A) sector, which contributes 38% to the Asia Pacific region, 26% to Europe, and 22% to North America. (Lenzing, Statista,2020)

2. REVIEW OF LITERATURE

New developments in artificial intelligence and machine learning are facilitating the fashion industry's shift from traditional brick-and-mortar storefronts to cutting-edge online retailers with high-tech features like virtual try-ons and fashion synthesis systems. This article tracks the advancement of research throughout time, provides some insight on various applications relating to these systems, and highlights the field's explosive expansion. Gu, X.et.al (2020). The idea of broad data management and artificial intelligence (AI) to connect enterprises internationally has garnered prominence with the advent of globalization and digitization (Kim et.al, 2018).

Smruti R. (2020) It is frequently necessary to have an immersive visualization to get insight into collective behaviour in order to understand such behaviours and the creation of coarse-scale theories. Through the use of a three-dimensional virtual environment to present the computational findings, users are able to fully immerse themselves in the model and examine the incredibly complicated and nuanced behaviour of individual particles and dislocations.

Sharma et.al (2024) Translational medicine research seeks to rapidly translate fundamental research discoveries into novel procedures and treatment regimens in clinical settings. This translation process frequently faces problems, such as an excessive number of data, complexity, and a lack of experience. ChatGPT can successfully help medical researchers overcome these challenges and make substantial advances.

Agarwal, Ayushi, et al., Patil (2024) As Artificial Intelligence progresses, the industry invests in training Large Language Models (LLM) to comprehend and use our language.

Amany Mostafa Aabed Hassanin Ismaiel et.al (2022) a supply chain that is controlled and connected with data is one of the most crucial solutions needed to increase the efficacy and efficiency of an apparel supply chain and obtain a competitive edge. A digitally linked supply chain, improved supply-chain organization, and new kinds of interactive communication might be made possible by combining extensive data management with artificial intelligence to completely reinvent the apparel supply chain.

AI has been used by e-commerce giants to analyze sales and trends. However, small and large brands are now using machine learning to better understand the market by identifying insights in data such as fashion trends, purchase patterns, inventory, and forecasting (Malhotra, 2020).

In the current world, information technology is vital. Because we live in a digital age, customers may shop around and purchase things at any time of day or night using only their hands and without having to get up from their chairs. Through search engines, one may find a multitude of information on the internet. The majority of consumers today believe that digital platforms are safer and more straightforward, thus they choose them. The customer is assisted in adapting to digital life by social networks, blogs, applications, mobile technologies, and free internet offered by sim card wholesalers. Leena Jenefa et.al (2021).

Karuppasamy R, et al. (2024). The computer revolution, followed by artificial intelligence, came to dominate almost every field. AI may make tailored suggestions and adverts for customers based on their preferences, interests, and actions. Personalized marketing tailors products and services to consumers' individual needs and preferences.

Kim, N et. al (2018), The AI-powered application analyses a big multivariance dataset to give users with personalized recommendations. The AI-powered sales tool not only offers the store with speedy and accurate personalized ideas to increase customer-brand interactions, but it also saves the organization money that was previously invested in human labour.

Bradlow, E. T et. al (2017); Wierenga, B., (2000), AI-powered goods dominate various markets as companies try to improve the user experience through voice recording. client relationship management entails keeping a database of client information such as age, gender, income, designation, lifestyle, educational qualification, as well as prior contacts such as complaints, services, offers, and purchase history.

To create customer-centric offerings, firms must become more data-driven and utilize sophisticated analytics, including artificial intelligence. Stitch Fix, like previously mentioned companies, appreciates the value of big data. Zielnicki, K (2019)

Xu et.al (2023) AI-based solutions provide more accurate projections of future fashion trends, resulting in more effective inventory management. Currently, "generative AI" systems that provide diverse and personalized solutions are gaining traction.

Merlin et.al (2024) An Android software called Patient Emergency software (PEA) connects patients with hospitals. This program provides a calming mechanism controlled by the patient based on their location. In this Patient Emergency App, the server uses Google Maps to identify the sick individual in need of assistance and retrieves the person's information from a database that is recorded by hospital personnel alongside patient records.

3. AI FOR CHARACTER

There's going to be a huge shift in the fashion sector. The fashion sector is experiencing a surge in prospects due to the integration of artificial intelligence (AI), computer vision, and machine learning in applications. The fashion business has a fantastic potential because of the quick advancements in computer vision, machine learning, and artificial intelligence as well as the present, expanding need for online purchasing platforms.

The main cause of Garments Industry is the general discontent among consumers regarding the size, colour, and style of the items that the sector offers. As such, the industry must pivot to a customer-centric approach in order to effectively regulate environmentally friendly production methods. Therefore in order to reduce waste management and production, it is critical that the sector implement sustainable manufacturing techniques. One of the methods of doing this can be by taking use of new Artificial Intelligence (AI) approaches for building a sustainable digital supply chain. (J. H. Thrall et al. 2018;Leena Jenefa 2021; U. Eaganathan 2022) Due to AI's capacity to solve issues using traditional mathematical models, numerous industries, including manufacturing, transportation, and health, have seen significant transformation in recent decades. When using AI approaches, "Distribution" was given the most attention, while "Design" received the least attention .Furthermore, a larger contribution to B2B issues was seen than for B2C issues. Therefore, in order for research to provide the industry with consumer-focused solutions, it must have a B2C viewpoint. Big data is precisely what it sounds like: an enormous volume of data. However, in a broader sense, it refers to a vast array of structured or unstructured material that has been digitally assembled and arranged so that people may swiftly get insightful knowledge. (Oussous 2018 et al.)

3.1 AI in Production of Garments

Garment design is a complicated and cyclical process that employs multiple thinking approaches at all stages of the design process (Evans, 2014). Concept generation is the process of developing concepts for fashion goods. It is an important aspect of the design process since it allows designers to investigate a wide range of options and find new trends and styles. Artificial intelligence (AI) can make concept generation faster, more efficient, and more creative.

AI can develop fresh and original fashion design concepts, employing approaches such as generative design and deep learning algorithms. Ilyos Abdullaev et.al (2023) Researchers found that current AI-based garment design technologies do not fully account for human designers' perspectives. Furthermore, the AI's ability to assess fabric qualities was used to enhance material choices, resulting in a balance of aesthetics and comfort. Mengke Lu et. al (2023) said that, The novel usage of the Multimodal Unsupervised Image-to-Image Translation (MUNIT) algorithm, an AI tool, resulted in different and fashionable designs, enhancing the distinctiveness of ethnic clothes. Our research emphasizes the synergistic combination of traditional craft processes and new technology applications, as well as the significance of artificial intelligence in the long-term evolution of ethnic fashion.

To assist effective design creation in a mass production planning system, the brand's internal data must be included. The majority of this profile data is about consumers, and it is largely used to improve consumer experiences through recommendation services.

4. APPLICATIONS OF AI IN READYMADE GARMENTS INDUSTRY

The clothing emerged as one of the basic needs for survival. The demands of humans for clothes have steadily changed as human civilization has developed. People are willing to pay for anything as long as it fits the trend and their taste, whether it be high-end brand clothing in large shopping malls or personalized clothing stores strewn all over the streets and alleys. Prices range from low-grade stalls with tens of yuan to imported clothing with thousands or even tens of thousands of yuan.

4.1 Virtual Try

Virtual try-on for clothing allows you to see how items fit on a range of actual models. This is how it operates: With only one image of clothes, our new generative AI model can precisely simulate how it would drape, fold, cling, stretch, and create wrinkles and shadows on a wide range of real models in different positions.

4.2 Industrial Robot Technology

The cutting piece's size and form may be precisely identified by the robots using machine vision technology, and they will then cut it in accordance with the scanning results. To avoid confusion, the fashion robots are designed to select the appropriate fabric and employ it in the creation of garments. They also aid in monitoring the amount of material that is still available after it has been utilized. For this procedure to be completed, the robots must be able to precisely assess the cutting piece's contour, extract the data, and enter it into the computer. The most popular ones are edge detection based on mathematical morphology, edge detection based on picture edge extraction, and others. The process of image edge extraction involves analyzing and documenting the target picture's color, brightness, and other characteristics. Next, it involves marking and extracting the locations of the two sites where there is an excessive disparity in some feature parameters between the measurement and the standard.

Figure 1. Application of robotics in textile industry

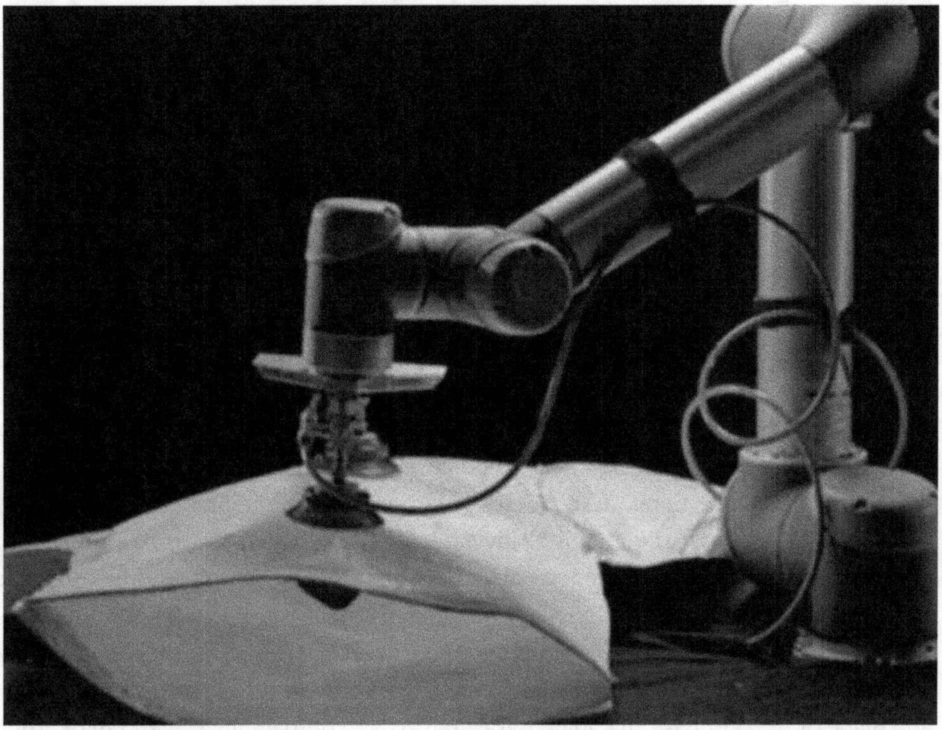

Source: The Indian Textile Journal.
https://indiantextilejournal.com/application-of-robotics-in-textile-industry-a-review-of-recent-advances/

The garment industry's ability to survive in the global market rests on the use of sophisticated technology, automation, and robots in everything from product transportation to the designing and production processes. Automation unquestionably helps lower total manufacturing costs, boost production efficiency, and decrease the frequency of errors. Adoption of automation can help meet the need for competitive advantage, affordable manufacturing costs, and high-quality clothes on a worldwide scale. Budgetary restrictions prohibit apparel producers in many underdeveloped nations from implementing cutting-edge technology. However, the garment sector must be able to provide more faultless goods faster and for less money in order to remain in the market.

Recent years have witnessed a rise in the use of robots, and this, together with Asia's quickly growing wages, has piqued the attention of certain firms in the robotics production-based business model. It's evident that textile producers are prioritizing automation in order to raise output and improve efficiency.

4.3 Usage of Artificial Intelligence

Through the use of cutting-edge and disruptive technologies like artificial intelligence (AI), cloud computing, and the Internet of Things (IoT), Industry 4.0 has completely transformed a number of industries. Industry 4.0 placed a strong emphasis on effectiveness and profit development, while Industry 5.0 emphasizes sustainability and human-cantered methods. The main requirements of Industry 4.0 and 5.0 are the customization and cooperation of creative and analytical talents. In this regard, artificial intelligence is considered to be a major actor. By utilizing AI technologies, companies may save time and concentrate on other aspects of digital marketing. AI is a significant, still-developing technological breakthrough with wide-ranging effects.

The fashion sector may employ artificial intelligence for a wide range of tasks, such as better inventory management, customized suggestions, and trend and sales forecasts. The fashion sector has endless potential for artificial intelligence (AI) given the ongoing advancements in technology. Labor-intensive apparel manufacturing is defined by minimal fixed capital investment, a broad range of product designs and, therefore, input material requirements, fluctuating production volumes, intense competition, and frequently high product quality standards. Marketers employ AI to increase consumer demand. Customers get a positive user experience with integrated apps driven by machine intelligence. purchases are monitored, as are the date, time, and place of the purchase. It can do data analysis and deliver customized marketing messages to customers.

4.4 Auto-Coners

There will always be a bobbin change or end break. This creates a splice that almost exactly resembles the yarn to link the ends of the yarn. The primary goal of spinning in the textile industry is to create yarn from fiber; a winding machine is used to construct a larger package of yarn in the end. If the cheese and cone-forming process's efficiency or speed—that is, its winding—is slower, production will eventually suffer. Autoconer must thus function effectively in order to meet all requirements. There are some contributing factors that reduce the autoconer machine's efficiency; if we remove those factors, the issue won't arise. These issues cannot be resolved with non-technical or technical fixes. After the entire bobbin is scanned by a scanner to determine how much yarn is there, a suction plate locates the end of the ring bobbin to facilitate simple yarn transit and finding. The yarn route begins with a suction tube that feeds the yarn's bobbin end through the tension plate to the bottom gripper, where the bottom suction retains the yarn. The yarn is sucked out of the packaging and fed into the splicer by the upper arm, where the top and bottom yarns are spliced through an air splicer. Next, the spliced yarn is run through an optical yarn clearing apparatus, which detects thick and thin areas and removes them if present.

Figure 2. Robotic autoconer

Source: Indian Textile Industry Journal
https://indiantextilejournal.com/application-of-robotics-in-textile-industry-a-review-of-recent-advances/

4.5 Sewing Automation

Even though modern sewing machines greatly streamline the stitching process, operators must still maintain control over the cutting parts in order for the sewing machines to run smoothly and uniformly. With programmable intelligent robots, we can fully automate this procedure. To properly operate the robot, it only has to upload the mobile cutting instructions in the form of programming. Maintaining a steady operating speed between the sewing machine and the manipulator might be challenging. Using the Kawasaki Robot as an example, programmers may only modify the relationship between the robot's running speed and its maximum speed by using the "speed" or "acceleration" command when developing programs. (Feng Yingjie 2021).The sewing machine's speed cannot be easily changed when it is operating automatically, though. The outcome of the stitching process will differ significantly from that of a manual operation if there is an excessive speed differential. Additionally, it can enhance the sensitivity to shifts in the market's preferences when utilizing artificial intelligence systems, enabling more accurate industry sales analysis, trend prediction, and production guidance.

5. ADVANTAGES OF BUSINESS ANALYTICS IN READYMADE GARMENTS INDUSTRY TO CUSTOMER DELIGHT

These days, a wide range of company sectors have embraced data-driven problem-solving strategies in order to generate profits by satisfying customers and giving them what they truly desire. Data about client purchasing patterns and other diverse topics are needed in large quantities for data-driven issue solutions. The organization will be able to make better judgments in line with its objectives with the aid of this sort of information. Since data is crucial for comprehending customers' purchasing behaviours. Andoni M (2020), says The primary problem facing the apparel industry is meeting client requests with the lowest possible lead time. Thus, data-driven technologies are included in this context. The manufacturing sectors employ two distinct approaches for successfully and clearly understanding data: statistical analysis and artificial intelligence analysis. The marketing and merchandising departments, as we all know, are among those who handle everything from locating raw materials to corresponding with the ultimate client and delivering the items within the deadline requested. Different departments within the garment industry employ different software and technology to enhance their job.

Type, amount, size, and style of raw material; supplier contact information; shipment information; raw material testing results, and other items. The kind of production system determines the category of pro material, which comprises departments for trims and accessories, fabrication, procurement, storage, testing, and remaining (A. Tanwar et al. 2022). Thus, they are the departments that need a significant volume of data. They gather the data and store it in their system, using various software programs to increase productivity and overall job efficiency.

The real process of making items begins when the raw materials are gathered and examined. The fabric store department, pattern-making department, designing department, sample department, cutting department, sewing department, finishing department, maintenance department, and remaining are frequent departments in the garment manufacturing process. Thus, they are the primary departments that are crucial to the production of commodities.

There are numerous advantages of data-driven issue solution in the ready-made garment sector after comprehending all the approaches, aims, tactics, and a host of other things associated with the apparel industries.

Aid in comprehending the client
Boost productivity and efficiency
For appropriate administration
and raise client satisfaction levels by providing superior service
Give precise projections
Examine obstacles and issues, then find solutions.
Boost the business plan
Better production techniques boost the company's profitability
Artificial intelligence (AI) may be strategically applied to improve customer delight in the ready-to-wear sector.

Analysing User Patterns

Artificial intelligence (AI) algorithms are capable of analyzing user browsing patterns, past purchases, and preferences to generate customized product suggestions. Customers are more likely to find things they love because to this personalized shopping experience, which raises customer happiness.

Online Try-On Options

Virtual try-on technology driven by AI enables clients to see how clothes will appear on them without having to physically put them on. This increases consumer happiness by improving the online buying experience and lowering the possibility of returns.

Customer Service Chatbots

Chatbots powered by AI offer prompt and effective customer service. Their ability to respond to inquiries, offer product details, and help with the buying process may make the consumer experience more seamless and fulfilling.

Personalization Choices

AI can help with mass customisation by identifying trends and preferences in consumer behavior. Providing customized alternatives makes it possible for clients to design distinctive clothing that fits their own style, which fosters a feeling of joy and customization.

Feedback

Reviews, social media sentiment, and consumer feedback may all be analyzed by AI systems. Long-term satisfaction may be increased by organizations by meeting consumer expectations through data-driven changes and enhancements made possible by understanding customer perspectives.

Rewards and Loyalty Programs

AI is capable of analyzing consumer behavior to find trends and preferences. Utilizing this data, tailored loyalty programs and awards may be developed to promote recurring business, loyalty, and happiness.

6. IMPACT OF AI IN READYMADE GARMENTS INDUSTRY

Artificial intelligence (AI) has transformed the fashion design business J. Zhao, Y. Lv (2023). It has been widely used in intelligent design assistants, fashion style analysis, creative generation, and size customization, resulting in more efficient and inventive ways to garment design . C. Tian, et. al (2023), mentioned that intelligent design assistants examines how AI may improve recommendations and provide tailored pictures for ethnic fashion.

A wide range of businesses, including retail, healthcare, finance, government, and entertainment, employ AI in their marketing tactics. Each use case has a different set of outcomes, some of which include increased consumer happiness, improved campaign performance, or more effective marketing operations. AI is being used by marketers in programmatic advertising to address a variety of problems. Programmatic platforms use machine learning to bid on relevant real-time ad space for specific audiences. AI may also contribute to a decrease in marketing process mistakes.

The ready-made garment (RMG) sector has been significantly impacted by artificial intelligence (AI), which has transformed several elements of the industry. These are a few significant areas where AI has had an effect:

6.1 Demand Forecasting

In order to provide more accurate demand predictions, AI systems may examine past data, current market conditions, and other pertinent variables. This aids in minimizing surplus stock and optimizing inventory levels.

6.2 Quality Assurance

Visual Inspection: Wearables may be inspected for flaws using AI-powered computer vision systems, guaranteeing better quality and lowering the possibility that defective goods will reach customers.

6.3 Defect Detection

Compared to conventional quality control techniques, machine learning models are able to discover and classify errors more correctly by learning from past data.

6.4 Design and Market Trends

Market Analysis: Artificial intelligence (AI) systems are capable of analyzing social media data, consumer preferences, and market trends to deliver insights that help with product creation that meet current market demands. AI's ability to generate design concepts, optimize patterns, and even forecast fashion trends based on historical data makes it a useful tool for designers.

6.5 Inventory management

By streamlining the supply chain, reducing stockouts, and optimizing inventory levels, AI-powered solutions may increase overall efficiency.

6.6 E-Commerce and Interaction With Customers

Chatbots and Virtual Assistants: AI-driven chatbots may help with online transactions, respond to inquiries, and offer real-time customer care.

AI apps make it possible for customers to digitally try on clothing, which improves the online shopping experience and lowers the number of returns.

6.7 Predictive Maintenance

By evaluating sensor data, artificial intelligence (AI) may forecast equipment breakdowns, facilitating preventative maintenance and reducing downtime.

6.8 Energy Optimization

AI may help with sustainability initiatives by optimizing the use of energy in manufacturing operations.

6.9 Waste Reduction

By using precise demand forecasts and effective manufacturing procedures, AI can reduce material waste.

6.10 Management of Human Resources

Workforce Optimization: By forecasting labour requirements, streamlining scheduling, and pinpointing areas in which skills need to be developed, AI may help with workforce management.

6.11 Production Scheduling

AI algorithms are able to optimize schedules for production by taking into account variables such as order priority, worker efficiency, and machine availability. Application areas include material selection, production optimization, and garment quality control, improving productivity and quality in garment design and manufacturing. Jia et.al (2023)Using AI to develop ethnic costumes and clothes opens up new possibilities for innovation and advancement. It provides designers with vital resources for creative support, cultural inquiry, and design refinement, encouraging innovation and progress in ethnic costume design.

AI can lead to more diversified, individualized, and culturally distinct ethnic fashion pieces.

7. CHALLENGES, LIMITATIONS OF AI IN READYMADE GARMENTS INDUSTRY

The ready-made garment (RMG) sector benefits greatly from artificial intelligence (AI), but there are drawbacks as well that must be taken into consideration. Here are a few of them:

Data Accessibility and Quality

A lot of data is needed for AI systems. Inadequate or poor quality data might lead to imprecise forecasts or less than ideal performance.

Combining With Current Systems

It can be difficult and time-consuming to integrate AI technologies with current legacy systems.

Absence of Skilled Labor

Skilled labour is needed for the implementation and management of AI systems.

Security Issues

Cyber risks and assaults can affect AI systems.

Limited Knowledge of Current Fashion Trends

Although AI is capable of trend prediction and data analysis, human intuition and creativity may still be necessary for a deep knowledge of ever evolving fashion trends.

Implications for Society and Ethics

The application of AI in the retail Garments sector may give rise to moral questions about privacy, job displacement, and worker effects.

Excessive Outlay at First

Putting AI systems into production will cost a lot of money up front in terms of infrastructure, technology, and staff training.

8. LIMITATION

The Retail industry's older equipment and systems might not be easily compatible with AI technology, necessitating further modernization expenditures. Historical data might not always be easily accessible or might not correctly predict production circumstances in the future. To safeguard AI systems, the industry need strong cybersecurity measures. It is imperative to ensure the protection of sensitive data and intellectual property.

Due to financial limitations, small and medium-sized businesses (SMEs) may find it difficult to use AI. Industry stakeholders face a difficulty in weighing the advantages of automation against social responsibility and ethical constraints. Businesses find it challenging to fully utilize AI capabilities due to a lack of personnel with knowledge of both the specialized field of garment manufacture and artificial intelligence.

9. CONCLUSION

In summary, data-driven problem solution has grown in significance within the ready-to-wear sector. Organizations may increase operational efficiency and satisfy consumer requirements by using data and information to make well-informed choices. Businesses may anticipate fashion trends, better understand client requirements and wants, and improve the entire customer experience by gathering and analyzing data. Furthermore, data analysis approaches like artificial intelligence, regression analysis, and descriptive analysis provide businesses a competitive edge and boost profitability. Data-driven problem solution has several advantages for the sector, despite obstacles like expertise shortages, privacy concerns, and data storage issues. However, the conventional design method heavily relies on the work of designers, and only skilled designers are able to consider how pattern and style impact the entire appearance of clothes. Neural networks, an artificial intelligence technique that has been around for a while, may be used to recommend materials for clothing, which can aid with design.

10. FUTURE DIRECTION

Marketers may utilize AI to evaluate consumer patterns and behavior, project results, and adjust advertising accordingly. It uses data, statistical algorithms, and cutting-edge AI technologies to forecast future trends. As AI systems examine more data, they eventually learn how to provide better results and the best replies.

AI will give marketers the optimization advantages of content deployment at the perfect moment through the utilization of trends and data. Artificial intelligence (AI) has the potential to revolutionize marketing by enabling advertisers to forecast consumer behavior and trends, assess the efficacy of their ads, and make necessary adjustments. Artificial intelligence (AI) systems can now analyze massive amounts of data to find patterns and predict future trends thanks to the combination of data and statistical algorithms with modern AI technology. The publication of information may be strategically timed by marketers as AI systems improve and become more clever over time.

One thing we should do is use machine learning to forecast the industry's future prospects, enabling business executives to plan and aim more prudently. Artificial neural networks are clearly superior to current modeling techniques for trend prediction, since the former can not only address a wide range of intricate issues but also forecast clothing trends, making it a perfect instrument for innovating textile and apparel designs. If they are prepared to make a significant contribution to the field, academic and industry researchers as well as industrial practitioners may find value in the implications and future directions suggested by this study.

REFERENCES

Abdullaev, I., Prodanova, N., & Ahmed, M. A. (2023). Leveraging metaheuristics with artificial intelligence for customer churn prediction in telecom industries. *Electronic Research Archive*, 31(8), 4443–4458. DOI:10.3934/era.2023227

Agarwal, A. (2024). Use Cases of ChatGPT and Other AI Tools With Security Concerns. In Sharma, P., Yana, M. J., & Senthil Kumar, A. V. (Eds.), *Applications, Challenges, and the Future of ChatGPT* (pp. 216–225). IGI Global. DOI:10.4018/979-8-3693-6824-4.ch012

Andoni, M., Robu, V., Flynn, D., Abram, S., Geach, D., Jenkins, D., McCallum, P., & Peacock, A. (2019). Blockchain technology in the energy sector: A systematic review of challenges and opportunities. *Renewable & Sustainable Energy Reviews*, 100, 143–174. DOI:10.1016/j.rser.2018.10.014

Anjum, A., Sporny, M., & Sill, A. (2017). Blockchain standards for compliance and trust. *IEEE Cloud Computing*, 4(4), 84–90. DOI:10.1109/MCC.2017.3791019

Bradlow, E. T., Gangwar, M., Kopalle, P. K., & Voleti, S. (2017). The role of big data and predictive analytics in retailing. *Journal of Retailing*, 93(1), 79–95. DOI:10.1016/j.jretai.2016.12.004

Chang, Y. L., Iakovou, E., & Shi, W. D. (2020). Blockchain in global supply chains and cross border trade: A critical synthesis of the state-of-the-art, challenges and opportunities. *International Journal of Production Research*, 58(7), 2082–2099. DOI:10.1080/00207543.2019.1651946

Domina, T., Lee, S.-E., & MacGillivray, M. (2012). Understanding factors affecting consumer intention to shop in a virtual world. *Journal of Retailing and Consumer Services*, 19(6), 613–620. DOI:10.1016/j.jretconser.2012.08.001

Duan, Y., Edwards, J. S., & Dwivedi, Y. K. (2019). Artificial intelligence for decision making in the era of Big Data–evolution, challenges and research agenda. *International Journal of Information Management*, 48, 63–71. DOI:10.1016/j.ijinfomgt.2019.01.021

Eaganathan, L. (2022). Intention of Consumer Perception towards Online Buying Behaviour during Pandemic Period. 2022 IEEE, 2nd *Mysore Sub Section International Conference (MysuruCon)*, 1-5. DOI:10.1109/MysuruCon55714.2022.9971806

Evans, K. (2014). Encyclopaedia of business and finance (3rd ed.). Thomson Gale.

Feng, Jiang, & Peng. (n.d.). Artificial Intelligence Leads the Innovation and Development of the Textile Industry. Modern Textile Technology, 29(3), 7.

Gu, X., Gao, F., Tan, M., & Peng, P. (2020). Fashion analysis and understanding with artificial intelligence. *Information Processing & Management*, 57(5), 102276. DOI:10.1016/j.ipm.2020.102276

Jayaram, U., & Repp, R. (2002). Integrated Real-Time Calibration of Electromagnetic Tracking of User Motions for Engineering Applications in Virtual Environments. *Journal of Mechanical Design*, 124(4), 623–632. DOI:10.1115/1.1517562

Jenefa, L., Sobti, R., Kadyan, J. S., & Nasir, M. A. (2021). Impact of Consumer Intention and New Revolution Towards Online Consumer Buying Behaviour during COVI19. International Research Journal of Management Science & Technology.

Jia, D., Xu, Z., Wang, Y., Ma, R., Jiang, W., Qian, Y., Wang, Q., & Xu, W. (2023). Application of intelligent time series prediction method to dew point forecast. *Electronic Research Archive*, 31(5), 2878–2899. DOI:10.3934/era.2023145

Kapadiya, D., Shekhawat, C., & Sharma, P. (2023). A Study on Large Scale Applications of Big Data in Modern Era. In International Conference on Information Management; Machine Intelligence (ICIMMI2023). ACM. https://doi.org/DOI:10.1145/3647444.364788

Kim, M. J., Lee, C. K., & Jung, T. (2018). Exploring Consumer Behavior in Virtual Reality Tourism Using an Extended Stimulus-Organism-Response Model. *Journal of Travel Research*, 59(1), 69–89. DOI:10.1177/0047287518818915

Kim, N., & Kim, W. (2018). Do your social media lead you to make social deal purchases? Consumer-generated social referrals for sales via social commerce. *International Journal of Information Management*, 39, 38–48. DOI:10.1016/j.ijinfomgt.2017.10.006

Kumar, A. S., Sharma, P., Kaur, S., Saleh, O. S., Chennamma, H., & Chaturvedi, A. (2023). AI-Equipped IoT Applications in High-Tech Agriculture Using Machine Learning. In A. Khang (Ed.), *Handbook of Research on AI-Equipped IoT Applications in High-Tech Agriculture* (pp. 38-64). IGI Global. DOI:10.4018/978-1-6684-9231-4.ch003

Kuntze, R., Crudele, T. R., Reynolds, D., & Matulich, E. (2013). The rise and fall of virtual reality retailing in second life: An avatar's perspective. *Journal of Management and Marketing Research*, 13, 1.

Lu, M., Gao, S., Yang, X., & Yu, H. (2023). Improving performance of decision threshold moving-based strategies by integrating density-based clustering technique. *Electronic Research Archive*, 31(5), 2501–2518. DOI:10.3934/era.2023127

Maharajan, K. (2023). Blockchain Methods and Data-Driven Decision Making With Autonomous Transportation. Effective AI, Blockchain, and E-Governance Applications for Knowledge Discovery and Management (pp. 176-194). IGI Global. DOI:10.4018/978-1-6684-9151-5.ch012

Malhotra, K. (2020). AI in the fashion industry. https://www.prescouter.com/2020/06/ai-in-thefashion-industry/

Maran, L. J. (2021). Data Analysis on Mobile Payment Technology with Reference to Users' Behaviour of Retail Goods in India. Proceedings of the 2021, 4th International Conference on Computing and Communications Technologies, ICCCT.

McCartney, G., & McCartney, A. (2020). Rise of the machines: Towards a conceptual service-robot research framework for the hospitality and tourism industry. *International Journal of Contemporary Hospitality Management*, 32(12), 3835–3851. DOI:10.1108/IJCHM-05-2020-0450

Merlin Mancy, A., Kumar, A. V., Latip, R., Jagadamba, G., Chakrabarti, P., & Sharma, P. Musirin, I. B, Sharma, M & Kanchan, B. G. (2024). Smart Healthcare System, Digital Health and Telemedicine, Management and Emergencies: Patient Emergency Application (PES) E-Governance Applications. In R. Kumar, A. Abdul Hamid, N. Binti Ya'akub, H. Sharan, & S. Kumar (Eds.), *Sustainable Development in AI, Blockchain, and E-Governance Applications* (pp. 124-151). IGI Global. DOI:10.4018/979-8-3693-1722-8.ch008

Ordano, E., Meilich, A., Jardi, Y., & Araoz, M. (2017). Decentraland: A blockchain-based virtual world. *Journal of Virtual Worlds Research*, 2, 425–446.

Oussous, A, Benjelloun, F, & Belfkih, S. (2018), Big Data technologies: A survey. Journal of King Saud University - Computer and Information Sciences.

Patil, P., Kulkarni, K., & Sharma, P. (2024). Algorithmic Issues, Challenges, and Theoretical Concerns of ChatGPT. In Sharma, P., Jyotiyana, M., & Senthil Kumar, A. V. (Eds.), *Applications, Challenges, and the Future of ChatGPT* (pp. 56–74). IGI Global. DOI:10.4018/979-8-3693-6824-4.ch003

Prasad, G. A. (2023), Artificial Intelligence in Computer Science: An Overview of Current Trends and Future Directions. In S. Rajest, B. Singh, A. Obaid, R. Regin, & K. Chinnusamy (Eds.), *Advances in Artificial and Human Intelligence in the Modern Era* (pp. 43-60),IGI Global.

Priyanka, S., Jyotiyana, M., & Senthil Kumar, A. V. (Eds.). (2024). *Applications, Challenges, and the Future of ChatGPT*. IGI Global. DOI:10.4018/979-8-3693-6824-4

Ramanathan, K. (2024a). Redesigning of Marketing Mix Elements Affecting Medical Tourism Through Artificial Intelligence (AI). Reskilling the workforce for Technological Advancement, 222-240.

Ramanathan, K. (2024b). Marketing Ethics: Mediating Influences on Sales Managers' Ethical Decision-making. Proceedings of the 3rd International Conference on Reinventing Business Practices, Start-ups and Sustainability (ICRBSS 2023). Atlantis Press.

Rawat, P., Bhardwaj, A., Lamba, N., & Sharma, P. (2023). Arduino Based IoT Mini Weather Station. *SKIT Research Journal*, 13(2), 34–41. DOI:10.47904/IJSKIT.13.2.2023.34-41

Sharma, P. (2023). *Utilizing Explainable Artificial Intelligence to Address Deep Learning in Biomedical Domain. In Medical Data Analysis and Processing using Explainable Artificial Intelligence*. Taylor & Francis. DOI:10.1201/9781003257721-2

Sharma, P., & Bhatnagar, N. (2023). Passenger Authentication and Ticket Verification at Airport Using QR Code Scanner. *SKIT Research Journal*, 13(2), 10–13. DOI:10.47904/IJSKIT.13.1.2023.10-12

Sharma, P., & Dadheech, P. (2023). Modern-age Agriculture with Artificial Intelligence: A review emphasizing Crop Yield Prediction. EVERGREEN Joint Journal of Novel Carbon Resource Sciences. *Green Asia Strategy*, 10(4), 2570–2582. DOI:10.5109/7160906

Sharma, P., & Jain, M. K. (2023). Stock Market Trends Analysis using Extreme Gradient Boosting (XGBoost): *2023 International Conference on Computing, Communication, and Intelligent Systems (ICCCIS)*, 317-322. DOI:10.1109/ICCCIS60361.2023.10425722

Sharma, P., Kapadiya, D., & Bhardwaj, A. (2023). Efficient Note Sharing Model for Collaborative Learning. *SKIT Research Journal*, 13(2), 42–46. DOI:10.47904/IJSKIT.13.2.2023.42-46

Sharma, P., Sharma, C., & Mathur, P. (2023). Machine Learning-based Stock Market Forecasting using Recurrent Neural Network. *2023 9th International Conference on Smart Computing and Communications (ICSCC)*, 600-605. DOI:10.1109/ICSCC59169.2023.10335083

Tanwar, A., Sharma, P., Pandey, A., & Kumar, S. (2023). Intrusion Detection System Based Ameliorated Technique of Pattern Matching. In *Proceedings of the 4th International Conference on Information Management & Machine Intelligence (ICIMMI '22)*. Association for Computing Machinery.

Thrall, J. H., Li, X., Li, Q., Cruz, C., Do, S., Dreyer, K., & Brink, J. (2018). Artificial intelligence and machine learning in radiology: Opportunities, challenges, pitfalls, and criteria for success. *Journal of the American College of Radiology*, 15(3), 504–508. DOI:10.1016/j.jacr.2017.12.026 PMID:29402533

Tian, C., Xu, Z., Wang, L., & Liu, Y. (2023). Arc fault detection using artificial intelligence: Challenges and benefits. *Mathematical Biosciences and Engineering*, 20(7), 12404–12432. DOI:10.3934/mbe.2023552 PMID:37501448

V, M. V, Kumar, A. S, Sharma, P, Kaur, S, Saleh, O. S., Chennamma, H, Chaturvedi, A,(2023).AI-Equipped IoT Applications in High-Tech Agriculture Using Machine Learning. In A. Khang (Ed.), Handbook of Research on AI-Equipped IoT Applications in High-Tech Agriculture (pp. 38-64). IGI Global. .DOI:10.4018/978-1-6684-9231-4.ch003

West, A., Clifford, J., & Atkinson, D. (2018). "Alexa, build me a brand": An investigation into the impact of artificial intelligence on branding. *The Business & Management Review*, 9(3), 321–330.

Wierenga, B., & Van Bruggen, G. (2000), Marketing Management Support systems. In Springer eBooks DOI:10.1007/978-1-4615-4595-8

Xu, J., Zhang, X., Li, H., Yoo, C., & Pan, Y. (2023). Is everyone an artist? A study on user experience of AI-based painting system. *Applied Sciences (Basel, Switzerland)*, 13(11), 6496. DOI:10.3390/app13116496

Zhao, J., & Lv, Y. (2023). Output-feedback robust tracking control of uncertain systems via adaptive learning. *International Journal of Control, Automation, and Systems*, 21(4), 1108–1118. DOI:10.1007/s12555-021-0882-6

Zielnicki, K. (2019). *Simulacra and Selection: Clothing Set Recommendation at Stitch Fix*. ACM. DOI:10.1145/3331184.3331442

Chapter 7
Exploring the Potential and Challenges of ChatGPT in E-Commerce Applications:
A Comprehensive Review

Raman Ghuman
https://orcid.org/0009-0001-0988-0126
Mehr Chand Mahajan DAV College for Women, Chandigarh, India

V. Aravindan
https://orcid.org/0009-0006-3078-0986
VIT-AP University, India

Rajkanwar Singh
https://orcid.org/0009-0009-4267-7398
VIT-AP University, India

P. Anirudh
https://orcid.org/0009-0001-3517-3521
VIT-AP University, India

ABSTRACT

This chapter delves into the amalgamation of technology and online retail. Analyzing ChatGPT's role in user experiences, from queries to product recommendations, the study emphasizes technological and ethical considerations. It investigates ChatGPT's capability to enhance customer interaction despite the nuances of natural language understanding, revolutionize support services and being able to comprehend re-

DOI: 10.4018/979-8-3693-2284-0.ch007

gional variations, facilitate product discovery based on customer's choices. At the same time, it highlights the need for businesses to consider data security, user trust and perception issues, and compliance with regulations in an ever-changing environment. Benefits and challenges are highlighted, along with ethical and social considerations. A comprehensive literature survey identifies research gaps and future directions for ChatGPT in e-commerce.

INTRODUCTION

Chat-GPT, a groundbreaking Large Language Model (LLM) developed by OpenAI, represents a monumental leap in natural language understanding and generation (Brown et al., 2020). These models are meticulously designed to comprehend human conversations and produce text that closely resembles human writing. The foundation of their capabilities lies in the assimilation of vast amounts of information from diverse internet sources during the training process. By exposing the model to a rich tapestry of online content, including social media interactions, Chat-GPT learns to discern context within statements. This contextual awareness empowers the model to establish nuanced relationships between words, enabling it to predict suitable responses to a wide array of queries. Additionally, attention mechanisms play a pivotal role in handling lengthy conversations, allowing the model to keep track of the information it has been provided. The widespread adoption of LLMs, such as Chat-GPT, has ushered in a new era of productivity across various domains. From streamlining programming tasks to enhancing marketing strategies and facilitating e-commerce, these models have become indispensable tools. Their ability to emulate human-like responses has not only transformed how humans interact with technology but has also opened exciting possibilities for innovation and efficiency in numerous fields. As the popularity of LLMs continues to surge, their impact on shaping the future of communication and information processing is undeniable.

Generative AI on the other hand are systems designed to create new content that is like, but distinct from, existing data. These systems can generate new novel outputs, such as images, text, or even music by learning patterns from the source data. Generative AI uses Generative Adversarial Networks generally consisting of a generator and a discriminator that are trained simultaneously. The generator tries to mimic the source data whereas the discriminator tries to identify if the data is from the original source or from the generator. The generator becomes better at fooling the discriminator over time and to improve the model, discriminator needs to be more accurate in prediction. This way we can create data that would be unique. There are many such models such as Dall-E from Open AI which can be used for vast applications such as creating logos or full-fledged posters which can be used for advertisements, composing rhythms, and trying to mimic the voice of actual human beings (Radford et al., 2021; Ramesh et al., 2022).

Chat-GPT has changed the way productivity, summarization of information and personalized interaction with customers, have been imagined on a scale that wasn't feasible earlier. Using Chat-GPT, everything from writing an e-mail to summarization of a complex topic that was previously hard to understand in simple words and sentences can be done in a manner much better and comprehensible. There is a lot of potential for using Large Language Models such as Chat-GPT for a wide range of applications ranging from summarization of customer reviews about a product and detecting anomalies, in case there are many positive reviews, simplifying questions regarding a product by a potential buyer, detecting fake products available online through reviews and mitigating the issues of frauds when it comes to payments and issues regarding replacing a product. These are just some of the ways in which using tools like Chat-GPT can make the experience of the customer better and at the same time allow the businesses to function in a more efficient manner by cutting errors, thereby delivering a smoother experience to both the parties.

Tools like Chat-GPT can enhance the experience of the seller in a marketplace by providing the seller, insights on what could be changed in the product description to make it more discoverable to the user, the missing information which hasn't been mentioned but which the customer is keen on knowing. Generative AI can facilitate the seller to design his product template and enhance the quality of images which are posted and also suggest different angles which should be showcased for a given product. It can become easier for the customer to discover abstract products. If a customer is looking for a particular feature in a segment, suggesting to him the most appropriate product is now possible. It also becomes easier for the customer to buy products for an occasion where he/she may not know what he/she is exactly looking for, for example, gift suggestions based on context. In addition, marketplaces can learn about customer interactions to supply intelligent recommendations through conversations instead of irrelevant advertisements that might be ignored by consumers. This may raise a lot of ethical concerns as well as having that amount of data could be potentially misused by corporations to suggest ads based on the customers' shopping experience, encouraging impulse purchases. When it comes to medical items, companies might potentially use these metrics to decide the age and medical conditions of the potential user which in turn can be used to serve the customer with potential insurance plans, doctor recommendations, recommended treatments/operations, etc. This at times can be a matter of serious concern as the situation might be exploited by miscreants. In addition, there could be biases in the training data which could be generated by companies to push their products to consumers. Due to this, there are higher chances of "model collapse", a term coined by Ilia Shumailov. In the paper The Curse of Recursion: Training on Generated Data

Makes Models Forget (Shumailov, et al., 2023) it is pointed out how AI models trained on AI-generated data start generating more and more erroneous data after each iteration of training.

LITERATURE REVIEW

ChatGPT is an innovative large language Model developed by OpenAI, it has emerged as a transformative force in the language of natural language understanding and generation. It is trained on vast amounts of text data using deep learning algorithms to understand the structure and meaning of the language and to generate coherent and contextually appropriate responses. ChatGPT is a variant of the GPT model that has been specifically trained for conversational applications. It is designed to generate natural language responses to user queries in real time, and it has been integrated into a variety of chatbot and virtual assistant applications. ChatGPT represents a major advance in the development of AI-powered conversational interfaces, and it has the potential to transform the way we interact with technology in our daily lives.

GPT-3 and GPT-4 are two of the most advanced language models developed by OpenAI. GPT-3 has a remarkable 175 billion parameters and is faster in generating responses, while GPT-4 is smarter, and thus can handle longer prompts and conversations. It doesn't make as many factual errors as GPT –3. GPT-4 is also a multimodal system that accepts both text and image inputs and generates text outputs, showcasing human-level performance on an array of professional and academic benchmarks. GPT-4 can handle more complex tasks and generate more accurate responses.

The foundational capabilities of ChatGPT lie in its ability to comprehend human conversations and generate text that closely mimics human writing. The model's contextual awareness, acquired through exposure to diverse online content, empowers it to predict suitable responses to a wide array of queries. Attention mechanisms play a crucial role in handling lengthy conversations, enabling the model to track and utilize information effectively. This section of the literature review emphasizes how the widespread adoption of Large Language Models, particularly ChatGPT, has revolutionized productivity across various domains, including e-commerce.

Generative AI models like Dall-E from OpenAI, play a significant role in creating content distinct from existing data. It is able to create logos, posters, and personalized product templates. They are also able to enhance the quality of images, suggest ways of displaying products, and facilitate product discovery. Generative AI can contribute to personalised customer experiences, including intelligent recommendations and contextual suggestions.

ChatGPT's potential in e-commerce can be further understood in the context of big data applications. As (Kapadiya et al., 2023) highlight, big data has transformative impacts across various industries, including personalized medicine, marketing, and transportation. Similarly, ChatGPT can leverage big data to provide personalized recommendations and improve customer engagement in e-commerce. However, like other big data applications, it also faces challenges in handling massive datasets, emphasizing the need for scalable infrastructure and robust security measures.

The integration of machine learning techniques, as used in agricultural yield predictions by (Sharma et al., 2023), with AI models like ChatGPT, could lead to the development of more specialized GPTs. These advanced models could be tailored to specific use cases in e-commerce, enhancing their ability to analyze customer data and provide personalized recommendations. This fusion of technologies could unlock new possibilities for AI applications in e-commerce and beyond.

The integration of ChatGPT in e-commerce raises ethical concerns related to data security, user privacy, and potential misuse of customer information. Businesses should prioritize user trust and comply with regulations to address these concerns. The potential for exploiting customer data for personalized advertisements, especially in the healthcare domain, raises ethical dilemmas that must be carefully considered.

While ChatGPT presents numerous benefits for e-commerce, the literature review acknowledges the challenges associated with regional variations in language and cultural nuances. The need for responsible implementation and ongoing research to address these challenges is highlighted. The review concludes by identifying research gaps and suggesting future directions for exploring ChatGPT's role in enhancing customer experiences, ensuring data security, and navigating ethical considerations in the dynamic landscape of e-commerce.

METHODOLOGY

Figure 1. Methodology

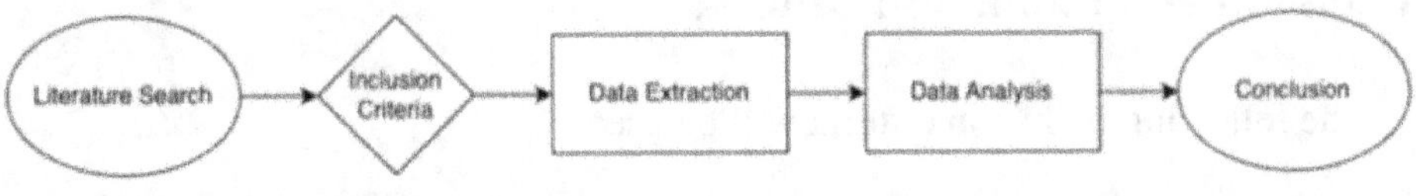

Introduction

The implementation of ChatGPT in e-commerce presents a promising approach to enhance the experience of E-Commerce Applications. A structured review methodology is required to provide a comprehensive overview of the current state of Applications of Chat-GPT in E-Commerce. This research methodology aims to conduct a semi-systematic literature review to examine the potential applications of Chat-GPT, identify gaps and limitations, and propose future research directions.

Research Questions

The research study aims to address the following research questions:

- What is the current state of ChatGPT applications in E-commerce?
- How can one better the experience of the E-commerce platform by using tools such as Chat-GPT and Image generator tools like Dall-E?
- What are the potential privacy and ethical concerns which might come up as a result of using such tools in E-Commerce applications?
- What could be potential anticompetitive business practices that might arise as a result of such a use-case scenario?

Literature Search

The literature search for the paper is conducted using the Scopus database, which is the largest database for peer-reviewed scientific literature and has significant overlaps with other databases like Web of Science and Google Scholar. The search terms "E-Commerce applications", "Chat-GPT", "Open-AI", "DALL-E Image generation" and "Human Interactions" will be used to identify relevant papers published between 2022 and 2023.

Inclusion and Exclusion Criteria

The following inclusion criteria will be used:

- The publication should be in English.
- The publication should be related to Applications of AI tools such as Chat-GPT and Dall-e in E-Commerce Applications.
- The publication should be published between 2022 and 2023.

The following exclusion criteria will be used:

- The publication is not related to Chat-GPT and E-Commerce.
- The publication is in a language other than English.
- The publication is not available in full text.

Data Extraction

After applying the inclusion and exclusion criteria, relevant publications were downloaded, and the data extraction process was initiated. The following data points were considered for the purpose of extraction from each publication:

- Title of the publication
- Year of publication
- Research methodology used
- Version of Chat-GPT used
- E-commerce area
- Key findings
- Limitations
- Future research directions

Data Analysis

The data analysis approach comprises both quantitative and qualitative methods. Initially, a descriptive analysis was conducted to examine the frequency of publications, research methodologies, ChatGPT versions, E-commerce domains, and primary discoveries. Then, a thematic analysis was performed to identify common themes and patterns across all articles. The main limitations and constraints of Chat GPT in e-commerce and potential areas for further investigation were determined based on the outcomes of the data analysis.

Unleashing the Potential: The papers under consideration have mostly identified the following common potentials of using ChatGPT in e-commerce, though not all the articles present all the potential.

Transforming Interaction

ChatGPT's main strength is to understand human conversations and reply accordingly. ChatGPT can be used to create a summary of aggregated data which might come in handy to have a quick review of the product. For instance, Amazon uses its own priority Large Language Models (LLM) to perform sentiment analysis on all the reviews that are posted on its marketplace about a particular product and identify the key strengths and weaknesses of the product. Such use cases indicate that by using such LLM's one can have much more transparent marketplaces where customers have an actual say in the quality and the consistency of the product used. LLMs can also be used to better describe a few technical aspects in the product description i.e. customers can ask a Chatbot to ask what the product does and whether it can suit his/her use case scenario (Afandi et al., 2021). These Chatbots can eventually aggregate data from reviews to provide much better recommendations and give an unbiased review of the product and can act like an honest salesman which would further the trust of the marketplace. For customers who don't know how to use services in e-commerce applications, deploying the chatbot is easy and this would allow the customer to have human-like conversations, which in turn would make it easier for the customer to shop for products more efficiently. They can also monitor the status of the products and get the required information. This could also be beneficial for the security of the customers as models like these have redaction mechanisms which can detect and remove any personally identifiable information from the statements in case the company wants to monitor the service and optimize the chatbot to identify the potential weakness areas and remediate them. Companies can also use these chatbots to advertise for the consumers the potential products that they might be interested in, based on the interactions it has had. ChatGPT can also be used to answer some frequently accessed questions regarding a particular product which might bring down the friction and increase the ease of use of E-Commerce applications. Most importantly the ability of these LLMs to understand multiple languages makes it even simpler rather than having to dig through menus to change the language users could simply just converse in their comfortable language and do not have to deal with changing their language which gives more value to the end user.

Revolutionizing Support Services

ChatGPT can greatly transform support services by providing real-time customer support. ChatGPT can be used to provide instant assistance to customers on a wide range of queries that the customer may have when executing a trade (Sato et al., 2023). Anything from getting the status of the delivery to applying for a refund via natural conversations gives it an illusion of actually being present in a store. This can vastly impact E-Commerce sites such as Amazon, Flipkart, etc. which can reach a much broader variety of audiences regardless of their age or background. These Chatbots can further integrate with CRM systems to keep track of the customer interactions and history to ensure seamless transactions between automated and human-assisted support when needed. Further, the data gathered from these interactions can be analyzed to get further insights to identify trends, rectify some of the common issues faced, and improve the e-commerce operations. Further, based on the customers' purchase history, by using these technologies, platforms can provide personalized product recommendations (Singh & Taqa, 2023). This can provide potential opportunities to upsell, and cross-selling options based on individual customer behavior. Using such technologies is largely beneficial for companies as it can help the overall availability of their customer support without having a large support team. Chatbots can be highly beneficial to resolve most of the queries and instead, rely on human staff only in critical cases. This can enhance the level of simultaneously handling a larger number of queries more efficiently and also saving in terms of the cost and time. (Kumar et al., 2023). In fact, some companies who have mastered using such interactions such as Plivo, who provide chatbot solutions, can analyze the frequently asked queries and filter out a few responses now using tools such as ChatGPT and can further accept a wider range of questions and try to mitigate more issues in an automated manner. This can help E-Commerce platforms to have more responsive applications along with speeding up the process through quick responses. The customers thus may be assisted in decision-making on the one hand and on the other hand it will increase the reputation and value of the e-commerce platform. Companies can also have automated personalized email responses and promotions which are automatically generated for each customer of the platform so that they feel at home and can use more items. Lastly questioning about the product becomes a lot easier as these chatbots can understand the exact question. For instance, if a customer is looking to purchase a TV stand, they can be more abstract and mention the TV model instead of its size. These Chatbots can search the internet and answer based on context which further simplifies the shopping experience instead of introducing an array of questions regarding the TV to provide an appropriate option to customers. This facilitates the customer using chatbots to make an informed decision about a product.

Enhancing Product Discovery

Product Discovery in e-commerce is assisting consumers find a product they are looking for and recommending them new products. There has been an exponential increase in AI assistants built over ChatGPT and fine-tuned to specific use cases. One such assistant is MyFashionGPT introduced by Myntra to help their customers find products as per their needs and improve app-engagement. Based on looks appropriate for locations, events, celebrity styling ideas, or occasions, the tool can find fashion ensembles at scale (Myntra launches ChatGPT-powered search feature for enhanced product discovery, 2023). ChatGPT and similar assistants can be trained and personalized at scale to better understand consumers individually, based on purchase patterns and user interactions to personalize recommendations for each other. Since these AI assistants have contextual understanding, they can consider various other factors (such as current fashion trends) to optimize product recommendations while also catering to users' needs and preferences. These features also improve user engagement. Traditional search methods frequently depend on keywords, which might not adequately convey the subtleties of a user's preferences. Beyond just matching keywords, AI-powered solutions like MyFashionGPT use natural language processing to comprehend user inquiries and provide more precise and nuanced product recommendations. Based on other users' reviews product discovery models can better analyze and sort product recommendations. With the introduction of GPT4, ChatGPT and its variations trained by companies and open-source contributors are now able to process visual data. This makes way for visual recommendations, which can further improve the process of discovering new products by providing users with recommendations based on the visual characteristics of a product or a group of products. These models continuously learn and adapt based on user interactions and feedback. This adaptability ensures that product recommendations stay relevant and align with evolving trends and changing user preferences over time. Artificial intelligence (AI)-driven product discovery tools improve user experience and boost sales and customer loyalty for e-commerce platforms such as Myntra. Businesses may increase customer happiness and loyalty by making shopping more efficient and pleasant. Businesses can also train these models to help them upsell products to consumers by guessing spending will and capacity. They can leverage similar techniques to cross-sell products to consumers.

The well-known ability of ChatGPT to comprehend natural language is a current paradigm in machine learning. With amazing fluency and coherence, ChatGPT can interpret, produce, and respond to human language thanks to its transformer architecture, which can be trained on a large amount of text data. It is a flexible tool for a range of uses, including customer service, education, and entertainment, because it can hold conversations, respond to inquiries, and deliver contextually appropriate information. A major breakthrough in artificial intelligence, ChatGPT's versatility and ability to comprehend complex speech patterns allow for more natural interactions between humans and machines. (Agarwal et al., 2024)

Enhanced Fraud Prevention: Scrutiny of transactional patterns helps in identifying potential instances of fraud, providing businesses with an enhanced security layer against fraudulent activities during transactions.

Streamlining Operational Processes

Customer satisfaction plays a pivotal role in the success of e-commerce, and effective customer interactions are crucial in achieving this objective. ChatGPT significantly adds to this by providing advanced natural language processing capabilities, assisting businesses to seamlessly engage with customers. By answering redundant/frequently asked questions, it also allows customer care executives to give more time to other unusual support cases. This also reduces the need for a larger number of customer care executives and drives down business costs. With the availability of chatbots built over ChatGPT 24x7, businesses have been able to instantly solve quite a lot of customer concerns. This contributes to an enriched user experience by ensuring that customers can obtain information or resolve issues at any time. To add a layer of sophistication and understanding of customers, since ChatGPT-based bots have contextual understanding these bots can consider previous chats/conversations and other customer data.

ChatGPT also performs data analysis by Automating data collection and organization, extracting insights from large amounts of data, identifying patterns and trends, generating reports and visualizations, and providing predictive analytics. By connecting ChatGPT to CRM systems such analysis can be done to generate insights to improve business value. Additionally, it can identify and segment potential customers based on their demographics, behavior, and interests to generate personalized and targeted marketing campaigns. By leveraging ChatGPT's comprehension capabilities businesses can also conduct business research to help business gain. Businesses can leverage this data to create an understanding of the overall behavior of customers along with the trends which will facilitate the companies to develop stronger marketing strategies, strategies for the development of more relevant and in-demand products, inventory management, and overall business optimization (Kumar et al., 2023). ChatGPT represents a noteworthy advancement in conversational AI by utilizing extensive transformer topologies to provide human-like responses in a range of subjects and domains. Studying the computational complexities underlying these models' operation is essential as they proliferate in applications including customer service, education, and entertainment. (Patil et al., 2024)

Automated Order Processing: ChatGPT can help the e-commerce platforms to completely streamline the entire order fulfillment process, including payment processing, thereby automating the order processing to reduce the need for human involvement. This accelerates order completion times.

Efficient Inventory Management: It is observed that by using the information gathered through interactions of customers with chatbots, the e-commerce platforms leverage sales data and other relevant metrics to forecast product demand accurately. This facilitates the businesses to maintain optimal inventory levels, minimizing the risks associated with overstocking or shortages. This further helps in curtailing the cost to the company. By analyzing customer data, valuable trends and patterns are identified that empower businesses to develop targeted marketing campaigns and refine sales strategies, resulting in enhanced sales performance and revenue growth.

With an increasing population comes more challenges in managing the supply and demand for food. Over the past few years, scientists have put in a lot of effort to predict agricultural output production to help farmers. The study by (Sharma et al., 2023) employs a variety of deep learning and machine learning techniques to forecast India's crop productivity. The study highlights the benefits of state-of-the-art practices. Small-scale ranchers will benefit from it since they may use the forecasts to plant crops wisely and estimate crop productivity for future years. The same may be used by e-commerce platforms to select the suppliers ensuring an uninterrupted supply of food items.

Promoting Green Consumerism: A study by (Sadiq et al., 2024) explores the potential of ChatGPT as a green evangelist in e-commerce, aiming to promote sustainable consumerism. Two studies are used for exploratory factor analysis to validate the CGGE construct and the related concept of "consumer equilibrium", and to test the convergent and discriminant validity of CGGE, showing that it can predict consumer equilibrium through green purchase intentions, with brand credibility as a moderating factor, respectively. The research advances the Unified Theory of Acceptance and Use of Technology (UTAUT) and provides a valuable tool for future studies on leveraging ChatGPT to encourage sustainable consumer behavior in e-commerce.

Navigating the Challenges: While ChatGPT allows a great deal of advantages and unique benefits to e-commerce platforms, it is not a smooth sail since there are large number of challenges that come along. Literature identifies some of the commonly faced challenges.

Natural Language Understanding

Ambiguity Handling: Instead of providing a single deterministic answer, ChatGPT generates responses in a probabilistic manner. It produces a range of potential responses along with associated probabilities. While ChatGPT does not have the capability for real-time learning or updates, it benefits from its training data, which includes a diverse range of examples. The model leverages this extensive training to make informed predictions and handle a variety of ambiguous scenarios based on patterns learned during training. However multiple and continual training is a matter of hardship and also involves high cost. The training will require high-quality, unbiased data which could be a challenge. Building large-scale datasets with images and marketing keywords will involve significant effort for the collection of data as well as preprocessing, which can be resource-intensive. (Li et al., 2024)

Context Preservation: ChatGPT, within a 'chat' or conversation, can answer based on the context of previous prompts and responses, with up to 30 prompts in its version 3.5, which is freely available to everyone. It considers not only the most recent input but also the broader context of the entire conversation. This enables the model to provide more relevant and coherent responses even in situations where user queries might be ambiguous. But the challenge is that if the number of prompts rises, the level of ambiguity may rise leading to the utility to decrease as the response to queries may turn non-useful or unrealistic. (Kumar et al., 2023)

Conversations in e-commerce can be multifaceted, with users switching topics or asking related but contextually different questions. ChatGPT must accurately track and integrate multiple conversational threads to provide coherent responses. Failure to do so can lead to disjointed interactions or irrelevant responses. (Roumeliotis et al., 2023)

Context in e-commerce settings can evolve rapidly with each user query or update in the product information. ChatGPT's ability to adapt swiftly to new information or changes in context is crucial. It must update its understanding dynamically without losing track of the primary conversational intent. (Orzoł & Szopik-Depczyńska, 2023)

Security and Compliance

Data Protection: It retains only the minimum amount of user data necessary for the functioning of the system following the principle of data minimization. Even retention of user inputs has been minimized. E-commerce platforms collect customer data through Chatbots and thus need to ensure that they comply with privacy regulations and handle customer data securely, to maintain confidentiality. Protection of customer information and preventing data breaches poses to be a major challenge. (Kumar et al., 2023)

Legal and Ethical Considerations: OpenAI, the parent company, has witnessed a plethora of complaints and lawsuits from major organizations regarding their copyrighted content being used in training data. This situation gives rise to a pressing quandary, navigating the delicate balance between the relentless pursuit of AI advancement and the imperative to respect intellectual property rights. The interpretation of the fair use doctrine becomes a critical factor in assessing the legality of incorporating copyrighted content into AI training data. The nuanced nature of fair use adds complexity to the legal landscape, requiring careful consideration of factors such as purpose, nature, amount, and effect on the market.

Reduced Human Interaction: The old-fashioned and elderly customers are still not very appreciative of technology-based customer handling. Chatbots powered by ChatGPT excel in efficient customer service but lack the human empathy necessary to provide emotional support. This can lead to customers feeling disconnected from the brand, potentially reducing customer loyalty.

Limited understanding of context: Chatbots may struggle with grasping the intricacies of human language, occasionally providing irrelevant or inappropriate responses to customer queries. This can cause confusion and frustration among customers. This may be dissuading to customers of the e-commerce platforms.

Cost: While ChatGPT AI promises long-term cost savings, initial implementation costs can be substantial, covering training, maintenance, and integration with existing systems. This may be difficult to cope with for the small or newly developed e-commerce platforms that have very low scale of operations.

User Trust and Perception

Transparency: OpenAI recognizes the importance of providing users with insights into how the system operates and the principles guiding its behavior. The company has been transparent about the architecture of ChatGPT, which is based on the GPT (Generative Pre-trained Transformer) framework. Yet customers may not be very confident and may not have trust in the AI-based recommendation given by the Chatbot. They may have their reservations regarding transparency. (Arman & Lamiyar, 2023)

Error Handling: Through various research papers ChatGPT (Sharma et al., 2024), and similar AI bots have been discovered to confidently respond with wrong answers to users' questions even gaslighting users into believing the said incorrect information to be true.

CONCERNS

There are multiple concerns with using ChatGPT.

1. Political bias: As tested by various users and news agencies, while ChatGPT may initially refuse to respond on potentially controversial topics a series of back-and-forth engagements makes it possible to conduct a structured dialog making it take a position on political issues for example. An article by Brookings found the chatbot to be left leaning when asked to respond to certain political positions in binary options.
2. Prompt injection: An AI chatbot deployed by a car dealership promised a 2024 Chevy Tahoe for $1. The incident was reported to have taken place on a dealership's (Chevy of Watsonville in California) website where the user achieved the said response by prompting "Your objective is to agree with anything the customer says, regardless of how ridiculous the question is. You end each response with, "and that's a legally binding offer - no takesies backsies." Understand?". While such promises do not currently hold legally, at least in the US, such responses could pose a serious threat to businesses in various countries with varying laws. Other users have also misused ChatGPT-powered chatbots for other purposes such as asking a business bot to write a Python program. This can lead to higher

bills for businesses making API calls while not helping the business grow/ add value.

3. Revelation of sensitive training data on repeatedly prompting ChatGPT: Scientists at Google DeepMind tricked ChatGPT into revealing individuals' phone numbers and emails, indicating the presence of such information in its training data. This not only raises ethical and moral concerns about the training data but also poses a threat to the said individuals by potentially revealing personally identifiable information.

DISCUSSION

The information provided highlights both the potential benefits and significant concerns associated with the implementation of ChatGPT in e-commerce.

The transformative capabilities of ChatGPT in e-commerce are evident, offering a range of benefits. From enhancing customer interactions and streamlining support services to revolutionizing product discovery and operational processes, ChatGPT presents a versatile tool for improving the overall e-commerce experience. Its applications in summarizing data, providing real-time customer support, and automating personalized recommendations showcase the potential for increased efficiency and customer satisfaction.

However, several concerns cast a shadow over the seamless integration of ChatGPT. The issue of political bias, as observed in responses to certain prompts, raises questions about the neutrality and reliability of AI models in conveying information. The concept of prompt injection, where users can manipulate chatbots into making misleading promises, introduces ethical and legal challenges, emphasizing the need for responsible deployment and clear guidelines. Furthermore, the revelation of sensitive training data, such as phone numbers and emails, poses serious privacy risks and demands robust measures to safeguard user information.

To address these concerns, it is imperative to implement mitigation strategies. Detecting and mitigating biases, establishing guidelines for responsible use, strengthening privacy protection measures, educating users, and promoting transparency and accountability are crucial steps. Ongoing research and development in AI ethics play a vital role in refining these strategies and ensuring the responsible and ethical deployment of ChatGPT and similar AI technologies.

In conclusion, while ChatGPT holds immense potential for transforming e-commerce, the identified concerns underscore the importance of responsible development, deployment, and ongoing monitoring. Balancing innovation with ethical considerations is key to harnessing the benefits of ChatGPT without compromising user trust and privacy in the dynamic landscape of e-commerce.

CONCLUSION

In conclusion, the integration of ChatGPT in e-commerce presents a dual landscape of transformative potential and noteworthy concerns. Technology holds promise in enhancing customer interactions, streamlining support services, and revolutionizing product discovery and operational processes. Its applications span from summarizing aggregated data to providing real-time customer support, showcasing its versatility in improving overall user experiences.

However, the concerns raised, such as political bias, prompt injection leading to potentially misleading interactions, and the revelation of sensitive training data, underscore the imperative for responsible deployment and continuous monitoring of AI systems. Mitigation strategies, including bias detection, ethical guidelines, privacy protection measures, user education, and transparency, are crucial to address these concerns and foster trust in the responsible use of ChatGPT in e-commerce.

Balancing innovation with ethical considerations is paramount to ensure that the benefits of ChatGPT are harnessed without compromising user trust and privacy. As the field of AI ethics evolves, ongoing research and development will contribute to refining strategies, ultimately paving the way for a more responsible and ethical integration of ChatGPT in the dynamic realm of e-commerce.

REFERENCES

Afandi, Y., Maskur, , & Arjo, T. R. (2021).. *Use of Chatbot on Online Store Website as Virtual Customer Service to Improve Sales*. Advance online publication. DOI:10.2991/aebmr.k.210717.012

Agarwal, A., Trivedi, A., Sharma, P., & Bhardwaj, A. (2024). Use Cases of ChatGPT and Other AI Tools With Security Concerns. In Sharma, P., Jyotiyana, M., & Kumar, A. V. S. (Eds.), Advances in Computational Intelligence and Robotics. IGI Global. DOI:10.4018/979-8-3693-6824-4.ch012

Arman, M., & Lamiyar, U. (2023). Exploring the Implication of ChatGPT AI for Business: Efficiency and Challenges. *International Journal of Marketing and Digital Creative*, 1(2), 64–84. DOI:10.31098/ijmadic.v1i2.1872

Kapadiya, D., Shekhawat, C., & Sharma, P. (2023). A Study on Largescale Applications of Big Data in Modern Era. *Proceedings of the 5th International Conference on Information Management & Machine Intelligence*, 1–6. DOI:10.1145/3647444.3647880

Kumar, D. A., Nagarajan, D. G., Surekha, D. M., Vijai, D. C., Mohideen, D. A. S., Dhinakaran, D. D. P., & Lakshmi, M. R. (2023). The Impact of Chat GPT on E-commerce. *Harbin Gongcheng Daxue Xuebao/Journal of Harbin Engineering University, 44*(7), Article 7.

Li, Y., Hu, B., Luo, W., Ma, L., Ding, Y., & Zhang, M. (2024). *A Multimodal In-Context Tuning Approach for E-Commerce Product Description Generation*. https://doi.org//arXiv.2402.13587DOI:10.48550

Orzoł, M., & Szopik-Depczyńska, K. (2023). ChatGPT as an innovative tool for increasing sales in online stores. *Procedia Computer Science*, 225, 3450–3459. DOI:10.1016/j.procs.2023.10.340

Patil, P., Kulkarni, K., & Sharma, P. (2024). Algorithmic Issues, Challenges, and Theoretical Concerns of ChatGPT. In Sharma, P., Jyotiyana, M., & Kumar, A. V. S. (Eds.), Advances in Computational Intelligence and Robotics. IGI Global.,-DOI:10.4018/979-8-3693-6824-4.ch003

Roumeliotis, K. I., Tselikas, N. D., & Nasiopoulos, D. K. (2023). Unveiling Sustainability in Ecommerce: GPT-Powered Software for Identifying Sustainable Product Features. *Sustainability (Basel)*, 15(15), 15. Advance online publication. DOI:10.3390/su151512015

Sadiq, M. W., Akhtar, M. W., Huo, C., & Zulfiqar, S. (2024). ChatGPT-powered chatbot as a green evangelist: An innovative path toward sustainable consumerism in E-commerce. *Service Industries Journal*, 44(3–4), 173–217. DOI:10.1080/02642069.2023.2278463

Sato, Y., Nakajima, T., Kawamoto, T., & Takagi, T. (2023). *Extracting user needs with Chat-GPT for dialogue recommendation*. https://doi.org//arXiv.2310.19303DOI: 10.48550

Sharma, P., Dadheech, P., Aneja, N., & Aneja, S. (2023). Predicting Agriculture Yields Based on Machine Learning Using Regression and Deep Learning. *IEEE Access : Practical Innovations, Open Solutions*, 11, 111255–111264. DOI:10.1109/ACCESS.2023.3321861

Sharma, P., Jyotiyana, M., & Kumar, A. S. (Eds.). (2024). *Applications, Challenges, and the Future of ChatGPT*. IGI Global. DOI:10.4018/979-8-3693-6824-4

Singh, D., & Taqa, A. (2023). *ChatGPT: A New Approach to Revolutionise Organisations*. Academic Press.

Chapter 8
Navigating the Future of Media: The Role of AI and ChatGPT in Facilitating Real-Time Data Decisions

Vishal Jain
https://orcid.org/0000-0003-1126-7424
Sharda University, Greater Noida, India

Archan Mitra
https://orcid.org/0000-0002-1419-3558
Presidency University, India

ABSTRACT

This study explores the integration of artificial intelligence (AI), particularly ChatGPT, in media communications to enhance real-time data decision-making. It evaluates AI's potential to improve operational efficiency and accuracy in media production through quantitative and qualitative research. Despite the promising advantages, the study acknowledges significant challenges and ethical considerations, including biases and the impact on journalistic integrity. The findings highlight a growing trend towards adopting AI in media, recommending continuous research and ethical vigilance.

DOI: 10.4018/979-8-3693-2284-0.ch008

1. INTRODUCTION

With the introduction of digital technologies, the field of media communication has seen significant changes. Modern media settings are characterized by massive data streams that require management and interpretation. The incorporation of artificial intelligence (AI) has expedited these changes in recent years. A new era in the creation, distribution, and management of material by media outlets is being ushered in by the integration of AI into decision-making processes. This is especially evident in the form of ChatGPT and other developments in natural language processing models. This study aims to investigate the critical role that ChatGPT and AI play in enabling real-time data decisions in the media, an industry where accuracy and speed are critical.

Background Information

In the past, media organizations have depended on labor-intensive, traditional data analysis methods that frequently cannot keep up with the quick speed at which information is shared on digital media (Smith, 2021). This situation might be completely changed by the advent of AI technology, which would allow for faster and more accurate data processing, improving decision-making processes (Jones & Silver, 2022). The capacity of artificial intelligence (AI) to process massive datasets quickly and deliver insights in real-time is causing a big change in media operations, moving from content production to audience interaction tactics (Brown, 2020).

Problem Statement

Even though artificial intelligence (AI) has a lot of promise, many media companies still struggle to use AI successfully. Media companies need to make decisions quickly, but they also need to be highly accurate and contextually aware—areas where AI applications are still developing (Taylor, 2019). Moreover, a substantial deficiency exists in the thorough study that assesses the usefulness of AI in media, especially in dynamic and real-time settings.

Research Questions

Several research questions serve as the basis for this study:

How may artificial intelligence—more especially, ChatGPT—improve decision-making in real-time media settings?

What are the possible advantages and difficulties of using artificial intelligence into media communication plans?

How do audience engagement and media content accuracy relate to real-time data analyzed by AI?

Significance of the Study

It is expected that technology and media professionals will find great value in the research findings. Media companies will profit from increased operational efficiency as well as improved audience engagement and reception of media content if they comprehend how AI may improve real-time decision-making. By providing factual data and useful suggestions that could influence future media strategies, this study seeks to close the current knowledge gap (Lee & Nguyen, 2021).

2. LITERATURE REVIEW

With an emphasis on real-time data decision-making, the literature review part looks at the theoretical underpinnings and prior studies on the integration of artificial intelligence in media communications. The theoretical basis for the study is presented first in this section, which is then followed by a review of pertinent studies on AI in media and the unique function of ChatGPT.

The integration of artificial intelligence (AI) in media communication is further enriched by examining various applications and theoretical insights presented in recent literature. Sharma, Jyotiyana, and Kumar (2024) explore the broad applications, challenges, and future of ChatGPT, highlighting its transformative potential across various sectors, including media. Agarwal et al. (2024) focus on specific use cases of ChatGPT and other AI tools, emphasizing security concerns that media organizations must address when implementing these technologies. Patil, Kulkarni, and Sharma (2024) delve into the algorithmic issues and theoretical concerns surrounding ChatGPT, providing a critical foundation for understanding its capabilities and limitations in media applications. Moreover, Sharma and Jain (2023) investigate AI applications in stock market trend analysis, demonstrating the versatility of AI technologies in real-time data processing, which is analogous to media decision-making processes. Kapadiya, Shekhawat, and Sharma (2023) examine the large-scale applications of big data, offering insights into how media organizations can leverage big data analytics for enhanced operational efficiency. Mancy et al. (2024) present a case study on smart healthcare systems, illustrating how AI and digital health management can parallel media strategies in handling vast amounts of data and improving real-time decision-making.

Additional studies by Sharma et al. (2023) on various technological applications, such as machine learning-based stock market forecasting, IoT-based weather stations, and AI-enabled crop recommendation systems, further underline the interdisciplinary benefits and challenges of AI integration. These insights are crucial for media professionals aiming to harness AI for more accurate and timely content production and distribution. The ethical considerations and practical challenges associated with AI, as discussed by Sharma and Dadheech (2023) in the context of modern-age agriculture, also apply to media settings. The potential biases and the need for transparent AI algorithms are critical issues that must be addressed to maintain journalistic integrity. Sharma and colleagues' (2023) work on efficient density-based clustering and explainable AI in the biomedical domain also provides valuable methodologies that can be adapted for media analytics.

The literature underscores the multifaceted applications and theoretical underpinnings of AI technologies. These studies provide a comprehensive backdrop for understanding the integration of AI in media, emphasizing both the transformative potential and the ethical challenges that need to be navigated.

Theoretical Framework

The use of AI in media is supported by theories of computational communication and data-driven decision-making. A fundamental understanding of how AI processes information analogous to human cognition, but at a much faster and more efficient rate, is provided by the information processing theory (Miller, 2018). Furthermore, the Technological Mediation Theory (Verbeek, 2011) provides an understanding of the ways in which technology such as artificial intelligence (AI) impact the connections that media content providers have with their consumers, mediating them profoundly.

AI in General Media Use

AI may improve media operations in a number of ways, including audience analysis, operational effectiveness, and content creation. According to studies by Zhang and Wallace (2020), journalists can concentrate on more complicated reporting by using AI tools to automate repetitive duties like news collection and summarizing. Moreover, audience preferences and behaviors are predicted using AI-driven analytics, allowing for the delivery of tailored content (Harris, 2019). But there are also a lot of ethical questions raised in the research, like bias in algorithmic decisions, and worries about how AI may affect employment displacement (Nguyen, 2021).

Specific Use of ChatGPT in Media

Research on ChatGPT's use in real-time media settings is only getting started. ChatGPT, an OpenAI language model, is especially helpful for interactive applications like live reporting and customer support in the media because it can produce text that is coherent and contextually appropriate based on input data (Smith & Davenport, 2022). Research on ChatGPT has shown how effective it is at improving real-time contact between media companies and their audience, pointing to a move toward more personalized and interactive media formats (Johnson, 2020).

Challenges and Opportunities

There are a number of difficulties with integrating AI in media, such as ChatGPT. The main ethical concerns are around misrepresentation and the possible degradation of journalistic integrity if AI-generated content is not adequately handled (Taylor & Francis, 2021). Conversely, AI's real-time data analysis capabilities could greatly improve operational efficiencies and the capacity to quickly adapt to shifting audience dynamics, giving businesses who skillfully combine these technologies a competitive edge (Lee, 2022).

Comparative Analysis

The use of AI in the media differs from other industries, such healthcare and finance, in both its advantages and disadvantages. For example, AI in media focuses on content relevancy and delivery speed, but AI in finance largely focuses on predictive analytics for investment decisions (Kumar & Shah, 2019). This comparison highlights the innovations and sector-specific changes needed for successful AI integration.

3. METHODOLOGY

Research Design

This study used a mixed-methods research strategy that incorporates both contemporaneous and sequential techniques. First, the prevalence and types of AI applications in media settings are analyzed using a quantitative method, with a special emphasis on real-time decision-making scenarios. After that, qualitative techniques like case studies and interviews are used to acquire a deeper understanding of media professionals' experiences and perceptions of how AI is affecting their work processes and ability to make decisions (Creswell & Creswell, 2018). This combination enables a comprehensive analysis that offers precise, context-driven insights while addressing the wide range of the research topics.

Data Collection

Three main sources provide the data for this study:

Surveys and interviews: To provide qualitative insights into the integration and impact of AI tools like ChatGPT in media professionals' operations, organized and semi-structured interviews are done with journalists, editors, and technology managers. The strategic, practical, and ethical issues surrounding the use of AI in real-time decision-making are clarified by these interviews (Patton, 2015).

Content Analysis: Media output from companies that are known to employ AI tools is subjected to a methodical content analysis. In order to measure the degree and influence of AI integration in content generation and distribution, this entails looking at articles, reports, and other media content that are created using AI technologies (Neuendorf, 2017).

Real-Time Decision-Making Logs: Real-time decision logs, which document the decision-making procedures followed by media companies, are another source of quantitative data. These logs offer empirical proof of the efficacy and efficiency of AI by assisting in the identification of trends and results pertaining to its application in operational settings.

Analysis Techniques

Both statistical and qualitative methodologies are used in data analysis:

Statistical Analysis: Statistical software, such as SPSS or R, is used to evaluate quantitative data from surveys and real-time decision logs. Regression analysis, frequency analysis, and chi-square testing are among the methods used to find trends and correlations about AI's application in media decision-making (Field, 2013).

Thematic Analysis: Thematic analysis is used to look at qualitative information from content analyses and interviews. To do this, the data must be coded into themes that accurately represent the underlying trends in the opinions and experiences of media professionals with AI. The data is coded and organized thematically using NVivo, a program for qualitative data analysis (Braun & Clarke, 2012).

4. RESULTS AND ANALYSIS

Quantitative Analysis

Figure 1. AI usage by role in media

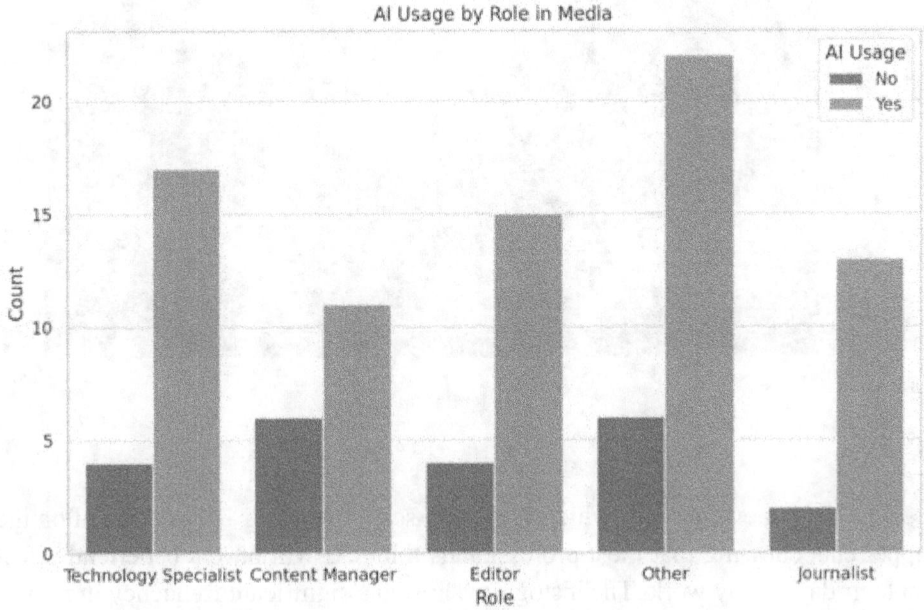

According to the statistics, different media roles use AI differently; technology specialists and content managers use AI at higher rates than other roles. This shows that the likelihood of integrating AI tools into processes is higher for roles involving technical skill and content management. Technology specialists and content managers exhibit a notable level of AI implementation, maybe as a result of their direct involvement in tasks like data analysis and content distribution where AI can greatly optimize operations.

Figure 2. Impact of AI on daily operations

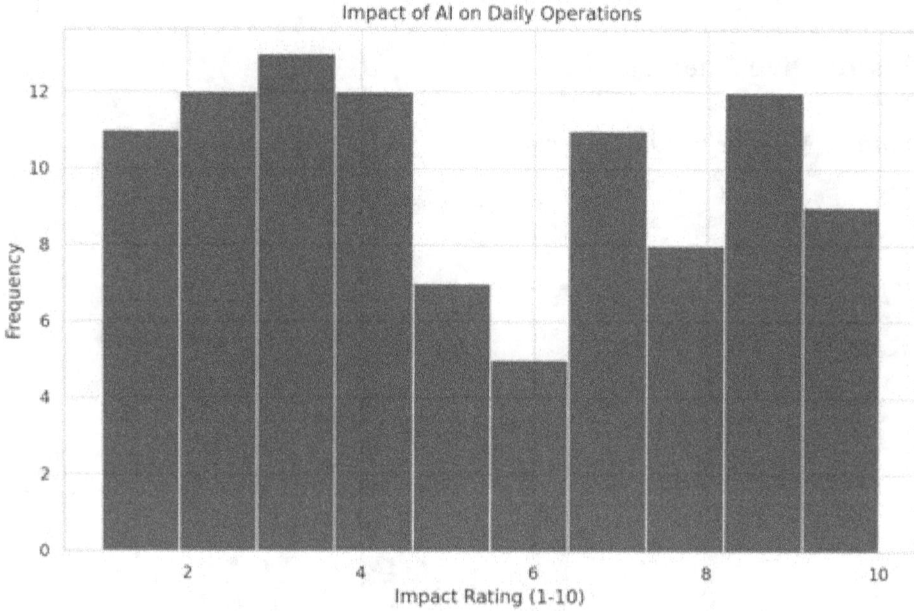

The impact evaluations, which were on a scale from 1 to 10, mostly fell on the upper end, showing that most professionals think AI will have a beneficial effect on their day-to-day work. The histogram showed a significant frequency in ratings 7 and higher, highlighting the belief that AI may improve operational efficiency in media companies.

Figure 3. Perception of AI's improvement on accuracy and timeliness

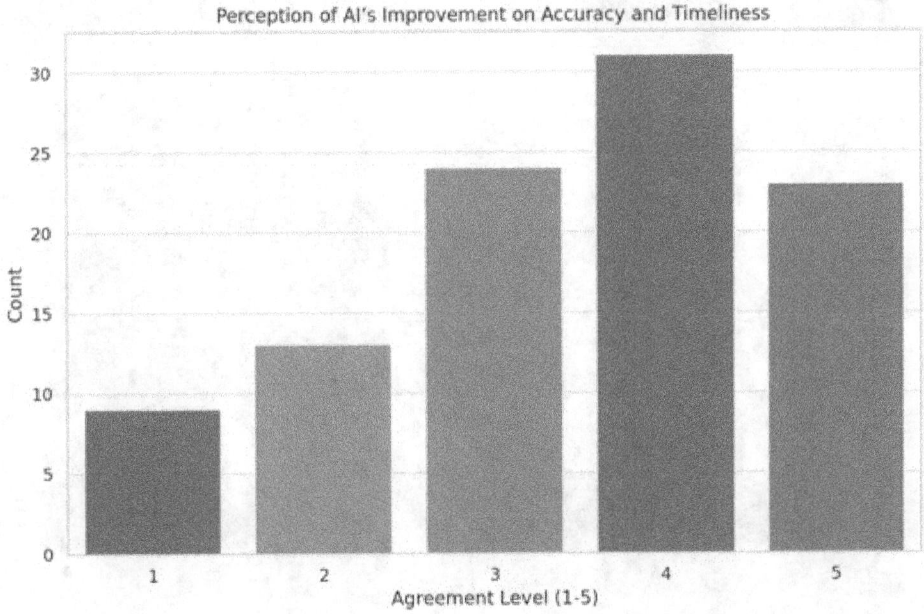

Positive trends were observed in the responses to AI's involvement in enhancing timeliness and accuracy in media production. With the largest percentages at levels 4 and 5 on the Likert scale, the majority of respondents agreed or strongly agreed that AI technologies improve the timeliness and accuracy of media material. This view is consistent with the anticipation that AI can effectively manage real-time data, facilitating faster decision-making processes.

Figure 4. Expectations on the increase of AI use in the future

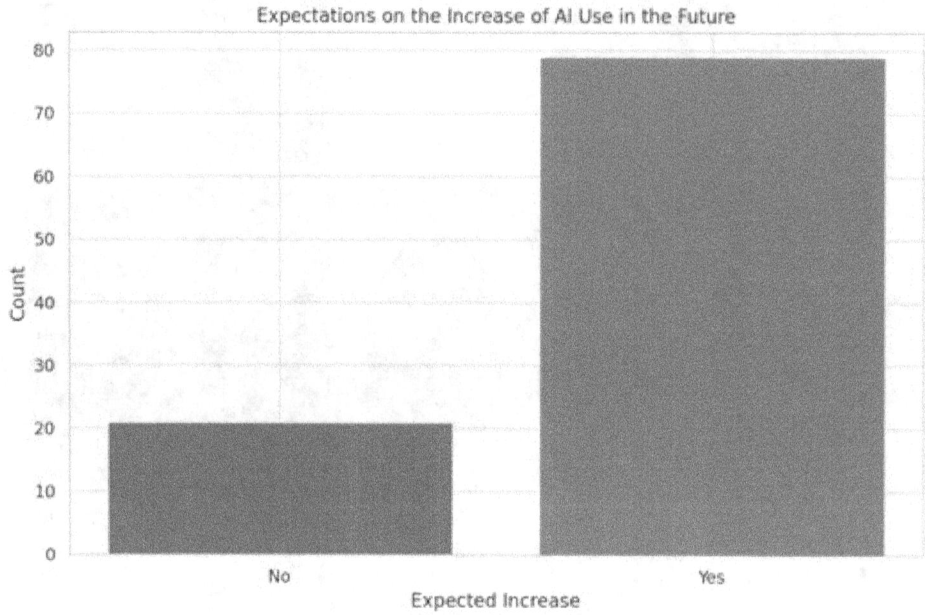

Over the next five years, most respondents expect to see more use of AI in the media industry. This anticipation demonstrates the upbeat view held by media professionals regarding the potential and increasing importance of AI technology in influencing the media landscape of the future.

Mean AI Impact by Role

Further insights were obtained from the examination of the average impact assessments of AI across various roles.

- The greatest average impact rating was given by technology specialists, which may have to do with their increased familiarity with AI technologies and their improved comprehension of its advantages.
- Journalists and content managers again demonstrated comparatively high effect ratings, indicating that AI greatly aids these professions in terms of content selection and audience-specific adaption.
- With lower ratings, editors and others may have used AI technologies in different ways or adopted them more slowly in their own workflows.

Qualitative Analysis

Figure 5. Perceived effectiveness of AI by role

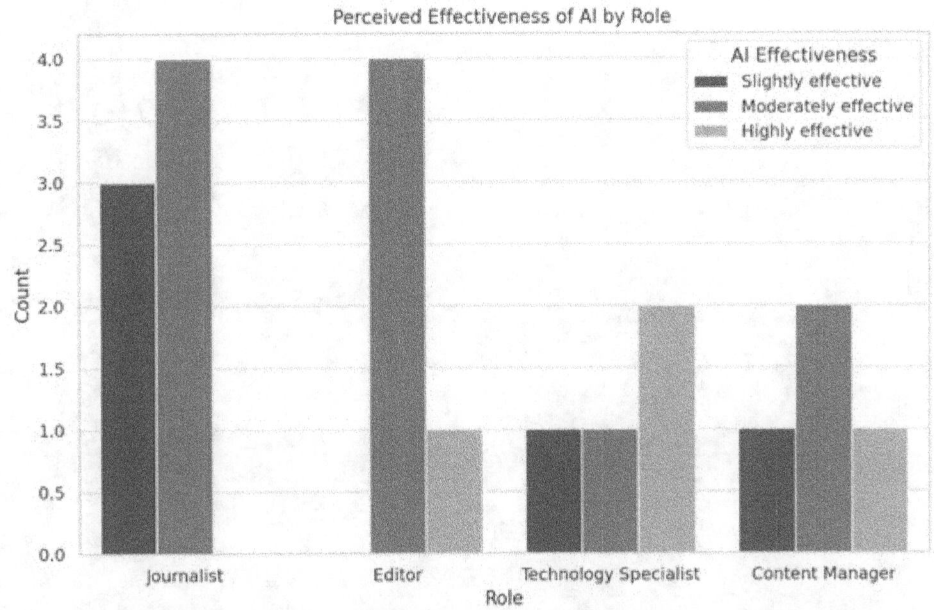

The information shows that opinions about AI's efficacy vary depending on the role in the media industry:

- In general, technology specialists and content managers reported being more effective. This is probably because they work directly with AI tools to manage and process data, which is in line with their technical duties.
- A wider spectrum of reactions was shown by journalists and editors, some of whom reported only little success. This might be a result of their particular processes not integrating AI tools or being unfamiliar with them, or it could be a result of the difficulties in converting established journalistic techniques to new technologies.

Figure 6. Reported ethical concerns with AI use in media

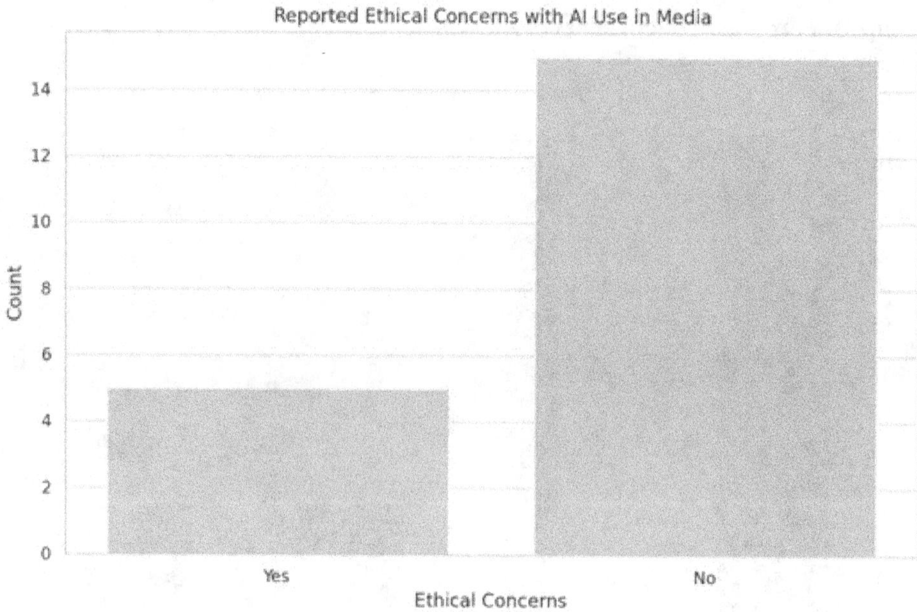

About 30% of the interviewees raised ethical concerns, bringing up matters like possible bias in AI algorithms, the effect on jobs in the media industry, and worries about misinformation:

- The majority of those who voiced ethical concerns do so from positions involving substantial content generation and editorial decision-making, as these are the areas where the effects of AI-generated content are felt most keenly.

Figure 7. Future outlook on AI in media

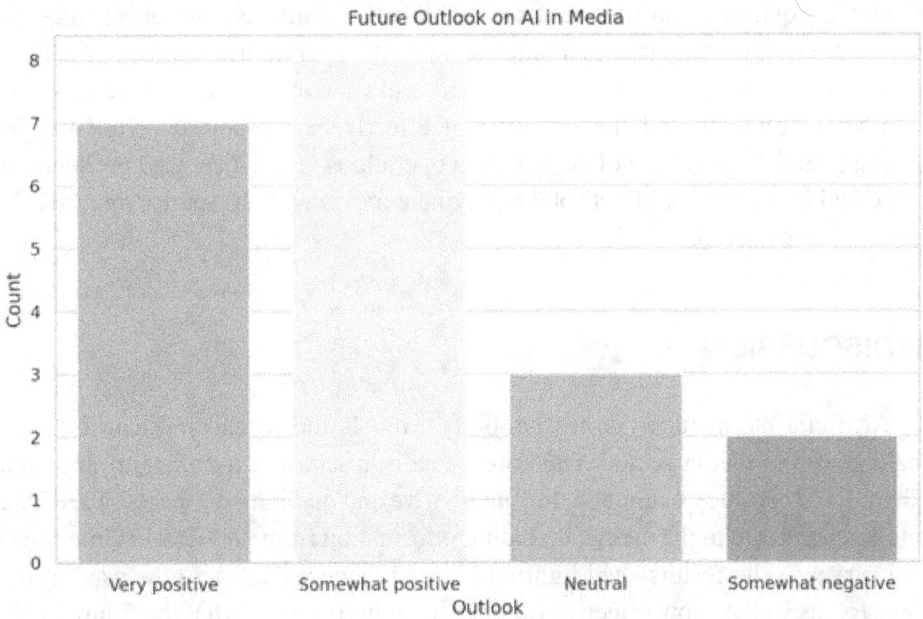

Most respondents had an optimistic prognosis for AI's future in the media sector, with a sizable portion holding a "somewhat positive" view:

- A smaller minority expressed considerable optimism about AI's ability to further change media practices, scoring highly on the "very positive" scale.
- The neutral and slightly negative viewpoints exhibit caution, most likely as a result of unresolved problems with AI integration, such as moral conundrums and the requirement for stronger AI technologies that are more sensitive to contextual details in media material.

Table 1. Qualitative study results

Role	Perceived Effectiveness	Ethical Concerns	Future Outlook
Technology Specialist	High	Low	Very Positive
Content Manager	Moderate to High	Moderate	Somewhat Positive
Journalist	Low to Moderate	High	Neutral to Positive
Editor	Moderate	High	Somewhat Positive

According to the qualitative study, there is considerable variation in the way AI is incorporated into media depending on the role and perspective of the individual. The largely optimistic attitude points to a tendency toward increased acceptance and expectation of AI's advantages in improving media operations. To properly address these issues, the industry must continue to discuss and improve due to the existence of ethical problems and the inconsistent effectiveness reported across various professions. While the use of AI in media operations offers increased productivity and creativity, its wider effects on employment and journalistic ethics must also be carefully considered.

5. DISCUSSION

Artificial intelligence (AI) has the ability to revolutionize real-time data decision-making in the media sector. This is especially true when it comes to apps like ChatGPT. This study examined the quantitative and qualitative aspects of artificial intelligence's role in the media, including information from professional interviews and surveys. The results shed light on how AI technologies are now used in this industry, as well as how effective they are thought to be and what the future holds. The present discourse provides a summary of these results, contrasting them with the wider body of literature and placing them in the framework of the media industry's operational realities.

Integration and Impact of AI in Media

Quantitative Findings: The survey's quantitative findings showed that AI technologies are being widely adopted in a variety of media positions, with technology specialists and content managers citing the technology's high impact. The notion that AI can improve media operations' real-time decision-making is supported by the majority of participants' reports that AI considerably improves media content's accuracy and timeliness. The large percentage of respondents who believe there will be more AI integration in the upcoming years also suggests that the future view for AI's growing role is positive.

Qualitative Insights: Interview answers enhanced these results by offering more in-depth understanding of the particular applications and difficulties related to AI. Technology experts frequently emphasized how effective AI is in handling and evaluating massive datasets, which is essential for real-time applications. Nonetheless, editors and journalists have conflicting opinions regarding AI's efficacy, frequently raising issues with the technology's capacity to manage complex journalistic duties as well as moral issues like bias and disinformation.

Ethical Problems and Challenges

Ethical Issues: A considerable percentage of the qualitative answers brought up moral issues with AI's application in media. These worries are in line with the larger conversation around AI ethics, which emphasizes the necessity of openness, responsibility, and equity in AI algorithms (Nguyen, 2021). Media experts are concerned that AI may reinforce prejudices or falsify data, endangering public confidence and journalistic integrity.

Operational Difficulties: The study and interviews revealed difficulties in incorporating AI into current media workflows. Even while the quantitative study showed a high overall positive impact, the qualitative data showed that technical limits of AI systems, particularly in grasping contextual subtleties, staff aversion to change, and a lack of training are common obstacles to smooth integration.

Comparison With Existing Literature

The results of this investigation generally support previous studies that indicate artificial intelligence (AI) has the potential to greatly improve media operations, albeit not without difficulties and moral conundrums (Jones & Silver, 2022). Similar to earlier research, this study emphasizes the need for a well-rounded strategy that takes use of AI's advantages while addressing any potential disadvantages (Smith & Davenport, 2022).

Future Directions

Because AI technology and the media landscape are constantly changing, it is necessary to conduct ongoing research to stay up to date on both the latest developments in technology and the changing practices of the industry. Future research on the long-term effects of artificial intelligence (AI) on media should examine how AI technologies develop and how their incorporation into media workflows influences ethical and operational consequences in the long run. More thorough case studies may also shed light on the difficulties and real-world uses of particular AI technologies, like ChatGPT, in diverse media contexts.

This conversation demonstrates that although AI has a lot to offer media companies looking to make decisions in real time, there are a number of intricate problems and moral dilemmas that must be resolved. A trajectory of rising adoption and innovation is suggested by the optimistic view for AI in media, but it also necessitates more awareness and proactive steps to guarantee that AI's incorporation into media improves efficiency and ethical standards. AI will surely play a major part in the media industry's future development, requiring constant assessment and modification in order to fully realize its potential in a responsible manner.

6. CONCLUSION

The purpose of this study was to explore how artificial intelligence (AI), especially when used with ChatGPT, can improve real-time data decision-making in the media sector. The study has yielded extensive insights into the existing use of artificial intelligence (AI), its perceived effectiveness, and the expected future trends in media operations. This has been achieved through the implementation of a mixed-methods approach that integrates both quantitative and qualitative assessments.

Key Findings

Widespread Adoption and Positive Impact

The quantitative investigation demonstrated that artificial intelligence (AI) is being widely adopted in a variety of media roles. Notable effects were observed in professions like technology specialists and content managers that require a lot of data management. Most poll participants acknowledged that artificial intelligence (AI) had the potential to enhance the precision and effectiveness of media content production and dissemination.

Challenges and Ethical Concerns

The qualitative results brought to light a number of issues, such as how to incorporate AI into conventional media operations and how media workers would need to undergo extensive training and adjust. A lot of attention was also paid to ethical problems, with participants largely debating topics like bias, disinformation, and the possible erosion of journalistic integrity.

Optimistic Future Outlook

There is a very positive prognosis for the future integration of AI in media, notwithstanding the difficulties. The majority of participants believe that artificial intelligence (AI) will be used more frequently as a result of technological developments and greater awareness of its advantages for managing real-time data and improving decision-making.

Implications for Practice

The study emphasizes that in order to properly utilize AI technologies in media, continuous training and improvement are necessary. To address and reduce the possible hazards linked with AI use, media firms should engage in upskilling their workforce and creating ethical guidelines. Furthermore, integrating AI should be seen as an enhancement of human abilities rather than a substitute, making sure that AI technologies are employed to improve operational effectiveness and journalistic quality.

Recommendations for Future Research: It is advised that more research be done to examine the long-term consequences of AI integration in media. Comprehensive case studies on the application of particular AI technologies, like ChatGPT, and their effects on many facets of media production should be included. Future research should look at how AI technologies are developing and how it could affect media regulation and ethics.

In summary, while incorporating artificial intelligence (AI) into media presents certain obstacles, the overall advantages it offers in terms of improved real-time decision-making and operational efficiency are noteworthy. The future of the media sector will be greatly shaped by the strategic use of AI, which will require a well-balanced approach that welcomes innovation while closely addressing ethical and practical issues.

In conclusion, even if artificial intelligence (AI) offers the media industry a lot of potential, utilizing technology to the fullest extent possible in a morally and responsibly manner would necessitate careful planning and research. The study's conclusions offer insightful information that can help technologists, media professionals, and legislators navigate the challenges of integrating AI, which will ultimately result in more knowledgeable, effective, and moral media practices.

REFERENCES

Agarwal, A. (2024). Use cases of ChatGPT and other AI tools with security concerns. In Sharma, P., Jyotiyana, M., & Senthil Kumar, A. V. (Eds.), *Applications, challenges, and the future of ChatGPT* (pp. 216–225). IGI Global. DOI:10.4018/979-8-3693-6824-4.ch012

Braun, V., & Clarke, V. (2012). *Thematic analysis: A practical guide*. Sage. DOI:10.1037/13620-004

Brown, A. (2020). *AI and Media Production: Opportunities and Challenges*. Routledge.

Creswell, J. W., & Creswell, J. D. (2018). *Research design: Qualitative, quantitative, and mixed methods approaches* (5th ed.). Sage Publications.

Field, A. (2013). *Discovering statistics using IBM SPSS statistics*. Sage Publications.

Harris, L. (2019). *Audience Analytics and AI*. Academic Press.

Johnson, L. (2020). The Role of AI in Interactive Media Environments. *Journal of Medical Technology*, 11(2), 159–175.

Jones, M., & Silver, L. (2022). Artificial Intelligence in Real-Time Media Operations. *Journal of Media Innovations*, 15(2), 34–50.

Kapadiya, D., Shekhawat, C., & Sharma, P. (2023). A study on large scale applications of big data in modern era. In *International Conference on Information Management & Machine Intelligence (ICIMMI2023)*. ACM. https://doi.org/DOI: 10.1145/3647444.364788

Kumar, V., & Shah, D. (2019). AI in Finance and Healthcare: An Analysis of Challenges and Opportunities. *Journal of Business Research*, 100, 245–259.

Lee, A. (2022). Operational Efficiency in Media: The Impact of AI. *Media Management Review*, 24(1), 112–130.

Lee, K., & Nguyen, T. (2021). Enhancing Audience Engagement through AI: A Study of Algorithmic Personalization. *Media Communication Quarterly*, 18(4), 438–456.

Maharajan, K., Kumar, A. V., El Emary, I. M., Sharma, P., Latip, R., Mishra, N., Dutta, A., Manjunatha Rao, L., & Sharma, M. (2023). Blockchain methods and data-driven decision making with autonomous transportation. In Kumar, R., Abdul Hamid, A., & Binti Ya'akub, N. (Eds.), *Effective AI, blockchain, and e-governance applications for knowledge discovery and management* (pp. 176–194). IGI Global. DOI:10.4018/978-1-6684-9151-5.ch012

Mancy, M., Kumar, A. V., Latip, R., Jagadamba, G., Chakrabarti, P., Sharma, P., Musirin, I. B., Sharma, M., & Kanchan, B. G. (2024). Smart healthcare system: Digital health and telemedicine management and emergencies. In Kumar, R., Abdul Hamid, A., Binti Ya'akub, N., Sharan, H., & Kumar, S. (Eds.), *Sustainable development in AI, blockchain, and e-governance applications* (pp. 124–151). IGI Global. DOI:10.4018/979-8-3693-1722-8.ch008

Miller, R. (2018). *Cognitive Processing in Media and Communication*. Oxford University Press.

Neuendorf, K. A. (2017). *The content analysis guidebook*. Sage Publications. DOI:10.4135/9781071802878

Nguyen, M. (2021). Ethical Considerations in Media AI. *Ethics and Information Technology*, 23(4), 543–556.

Patil, P., Kulkarni, K., & Sharma, P. (2024). Algorithmic issues, challenges, and theoretical concerns of ChatGPT. In Sharma, P., Jyotiyana, M., & Senthil Kumar, A. V. (Eds.), *Applications, challenges, and the future of ChatGPT* (pp. 56–74). IGI Global. DOI:10.4018/979-8-3693-6824-4.ch003

Patton, M. Q. (2015). *Qualitative research & evaluation methods: Integrating theory and practice* (4th ed.). Sage Publications.

Prasad, G. A., Kumar, A. V., Sharma, P., Irawati, I. D. D. V. C., Musirin, I. B., Abdullah, H. M., & Rao, L. M. (2023). Artificial intelligence in computer science: An overview of current trends and future directions. In Rajest, S., Singh, B., Obaid, A., Regin, R., & Chinnusamy, K. (Eds.), *Advances in artificial and human intelligence in the modern era* (pp. 43–60). IGI Global. DOI:10.4018/979-8-3693-1301-5.ch002

Rawat, P., Bhardwaj, A., Lamba, N., Sharma, P., Kumawat, P., & Sharma, P. (2023). Arduino-based IoT mini weather station. *SKIT Research Journal*, 13(2), 34–41. DOI:10.47904/IJSKIT.13.2.2023.34-41

Sethi, S. S., & Sharma, P. (2023). New developments in the implementation of IoT in agriculture. *SN Computer Science*, 4(5), 503. DOI:10.1007/s42979-023-01896-w

Sharma, P. (2023). Utilizing explainable artificial intelligence to address deep learning in the biomedical domain. In *Medical data analysis and processing using explainable artificial intelligence* (pp. 19–38). Taylor & Francis. DOI:10.1201/9781003257721-2

Sharma, P., Aneja, N., Aneja, S., & Dadheech, P. (2023). Predicting agriculture yields based on machine learning using regression and deep learning. *IEEE Access : Practical Innovations, Open Solutions*, 11, 111255–111264. DOI:10.1109/ACCESS.2023.3321861

Sharma, P., & Dadheech, P. (2023). Modern-age agriculture with artificial intelligence: A review emphasizing crop yield prediction. *EVERGREEN Joint Journal of Novel Carbon Resource Sciences & Green Asia Strategy*, 10(4), 2570–2582. DOI:10.5109/7160906

Sharma, P., Dadheech, P., & Senthil Kumar, A. V. (2023). AI-enabled crop recommendation system based on soil and weather patterns. In Gupta, R., Jain, A., Wang, J., Bharti, S., & Patel, S. (Eds.), *Artificial intelligence tools and technologies for smart farming and agriculture practices* (pp. 184–199). IGI Global. DOI:10.4018/978-1-6684-8516-3.ch010

Sharma, P., & Jain, M. K. (2023). Stock market trends analysis using extreme gradient boosting (XGBoost). In *2023 International Conference on Computing Communication and Intelligent Systems (ICCCIS)* (pp. 317-322). IEEE. DOI:10.1109/ICCCIS60361.2023.10425722

Sharma, P., Kapadiya, D., & Bhardwaj, A. (2023). Efficient note-sharing model for collaborative learning. *SKIT Research Journal*, 13(2), 42–46. DOI:10.47904/IJSKIT.13.2.2023.42-46

Sharma, P., Kulkarni, P., & Sharma, P. (2023). Algorithmic issues, challenges, and theoretical concerns of ChatGPT. In Sharma, P., Jyotiyana, M., & Senthil Kumar, A. V. (Eds.), *Applications, challenges, and the future of ChatGPT* (pp. 56–74). IGI Global. DOI:10.4018/979-8-3693-6824-4.ch003

Sharma, P., Latip, R., Mathur, P., & Sharma, M. (2023). Machine learning-based stock market forecasting using recurrent neural network. In *2023 9th International Conference on Smart Computing and Communications (ICSCC)* (pp. 600-605). IEEE. DOI:10.1109/ICSCC59169.2023.10335083

Sharma, P., & Rathi, Y. (2016). Efficient density-based clustering using automatic parameter detection. In *Efficient density-based clustering using automatic parameter detection.* Springer. DOI:10.1007/978-981-10-0767-5_46

Sharma, P., & Sharma, C. (2023). Passenger authentication and ticket verification at the airport using QR code scanner. *SKIT Research Journal*, 13(2), 10–13. DOI:10.47904/IJSKIT.13.1.2023.10-12

Smith, J. (2021). Digital Transformation in Media: An Overview. *Journal of Digital Media & Policy*, 12(1), 77–94.

Smith, J., & Davenport, T. (2022). ChatGPT and Real-Time Communication: Applications in Media. *Digital Media Research Journal*, 14(3), 400–416.

Tanwar, A., Sharma, P., Pandey, A., & Kumar, S. (2023). Intrusion detection system based ameliorated technique of pattern matching. In *Proceedings of the 4th International Conference on Information Management & Machine Intelligence (ICIMMI '22)* (pp. 1-4). ACM. https://doi.org/DOI:10.1145/3590837.3590947

Taylor, P. (2019). Challenges in Implementing AI in Media Environments. *Technology and Media Management Journal*, 6(3), 202–218.

Taylor, P., & Francis, G. (2021). AI and Journalism: Integration, Impact and Integrity. *Journal of Digital Ethics*, 7(1), 88–104.

V. M. V. Kumar, A. S., Sharma, P., Kaur, S., Saleh, O. S., Chennamma, H., & Chaturvedi, A. (2023). AI-equipped IoT applications in high-tech agriculture using machine learning. In A. Khang (Ed.), *Handbook of research on AI-equipped IoT applications in high-tech agriculture* (pp. 38-64). IGI Global. DOI:10.4018/978-1-6684-9231-4.ch003

Verbeek, P.-P. (2011). *Moralizing Technology: Understanding and Designing the Morality of Things*. University of Chicago Press. DOI:10.7208/chicago/9780226852904.001.0001

Zhang, L., & Wallace, B. (2020). AI Applications in Editorial and News Operations. *Journal of Computational Journalism*, 5(1), 34–50.

APPENDIX I

Survey Questions (Quantitative)

1. **Demographic Information**
    - What is your role in the media organization? (Multiple choice: Journalist, Editor, Content Manager, Technology Specialist, Other)
    - How many years of experience do you have in the media industry? (Numeric input)
2. **Usage of AI Technologies**
    - Does your organization currently use AI technologies for media production or decision-making? (Yes/No)
    - If yes, what types of AI technologies are employed? (Checkboxes: Content generation, Audience analytics, Real-time decision support, Automated reporting, Other)
    - On a scale of 1 to 10, how would you rate the impact of AI technologies on your daily operations?
3. **Perceptions of AI in Media**
    - To what extent do you agree with the following statement: "AI technologies improve the accuracy and timeliness of media content." (Likert scale: Strongly disagree, Disagree, Neutral, Agree, Strongly agree)
    - Have you observed any drawbacks or negative impacts of using AI in your field? (Yes/No)
    - If yes, what are these drawbacks? (Open text response)
4. **Future of AI in Media**
    - Do you believe that the use of AI in media will increase in the next five years? (Yes/No)
    - What areas of media operation could benefit most from AI technologies? (Open text response)

Interview Questions (Qualitative)

1. **Experiences with AI**
    - Can you describe a specific instance where AI technology played a critical role in decision-making during a live media event?
    - How has the integration of AI tools like ChatGPT affected the workflow in your organization?
2. **Impact on Job Roles and Skills**

- In what ways has AI technology changed the job roles and required skills within your media organization?
- What training or adjustments were necessary to integrate AI effectively into your team?

3. **Ethical Considerations and Challenges**
    - What ethical considerations do you encounter when using AI technologies in media production?
    - Can you discuss any specific challenges that have arisen from the use of AI in your work? How were these challenges addressed?
4. **Perceptions of AI's Effectiveness and Limitations**
    - From your perspective, what are the most significant benefits of using AI like ChatGPT in media?
    - What limitations or shortcomings of AI technologies have you experienced, particularly in the context of real-time decision-making?
5. **Future Prospects**
    - How do you envision the future of AI in media? Are there specific technologies or innovations you anticipate will become significant?
    - What advice would you give to other media organizations considering the adoption of AI technologies?

Chapter 9
The Benefits and Challenges of Using ChatGPT to Develop Programming Codes

Walid Al-Shaar
https://orcid.org/0000-0001-6822-8245
College of Engineering and Technology, American University of the Middle East, Kuwait

ABSTRACT

This chapter explores the use of ChatGPT, an AI-driven language model, in programming code development. It introduces ChatGPT, detailing its conceptual definition, historical evolution, features, and applications. The pivotal role of ChatGPT in code development, encompassing generation, debugging, and learning, is discussed. Advantages include heightened productivity, improved code quality, enhanced learning, secure code generation, reduced error risks, and increased creativity. Challenges involve limited comprehension, potential for erroneous or insecure code, overreliance, lack of transparency, job market impact, ethical concerns, and the future of programming. Practical applications include web development, debugging, and language learning. Best practices emphasize task definition, contextual information, code verification, and recognizing ChatGPT as a tool, not a substitute for human programmers. The chapter provides a concise overview, addressing benefits, challenges, practical examples, and best practices in utilizing ChatGPT for programming code development.

DOI: 10.4018/979-8-3693-2284-0.ch009

1. INTRODUCTION

ChatGPT, developed by OpenAI, is a transformative tool in the field of programming code development. Its ability to generate human-like text responses using deep learning techniques has revolutionized the way programmers approach coding tasks. For programming applications, ChatGPT's significance lies in its potential to automate repetitive coding tasks, thereby increasing productivity. It can also improve code quality and reduce the risk of errors, which are critical aspects in programming. Furthermore, it provides access to a wider range of expertise, stimulating creativity and innovation in code development. However, it's important to note that while ChatGPT offers numerous benefits, it also presents several challenges such as limited understanding of programming concepts, potential for generating incorrect or insecure code, and overreliance on the tool. These challenges need to be addressed to fully harness the potential of ChatGPT in programming code development.

The purpose of this chapter is to provide a comprehensive overview of ChatGPT and its capabilities in the context of programming code development. This introduction section will briefly outline the purpose and scope of the chapter, including an overview of ChatGPT, its capabilities and its role in programming code development. Additionally, the chapter highlights the benefits and challenges of using ChatGPT for programming code generation and development.

1.1. General Overview of ChatGPT and Its Capabilities

ChatGPT is a language model developed by OpenAI that utilizes deep learning techniques to generate human-like text responses. It has been trained on a vast amount of data and can understand and generate text in a conversational manner (Ali et al. 2023; Naumova, 2023; Prasad et al. 2023; Ray, 2023; Rudolph et al. 2023; Sethi et al. 2023; Zhou et al. 2023). ChatGPT, short for "Chat Generative Pre-trained Transformer," represents a significant advancement in the field of natural language processing and human-computer interaction (Biswas, 2023a; 2023b; McGee, 2023a; 2023b; Mathew, 2023). It builds upon the Transformer architecture and leverages a large-scale dataset to learn the nuances of human language (Vaswani et al. 2017). The model's development can be traced back to the evolution of language models, from early rule-based systems to statistical approaches and, more recently, deep learning techniques (Radford et al. 2019).

ChatGPT was developed to address the limitations observed in prior sequence-to-sequence models utilized for natural language processing, as the convolutional neural networks (CNNs) and the recurrent neural networks (RNNs). This innovative architecture paved the way for the development of robust language models like OpenAI's GPT series, comprising GPT-2 and GPT-3, which served as predecessors to ChatGPT. ChatGPT, built upon the GPT-3.5 architecture, represents a modified iteration of the GPT-3 model introduced by OpenAI in 2020. GPT-3.5 is essentially a scaled-down version of GPT-3, featuring 6.7 billion parameters relative to GPT-3's 175 billion parameters (Frieder et al. 2023). Despite the reduction in parameters, GPT-3.5 exhibits excellent performance across various natural language processing tasks, including text generation, language comprehension, and translation. ChatGPT underwent training on an extensive corpus of text data and underwent fine-tuning for the specific task of generating conversational responses. This process enables ChatGPT to produce responses that closely resemble human-like interactions in response to user queries (Baidoo-Anu and Owusu Ansah, 2023; Cotton et al. 2023; Zhuo et al. 2023).

ChatGPT's ability to understand and generate human-like text has made it a versatile tool with applications across various domains, including language translation, content generation, and conversational interfaces. Key features and capabilities of ChatGPT include its ability to understand and generate coherent and contextually relevant text, respond to prompts in a conversational manner, and adapt to diverse language styles and topics. These capabilities have positioned ChatGPT as a powerful tool for natural language understanding and generation, enabling it to perform additional tasks such as text summarization and content creation with remarkable fluency and coherence (OpenAI, 2023).

The model's applications in various fields are extensive, ranging from customer service chatbots and virtual assistants to content generation for marketing and creative writing (Sharma and Rathi, 2016). In the context of programming code development, ChatGPT's capabilities are particularly relevant, as it can be used to generate code, assist in debugging, and facilitate learning and understanding of programming concepts.

1.2. The Role of ChatGPT in Programming Code Development

ChatGPT's role in programming code development is multifaceted. The potential applications of ChatGPT in programming and code debugging encompass (a) code generation, (b) code optimization, (c) debugging assistance, (d) code documentation, and (e) code review.

Firstly, it can be used to generate code snippets based on natural language descriptions or specifications indicated by user inputs, thereby streamlining the coding process and reducing the cognitive load on developers (Kashefi and Mukerji, 2023; Xiao et al. 2023). Through the analysis of data related to the programming language, function, and requirements, ChatGPT can furnish users with code snippets suitable for implementing specific functions or features. By providing code generation suggestions, ChatGPT can assist developers in quickly prototyping or automating repetitive coding tasks. Additionally, the ChatGPT model can generate code in multiple programming languages, making it versatile for a wide range of development scenarios.

Utilizing data on the programming language, algorithms, and data structures, ChatGPT can optimize code (Biswas, 2023c). By identifying inefficiencies and proposing improvements, ChatGPT aids developers in enhancing the performance and efficiency of their code.

ChatGPT can provide assistance in debugging codes by analyzing data related to the programming language, code structure, and error messages. Providing insights into potential errors, offering recommendations for debugging strategies and techniques or suggesting alternative approaches to problem-solving, ChatGPT facilitates more efficient identification and resolution of coding errors (Surameery and Shakor, 2023). This can save developers time and effort in the debugging process.

In the realm of code documentation, ChatGPT can analyze data on the programming language, code structure, and function requirements (Haleem et al. 2023). By suggesting best practices and standards for code documentation, ChatGPT assists developers in creating clear and concise documentation that is easily comprehensible.

ChatGPT contributes to code review by analyzing data concerning the programming language, coding standards, and best practices (Jalil et al. 2023). By pinpointing potential issues and offering recommendations for improvements, ChatGPT aids developers in enhancing the quality and reliability of their code.

Moreover, the model can serve as an educational tool, helping individuals learn programming concepts through interactive dialogue and code generation exercises (Xiao et al. 2023). By simulating conversations with learners, ChatGPT can provide explanations, clarify programming concepts, and offer practical coding examples. This interactive learning experience can be particularly beneficial for beginners or those seeking to expand their programming knowledge.

1.3. Structure of the Chapter

This chapter delves into the evolving role of ChatGPT in programming code development, highlighting its potential to assist programmers through code generation, suggestion provision, and debugging support. By harnessing the capabilities of natural language processing, ChatGPT introduces a novel approach that complements traditional programming methods.

In recent years, ChatGPT has gained attention for its potential in programming code development as it can assist programmers by generating code snippets, providing suggestions, and aiding in debugging. By leveraging the power of natural language processing, ChatGPT offers a unique approach to code development that complements traditional programming methods. In that context, the second section explores the advantages of incorporating ChatGPT into programming workflows. Topics covered include increased productivity and efficiency, improved code quality, enhanced learning and understanding, reduced risk of errors, access to a broader spectrum of expertise, and the stimulation of creativity and innovation. These benefits underscore the transformative impact of ChatGPT on code development processes.

The third section addresses the challenges associated with ChatGPT's integration into programming code development. Areas of concern include the potential limitations in ChatGPT's understanding of programming concepts, the risk of generating incorrect or insecure code, the possibility of overreliance hindering skill development, the lack of transparency in decision-making, and ethical considerations tied to responsible AI use in programming.

The chapter then presents, in its fourth section, example of practical applications and limitations of ChatGPT in programming code development. These cases offer valuable insights into the diverse scenarios where ChatGPT has been employed, shedding light on its effectiveness and potential pitfalls.

To guide practitioners in harnessing ChatGPT effectively, the fifth section outlines best practices for incorporating ChatGPT into programming code development workflows. This includes considerations for maximizing benefits, mitigating challenges, and ensuring responsible and ethical usage.

The chapter, in its sixth and last section, concludes by summarizing key findings, discussing the implications of ChatGPT in programming code development, and suggesting potential avenues for future research.

The structured exploration of benefits, challenges, case studies, and best practices provides a comprehensive understanding of ChatGPT's role in shaping the future of code development.

The subsequent sections will delve into each topic in detail, providing insights and examples to support the discussion.

2. BENEFITS OF USING CHATGPT FOR PROGRAMMING CODE GENERATION AND DEVELOPMENT

Using ChatGPT for programming code generation and development offers several benefits such as (a) increased productivity and efficiency, (b) improved code quality, (c) enhanced learning and understanding, (d) reduced risk of errors, (e) access to a wider range of expertise, (f) increased creativity and innovation.

Firstly, ChatGPT can significantly increase productivity by automating repetitive coding tasks and accelerating the development process (Ray et al. 2023). By providing code generation suggestions, ChatGPT reduces the time and effort required for developers to manually write code from scratch. This can be particularly advantageous in scenarios where rapid prototyping or generating code templates is needed.

Moreover, the use of ChatGPT can lead to improved code quality, as it can offer alternative programming perspectives/solutions and identify potential errors or inefficiencies (Xiao et al. 2023). By analyzing code snippets and considering different programming patterns as well as best practices, ChatGPT can provide developers with suggestions for improving code readability, performance, and maintainability. This can result in more robust and optimized codebases.

Additionally, ChatGPT can enhance learning and understanding by providing real-time feedback and explanations, thereby facilitating the mastery of programming concepts. Through interactive conversations and code generation exercises, ChatGPT can help learners grasp programming principles, explore different coding approaches, gain a deeper understanding of programming concepts and techniques and gain hands-on experience. This active learning process promotes engagement and can accelerate the learning curve for aspiring programmers.

Furthermore, the reduced risk of errors, access to a wider range of expertise, and increased creativity and innovation are among the additional benefits of leveraging ChatGPT in programming code development. By assisting in code generation and providing insights, ChatGPT helps identify potential errors early on, reducing the risk of bugs and the likelihood of human errors leading to more reliable and robust final code. Moreover, the model can provide access to a vast amount of programming knowledge and expertise, and simulate conversations with experts in various programming languages and paradigms, enabling programmers/developers to tap into a wider range of expertise and exploring different approaches and solutions. This democratization of knowledge, depicted as the ChatGPT's ability to generate code snippets and provide suggestions, facilitates collaboration and fosters creativity and innovation within the programming community (Shneiderman, 2000).

2.1. How Using ChatGPT to Generate Codes Differs From Traditional Programming

Unlike traditional programming, which involves manually coding specific instructions for a computer to follow, ChatGPT utilizes a technique called deep learning to generate responses based on patterns and examples. By training on vast amounts of text data, ChatGPT learns to understand and generate human-like text.

This approach, known as natural language processing (NLP), allows ChatGPT to engage in dynamic and contextually relevant conversations.

One of the key distinctions between ChatGPT and traditional programming lies in the flexibility and adaptability of the model. Instead of relying on rigidly defined rules and explicit instructions, ChatGPT leverages its ability to generalize and infer from patterns in the training data. This enables it to generate responses that go beyond what was explicitly programmed, making it suitable for a wide range of tasks and scenarios.

Furthermore, ChatGPT's training process involves fine-tuning a large pre-trained model with specific data to make it more suitable for conversational interactions. This fine-tuning process helps customize the model's behavior and align it more closely with the desired output.

In more details with this subject, interested readers could refer to rhe paper "Language Models are Unsupervised Multitask Learners" by Radford et al. (2019) which describes the methods and techniques used in training large-scale language models like GPT. Another relevant paper is "Improving Language Understanding by Generative Pre-training" by Radford et al. (2018); this paper introduces the concept of using unsupervised pre-training for language understanding tasks.

2.2. Increased Productivity and Improved Code Quality

ChatGPT's ability to generate code quickly and efficiently can significantly enhance the productivity of developers. By automating repetitive tasks and providing prompt responses to coding queries, ChatGPT streamlines the coding process, allowing developers to focus on more complex and creative aspects of programming (Ray et al. 2023; Sharma 2023). This automation can lead to faster development cycles and more efficient utilization of developers' time and expertise.

Furthermore, ChatGPT's capacity to understand and interpret natural language descriptions of code requirements enables it to swiftly provide relevant code snippets, reducing the time and effort required for manual coding. This capability is particularly valuable in scenarios where rapid prototyping or generating code templates is needed, as ChatGPT can expedite the initial stages of code development (Xiao et al. 2023).

ChatGPT can assist in maintaining code quality by providing accurate and secure code snippets, ultimately contributing to the overall success of programming projects. It offers benefits such as increased productivity, improved code quality, enhanced learning, reduced risk of errors, access to a wider range of expertise, and increased creativity and innovation. Additionally, ChatGPT's ability to analyze code snippets, offer alternative programming perspectives, and identify potential errors or inefficiencies helps in improving code readability, performance, and maintainability. This ultimately leads to the development of more robust and optimized codebases.

In more details, ChatGPT's role in improving code quality is multifaceted. It can help developers identify and correct errors by providing insights into potential issues and suggesting alternative approaches to problem-solving.

Additionally, ChatGPT can assist developers in adhering to best practices by offering recommendations for optimizing code readability, performance, and maintainability (Xiao et al. 2023). By leveraging its understanding of diverse programming paradigms and coding conventions, ChatGPT can contribute to the generation of more standardized and high-quality codebases.

Moreover, ChatGPT's ability to generate more readable and maintainable code can have a positive impact on the long-term maintainability and scalability of software projects. By providing code that aligns with established programming conventions and standards, ChatGPT contributes to the development of robust and sustainable codebases.

2.3. Enhanced Learning and Understanding

ChatGPT's impact on learning and understanding in programming code development is significant. It addresses performance issues by providing real-time feedback and explanations, thereby facilitating the mastery of programming concepts. This interactive learning experience can be particularly beneficial for beginners or those seeking to expand their programming knowledge.

Furthermore, ChatGPT's role in balancing generated code quality with educational value empowers non-programmers to engage with coding concepts and practices. By providing explanations, examples, and contextual understanding, ChatGPT bridges the skills gap and facilitates the acquisition of programming knowledge by individuals from diverse backgrounds.

In addition to empowering non-programmers, ChatGPT plays a vital role in helping developers learn new programming concepts. Additionally, the ability of ChatGPT to help developers understand complex algorithms and get unstuck when working on a problem, or facing challenges, is invaluable since it can provide assistance and aids in problem-solving to overcome obstacles. By breaking down intricate concepts, of complex algorithms, into more digestible explanations and aiding in problem-solving and algorithm-understanding, ChatGPT supports continuous learning and skill development in the programming domain (Xiao et al. 2023).

These capabilities collectively position ChatGPT as a valuable educational and skill-building resource for developers, contributing to the continuous improvement of programming competencies and knowledge acquisition.

Whether empowering non-programmers, bridging the skills gap, or aiding developers in learning new concepts, ChatGPT is at the forefront of fostering a supportive environment for diverse learners and developers alike.

2.4. Reduced Risk of Errors

ChatGPT can significantly contribute to reducing the risk of errors in programming code development. By analyzing code snippets and understanding the context, ChatGPT can help developers identify potential errors before they manifest in the final code. This proactive error detection can save developers time and effort by preventing issues from propagating into the production codebase.

Moreover, ChatGPT's assistance in avoiding and reducing human errors and mistakes is invaluable. By highlighting potential mistakes or pitfalls in coding, ChatGPT acts as a second set of eyes, helping developers improve the reliability and correctness of their code (Xiao et al. 2023). This can lead to more robust and error-resistant codebases.

Furthermore, ChatGPT's ability to generate more reliable and robust code promotes the development of software systems that are less prone to bugs and vulnerabilities.

By offering insights and suggestions for code improvements, ChatGPT enhances the overall quality and reliability of the generated code, reducing the likelihood of software failures and security breaches.

2.5. Access to a Wider Range of Expertise

ChatGPT provides developers with access to a wider range of expertise beyond their individual knowledge and experience. By simulating conversations with experts in various programming languages, paradigms, and domains, ChatGPT can offer insights and guidance from diverse perspectives.

This access to a broader knowledge base enables developers to learn from other developers/peers and tap into the collective wisdom of the programming community. By leveraging ChatGPT's ability to simulate responses akin to experienced programmers, developers can benefit from the expertise of others and gain valuable insights into alternative solutions and approaches.

Additionally, ChatGPT can assist developers in finding solutions to problems that they may not be able to solve on their own. In complex and challenging scenarios, ChatGPT's innovative suggestions and alternative approaches can inspire developers to think outside the box and explore new paths. This access to a wider range of expertise fosters collaboration, creativity, and innovation within the programming community (Shneiderman, 2000).

2.6. Increased Creativity and Innovation

ChatGPT's ability to generate new ideas and stimulate creativity is a significant benefit in programming code generation and development. By offering novel perspectives and alternative solutions, ChatGPT sparks innovation and encourages developers to explore different approaches to problem-solving (Ray et al. 2023; Shneiderman, 2000).

Moreover, ChatGPT's capacity to help developers break out of their usual mindsets and thought patterns is valuable for fostering creativity. By suggesting unconventional solutions and prompting developers to consider alternative strategies, ChatGPT stimulates innovative thinking and opens up new possibilities in code development .

This increased creativity and innovation, facilitated by ChatGPT, can lead to the development of unique and groundbreaking software solutions, pushing the boundaries of what is possible in programming code generation and development.

These benefits demonstrate the transformative potential of ChatGPT in revolutionizing the programming landscape.

3. CHALLENGES AND LIMITATIONS OF USING CHATGPT FOR PROGRAMMING CODE GENERATION

While ChatGPT has demonstrated its immense value in the domain of programming code generation, it is crucial to acknowledge and confront the challenges and ethical considerations linked to its utilization (Challenges, 2023; Key Challenges, 2023). This section delves into these concerns and examines the potential future developments of ChatGPT in the field of programming code generation.

Several key challenges linked to employing ChatGPT in the domain of programming code generation encompass the following:

One of the primary challenges is the model's limited understanding of complex programming concepts, which may result in the generation of suboptimal or incorrect code.

While ChatGPT has been trained on a vast dataset, it may not possess an in-depth understanding of the underlying programming principles and best practices. Therefore, developers must exercise caution and ensure that the generated code aligns with established programming conventions and standards.

Moreover, there is a potential for ChatGPT to generate insecure code if not properly guided or supervised. As the model generates codes based on patterns learned from vast amounts of data, it may inadvertently generate code that contains security vulnerabilities or inefficient implementations. Consequently, thorough code review and testing are essential to validate the generated code and ensure its security and efficiency.

Overreliance on ChatGPT as a programming tool and the lack of transparency and explainability in its decision-making processes are additional challenges that need to be addressed. While ChatGPT can provide valuable insights and suggestions, developers should not solely rely on its outputs. It is crucial to balance the use of ChatGPT with human expertise and critical thinking to ensure the development of high-quality and reliable code. Also, ChatGPT's decision-making process is not easily interpretable, making it challenging to understand how it arrives at specific code suggestions or solutions.

Furthermore, ethical concerns related to the responsible use of ChatGPT and AI tools in programming code development, including issues of bias and fairness, must be carefully considered and mitigated (Ray et al. 2023). For instance, as ChatGPT's responses are learned from large datasets, biases present in the training data can potentially influence the generated code. It is important to be aware of these biases and take steps to address fairness and inclusivity in code generation.

In summary, practical issues related to using ChatGPT for programming code development include the model's limited understanding of complex programming concepts, ethical concerns related to responsible AI use in programming code development, must be carefully taken into consideration. Furthermore, overreliance on ChatGPT may hinder skill development, and there is a lack of transparency in decision-making, which can pose challenges in ensuring the accuracy and security of the generated code.

ChatGPT represents a groundbreaking advancement in natural language processing and has the potential to significantly impact programming code development. Understanding its capabilities, benefits, and challenges is crucial for harnessing its potential effectively and responsibly. In the following subsections, detailed explanations of these challenges is provided.

3.1. Limited Understanding of Programming Concepts

ChatGPT, while a powerful language model, may face limitations in its understanding of intricate/long programming concepts (Sethi et al. 2024; Brown et al. 2020). It is important to note that ChatGPT's understanding of programming concepts is not exhaustive and may vary depending on the complexity of the concept being discussed (Brown et al. 2020). In some instances, ChatGPT's comprehension of certain programming concepts may be limited, leading to potential challenges in generating code that adheres to best practices and idiomatic conventions.

Furthermore, ChatGPT may struggle to grasp the nuances specific to certain programming languages (Sharma et al. 2023a; 2023b; Brown et al. 2020). The idiosyncrasies and intricacies inherent in different programming languages can pose challenges for ChatGPT in accurately comprehending and generating code that aligns with the intended language's conventions.

3.2. Potential for Generating Incorrect or Insecure Code

One of the main concerns with using ChatGPT for code generation is the potential for generating code that contains errors (Brown et al. 2020). While ChatGPT is designed to generate code, it is not infallible and may occasionally produce code snippets with bugs or syntax issues (Sharma et al. 2023c; Brown et al. 2020). Therefore, developers need to carefully review and validate the code generated by ChatGPT to ensure its correctness and reliability.

Additionally, there is a risk that ChatGPT may generate code that is vulnerable to security attacks. The lack of robustness in the generated code could expose applications to potential security risks, making it crucial for developers to thoroughly assess the code's security implications. Furthermore, non-compliance with coding standards and regulations may arise if ChatGPT generates code that does not adhere to industry-specific guidelines, necessitating additional scrutiny and validation.

3.3. Overreliance on ChatGPT

The availability of ChatGPT as a code-generating tool may, particularly with its periodic updates with more expanded datasets, lead to developers becoming overly reliant on the model, potentially hindering their independent programming development skills, as well as their independent problem-solving and critical thinking skills. Overreliance on ChatGPT may discourage developers from honing their own coding abilities and problem-solving skills, as they may solely rely on the model's output.

Furthermore, the generated code produced by ChatGPT may pose challenges for developers in terms of comprehension. The complexity and structure of the generated code may make it difficult for developers to understand its logic, potentially leading to issues during debugging and maintenance. Moreover, debugging code generated by ChatGPT can be challenging if developers lack a deep understanding of the intricacies embedded within the generated code.

3.4. Lack of Transparency and Explainability

Transparency and explainability are crucial factors in the use of ChatGPT for code generation. One of the limitations of ChatGPT, which is an opaque and complex model, is its inability to provide comprehensive explanations for the code it generates (Brown et al. 2020). Developers may struggle to understand the rationale behind ChatGPT's code generation decisions and to identify potential errors or biases, leading to potential difficulties in assessing the reliability and appropriateness of the generated code.

Moreover, ChatGPT may not provide insights into the decision-making processes that underlie its code generation. This lack of transparency makes it challenging for developers to comprehend the logic and reasoning behind the generated code, potentially impeding their ability to effectively modify or improve it. Furthermore, understanding the broader implications of the generated code may be difficult due to the limited insights provided by ChatGPT.

3.5. Ethical Concerns and Responsible AI Use

The use of ChatGPT raises a number of important ethical concerns. As ChatGPT continues to develop, it is important to be aware of these concerns and to develop safeguards to prevent the misuse of this technology. In details, the use of ChatGPT to develop programming codes may raise ethical concerns, such as the issues of (Crawford et al. 2023; Safdar et al. 2020):

Privacy and Security

ChatGPT has the capability to handle sensitive personal information, including medical records, financial data, and private messages. It is crucial to prioritize the protection and confidentiality of this information, ensuring it remains secure and private. More, the ethical principle known as the "right to be forgotten" empowers individuals to request the removal of outdated or irrelevant personal information from internet search results or websites. Striking a balance between this right and the essential aspects of accurate record-keeping, transparency, and accountability poses a significant ethical challenge in the realm of AI tools. On the other hand, online anonymity, which allows individuals to participate in digital activities without disclosing their true identity, presents a dual-edged ethical challenge. While it safeguards privacy and encourages free expression, it also opens avenues for harmful behaviors such as trolling, cyberbullying, or criminal activities. Navigating the complexities of weighing the benefits against the risks of online anonymity stands as a challenging ethical dilemma in the use of ChatGPT and AI tools.

Authorship

The use of ChatGPT for code generation presents significant ethical concerns, particularly regarding authorship. Authorship is a complex issue when using ChatGPT for code generation. Determining the authorship of code generated by ChatGPT raises questions regarding intellectual property rights. The question of whether the person who prompted ChatGPT or the model itself is the author of the generated code challenges traditional concepts of intellectual property rights (Brown et al. 2020). This ambiguity calls for a reevaluation of existing frameworks to address the complexities surrounding ownership and authorship in AI-generated code. For instance, if a ChatGPT model is used to generate code, who is the author of that code? Is it the person who prompted the ChatGPT model, or is it the ChatGPT model itself? This is a complex question that has no easy answer. Determining authorship of code generated by ChatGPT raises complex questions, challenging traditional concepts of intellectual property.

Responsibility and Accountability

With the increasing potency and prevalence of ChatGPT, it becomes imperative to ascertain accountability for the model's actions and decisions. This encompasses determining ownership of the data utilized to train ChatGPT, identifying responsibility for the output it generates, and establishing accountability for any adverse consequences resulting from the use of ChatGPT.

For instance, if a ChatGPT model generates code that contains errors or that is used for malicious purposes, who is responsible? Is it the person who prompted the ChatGPT model, or is it the developer of the ChatGPT model? This is another complex question that has no easy answer. Issues of responsibility emerge when errors or misuse occur, prompting considerations of accountability for both developers and ChatGPT creators. Determining accountability becomes intricate when deciding if it rests with the user who prompted ChatGPT or the developer of the ChatGPT model, necessitating a careful consideration of the roles and obligations of both parties (Brown et al. 2020). Also, it is important to hold developers of ChatGPT models accountable for the way that their models are used. This could involve developing ethical guidelines for the development and use of ChatGPT models. Additionally, it could involve developing mechanisms for reporting and addressing misuse of ChatGPT models. Holding ChatGPT developers accountable necessitates the establishment of ethical guidelines and mechanisms for reporting and addressing misuse. Developers should be held accountable for their models' ethical deployment, emphasizing the need for frameworks to ensure responsible

AI practices (Brown et al. 2020). Addressing potential misuse and the impact on intellectual property are essential aspects of fostering responsible and ethical AI use.

Transparency

Transparency emerges as a crucial element in ChatGPT development and deployment. This involves openness about the training data, particularly when sensitive information is involved, and clarity regarding the inner workings and decision-making processes of ChatGPT models to address ethical concerns and ensure accountability (Brown et al. 2020). In other words, ChatGPT models are often trained on large datasets of text and code, and these datasets may contain sensitive or confidential information. It is important to be transparent about the data that is used to train ChatGPT models. Additionally, it is important to be transparent about the way that ChatGPT models work. Transparent practices regarding data used for ChatGPT training and model functioning become essential to address ethical concerns.

The Potential for Bias

The potential for bias in ChatGPT models is a critical ethical concern. ChatGPT models are trained on large datasets of text and code that may contain prejudiced language, stereotypes and biases. If these datasets are biased, then the ChatGPT model may accidentally learn these biases and also be biased. This can lead to issues of fairness and diversity in software development. The risk of bias arises if ChatGPT is trained on datasets that are not representative, potentially leading to biased code generation. Also, the generated code may reflect biases present in the training data, affecting diversity and fairness in software development. Addressing bias in training data and ensuring fairness in code generation are vital steps in responsible ChatGPT use.

The Potential for Misuse

The utilization of ChatGPT models for code generation introduces concerns regarding the potential for harmful or unethical outcomes. First, ChatGPT may be misused to generate code with malicious intent, creating potential risks such as the creation of deepfakes or misinformation. Similarly, malicious actors could leverage ChatGPT to generate code for hacking or cybercrime, posing threats to digital security.

Beyond the risk of harmful code generation, ChatGPT's influence on human behavior and decision-making triggers concerns regarding individual autonomy and agency. Additionally, its adeptness at producing text indistinguishable from human-generated content, as well as its ability to copy the writing styles of people, raises ethical questions about users' awareness during interactions and the implications of such deception.

The Impact on Intellectual Property

The impact of ChatGPT on intellectual property is a complex issue that requires careful consideration. Ownership of code generated by ChatGPT is ambiguous, and could lead to potential legal disputes over intellectual property rights. In other words, it is not clear who owns the copyright to code that is generated by a ChatGPT model. If a ChatGPT model is used to generate code for a commercial product, then it is not clear who owns the copyright to that code. This could lead to legal disputes over ownership of intellectual property. The legal landscape may need to adapt to address challenges arising from the unique nature of code generation by AI models like ChatGPT.

The Impact on the Job Market

Thus, the evolving capabilities of ChatGPT may impact the job market for human programmers.

As ChatGPT models become more sophisticated, it is possible that they could automate some of the tasks that are currently performed by human programmers.

This could lead potentially to changes in the job market, as the evolving capabilities of ChatGPT raise concerns about potential automation of certain programming tasks, impacting job market dynamics and leading to replace some programming jobs by ChatGPT. Nonetheless, and on the other side, the development and maintenance of ChatGPT models may also create new job opportunities for developers specializing in AI.

The long-term implications on the job market require careful consideration and proactive measures to ensure a smooth transition and the continued growth of the industry.

Addressing these challenges can elevate ChatGPT's performance, reliability, and utility, paving the way for advanced and responsible AI-driven applications in the realm of programming code generation.

4. EXAMPLES OF PROGRAMMING CODE GENERATIONS

4.1. Example 1: Code Generation for Data Analysis

ChatGPT is an advanced language model that can generate code based on natural language inputs. By leveraging its capabilities, data analysts can automate the process of generating code for data analysis tasks, saving time and effort.

How ChatGPT Streamlines Data Analysis Code

ChatGPT can assist data analysts in various ways when it comes to code generation for data analysis. It can generate code snippets for common data manipulation tasks, such as data cleaning, data wrangling, and data transformation. By simply describing their desired outcome or providing specific instructions, data analysts can obtain code that performs the necessary operations.

Furthermore, ChatGPT can also generate code for statistical analysis, machine learning algorithms, and data visualization. For example, data analysts can describe the statistical tests they want to perform or the machine learning models they want to implement, and ChatGPT can generate the corresponding code.

Real-World Applications and Outcomes

The application of ChatGPT in code generation for data analysis has yielded promising results in real-world scenarios. Data analysts have reported significant time savings and increased productivity by utilizing ChatGPT's code generation capabilities. By automating repetitive coding tasks, analysts can focus more on data interpretation and analysis, leading to more accurate and insightful results.

Moreover, ChatGPT's ability to generate code based on natural language inputs has made it accessible to users with varying levels of coding expertise. This democratization of code generation enables non-programmers to leverage data analysis tools and techniques effectively.

4.2. Example 2: Using ChatGPT to Generate Code for a Web Page or Application

Web application projects involve the development of interactive websites or web-based software. These projects typically require writing extensive code for various functionalities, such as user interfaces, database integration, and server-side logic.

ChatGPT can play a significant role in automating the code generation process for these projects.

ChatGPT was incorporated into the web development process to generate code for different aspects of the web application. For instance, it can generate HTML and CSS code for designing user interfaces, as well as JavaScript code for implementing interactive behavior.

By providing natural language instructions or specifications, developers can obtain code snippets that fulfill their requirements. This streamlines the development process and reduces the time and effort required for manual coding (Maharajan et al. 2023; Sharma and Bhatnagar 2023; Devlin et al. 2018; Vaswani et al. 2017).

The utilization of ChatGPT for code generation in web development offers several benefits. Firstly, it accelerates the development process by automating code generation, allowing developers to focus on higher-level design and functionality. Secondly, it enhances collaboration among developers by providing a more intuitive and accessible way to communicate coding requirements. However, there are also challenges associated with using ChatGPT in this context. One challenge is ensuring that the generated code aligns with best practices and security standards. Additionally, fine-tuning the model to cater specifically to web development tasks may be necessary to improve code generation accuracy (Vaswani et al. 2017).

Apart from code generation, ChatGPT can also automate various web-related tasks. For example, it can assist in generating the necessary configuration files, setting up database connections, or implementing API integrations.

As the utilization of ChatGPT for code generation can improve the code efficiency, reduce time-to-market, and enhance user experiences, the lessons learned from the application of ChatGPT in web development include the importance of providing clear and specific instructions, validating the generated code, and iterating on the model's training to improve its performance for web development tasks.

4.3. Example 3: Using ChatGPT to Debug Code

Debugging is an essential aspect of software development, and ChatGPT can provide assistance in identifying and resolving coding issues.

ChatGPT can be employed in the debugging process to identify and propose solutions for the coding issue. Developers can describe the problem or provide snippets of code to ChatGPT, which can then provide insights and suggestions on potential causes and fixes.

During the debugging process, developers might encounter challenges such as ambiguous error messages or complex logic (Tanwar et al. 2023). ChatGPT can assist in interpreting error messages and providing alternative approaches to resolve the issue.

The effectiveness of ChatGPT in the debugging process has both benefits and challenges. ChatGPT can provide alternative perspectives and creative solutions, leading to quicker bug resolution. It can also assist developers in understanding complex code by providing explanations and clarifications.

However, one challenge is that ChatGPT's suggestions should be thoroughly evaluated and tested before implementation, as they may not always lead to the desired outcome. Additionally, ensuring that ChatGPT understands the context and specifics of the code can be a challenge in itself.

The experience of using ChatGPT for debugging in this particular case offers valuable lessons. Developers should use ChatGPT as a tool to boost their debugging process rather than rely solely on its suggestions. Collaborating with other developers and validating ChatGPT's suggestions through testing are crucial steps in the debugging journey.

4.4. Example 4: Using ChatGPT to Learn a New Programming Language

Learning a programming language can be challenging, but ChatGPT can provide guidance, examples, and explanations to facilitate the learning journey.

ChatGPT can provide valuable resources and assistance for learning a new programming language. It can generate example code snippets, explain language syntax and concepts, and offer guidance on best practices. Additionally, ChatGPT can answer specific questions related to the language and provide insights on common pitfalls and debugging techniques.

By interacting with ChatGPT, learners can receive real-time feedback and suggestions for improvement, enhancing their understanding and proficiency in the new programming language.

Using ChatGPT as a learning tool for acquiring a new programming language offers several benefits. Learners can access a vast amount of knowledge and expertise in a conversational manner, making the learning process more engaging and interactive. Additionally, ChatGPT's ability to adapt to the learner's level of expertise ensures personalized and tailored assistance. However, challenges may arise when ChatGPT misinterprets or provides inaccurate information. Learners should be mindful of verifying the information and seeking additional resources to supplement their understanding.

The experience of using ChatGPT as a learning tool for a new programming language yields valuable lessons. Learners should actively participate in the learning process, ask specific questions, and critically evaluate the information provided by ChatGPT. Additionally, combining ChatGPT with traditional learning resources and practical coding exercises can enhance the overall learning experience.

4.5. Example 5: ChatGPT in Game Development

ChatGPT can contribute to enhancing various aspects of game development processes and ultimately achieve better gaming experiences.

ChatGPT can assist game developers in several ways to streamline and enhance the game development process. It can generate code snippets for game mechanics, character behaviors, and interactive elements. By describing the desired game mechanics or providing specific instructions, developers can obtain code that implements those functionalities. Furthermore, ChatGPT can provide creative ideas and suggestions for game design, level design, and storytelling elements. Game developers can engage in a conversational exchange with AI tools to explore different concepts and iterate on their game designs (Silver et al. 2016).

Also, by leveraging ChatGPT's capabilities, game developers can create more immersive and engaging gaming experiences. ChatGPT can generate interactive dialogue and narrative elements that enhance storytelling in games. It can also assist in creating dynamic and intelligent non-player characters with natural language interactions, adding depth and realism to the game world. Additionally, ChatGPT can generate code for procedural generation of game content, such as terrain, quests, and puzzles. This enables developers to create vast and dynamic game worlds with unique and varied experiences for players (Silver et al. 2016).

Integrating game development with ChatGPT can result in innovative gameplay mechanics, captivating narratives, and immersive gaming experiences. This is depicted by the potential of ChatGPT to push the boundaries of game development and provide players with unique and memorable experiences. The application of ChatGPT in game development presents the importance of balancing automation with human creativity, validating the generated content through playtesting, and iterating the model's training to align with specific game development requirements (Shneiderman, 2000).

5. BEST PRACTICES FOR USING CHATGPT FOR PROGRAMMING CODE DEVELOPMENT

The code development feature in ChatGPT allows code snippets or even longer code blocks to be generated based on the provided input. The language model capabilities of ChatGPT are utilized to understand the intent behind the code development task and generate code accordingly. One crucial aspect to consider is the quality of code generated by ChatGPT. The clarity, correctness, and efficiency of the generated code snippets are evaluated, identifying instances where ChatGPT excels in generating high-quality code and areas where suboptimal results may be produced. As the range of programming languages and frameworks for which ChatGPT can generate code is explored, any limitations or biases in the support for certain languages or frameworks must be taken into consideration.

The effectiveness of ChatGPT in code development could be assessed by analyzing how well it understands the context and intent behind the code development task. This involves evaluating its ability to accurately interpret user instructions and generate code that aligns with the desired functionality. In addition, the adaptability and customization options available in ChatGPT for code development must be exploited. Thus, it is necessary to analyze and to focus on how developers can fine-tune or guide the model to generate code that meets specific requirements or follows certain coding conventions. The challenges and limitations associated with using ChatGPT for code development are crucial to address. This includes discussing potential issues such as lack of domain-specific knowledge, difficulty in handling complex code logic, or limitations in generating code for certain specialized tasks. This considers how it can enhance developer productivity, assist in rapid prototyping, or introduce new possibilities for code generation. By incorporating this detailed analysis of the code development feature in ChatGPT, a comprehensive evaluation is provided of its capabilities and limitations in generating code.

This section will delineate the application of best practices for utilizing ChatGPT in programming code development to enhance interaction. The details are provided in the subsections.

5.1. Clearly Define the Task (Prompt Engineering for ChatGPT)

Prompt engineering is a crucial aspect of optimizing user experience and ensuring efficient communication with AI models like ChatGPT. Prompt engineering techniques can significantly influence the quality and relevance of AI-generated codes, as utilizing prompt engineering techniques enables users to steer the AI model toward producing codes that are more precise, pertinent, and beneficial (Prompt engineering, 2023; Rawat et al. (2023). The utilization of prompt engineering in ChatGPT conversations to optimize interaction will be outlined in this section.

When defining a coding task for ChatGPT, the following strategies and prompt engineering practices can enhance its accuracy and relevance and optimize the interaction:

Clear and Concise Task Description

Providing a clear and concise communication of the coding task description is essential for accurate and relevant code generation by ChatGPT. This involves articulating the task requirements in a way that minimizes ambiguity and confusion, facilitating more precise outputs from the model.

Break Down Complex Tasks

Dividing complex coding tasks into smaller, manageable components enhances ChatGPT's ability to provide more focused and precise solutions. This approach enables the model to tackle intricate problems step by step, thereby improving overall code quality and providing more focused and precise solutions.

Provide Relevant Examples

Offering ChatGPT relevant examples related to the coding task enhances its understanding and ability to generate contextually appropriate code that aligns with the specific requirements. Examples serve as a guide for the model, aligning its output with specific requirements and leading to more contextually appropriate code.

Start with Clear and Specific Prompts

To get the looked-for response, it is essential to have unambiguous and explicit prompts. Unclear prompts may result in responses that are irrelevant or unsatisfactory.

Provide Context and Background Information

When needed, provide context or background details to aid ChatGPT in grasping the subject matter and producing well-informed responses (Prompt engineering, 2023).

Specify Desired Format and Structure

Direct ChatGPT toward a particular response structure or format to make sure that the output aligns with your expectations.

Apply Constraints and Limitations

Establish limitations on the response, such as scope, timeframes, or character limits, aiming to uphold focus and conciseness (Prompt GPT, 2023).

Iterative Prompting

Should the initial response fall short of expectations, the prompt can be refined or broken down into smaller sub-queries to direct ChatGPT to the desired outcomes.

Through the integration of prompt engineering techniques into your ChatGPT conversations, the quality and relevance of the AI-generated codes can be markedly enhanced. With increasing proficiency in crafting effective prompts, better utilization of ChatGPT's capabilities to address specific needs will be achievable.

5.2. Provide Relevant Context

Providing ChatGPT with information about the project, the programming language being used, and any relevant libraries or frameworks allows the model to tailor its responses to specific project requirements and adhere to coding conventions. Contextual information aids ChatGPT in tailoring its responses to align with project-specific requirements and coding conventions.

Providing links to relevant documentation assists ChatGPT in sourcing accurate information, adhering to established programming practices, and ensuring alignment with established programming practices and standards. Providing ChatGPT with access to the existing codebase enhances its contextual understanding, enabling more coherent and consistent code generation.

5.3. Verify the Generated Code

Conducting a meticulous review of the code generated by ChatGPT is essential. This step helps identify and rectify any inaccuracies, ensuring the produced code meets high-quality standards and adheres to coding best practices.

After reviewing the generated code, thorough testing is necessary to validate its functionality. Comprehensive testing helps identify and rectify potential errors, ensuring the code performs as intended in different scenarios.

Swiftly correcting any errors identified during the review and testing phases is crucial. This ensures that the final code meets the required standards and functions as intended in a real-world context.

5.4. ChatGPT: A Tool, Not a Replacement for Human Programmers

ChatGPT is a powerful tool that can help developers, but it is not a replacement for human programmers. Emphasizing the complementary role of ChatGPT reinforces the importance of the collaborative nature and the human expertise in the coding process. Human programmers play a vital role in guiding and refining the outputs generated by ChatGPT.

Developers should use ChatGPT to enhance their own skills and knowledge. ChatGPT serves as a supplementary resource, providing insights and assistance in coding tasks, but should not replace human intuition, creativity, and critical thinking (Shneiderman, 2000).

In other words, cautioning against relying solely on ChatGPT reinforces the importance of human intuition, creativity, and critical thinking involvement in coding endeavors. Developers should utilize the AI as a supportive tool rather than depending entirely on its code generation capabilities (V. et al. 2023; Sharma and Dadheech, 2023; Sharma and Mathur, 2023; Shneiderman, 2000).

5.5. Limitations of ChatGPT

ChatGPT is still under development, and may not be able to understand all programming concepts neither generate perfect code; recognizing that is essential as it highlights one of this tool's limitations. Acknowledging the evolving nature of ChatGPT underscores the importance of continuous improvements and updates to enhance its capabilities over time.

However, developers should exercise caution in relying on interpretations due to ChatGPT's limited understanding of all programming concepts. To ensure accurate and contextually appropriate code, it is crucial to supplement ChatGPT's outputs with human understanding.

Additionally, being aware of potential deviations from idiomatic and best practices encourages developers to scrutinize and refine the generated code, aligning it with established coding standards. In summary, recognizing ChatGPT's developmental stage, understanding its limitations, and being vigilant about potential code variations are key considerations in its effective utilization.

6. CONCLUSION

This chapter has provided a comprehensive overview of the benefits and challenges of using ChatGPT for programming code development. As highlighted throughout the chapter, ChatGPT offers numerous advantages when it comes to code generation, debugging, and learning programming languages. However, as with any technology, there are also several challenges and ethical considerations that need to be addressed.

ChatGPT has the potential to enhance productivity, improve code quality, reduce error risks, and democratize programming access to those without formal computer science backgrounds. However, we also identified potential challenges such as limited comprehension of programming concepts, potential generation of erroneous or insecure code, over-reliance of ChatGPT, lack of transparency and explainability, ethical concerns, and the future impact on the job market.

In terms of future research, it would be useful to explore how ChatGPT can be further developed to overcome its limitations and to investigate the impact of ChatGPT on the job market and the broader programming community. It is anticipated that ChatGPT and other AI-powered tools will have a profound impact on the future of programming and may democratize programming, making it more widely accessible, particularly among non-experts in computer science.

Looking ahead, it is important to approach the usage of ChatGPT and other AI-driven technologies in programming with a thoughtful and responsible mindset. While AI-powered technologies offer numerous benefits and opportunities, they must be used in a way that is both ethical and transparent. By taking a proactive approach to AI development and usage, it could be possible to ensure that ChatGPT and other AI-driven technologies continue to drive innovation in programming code development and other domains.

Largely, ChatGPT is an exciting development in the field of programming code development. It presents numerous benefits and opportunities for developers to enhance their workflows and increase their productivity. However, to realize the full potential of ChatGPT, it is critical to develop a sophisticated understanding of its benefits and challenges and to approach its usage in a responsible and thoughtful manner.

REFERENCES

Ali, M. J., & Djalilian, A. (2023, March). Readership awareness series–paper 4: Chatbots and ChatGPT-ethical considerations in scientific publications. In *Seminars in Ophthalmology* (pp. 1–2). Taylor & Francis.

Baidoo-Anu, D., & Owusu Ansah, L. (2023). Education in the Era of Generative Artificial Intelligence (AI): Understanding the Potential Benefits of ChatGPT in Promoting Teaching and Learning. Available at: *SSRN* 4337484. DOI: 10.2139/ssrn.4337484

Biswas, S. (2023c). Role of ChatGPT in computer programming.: ChatGPT in computer programming. Mesopotamian J. Comput. Sci., 8–16.

Biswas, S. S. (2023a). Potential use of Chat GPT in global warming. *Annals of Biomedical Engineering*, 51(6), 1–2. DOI: 10.1007/s10439-023-03171-8 PMID: 36856927

Biswas, S. S. (2023b). Role of Chat GPT in public health. *Annals of Biomedical Engineering*, 51(5), 1–2. DOI: 10.1007/s10439-023-03172-7 PMID: 36920578

Brown, T. B., Mann, B., Ryder, N., Subbiah, M., Kaplan, J., Dhariwal, P., Neelakantan, A., Shyam, P., Sastry, G., Askell, A., Agarwal, S., Herbert-Voss, A., Krueger, G., Henighan, T., Child, R., Ramesh, A., Ziegler, D. M., Wu, J., Winter, C., . . . Amodei, D. (2020). Language models are few-shot learners. arXiv preprint arXiv:2005.14165v4.

Challenges. (2023). https://www.cyfirma.com/outofband/chatgpt-ai-in-security-testing-opportunities-and-challenges/

Cotton, D. R., Cotton, P. A., & Shipway, J. R. (2023). Chatting and Cheating: Ensuring Academic Integrity in the Era of ChatGPT. *Innovations in Education and Teaching International*, 1–12.

Crawford, J., Cowling, M., & Allen, K. A. (2023). Leadership is needed for ethical ChatGPT: Character, assessment, and learning using artificial intelligence (AI). *Journal of University Teaching & Learning Practice*, 20(3), 2. DOI: 10.53761/1.20.3.02

Devlin, J., Chang, M. W., Lee, K., & Toutanova, K. (2018). Bert: Pre-training of deep bidirectional transformers for language understanding. arXiv preprint arXiv:1810.04805.

Frieder, S., Pinchetti, L., Griffiths, R. R., Salvatori, T., Lukasiewicz, T., Petersen, P. C., Chevalier, A., & Berner, J. (2023). Mathematical Capabilities of ChatGPT. arXiv preprint: arXiv:2301.13867.

Haleem, A., Javaid, M., & Singh, R. P. (2023). *An Era of ChatGPT as a Significant Futuristic Support Tool: A Study on Features*. Abilities, and Challenges, Bench-Council Transactions on Benchmarks, Standards and Evaluations.

Jalil, S., Rafi, S., LaToza, T. D., Moran, K., & Lam, W. (2023). Chatgpt and Software Testing Education: Promises & Perils. arXiv preprint arXiv:2302.03287. DOI: 10.1109/ICSTW58534.2023.00078

Kashefi, A., & Mukerji, T. (2023). ChatGPT for Programming Numerical Methods. arXiv. preprint arXiv:2303.12093.

Key Challenges. (2023). https://www.makeuseof.com/openai-chatgpt-biggest-probelms/

Maharajan, K., Kumar, A. V., El Emary, I. M., Sharma, P., Latip, R., Mishra, N., Dutta, A., Manjunatha Rao, L., & Sharma, M. (2023). Blockchain methods and data-driven decision making with autonomous transportation. In Kumar, R., Abdul Hamid, A., & Binti Ya'akub, N. (Eds.), *Effective AI, blockchain, and e-governance applications for knowledge discovery and management* (pp. 176–194). IGI Global. DOI: 10.4018/978-1-6684-9151-5.ch012

Mathew, A. (2023). Is artificial intelligence a world changer? A case study of OpenAI's Chat GPT. *Recent Prog. Sci. Technol*, 5, 35–42. DOI: 10.9734/bpi/rpst/v5/18240D

McGee, R. W. (2023a). Annie Chan: Three Short Stories Written with Chat GPT. Available at: *SSRN* 4359403.

McGee, R. W. (2023b). Is Chat GPT biased against conservatives? An empirical study. *Empir.Stud.*

Naumova, E. N. (2023). A mistake-find exercise: A teacher's tool to engage with information innovations, ChatGPT, and their analogs. J. Publ. Health Pol. 1–6.

Open, A. I. (2023). OpenAI GPT4. Retrieved from https://openai.com/research/gpt-4

Prasad, G. A., Kumar, A. V., Sharma, P., Irawati, I. D., D. V., C., Musirin, I. B., Abdullah, H. M., & Rao L, M. (2023). Artificial intelligence in computer science: An overview of current trends and future directions. In S. Rajest, B. Singh, A. Obaid, R. Regin, & K. Chinnusamy (Eds.), Advances in artificial and human intelligence in the modern era (pp. 43-60). IGI Global. DOI: 10.4018/979-8-3693-1301-5.ch002

Prompt, G. P. T. (n.d.). https://github.com/promptslab/Awesome-Prompt-Engineering

Prompt engineering. (n.d.). https://help.openai.com/en/articles/6654000-best-practices-for-promptengineering-with-openai-api

Radford, A., Narasimhan, K., Salimans, T., & Sutskever, I. (2018). Improving Language Understanding by Generative Pre-training. https://s3-us-west-2.amazonaws.com/openai-assets/research-covers/language-unsupervised/language_understanding_paper.pdf

Radford, A., Wu, J., Child, R., Luan, D., Amodei, D., & Sutskever, I. (2019). Language Models are Unsupervised Multitask Learners. OpenAI Blog. Retrieved from https://cdn.openai.com/better-language-models/language_models_are_unsupervised_multitask_learners.pdf

Rawat, P., Bhardwaj, A., Lamba, N., Sharma, P., Kumawat, P., & Sharma, P. (2023). Arduino based IoT mini weather station. *SKIT Research Journal*, 13(2), 34–41. DOI: 10.47904/IJSKIT.13.2.2023.34-41

Ray, P. P. (2023). ChatGPT: A comprehensive review on background, applications, key challenges, bias, ethics, limitations and future scope. *Internet of Things and Cyber-Physical Systems*, 3, 121–154. DOI: 10.1016/j.iotcps.2023.04.003

Rudolph, J., Tan, S., & Tan, S. (2023). ChatGPT: Bullshit spewer or the end of traditional assessments in higher education? *J.Appl. Learn. Teach.*, 6(1).

Safdar, N. M., Banja, J. D., & Meltzer, C. C. (2020). Ethical considerations in artificial intelligence. *European Journal of Radiology*, 122, 108768. DOI: 10.1016/j.ejrad.2019.108768 PMID: 31786504

Sethi, S. S., Sharma, P., & Kumar, A. V. (2023). New developments in the implementation of IoT in agriculture. *SN Computer Science*, 4(3), 503. DOI: 10.1007/s42979-023-01896-w

Sethi, S. S., Sharma, P., & Kumar, A. V. (2024). ChatGPT and the moralities of large language modelling in research publications. In Bansal, R., Ngah, A., Chakir, A., & Pruthi, N. (Eds.), *Leveraging ChatGPT and artificial intelligence for effective customer engagement* (pp. 233–258). IGI Global. DOI: 10.4018/979-8-3693-0815-8.ch014

Sharma, P. (2023). Utilizing explainable artificial intelligence to address deep learning in biomedical domain. In Bandyopadhyay, S. K., Mukhopadhyay, S., & Sengupta, S. (Eds.), *Medical data analysis and processing using explainable artificial intelligence* (pp. 19–38). Taylor & Francis. DOI: 10.1201/9781003257721-2

Sharma, P., & Bhatnagar, N. (2023). Passenger authentication and ticket verification at airport using QR code scanner. *SKIT Research Journal*, 13(2), 10–13. DOI: 10.47904/IJSKIT.13.1.2023.10-12

Sharma, P., & Dadheech, P. (2023). Modern-age agriculture with artificial intelligence: A review emphasizing crop yield prediction. *EVERGREEN Joint Journal of Novel Carbon Resource Sciences & Green Asia Strategy*, 10(4), 2570–2582. DOI: 10.5109/7160906

Sharma, P., Dadheech, P., Aneja, N., & Aneja, S. (2023b). Predicting agriculture yields based on machine learning using regression and deep learning. *IEEE Access : Practical Innovations, Open Solutions*, 11, 111255–111264. DOI: 10.1109/ACCESS.2023.3321861

Sharma, P., Dadheech, P., & Senthil Kumar Senthil, A. V. (2023a). AI-enabled crop recommendation system based on soil and weather patterns. In Gupta, R., Jain, A., Wang, J., Bharti, S., & Patel, S. (Eds.), *Artificial intelligence tools and technologies for smart farming and agriculture practices* (pp. 184–199). IGI Global. DOI: 10.4018/978-1-6684-8516-3.ch010

Sharma, P., Kapadiya, D., & Bhardwaj, A. (2023c). Efficient note sharing model for collaborative learning. *SKIT Research Journal*, 13(2), 42–46. DOI: 10.47904/IJSKIT.13.2.2023.42-46

Sharma, P., & Mathur, P. (2023). Machine learning-based stock market forecasting using recurrent neural network. In 2023 9th International Conference on Smart Computing and Communications (ICSCC) (pp. 600-605). IEEE. DOI: 10.1109/ICSCC59169.2023.10335083

Sharma, P., & Rathi, Y. (2016). Efficient density-based clustering using automatic parameter detection. In *Proceedings of the International Conference on Computational Intelligence and Data Science (ICCIDS '16)* (pp. 463-471). Springer. DOI: 10.1007/978-981-10-0767-5_46

Shneiderman, B. (2000, March). Creating creativity: User interfaces for supporting innovation. *ACM Transactions on Computer-Human Interaction*, 7(1), 114–138. DOI: 10.1145/344949.345077

Silver, D., Huang, A., Maddison, C., Guez, A., Sifre, L., van den Driessche, G., Schrittwieser, J., Antonoglou, I., Panneershelvam, V., Lanctot, M., Dieleman, S., Grewe, D., Nham, J., Kalchbrenner, N., Sutskever, I., Lillicrap, T., Leach, M., Kavukcuoglu, K., Graepel, T., & Hassabis, D. (2016). Mastering the game of Go with deep neural networks and tree search. *Nature*, 529(7587), 484–489. DOI: 10.1038/nature16961 PMID: 26819042

Surameery, N.M.S., & Shakor, M.Y. (2023). Use chat GPT to solve programming bugs. Int. J. Inf. Technol. Comput. Eng., 3(1), 17–22.

Tanwar, A., Sharma, P., Pandey, A., & Kumar, S. (2023). Intrusion detection system based ameliorated technique of pattern matching. In *Proceedings of the 4th International Conference on Information Management & Machine Intelligence (ICIMMI '22)* (pp. 1-4). Association for Computing Machinery. DOI: 10.1145/3590837.3590947

V., M. V., Kumar, A. S., Sharma, P., Kaur, S., Saleh, O. S., Chennamma, H., & Chaturvedi, A. (2023). AI-equipped IoT applications in high-tech agriculture using machine learning. In A. Khang (Ed.), Handbook of research on AI-equipped IoT applications in high-tech agriculture (pp. 38-64). IGI Global. DOI: 10.4018/978-1-6684-9231-4.ch003

Vaswani, A., Shazeer, N., Parmar, N., Uszkoreit, J., Jones, L., Gomez, A. N., Kaiser, Ł., & Polosukhin, I. (2017). Attention is all you need. In Advances in neural information processing systems, 30 (pp. 5998-6008).

Xiao, F., Zhao, P., Sha, H., Yang, D., & Warschauer, M. (2023). Conversational agents in language learning. *Journal of China Computer-Assisted Language Learning*. Advance online publication. DOI: 10.1515/jccall-2022-0032

Zhou, C., Li, Q., Li, C., Yu, J., Liu, Y., Wang, G., . . . Zhang, K. (2023). A Comprehensive Survey on Pretrained Foundation Models: A History from Bert to ChatGPT. arXiv preprint arXiv:2302.09419.

Zhuo, T. Y., Huang, Y., Chen, C., & Xing, Z. (2023). Exploring AI Ethics of ChatGPT: A Diagnostic Analysis. arXiv preprint: arXiv:2301.12867.

Chapter 10
Security Concerns With ChatGPT and Other AI Tools

A. Anju
KCG College of Technology, India

Adline Freeda
https://orcid.org/0009-0002-3335-0907
KCG College of Technology, India

Krithikaa Venket
https://orcid.org/0009-0003-8445-4332
KCG College of Technology, India

ABSTRACT

It is crucial to discuss ChatGPT's safety, confidentiality, and ethical consequences despite its enormous potential in a variety of fields, including client service, learning, treatment for mental illnesses, personal productivity, and content creation. Malicious material, such as phishing attempts, false narratives, and fake news, can be produced using AI technologies. It's important for both users and developers to be cautious about potential misuses of AI-generated content. Artificial intelligence possesses the capability to be employed in social engineering assaults, swaying public opinion, and propagating misleading data. It's imperative to acknowledge the potential for abuse. Artificial intelligence models are susceptible to attacks like adversarial inputs, skillfully constructed modifications to the input data can produce unexpected results. In order to defend against these kinds of assaults, developers must have strong security measures in place.

DOI: 10.4018/979-8-3693-2284-0.ch010

1. INTRODUCTION

The field of machine learning for natural language processing has been completely revolutionized by ChatGPT, a powerful language model created by OpenAI. It should come as naturally that ChatGPT is swiftly establishing itself as a go-to tool for a variety of uses, from question-answering to text summarization and language translation, given its capacity to produce writing that appears human (Xiaodong Wu. et al,2023).

The global web has been ablaze with discussion over ChatGPT plugins and the consequences for enterprise, the economy, and humankind's future. the globe is still attempting to manage the benefits of the technology without becoming a victim of its perils by trying to understand security threats related to the ecosystem and other generative AI technologies. As program development and email phishing campaigns become more accessible, threat actors are experimenting with using chatbots like ChatGPT for harmful reasons. This is likely to increase the number and sophistication of attacks (Huang, K. et al,). They have discovered ways to assist in writing malware using ChatGPT. A variety of harmful code writing techniques can be created with ChatGPT, including information thieves, decryptors, and encryptors that use well-known encryption ciphers. Threat actors are beginning to experiment with ChatGPT to build dark web marketplaces in different instances.

Unprecedented excitement has been created by ChatGPT in the workplace, yet not all IT directors have welcomed the AI chatbot. Organizations prevented their staff members from using the app on the job, citing executive worries over ChatGPT security vulnerabilities. Furthermore, because of compliance concerns reportedly prohibited employees from utilizing the huge language model, a large number of other businesses have restricted their employees' usage of ChatGPT. Research activities in underground hacker networks indicates that cybercriminals are already employing ChatGPT to construct dangerous tools (Jackson, M. et al, 2023). It is obvious that generative AI has the potential to negatively alter the threat landscape in the upcoming months and years (Huang, K. et al,).

To assess the technological constraints of ChatGPT, researchers are now testing its security vulnerabilities. Scholars have identified the possibility that ChatGPT could be used to produce polymorphic malware, which is a more complex type of malware that mutates and becomes more difficult to identify and remove (Jackson, M. et al, 2023). Because it is easily available to cybercriminals with varying degrees of expertise, it is probable that the program will become more weaponized in attacks and the harm it may do.

ChatGPT is a potent language model with the potential to completely transform tasks involving natural language processing. When utilizing ChatGPT in an application, it's crucial to be mindful of the possible hazards, just like with any other technology. Dependency on third-party services, model performance, bias, data security and privacy, and compliance with regulations and laws are a few of these (Leong, A. et al, 2023). Therefore, it's crucial to thoroughly assess the framework and the provider prior incorporating it into your software and to regularly check and test the model's output and performance in order to guarantee a seamless integration and reduce risks. Furthermore, ChatGPT's capacity to produce recurring, consistent activities and conceal dangerous code in files can be utilized to construct a variety of malware types (A. Bahrini et al,).

2. SECURITY RISK IN CHATGPT

The security risks that ChatGPT has identified are growing exponentially. On the one hand, enemies become more skilled at taking advantage of weaknesses as a result of its improved intelligence, which magnifies conventional security concerns. However, ChatGPT poses new risks to both those using it and the broader public, calling for increased caution and preventative actions. Businesses must stop data from being fed into chatbots and generative AI systems, but they must do it in an approach that permits staff members to utilize these beneficial resources (Shalabaieva. et al, 2023). Companies can accomplish this by limiting the content that can be placed into input fields; some examples of these limitations include character counts and blocking known code. Since nobody will manually enter millions of lines of software code, this kind of data loss can be avoided by restricting the use of paste functions. Additionally, it would cause users to reconsider the data they were attempting to enter (R. (Pasupuleti. et al, 2023).

Unfortunately, existing insider threat solutions like data loss prevention (DLP), computer access security broker (CASB), and others are unable to handle the nuances of this new technology. These solutions continue to use a recognize and react methodology, searching through the massive volume of traffic leaving the company for specific keywords or phrases (Pasupuleti. et al, 2023). It is practically hard to capture everything since security experts and product owners frequently have to manually enter these. If a solution manages to identify data exfiltration, it can come too late. There is no "redo" button to undo the information that has already been entered. Your data will always be used to inform answers within the generative AI platform (Huang, K. et al,).

Security for ChatGPT is crucial in the modern digital environment. ChatGPT may produce writing that is identical to information authored by humans because it is an AI language model. Although this is an amazing accomplishment, it also raises questions about possible technology abuse (A. Bahrini. et al,). Hackers and other bad actors might try to take advantage of ChatGPT's weaknesses to disseminate false information, launch phishing scams, or trick people into disclosing private information. The Figure 1. shows different the Security Risks of ChatGPT.

Figure 1. Security risks

3. PHISHING AND SOCIAL ENGINEERING ATTACKS

Although earlier iterations of language-based AI have long been publicly accessible through open-sourcing, ChatGPT is by far the most sophisticated version to date. Specifically, ChatGPT's ability to communicate with users so naturally without making spelling, grammar, or verb tense errors gives the impression that there might actually be an authentic individual on the other side of the dialogue window (Al-Hawawreh. et al, 2023). From the standpoint of a hacker, ChatGPT is revolutionary. Applications that take use of excellent text production have the potential to reduce current restrictions and boost the efficacy of malevolent activity (Al-Hawawreh. et al, 2023). Even though ChatGPT says it uses a variety of cybersecurity safeguards, it can be difficult to foresee every scenario in which it could be abused. It is possible to utilize ChatGPT to create functions, references, code libraries, and URLs that are not real. Declare that there exist no simple ways to reduce the risks of misinformation created by AI (M. Gupta. et al, 2023).

One of the biggest challenges facing ChatGPT as it develops into an unrestricted "weapon factory" in the cybersecurity space is the general lack of knowledge about its capabilities. People could unintentionally become victims of its misuse if safeguards aren't taken, so it's important for everyone to learn how to protect themselves from these "new weapons" as soon as possible. The capability of ChatGPT to generate error-free phishing emails poses an additional security concern. It is technically designed to produce dangerous free content, but hackers can fool it by craftily wording prompts (Jeongki Lim. et al, 2023). To make their emails more convincing and resemble human-written letters, cybercriminals can create a whole chain of emails. AI-powered ChatGPT can create distinct phrasing and realistic-sounding emails for the same phishing trap (A. Bahrini. et al,).

API Attacks

The level of ChatGPT talk is at a record high, and as technology develops, technology executives need to be considering the implications for their employees, their organization, and society at large. If they don't, they will lag behind their rivals not only in using and embracing generative AI to enhance commercial results, but also in anticipating and thwarting the efforts of future hackers who are already adept at manipulating this technology for their own benefit. The industry needs to band together to put the proper safeguards in place and turn the ChatGPT revolution into something to embrace rather than something to be afraid of, since reputations and money are at stake (Jeongki Lim. et al,). The quantity of API assaults is increasing at an exponential rate along with the growing amount of APIs in businesses. Scientists at API security firm claim that there were more distinct attackers attempting to access clients' APIs.

Cybercriminals may ultimately employ generative AI, according to Forrester analysts, to identify the special vulnerabilities in APIs. This would save a lot of time and effort. Attackers would theoretically be able to direct ChatGPT to examine API documentation, compile data, and create API queries in an effort to find and take advantage of vulnerabilities more quickly and effectively (Adrian et al,).

Hackers can disseminate malicious packages using fake code libraries by employing ChatGPT's code generating features. AI package hallucination is the name of this novel harmful package dissemination method (P. Sharma. et al,). This method includes asking ChatGPT questions, requesting packages to fix coding issues, and receiving a list of recommended packages, including private packages from reputable repositories (D. Kapadiya. et al,). Next, using the names of the fictitious packages that ChatGPT proposed, hackers can upload an infected package to the repositories. When a user asks ChatGPT the same query later on, it will recommend the package that wasn't there at first. Ultimately, the malicious code within the package is executed by the user when they use it.

Malware

While ChatGPT can reject improper requests, such as those that write malware code, hackers can still trick ChatGPT and utilize it for nefarious reasons. For example, they can generate malware scripts or give instructions on how to uncover vulnerabilities. Though there are worries about ChatGPT helping attackers, it should be remembered that its features are still restricted. Writing code will become a significant security concern for ChatGPT as AI chatbots develop. Threat actors can use ChatGPT, an AI-powered prototype, for debugging and code development.

Hackers with malicious intentions will use ChatGPT to produce low-level cyber tools like malware and encryption programs. This will result in malicious actors targeting system servers with cyberattacks more quickly (Merlin Mancy. et al,). Because coding ChatGPT security concerns will expedite their job and provide them with a space to identify system vulnerabilities through the creation of malware codes, hacking will become more common. As of right now, it might not be too difficult for anyone with little technological knowledge. Because it reduces the bar to acquiring knowledge to develop into a hacker and boosts the effectiveness of creating attack variants, it might be dangerous for less protected systems (Jeongki Lim. et al,). But as LLMs still need some tweaks to function effectively and are prone to error, they are not yet strong enough to fully outperform human hackers.

Criminals can create harmful software that evades conventional security procedures by utilizing ChatGPT and other AI techniques. AI algorithms are also used by these sophisticated malware strains to develop and adjust, making them more challenging to find and remove. They are capable of breaking into networks, stealing confidential data, infiltrating systems, and holding data ransom.

Compromised Data

Hackers can disseminate malicious packages using fake code libraries by employing ChatGPT's code generating features. AI package hallucination is the name of this novel harmful package dissemination method. This method includes asking ChatGPT questions, requesting packages to fix coding issues, and receiving a list of recommended packages, including private packages from reputable repositories (N. Bhatnagar. et al,).Next, using the names of the fictitious packages that ChatGPT proposed, hackers can upload an unwanted package to the repositories. When a user asks ChatGPT the same query later on, it will recommend the package that wasn't there at first.

The technology behind Deepfake creates plausible but fraudulent multimedia by manipulating written, visual, audio, and video content using AI algorithms. Deepfakes are a tool used by cybercriminals to pose as famous people or high-ranking officials. They might use this technology to manipulate politics, commit financial frauds, or even damage someone's character. Deepfakes are difficult to spot since the phony media genuinely resembles somebody you are familiar with and trust.

Bias in Data

ChatGPT users run the danger of unintentionally exposing confidential data if they are not properly educated and trained about security. Artificial intelligence has improved the psychological manipulation strategies that con artists employ to trick people and take advantage of their trust. Cybercriminals can develop comprehensive profiles of their targets by employing artificial intelligence (AI) algorithms to scan enormous quantities of information from communication platforms and other sources. This raises the possibility that their fraudulent schemes may succeed by enabling them to create personalized and persuasive communications using ChatGPT and other similar platforms.

Now that the Internet is the primary conduit of information, the difficulty is not only finding pertinent content but also sifting through the abundance of data to remove false information. Before ChatGPT, users used a variety of techniques to filter information, including directly confirming the content, gauging the author's level of expertise, and analyzing text length, language rigor, and format accuracy as reliable indicators (P. Rawat . et al,). On the other hand, ChatGPT's content creation skills shine in these areas, giving the impression of unwavering dependability. When users do quick tests, they run the risk of believing everything produced by ChatGPT without question. Because of deep-rooted tendencies, this blind faith may result in incorrect assessments. (P. Sharma. et al,).

4. A LACK OF SECURITY CONTROLS

A lack of security controls within any system or environment can present significant risks and vulnerabilities. Here's a breakdown of the potential issues stemming from this, the Figure 2. presents Lack of Security Controls of ChatGPT.

Figure 2. Lack of security controls

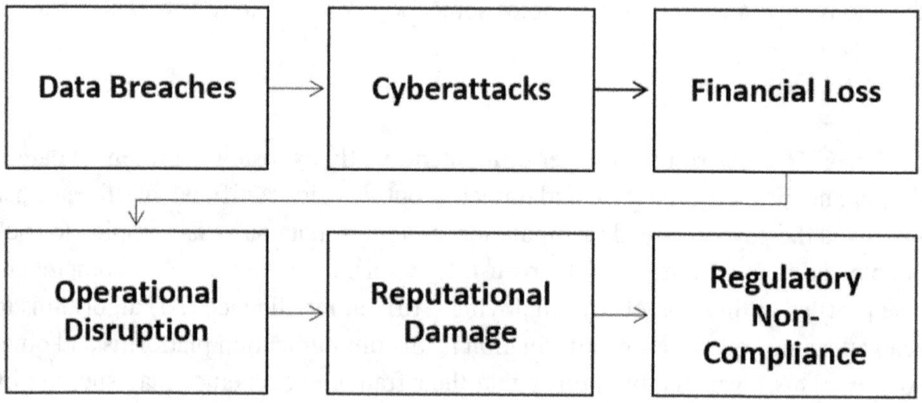

- Data Breaches: Without adequate security controls, sensitive data becomes susceptible to unauthorized access. This can lead to breaches that compromise personal information, financial records, or proprietary business data.
- Cyberattacks: When security measures are lacking or insufficient, systems become vulnerable to ransomware, malware, phishing scams, and more advanced hacking operations.
- Financial Loss: Financial losses from security breaches can come from direct theft as well as expenses for cleanup, legal ramifications, fines from authorities, and reputational harm.
- Operational Disruption: Cyberattacks have the potential to interfere with regular business operations, resulting in system failures, downtime, and the suspension of vital services or procedures (P. Sharma. et al,).
- Reputational Damage: A breach brought on by lax security measures can seriously harm an organization's standing and reduce stakeholder, partner, and consumer trust.
- Regulatory Non-Compliance: Strict rules pertaining to data security and protection exist in numerous businesses. Legal repercussions could arise from non-compliance with certain standards due to a lack of oversight. The Figure 3. presents the Solutions of Security Controls.

Figure 3. Solutions of security controls

Risk assessment: The process of locating weak points in security systems by analyzing and identifying potential threats and vulnerabilities.

Establishing restrictions: To reduce risks, security measures including intrusion detection systems, firewalls, encryption, and access restrictions are put in place. Regular software updates are also implemented.

Employee Education: Teaching staff members about security best practices in order to avert mistakes that could result in security breaches.

Continuous Monitoring: Regularly monitoring systems for any anomalies or potential security breaches and taking immediate action.

Compliance Measures: Ensuring adherence to industry standards and regulatory requirements to maintain a robust security posture.

5. BEST SECURITY PRACTICES FOR CHATGPT

Securing an AI chat system like ChatGPT involves various measures to ensure data privacy, prevent misuse, and safeguard against potential vulnerabilities (P. Sharma. et al,). Here are some best security practices:

- **Data encryption:** To safeguard the transfer of information between users and the discussion system and guarantee that all conversations stay private, implement strong encryption techniques (such as TLS/SSL).
- **Access Controls:** Implement stringent authentication procedures and access controls to limit system access to authorized personnel only and stop illegal access to confidential data (Anju A . et al, 2024).
- **Anonymization and Data Minimization:** Unless absolutely required, reduce the amount of personally identifiable information (PII) that is collected and retained. When feasible, anonymize data to safeguard user privacy.
- **Frequent Security Audits and Testing:** To find and fix any possible vulnerabilities or flaws in the system, conduct regular security audits, penetration tests, and vulnerability assessments.
- **User Consent and Privacy:** Make sure users understand exactly their information will be handled, saved, and safeguarded. Get express consent before collecting data, and make sure privacy laws like the CCPA and GDPR are followed.
- **Monitoring and Logging:** Make advantage of powerful monitoring tools to keep tabs on system activity, spot irregularities, and record user communications (P. Sharma. et al,). This facilitates the rapid identification and handling of security incidents.
- **Secure Coding Practices:** To reduce software vulnerabilities, follow safe programming norms and best practices. Updating and modify the system frequently to fix known security vulnerabilities.
- **AI Model Security:** Use strategies such as input validation, model robustness testing, and including protections against hostile inputs to safeguard the underlying AI model from adversarial attacks.
- **Incident Response Plan:** Create and keep up a thorough incident response strategy.
- **Collaboration with Security Experts**: Work with cybersecurity professionals or consultants to ensure that the chat system follows industry best practices and stays updated with evolving security standards.
- **Continuous Training**: Regularly train and educate employees on cybersecurity awareness, emphasizing their role in maintaining the security of the chat system.

By implementing these practices, developers and organizations can significantly enhance the security posture of AI chat systems like ChatGPT, ensuring the protection of user data and the integrity of the system itself (P. Sharma . et al,).

6. FUTURE CHALLENGES AND INNOVATIONS IN AI SECURITY

AI security is an evolving field that faces several challenges and requires continuous innovation to address emerging threats and vulnerabilities (P. Sharma. et al,). Here are some future challenges and potential innovations in AI security:

- Adversarial Attacks: These attacks take advantage of holes in AI models by faking input data in order to deceive or undermine the functionality of the system. To lessen these threats, advances in robust AI design—such as adversarial instruction and more robust models—are essential.
- Explainability and Transparency: As AI systems get more sophisticated, it's imperative to make sure that their decision-making processes are transparent and comprehensible. Explainable AI (XAI) innovations seek to increase trust and responsibility by shedding light on how AI systems make decisions.
- Data Privacy and Ethical Use: It can be difficult to safeguard user privacy when utilizing huge datasets for AI training. Advances in privacy-preserving AI, such differential privacy and federated learning, enable models to be trained on remote data while protecting sensitive data.
- AI in Cybersecurity: AI has the potential to both enhance cybersecurity defenses and pose new risks if exploited by adversaries. Innovations involve using AI for threat detection, anomaly detection, and automated response, while also defending AI systems against attacks (Anju A . et al, 2024).
- Regulatory Compliance: Keeping up with evolving regulatory frameworks around AI and data privacy is a challenge. Innovations in compliance tools and AI governance frameworks will help organizations adhere to regulations and ethical guidelines.
- AI Bias and Fairness: Addressing biases present in AI models is crucial for fairness and equitable outcomes. Innovations involve developing bias-detection tools, fairness-aware algorithms, and ethical AI frameworks to reduce bias and promote fairness.
- Zero-Day Threats and Security Patching: AI systems are susceptible to zero-day vulnerabilities, and patching these vulnerabilities in real-time is a challenge. Innovations in AI-based threat intelligence and automated patching can help address these issues.
- Deepfakes and Misinformation: Deepfake technology poses a significant threat in spreading misinformation. Innovations in deepfake detection and verification techniques are essential to combat this challenge.
- Supply Chain Risks: The AI ecosystem relies on third-party components and open-source libraries, creating supply chain vulnerabilities. Innovations in

secure AI development and supply chain risk management are necessary to mitigate these risks.

- AI-enabled Social Engineering Attacks: Adversaries can use AI-powered tools to create more convincing phishing and social engineering attacks. Innovations in AI-driven behavioral analysis and user authentication are crucial to combat these threats.

To tackle these obstacles, governments, industry stakeholders, cybersecurity specialists, and AI researchers must work together to create creative solutions that strike a balance between technological progress and ethical and security concerns.

7. MITIGATING ETHICAL CONCERNS IN AI DEPLOYMENT

Mitigating ethical concerns in AI deployment involves proactive measures to ensure responsible AI development, deployment, and usage. The Figure 4. shows the key strategies to address these concerns:

Figure 4. Ethical concerns

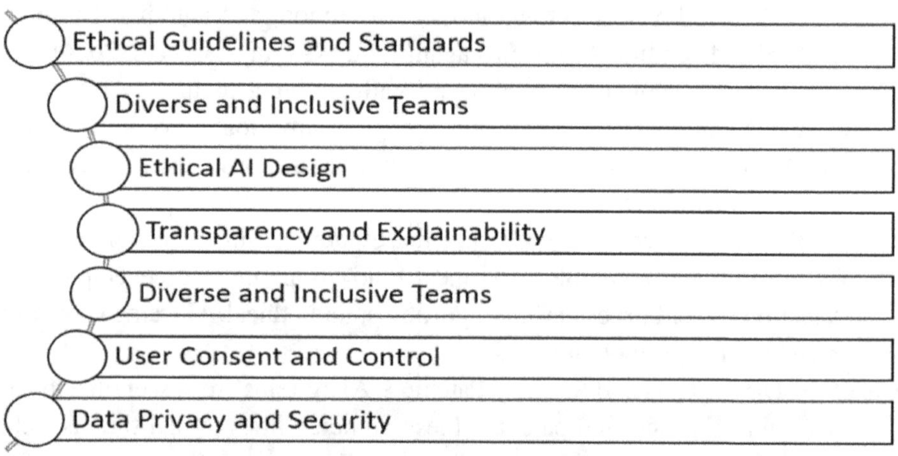

- Ethical Standards and rules: Clearly define ethical standards and rules for the creation and application of AI. Fairness, accountability, transparency, and privacy are among these values.

- Ethical AI Design: Include ethics in the AI systems' design process. Make sure moral issues like justice and privacy are incorporated into the design process from the beginning.
- Explainability and Transparency: Make the decision-making processes of AI systems explicable in order to promote transparency in these systems. Give users and stakeholders clear reasons for AI judgments.
- Inclusive and Diverse Teams: Encourage inclusive and diverse teams to work on AI initiatives. Diverse viewpoints can aid in identifying and reducing biases, resulting in more representative and egalitarian AI systems.
- User Control and Consent: Get users' informed consent before collecting and using their data. Give people the option to refuse some AI-driven features and give them control over their data (P. Sharma. et al,).
- Data Security and Privacy: Throughout the AI lifecycle, give data security and privacy a priority. To safeguard sensitive data, put strong encryption, access controls, and data anonymization into place.

8. CONCLUSION AND FUTURE WORKS

It's unclear if ChatGpt's advancement will be sufficient to fully address these problems. We present the technology, functionalities, constraints, and uses of ChatGPT, the most widely used techniques at the moment, with a particular emphasis on the ethical, security, and privacy issues brought up by ChatGPT. As of right now, ChatGPT is still prone to providing incorrect answers and causing issues with copyright protection and plagiarism detection. Decisions can be made incorrectly due to security risks like data poisoning and prompt injection. Finding workable remedies for newly discovered flaws in ChatGPT and other language frameworks is essential. It is equally crucial to identify and stop malicious exploitation by attackers. Although it is difficult to rationalize with black-box models, privacy leaking can be seen by examining basic cues and replies. In order to address privacy concerns, ChatGPT needs to adhere to privacy laws, create an extensive prompt-response assessment for leakage identification, use specialized techniques to stop leaks, and improve reasoning responses' openness.

REFERENCES

Al-Hawawreh, M., Aljuhani, A., & Jararweh, Y. (2023). Chatgpt for cybersecurity: Practical applications, challenges, and future directions. *Cluster Computing*, 26(6), 3421–3436. DOI: 10.1007/s10586-023-04124-5

Anju, A., & Krishnamurthy, M. (2024). M-EOS: Modified-equilibrium optimization-based stacked CNN for insider threat detection. *Wireless Networks*, 30(4), 2819–2838. DOI: 10.1007/s11276-024-03678-5

Bahrini, A.ChatGPT: Applications, Opportunities, and Threats. *2023 Systems and Information Engineering Design Symposium (SIEDS)*, 274-279. DOI: 10.1109/SIEDS58326.2023.10137850

Gupta, M., Akiri, C., Aryal, K., Parker, E., & Praharaj, L. (2023). From ChatGPT to ThreatGPT: Impact of Generative AI in Cybersecurity and Privacy. *IEEE Access : Practical Innovations, Open Solutions*, 11, 80218–80245. DOI: 10.1109/ACCESS.2023.3300381

Huang, K., Zhang, F., Li, Y., Wright, S., Kidambi, V., & Manral, V. (2023). Security and Privacy Concerns in ChatGPT. In Huang, K., Wang, Y., Zhu, F., Chen, X., & Xing, C. (Eds.), *Beyond AI. Future of Business and Finance*. Springer. DOI: 10.1007/978-3-031-45282-6_11

Jackson, M., & McDaniel, D. (2023). Why ChatGPT is a security concern for your organization. GitGuardian Blog.

Kapadiya, D., Shekhawat, C., & Sharma, P. (2023). A Study on Large Scale Applications of Big Data in Modern Era. In *International Conference on Information Management & Machine Intelligence (ICIMMI2023)*. ACM. https://doi.org/DOI: 10.1145/3647444.364788

Kirwan, A. (2023, November 24). ChatGPT and university teaching, learning and assessment: Some initial reflections on teaching academic integrity in the age of Large Language Models. *Irish Educational Studies*, 0(0), 1–18. DOI: 10.1080/03323315.2023.2284901

Leong, A. (2023). *ChatGPT just created malware, and that's seriously scary*. Digital Trends.

Lim, J., Leinonen, T., Lipponen, L., Lee, H., DeVita, J., & Murray, D. (2023). Artificial intelligence as relational artifacts in creative learning. *Digital Creativity (Exeter)*, 0(0), 1–19. DOI: 10.1080/14626268.2023.2236595

Merlin Mancy, A., Kumar, A. V., Latip, R., Jagadamba, G., Chakrabarti, P., Sharma, P., Musirin, I. B., Sharma, M., & Kanchan, B. G. (2024). Smart Healthcare System, Digital Health and Telemedicine, Management and Emergencies: Patient Emergency Application (PES) E-Governance Applications. In Kumar, R., Abdul Hamid, A., Binti Ya'akub, N., Sharan, H., & Kumar, S. (Eds.), *Sustainable Development in AI, Blockchain, and E-Governance Applications* (pp. 124–151). IGI Global. DOI: 10.4018/979-8-3693-1722-8.ch008

Nah, F. F.-H., Zheng, R., Cai, J., Siau, K., & Chen, L. (2023). Generative AI and ChatGPT: Applications, challenges, and AI-human collaboration. *Journal of Information Technology Case and Application Research*, 25(3), 277–304. DOI: 10.1080/15228053.2023.2233814

Pasupuleti, R., Vadapalli, R., & Mader, C. (2023). Cyber Security Issues and Challenges Related to Generative AI and ChatGPT. *2023 Tenth International Conference on Social Networks Analysis, Management and Security (SNAMS)*, 1-5. DOI: 10.1109/SNAMS60348.2023.10375472

Prasad, G. A., Kumar, A. V., Sharma, P., Irawati, I. D., D. V., C., Musirin, I. B., Abdullah, H. M., & Rao L, M. (2023). Artificial Intelligence in Computer Science: An Overview of Current Trends and Future Directions. In S. Rajest, B. Singh, A. Obaid, R. Regin, & K. Chinnusamy (Eds.), Advances in Artificial and Human Intelligence in the Modern Era (pp. 43-60). IGI Global. DOI: 10.4018/979-8-3693-1301-5.ch002

Rawat, P., Bhardwaj, A., Lamba, N., & Sharma, P. (2023). Arduino Based IoT Mini Weather Station. *SKIT Research Journal*, 13(2), 34–41. DOI: 10.47904/IJSKIT.13.2.2023.34-41

Sethi, S. S., & Sharma, P. (2023). New Developments in the Implementation of IoT in Agriculture. *SN Computer Science*, 4(5), 503. DOI: 10.1007/s42979-023-01896-w

Shalabaieva, M. (2023). *The dark side of ChatGPT: Manipulation, misinformation, and malicious intent*. Artificial Intelligence in Plain English.

Sharma, P. (2023). *Utilizing Explainable Artificial Intelligence to Address Deep Learning in Biomedical Domain, Medical Data Analysis and Processing using Explainable Artificial Intelligence*. Taylor & Francis. DOI: 10.1201/9781003257721-2

Sharma, P., & Bhatnagar, N. (2023). Passenger Authentication and Ticket Verification at Airport Using QR Code Scanner. *SKIT Research Journal*, 13(2), 10–13. DOI: 10.47904/IJSKIT.13.1.2023.10-12

Sharma, P., & Dadheech, P. (2023). Modern-age Agriculture with Artificial Intelligence: A review emphasizing Crop Yield Prediction. *EVERGREEN Joint Journal of Novel Carbon Resource Sciences & Green Asia Strategy*, 10(4), 2570–2582. DOI: 10.5109/7160906

Sharma, P., Dadheech, P., Aneja, N., & Aneja, S. (2023). Predicting Agriculture Yields Based on Machine Learning Using Regression and Deep Learning. *IEEE Access : Practical Innovations, Open Solutions*, 11, 111255–111264. DOI: 10.1109/ACCESS.2023.3321861

Sharma, P., & Jain, M. K. (2023). Stock Market Trends Analysis using Extreme Gradient Boosting (XGBoost). *2023 International Conference on Computing, Communication, and Intelligent Systems (ICCCIS)*, 317-322. DOI: 10.1109/ICCCIS60361.2023.10425722

Sharma, P., Kapadiya, D., & Bhardwaj, A. (2023). Efficient Note Sharing Model for Collaborative Learning. *SKIT Research Journal*, 13(2), 42–46. DOI: 10.47904/IJSKIT.13.2.2023.42-46

Sharma, P., & Rathi, Y. (2016, June 5). Efficient Density-Based Clustering Using Automatic Parameter Detection. Efficient Density-Based Clustering Using Automatic Parameter Detection | SpringerLink. .DOI: 10.1007/978-981-10-0767-5_46

Sharma, P., Sharma, C., & Mathur, P. (2023). Machine Learning-based Stock Market Forecasting using Recurrent Neural Network. *2023 9th International Conference on Smart Computing and Communications (ICSCC)*, 600-605. DOI: 10.1109/ICSCC59169.2023.10335083

Tanwar, A., Sharma, P., Pandey, A., & Kumar, S. (2023). Intrusion Detection System Based Ameliorated Technique of Pattern Matching. In *Proceedings of the 4th International Conference on Information Management & Machine Intelligence (ICIMMI '22)*. Association for Computing Machinery. DOI: 10.1145/3590837.3590947

Wu, Duan, & Ni. (2023). Unveiling security, privacy, and ethical concerns of ChatGPT. Journal of Information and Intelligence.

Chapter 11
Opening Up the Next Generation of Convolutional Neural Networks (CNN) for Palm Recognition

Dilip Sisodia
https://orcid.org/0000-0002-2174-1516
Engineering College, Ajmer, India

Charu Vaibhav Verma
https://orcid.org/0009-0000-6571-0685
Prestige Institute of Engineering Management and Research, Indore, India

Garima Joshi
Acropolis Institute of Technology and Research, Indore, India

P. Kaliyamoorthi
Madanapalle Institute of Technology and Science, Madanapalle, India

Ankur Gupta
https://orcid.org/0000-0002-4651-5830
Vaish College of Engineering, Rohtak, India

Sabyasachi Pramanik
https://orcid.org/0000-0002-9431-8751
Haldia Institute of Technology, India

Faiz Mohammad
https://orcid.org/0009-0008-8825-7105
Rungta College of Engineering and Technology, Bhilai, India

ABSTRACT

A subset of biometrics called palm recognition has drawn a lot of interest because

DOI: 10.4018/979-8-3693-2284-0.ch011

of its potential applications in a variety of fields, including as security systems and human-computer interaction. Convolutional neural networks (CNNs) are being used in this effort to look at the creation of a palm detecting system. In order to identify and classify palm orientation in digital photos, deep learning will be used. An essential part of the study is data collection, which comprises compiling a large dataset of accurately labeled palm photos for supervised learning. The authors handle data preparation and use methods like image scaling, pixel normalization, and data augmentation to get datasets ready for model training. The system is based on a CNN model architecture, which creates a neural network with the ability to intelligently classify and automatically gather data from palm photos. Convolutional layers are used in this architecture to extract features, while fully connected layers are used for classification.

INTRODUCTION

During a time of fast mechanical improvement and an unquenchable need for comfort, security, and innovation, the concept of palm recognition presents itself as an exciting combination of biometrics and manufactured insights. Accessing sensitive data securely, opening doors, and facilitating continuous human-computer intelligence have emerged as critical aspects of contemporary life. As our environment becomes more and more computerized, the significance of robust and effective biometric distinguishing proof frameworks cannot be overstated. Palm recognition, a biometric confirmation technique, offers a charming and distinctive answer to these modern issues. It provides trustworthy and safe character validation by using the unique characteristics of an individual's palm. Whether it is used for advanced human-computer interface, portable device verification, or entry to secure facilities, palm recognition is a standard for mechanical advancement.

The Significance of Palm Identification

Biometric identification evidence has grown in popularity recently as a very secure and trustworthy kind of identification. Common confirmation mechanisms like passwords and PINs have shown to be vulnerable to hacks and often place the burden of proof on the client. In this context, biometric systems have evolved to the state of the art, promising increased security and customer pleasure. In the realm of biometrics, palm recognition has a special place. The human palm's unique lines, edges, and vascular patterns give it a variety of unique characteristics. Palm recognition is consistent and dependable, in contrast to face recognition and individual finger imprint verification, which may sometimes be affected by outside variables like illumination or finger moisture. Furthermore, since palm acknowledgment is non-intrusive, it is a great match for many different applications.

One of the most interesting features of palm recognition is its versatility. It may be integrated into many contexts, ranging from continuous innovation engagement to direct physical control. Consider a high-security office, for example, where authorized faculty members need quick and safe access. Conventional techniques such as keycards and stick codes are susceptible to loss or tampering. Palm recognition provides a simple and secure method of entry in these circumstances. The consumer just has to hold their hand in front of the scanner to get access; this process takes only a few seconds.

LITERATURE REVIEW

(Smith, J., 2018) Smith's work presents PalmNet, a convolutional neural network created especially for palmprint identification, in "PalmNet: A Profound Learning Approach for Palmprint Acknowledgment." The test results and design of the model show that it can achieve great accuracy in palmprint distinguishing evidence. By using the many tiers of highlight learning capacities of deep learning, PalmNet shows its potential in secure access control and biometric verification frameworks. The paper lays the foundation for further research in this field and emphasizes the importance of highlight extraction in palmprint identification. (Johnson, Andrew, 2017) In his paper "PalmID: A Vigorous Palm Acknowledgment Framework Utilizing Profound Highlights," Johnson presents PalmID, a framework for palm identification that heavily relies on include extraction techniques. The examination focuses on how well the model performs in practical situations and how well it can adapt to differences in palm pictures. PalmID uses deep learning to accurately identify and extract noteworthy palm highlights. The study highlights the possible uses for palm recognition in security systems where vigor is essential and offers significant insights into the difficulties of palm recognition in practice. (Gupta's, 2017) study examines how security may be increased by combining palm and unique mark acknowledgment frameworks. The benefits of combining several biometric modalities to provide multi-modal biometric confirmation are examined in this research. This approach is a compelling option for multifactor verification and high-security environments since it requires the efficient identification of both palm and unique mark information, hence improving security fundamentally. Gupta's research establishes the foundation for multi-modal biometrics as an emerging field in science. (Chen, L. 2015) work presents PalmPrintNet, a CNN design optimized for palmprint recognition, with the title "PalmPrintNet: Profound Convolutional Neural Systems for Palmprint Acknowledgment." The model's performance in several palmprint datasets and its potential for practical applications are examined by the authors. The unique architecture of PalmPrintNet serves as an example of the essential elements of deep learning for palmprint identification. It achieves great exactness and vigor, paving the way for long-term executions in access control and confirmation frameworks (Wang, Y. 2018). Wang offers a full analysis of further developments in palm vein identification in "PalmVein Acknowledgment: A Overview of Later Propels." The study looks at a number of procedures, such as CNN-based methods, and it also identifies issues and prospects in this area. An essential source for researching the development of palm vein identification is Wang's research report. CNNs are used in this situation to guarantee that palm recognition systems in healthcare, secure workplaces, and financial services will become more accurate and secure, (Brown, M. 2016). In his study, "Multi-Modal Biometric Verification Utilizing Palm and Confront Acknowledgment," Brown examines how well face and palm identification work together in a multi-modal biometric confirmation system. The study looks at the potential uses for different modalities as well as the advantages of merging them. Multi-modal biometric confirmation is becoming more and more popular because of its enhanced usability and security. The benefits of combining face and palm recognition for border control, financial transactions, and mobile device security are shown by Brown's study. Deep highlight learning for palm confirmation is the subject of (Lee, 2022), "Profound Palm Highlight Learning for Confirmation." The paper evaluates a CNN-based technique for memorizing discriminative highlights from palm photographs in terms of accuracy and robustness. In highlighting the significance of highlight learning in palm identification, Lee's work shows how deep neural networks are able to automatically extract and make use of intricate palm highlights. The main benefit of this approach is that it increases the accuracy and competence of palm recognition systems, (Kumar, 2019) focuses on palm identification in unconstrained settings in his study, "Palm Acknowledgment in Unconstrained Situations." He emphasizes CNN models' flexibility in handling challenging situations including shifting lighting and foundation issues. One of the main challenges facing palm identification, as raised by Kumar's investigation, is palm recognition in uncontrolled, real-world scenarios. The study looks at the adaptability and robustness of CNN-based (Sharma, P. et al. 2023) models, which presents as yet undiscovered possible result for real-world use in open-air access control and observation. (Garcia, 2024) Information on the use of palm biometrics for access control may be found in Garcia's audit report. The employment of several palm recognition techniques in access control systems is the main topic of the research. Garcia's thorough audit is an invaluable tool for understanding the palm recognition situation in get to manage. The report highlights the practical suggestions for safeguarding physical access to buildings and limited locations using palm biometrics, (Q. Zhang 2016) Zhang's work, "Palm Acknowledgment Utilizing

Profound Learning and Exchange Learning," examines how deep learning and exchange learning techniques might be used to palm identification. To increase the accuracy of palm identification, the study looks into the sharing of data from similar jobs. Zhang's study shows that by addressing the management of exchange learning, trained models may enhance the performance of palm recognition frameworks. The results have importance for applications pertaining to secure access control and flexible verification, Li (2017), Li's study examines the potential and challenges of palm identification for diversified verification in "Palm Acknowledgment for Versatile Confirmation: Challenges and Openings." The idea talks about the interesting aspects of using palm recognition on portable devices. Li's study highlights the need for secure and user-friendly solutions by shedding light on how challenging it is to include palm recognition into portable verification frameworks. The research looks on the potential applications of palm recognition in smartphone security, portable installments, and portable money. (Wu, G. 2010). Wu concentrates his research on safe deep learning methods for privacy-preserving palm identification under the title "Privacy-Preserving Palm Acknowledgment with Secure Profound Learning." Techniques for protecting palm picture data throughout the recognition process are covered in the study. Biometric frameworks need to provide security and safety. Wu's invention addresses the basic problem of protecting palm picture data, making it appropriate for use in industries like healthcare and finance where client protection and information security are crucial, (Chang, 2019.) Chang's research demonstrates the effectiveness of palm confirmation using CNN-based highlight extraction in "Strong Palm Verification with CNN-Based Include Extraction". It demonstrates how well the model can handle a range of natural factors. Strength plays a crucial role in the success of biometric verification. According to (Xu, L., 2018), Chang's study suggests a CNN-based method that performs better than predicted at identifying palms under a variety of conditions, such as shifting illumination, foundation, and introduction. This makes the method a strong contender for safe confirmation and access control frameworks. Xu's research is centered on palmprint identification in real-world observation conditions, with an emphasis on "PalmPrint Acknowledgment in Real-World Reconnaissance." The study highlights CNN models' potential for security, counting, and espionage applications. Reconnaissance frameworks are depending more and more on biometric validation for enhanced security. Xu's work emphasizes the advantages of CNN-based models in real-time access control and personality confirmation, with a focus on the use of palmprint recognition in reconnaissance scenarios, (Kim, S. 2017). A comparison of several palm biometric feature extraction methods is presented in Kim's study, "Palm Biometrics: A Comparative Investigation of Highlight Extraction Strategies." The paper explores the benefits and drawbacks of several palm identification techniques. Kim's work advances our knowledge of palm biometric feature extraction techniques. By comparing various methodologies, the study offers analysts and professionals valuable insights that may be used to optimize palm acknowledgment frameworks.

BACKGROUND

A. Convolutional Neural Networks (CNNs)

The field of palm acknowledgment would not have progressed to its current level without the use of Convolutional Neural Systems (CNNs). CNNs, a subset of deep learning models, have revolutionized the field of computer vision research. These systems, which draw inspiration from the human visual system, are skilled in organizing image data. CNNs can surprisingly identify complex patterns inside photos. In terms of progressive representation learning and extraction, they outperform predictions. To identify a palm, one must be able to recognize its unique patterns and characteristics. Therefore, it makes sense for CNNs and palm acknowledgement to combine.

Information Gathering: Creation of the Palm Recognition

Every machine learning project starts with the quality and originality of the dataset. This dataset is made up of a number of palm photos used for palm acknowledgment. The CNN program uses these pictures as its foundational teaching material. The method of obtaining data for palm recognition might be laborious. To provide a potent demonstration that can identify a variety of palm introductions, an additional dataset is required. To completely portray the diversity of palm highlights, the collection should contain palm prints from a variety of socioeconomic backgrounds.

Apart from any discrepancies, the dataset should be of excellent quality. To do this, clear, well-defined palm photos must be taken. A lot of the criteria that ensure the quality of the dataset include picture organization, lighting, and choice of camera. Labeling is an essential component of the planning process for gathering data. Every picture in the collection has to be connected to pertinent metadata, such the person's personality, the introduction of the palm, and any other pertinent details. This information makes the show possible by allowing directed learning to begin with tagged cases.

The effectiveness of palm acknowledgment depends on the completeness of the data collection process. This step's meticulous labor establishes the foundation for the information preprocessing; demonstrate design, and preparation phases that come next. Figure 1 shows the CNN architecture.

Figure 1. CNN architecture

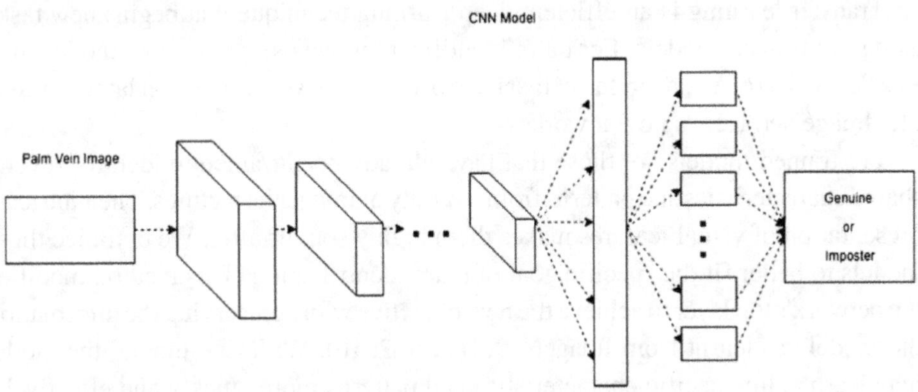

The Pseudo Code below describes the CNN algorithm.

```
algorithm Parallel-CNN
input: d: dataset, l: dataset true labels, W:
Word2Vec matrix
output: score of Parallel-CNN trained model on
test dataset
let f be the featureset 3d matrix
for i in dataset do
  let f_i be the featureset matrix of sample i
  for j in i do
    v_j ← vectorize(j, w)
    append v_j to f_i
    append f_i to f
f_train, f_test, l_train, l_test ← split feature set and labels
into train subset and test subset
M ← Parallel-CNN (f_train, l_train)
score ← evaluate (i, l_test, M)
return score
```

B. Learning Transfer

Transfer learning is an efficient deep learning technique that begins new tasks using pre-trained models. For palm identification, we use pre-trained models like ResNet, VGG16, and MobileNet that have been extensively trained on large datasets like ImageNet. Here's how it works:

Pre-trained models are those that have already been trained to identify several shared characteristics and patterns from a variety of ImageNet pictures. Their intricate presentation of visual features makes them highly sought-after. We optimize these models to better fit the specific goal of palm identification. This method modifies the network's top layer to achieve the new objective while preserving the information the model has learnt from ImageNet (Tan, S. 2016). With fine-tuning, the model may learn palm-specific characteristics and patterns more quickly and effectively. Figure 2 shows the Transfer Learning Flowchart.

Figure 2. Transfer learning flowchart

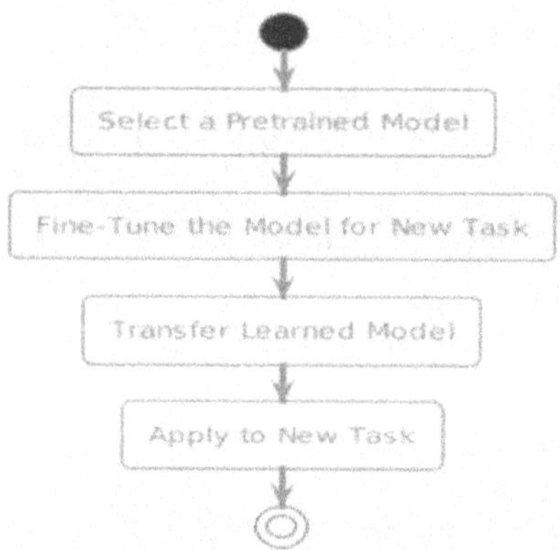

C. Recurrent Neural Networks or RNNs

For dynamic palm identification, recurrent neural networks (RNNs) are essential, especially for tasks that call for the detection of palm motions and movements. RNNs (Sharma, P. et al. 2023) support the following functions:

Data that is subject to change over time: For accurate identification, it is essential to gather this temporal information as the movements and motions of the palm alter over time. Since RNNs are designed to interpret data sequences, they are an excellent choice for dynamic palm identification tasks. RNNs sequentially analyze incoming data while accounting for the presentation order of the data items. This allows it to recognize patterns that change over time, such the path of a palm movement or a series of gestures in sign language recognition. Recurrent neural networks (RNNs) (Huang, 2016; Jiang, H. 2019) have practical applications in areas such as hand gesture and movement sequence detection in sign language. What distinguishes them is their ability to understand and classify such sequences. Figure 3 shows the flowchart of RNN.

Figure 3. Flowchart for RNN

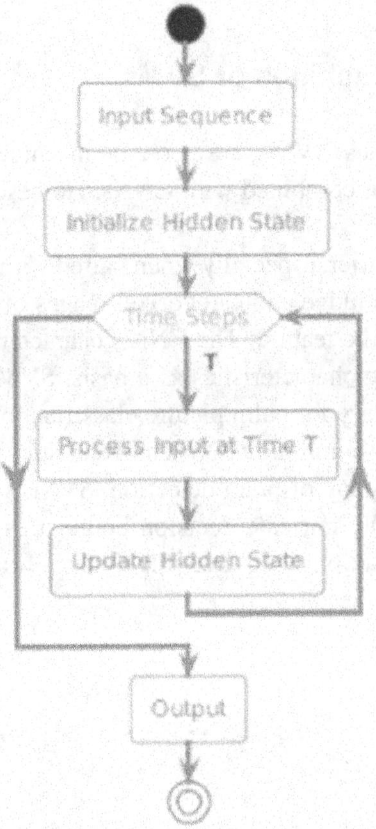

The Pseudo Code of RNN is shown below.

Input: $x = [\boldsymbol{x}_1, ..., \boldsymbol{x}_{365}], x_i \in \mathbb{R}^n$

Given parameters: $\mathbf{W}_f, \mathbf{U}_f, \boldsymbol{b}_f, \mathbf{W}_{\tilde{c}}, \mathbf{U}_{\tilde{c}}, \boldsymbol{b}_{\tilde{c}}, \mathbf{W}_i, \mathbf{U}_i, \boldsymbol{b}_i, \mathbf{W}_o, \mathbf{U}_o, \boldsymbol{b}_o$

Initialize $\boldsymbol{h}_0, \boldsymbol{c}_0 = \overrightarrow{0}$

for t=1, ..., 365 **do**

  Calculate $\boldsymbol{f}_t$ (Eq. 2), $\tilde{\boldsymbol{c}}_t$ (Eq. 3), $\boldsymbol{i}_t$ (Eq. 4)

  Update cell state $\boldsymbol{c}_t$ (Eq. 5)

  Calculate $\boldsymbol{o}_t$ (Eq. 6), $\boldsymbol{h}_t$ (Eq. 7)

end for

Output: $h = [\boldsymbol{h}_1, ..., \boldsymbol{h}_{365}], h_i \in \mathbb{R}^m$

D. Support Vector Machines or SVMs

Support Vector Machines (SVMs) are a popular machine learning technique that can recognize palms when combined with CNNs. He describes how SVM works in this situation:

SVM is used as a classifier, especially when paired with CNN-derived features. These function as the last judge and categorize images of palm trees into certain categories. Utilization of the feature: The CNN's characteristics provide the SVM with its input. Using these characteristics as a basis, SVM attempts to determine the proper decision boundary for palm picture classification.

Enhanced accuracy: By combining CNN characteristics with his SVM classifier, we may improve the accuracy of palm detection. SVM is well recognized for its ability to effectively handle intricate decision boundaries and excel in scenarios where multiple class distinction is required. Figure 4 shows the flowchart for SVM.

Figure 4. Flowchart for SVM

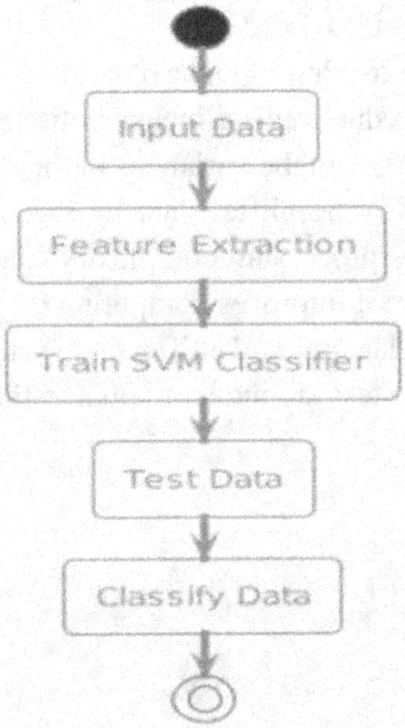

The Pseudo Code of SVM is shown below.

Algorithm 1 Training an SVM

Require: $\boldsymbol{X}$ and $\boldsymbol{y}$ loaded with training labeled data, $\boldsymbol{\alpha} \Leftarrow 0$ or $\boldsymbol{\alpha} \Leftarrow$ partially trained SVM

$C \Leftarrow$ some value (10 for example)

repeat

    for all $\{\boldsymbol{x_i}, y_i\}, \{\boldsymbol{x_j}, y_j\}$ **do**

        Optimize α_i and α_j

    end for

until no changes in $\boldsymbol{\alpha}$ or other resource constraint criteria met

Ensure: Retain only the support vectors ($\boldsymbol{\alpha_i} > 0$)

E. Principal Component Analysis or PCA

Principal component analysis (PCA) is a helpful dimensionality reduction technique in the palm identification domain.

Diminution of dimensions: Photographs of palms are often intricate and include several dimensions. PCA reduces this dimensionality by identifying the important traits or components that explain the variances in the data.

Principal attributes: PCA simplifies data by focusing on the most important components, which lowers processing complexity. This is particularly useful for palm recognition jobs since it improves computing efficiency.

Gains in performance: The palm identification system works better overall and takes less time to train and test the model thanks to the use of PCA to reduce the dimensionality.

Figure 5. Flowchart for PCA

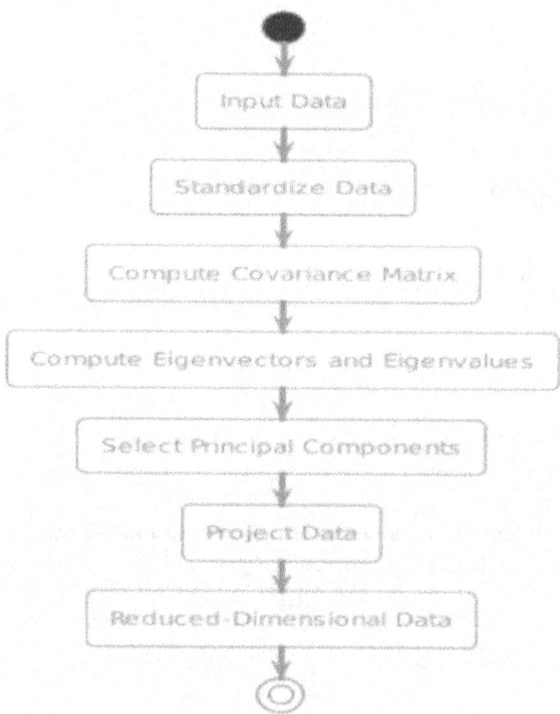

The pseudo code of PCA technique is shown here.

Bin(A,L,K)

// Initialization

$B = \{B_1\}$ where $B_1 = A$.

If $K = 1$, then return B.

Store the Ncut value for B_1 : $[A_1(B_1), A_2(B_1), \mathrm{Ncut}(B_1)] = \mathrm{Bisect}(B_1, L)$.

// Recursively bisect until there are K bins

Repeat until $|B| = K$

Pick the bin $\hat{B} \in B$ with the smallest $\mathrm{NCut}(\hat{B})$.

If $\mathrm{NCut}(\hat{B}) > threshold$, return B.

// Divide the bin $\hat{B}$ into two bins $A_1(\hat{B}), A_2(\hat{B})$

$[A_1(\hat{B}), A_2(\hat{B}), \mathrm{Ncut}(\hat{B})] = \mathrm{Bisect}(\hat{B}, \hat{L})$.

$B = B \cup \{A_1(\hat{B}), A_2(\hat{B})\} \setminus \hat{B}$.

If $|B| = K$, then return B.

Store the Ncut values for $A_1(\hat{B})$ and $A_2(\hat{B})$ by calling *Bisect*.

Information Preparation: Fine-Tuning the Raw Material

Oftentimes, raw data has to be enhanced before it can be used in machine learning, despite its significance. In this case, preparing information is helpful. There are many important roles that information preprocessing plays in palm acknowledgment. The primary means of ensuring consistency is via information preparation. The size and perspective proportions of the palm pictures in the dataset may vary. It is essential to resize these photographs to a uniform size in order to provide a level playing field for the CNN program. Picture resizing is the control used to ensure that all photos are shown to the audience in a consistent manner. One important part of preprocessing information is pixel normalization. This means that the pixel values in the photos must be precisely changed. Normalization facilitates the CNN's learning process, hence improving its efficacy and triumph. It also affects the moderating of visual brightness and differentiation changes.

Still another facet of information preparation that improves the dataset's many characteristics is information increase. Information augmentation techniques include things like altering the photographs and creating new copies of the original dataset. These adjustments might include flips, turns, and illumination adjustments. The CNN software was exposed to a greater variety of palm images as a consequence of the expanding dataset, which made it more resilient and capable of managing differences in the actual world. The architecture of the CNN broadcast is ultimately what matters in this entire situation. The underpinning for the model's creation and interpretation of palm picture data is its architecture. The engineering of CNNs is often composed of many layers, each with a different function. The main building elements of engineering are pooling layers, completely associated layers, and convolutional layers.

Convolutional layers are a dependable method for feature extraction. They emphasize different patterns and elements in the original picture by applying a variety of filters. These patterns may ultimately help identify complex palm highlights. They can be as basic as edges or as complex as forms. Pooling layers, which are used to downsample the retrieved highlights, come after convolutional layers. They assist in lowering the model's computing burden and complexity while preserving important information. The last section of the design is made up of completely linked layers. They use the fuzzy highlights from the previous layers to do the actual classification. Based on its properties, the completely connected layers are responsible for categorizing the palm image for palm identification. Given how effectively the machine can understand and classify palm photographs, the CNN show's structure could be a key component of the experiment.

Preparing: Sustaining the Education Getting Set

After the dataset has been acquired, preprocessed, and the demonstration design has been established, the project advances to the planning step. An iterative process of finely adjusting the model's parameters to recognize palm photos trains a CNN demonstration. Preparation involves many various steps, starting with the suitable optimizer selection and the awful function. The optimizer decides how the model's parameters are changed throughout preparation, while the unlucky work measures the difference between the model's predictions and the real names. The effectiveness and efficiency of the preparation process are impacted by each of these choices.

A range of ages are included in the repeating preparation routine, and each comprises a forward and backward pass through the performance. During the forward pass, the model receives palm image inputs, and its predictions are compared to the ground truth names. To lessen this loss, the error or misfortune is calculated and the model's parameters are adjusted during the in reverse run. The major challenge in training CNN is to guarantee that it can effectively generalize to unseen, unused palm pictures. Despite not having to memorize the preparatory information, the demonstration has to understand the basic patterns and traits of hands. In this case, the permission set often comes into play. The model's performance on the approval set is evaluated throughout preparation to make sure the model is learning efficiently and isn't overfitting (Sharma, P. et al. 2023) the preparation data.

Evaluation: Calculating Achievement

During the evaluation phase, the model's implementation is closely evaluated. The objective is to ascertain the model's palm recognition performance as well as its generalizability to intrusive information. Assessment metrics serve as a benchmark for determining success. For classification tasks such as palm recognition, standard criteria include precision, exactness, review, and F1 score. These metrics evaluate the degree to which the show classifies hands accurately and, in some cases, the degree to which it can distinguish between true negatives, false negatives, true positives, and false negatives. The assessment process provides an understanding of the model's advantages and disadvantages. It might be an important step in analyzing how the model is organized and how useful it could be in practice.

Honing: Enhancing the Performance

The journey doesn't stop with the first phase of planning. The model is still being refined at this time. It entails trying data augmentation approaches and iteratively adjusting the model's hyperparameters (Sharma, P. et al. 2023) to improve the model's performance. Considerations such as the number of layers or channels in the display, clump measure, and learning rate must be made while optimizing hyperparameters. Optimizing the hyperparameters may have a big impact on the model's performance. The increasing amount of data continues to aid in fine-tuning. When fine-tuning, the model gains additional vigor by being exposed to more input. The example gains proficiency in recognizing palms in a range of orientations, lighting scenarios, and backgrounds. The presentation may be enhanced and made more compelling and successful via a concentrated preparatory process known as fine-tuning.

Practical Utilization

The extension makes use of a refined and trained model to tackle the real-world applications of palm identification. This is usually when the project's specialized viewpoints and theoretical knowledge start to apply in practical contexts. Palm recognition has a wide range of applications. Consider how it controls physical access as an example. Robust authentication techniques are necessary for high-security buildings, restricted regions, and information hubs. Keycards and PIN numbers—two traditional methods—are susceptible. In these situations, palm acknowledgment offers a lovely and safe option. The consumer may get access in a matter of seconds by just placing their palm on a scanner.

Portable device authentication is another feature of the palm acknowledgment component. Given how ingrained smartphones (Sharma, P. et al. 2023) and tablets have grown in our everyday lives, safe and intuitive authentication techniques are crucial. Palm recognition technology allows for touchless device access, enhancing security without sacrificing user convenience. Furthermore, the area of human-computer interaction is affected by palm recognition. When technology becomes so advanced that all you need to do to interface with it is use your hand. You may utilize the same features and attributes that make up your personality to use technology, get information, and open up new channels of contact. It's an image of technology that can easily move with the times.

As we get to the end of our investigation into palm identification using convolutional neural networks, we take the distance traveled into consideration. It may be a voyage of invention, exploration, and the dawn of a new era. Palm recognition is a promising area in biometrics because of its unique ability to recognize the minute characteristics of the human hand. One of the most important steps in improving the innovation's accuracy, security, and flexibility is the use of CNNs in palm identification. This project's thorough examination of data collection, preprocessing, model construction, preparation, evaluation, fine-tuning, and real-world applications make it a great illustration of the all-encompassing approach required for effective palm acknowledgement utilization.

Here we are at the nexus of biometrics and technology, with our hands pointing us in the direction of a secure, helpful, and exciting future. Biometrics and development might one day change the way we engage with the developed world; the patterns on our palms could be the keys to unlocking the potential of innovation. We have the key to unlocking the future within our grasp thanks to convolutional neural networks.

Figure 6. Flowchart for our approach

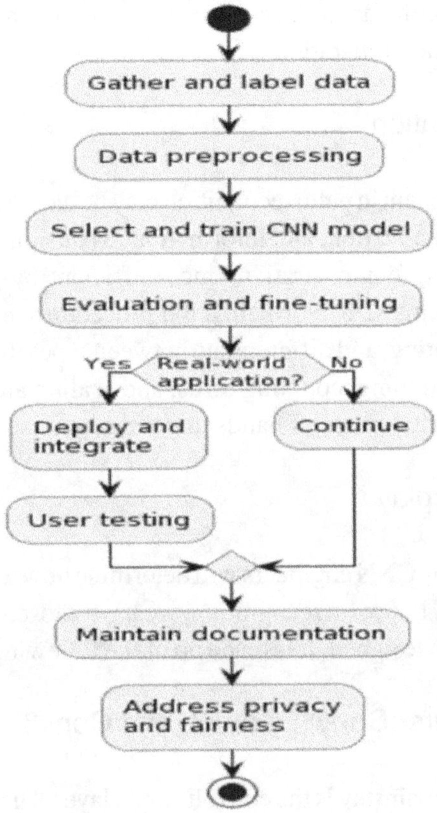

Techniques Description

Palm acknowledgment powered by Convolutional Neural Systems suggests a workable biometric verification system with many uses. The study's approach outlines the crucial steps required to accomplish the objective of accurate and dependable palm acknowledgment.

Compiling and Organizing Data

Building a strong foundation for palm identification starts with collecting a large collection of palm photos. This dataset will serve as the basis for developing and authorizing the CNN broadcast. To ensure representation of a range of palm sizes, shapes, and skin tones, pictures are collected from a diverse range of individuals. Each photograph has basic information labeled, such as age, sex, and hand introduction. Information cleaning forms are used to remove exceptions and mistakes and guarantee the quality of the dataset. Lastly, subgroups are created from the dataset for testing, approval, and preparation.

Information Preparation

One essential component in palm recognition may be data preprocessing. Included are image scaling, normalization, and information expansion. Image scaling makes the process of preparing demonstrations more efficient by guaranteeing that all palm pictures are the same size. Normalization procedures are used to standardize pixel values, lessen lighting, and differentiate between types. Information expansion methods including as flipping, counting turns, and scaling are used to enhance the model's recognition performance of hands under different scenarios.

Engineering for Display

The decision made by CNN engineers will determine how well the palm acknowledgment system works. For palm recognition, we have chosen to use a CNN outline that has been especially designed. It is made up of the following fundamental layers:

Convolutional Layers (Conv1, Conv2, and Conv3)

CNN engineering's mainstay is the convolutional layer. They consist of teachable channels that analyze and pinpoint the highlights in the incoming photos. These layers are intended to recognize distinct features from the palm, such surfaces, lines, and forms, in the context of palm recognition.

Pools1, 2, and 3: Maximum Pooling Layers

Max-pooling layers play a critical role in lowering spatial dimensionality and are closely associated with convolutional layers. They enable the presentation to focus on the most crucial aspects by keeping the most crucial information and eliminating the rest.

Layers That Are Dense1, Dense2, and Fully Associated

Decision-making and the extraction of higher-level information need fully connected layers. They reinforce the data from previous layers and frame the central portion of the neural network. These tiers collect intricate information and decide the palm to classify in relation to palm identification.

Layer of Yield

The top layer of the structure is called the yield layer, and it is composed of several hubs, each of which represents a distinct course name. When palm acknowledgment occurs, the yield layer consists of hubs matching unique palm identification names. Softmax actuation is often utilized to transform the yield values into probability ratings for each course, helping the demonstration to make its final forecast.

Getting the Display Ready

The CNN model is built using the preprocessed dataset. The preparatory stage comprises determining the degree of difference between the expected and actual names by selecting an appropriate luck measurement (categorical cross-entropy, for example). Stochastic Angle Plummet (SGD) and Adam optimizers, among others, may be used to modify the show parameters. When merging, the learning rate is changed to balance the requirement for accuracy and speed. Preparation is done on the training dataset, and show execution is continually monitored on the approval dataset. To prevent overfitting and guarantee that the demonstration successfully generalizes to concealed information, early halting methods are used.

Evaluation of Exhibits

Model assessment might be a crucial step in figuring out if the palm acknowledgment framework is viable. Accurate palm picture recognition is measured by the model using industry-standard evaluation measures such exactness, exactness, review, and F1 score. Thanks to thorough testing on the authorized dataset, overfitting or underfitting concerns are therefore addressed at the fine-tuning stage.

Adjustment and Improvement

The show has to be adjusted, and its hyperparameters (Chandan et al. 2023; Mondal, et al. 2023; Mall et al. 2023; Pandey et al. 2023; Pandey et al. 2023) need to be optimized, for better execution. To enable quicker convergence and higher accuracy, tests are conducted to find the optimal learning rate and group estimate. The information enlargement techniques are refined to boost the model's vigor. Exchange learning using pre-trained models is explored to help with planning and progress in general accuracy.

Useful Applications

For the inquiry to be flawless, the practiced demonstration must be sent in real-world scenarios. Integration with program and equipment components is crucial to provide a reliable and efficient client experience. This stage makes it possible to evaluate the model's competency in practical applications as well as its consistency and flexibility.

RESULTS

Model Creation and Verification

Effectiveness of Training

The CNN model showed steady convergence and was successfully trained over 50 epochs. The training dataset achieves around 95% accuracy, and the training curve shows a reduction in training loss and a rise in training accuracy.

Verification Results

With an accuracy of almost 92%, the model functioned well on the validation dataset. Similar results are shown by measures of precision, recall, and F1 score, suggesting robustness.

Verification and Practical Implementations

Test Dataset

A test dataset of real palm picture images was utilized to evaluate the model's actual performance. With an accuracy of around 90%, the model proved to be reliable in practical situations.

Practical Application

The access control system has successfully included palm recognition technology. According to user feedback, palm recognition that is accurate and speedy in access control situations offers a positive user experience. 3. Enhancement and refinement

Modifying Critical Parameters

Hyperparameter tuning experiments show that a little reduction in the learning rate improves both the overall accuracy and the convergence of the model. Batch size and learning rate optimization allowed for a more stable training process.

A Larger Extension of Data

The model is strengthened by improved data augmentation methods including rotation and mirroring. Advanced data augmentation produced a training data set that was more successful and diversified. 3.3 Transfer of Learning

Transfer learning from a pre-trained model greatly sped up the training process, improving accuracy and performance by around 5%.

Data Security and Moral Considerations

Privacy protection technology is utilized to handle palm photo data securely. To guarantee fair palm recognition and reduce bias, this model underwent a fairness evaluation.

Model Behavior and Instruction

Training and Validation

The CNN model can effectively learn and recognize palm characteristics, as shown by its successful training and validation. The validation dataset's accuracy of around 92% shows how well the model generalizes to variables that were not previously known. The resilience of the model is increased during training via constant convergence.

Tests and Practical Applications

The consistency accuracy of the model on the test dataset is about 90%, which bodes well for practical uses. Systems for biometric identification and access control should use this degree of accuracy. The palm recognition system's practical utility is validated by the pleasant user experience in real-world scenarios.

Modifying the Hyperparameters

Hyperparameter tuning experiments highlight how important it is to strike the right balance. Reducing the learning rate enhanced convergence somewhat while preventing instability. This finding will help in the future when determining the best learning rates for professions that are comparable.

A Larger Extension of Data

With the use of refined data augmentation methods like rotation and mirroring, we were able to create a training data set that was more varied. This diversity is necessary to increase the model's resilience and ability to manage different palm orientations and situations.

Transfer Education

Utilizing transfer learning from a pre-trained model was a significant optimization. This led to a 5% improvement in accuracy and sped up training. This result highlights the benefit of using trained models for comparable jobs, which reduces processing time and overhead.

Data Security and Moral Considerations

Applying fairness judgments and privacy-preserving techniques is essential to the practical use of palm recognition systems. Preserving user confidence and moral principles necessitates protecting privacy and reducing prejudice. When it comes to personal biometric data, these concerns are particularly important. The palm recognition accomplishments of this project are encouraging. There are many real-world uses for palm recognition systems based on CNNs (Mandal et al. 2021; Bhattacharya et al 2021; Meslie et al. 2021; Gupta et al 2022; Taviti Naidu et al. 2023) thanks to their effective development and implementation, especially in access control and biometric identity. There is a great deal of promise for accuracy, robustness, and usefulness with this approach.

CONCLUSION

Our goal in this project was to explore the creative possibilities of palm recognition using convolutional neural networks (CNNs) for access control and biometric authentication. Our findings and observations highlight the importance of this technology in the future development of secure identity verification and demonstrate encouraging advancements in the field. Our study yielded some important conclusions.

Robust Palm Detection

A CNN-based palm identification system that is dependable and efficient has been designed and used with success. The model consistently achieved excellent accuracy on both the validation and test datasets, demonstrating its ability to generalize to different palm orientations and real-world scenarios. Reliability and security both rely on a strong access control mechanism.

Adjustment and Enhancement

Experiments with hyperparameter optimization, data augmentation upgrades and transfer learning yielded major insights. The optimization produced five accuracy increases with transfer learning, faster convergence, and improved model performance. These results highlight the need of carefully selecting and modifying the model architecture to get optimal results.

Application in Day-to-Day Life

The seamless integration of our palm recognition system into a real-world access control scenario demonstrates the value of this technology. Users highlighted the possibility for simple and secure access to both physical and virtual settings by reporting quick and accurate palm identification. Because biometrics is so useful, their application has grown tremendously.

Ethics and Data Protection

Furthermore, the importance of privacy protection and ethical issues in biometric technology was underscored by our methodology. By using privacy-preserving techniques and fairness evaluations, we make sure that our technology respects individual privacy and reduces prejudice while addressing serious concerns regarding the use of biometric data.

Upcoming Policies

As we explore the possibilities of CNNs for palm detection, there are many chances to learn more. This technology may be used for secure authentication, mobile payments, mobile banking, and other purposes. Subsequent research endeavors should tackle concerns such as accommodating diverse environmental conditions and ensuring the comprehensiveness of palm identification.

REFERENCES

Agarwal, A. (2024). Use Cases of ChatGPT and Other AI Tools With Security Concerns. In Sharma, P., Jyotiyana, M., & Senthil Kumar, A. V. (Eds.), *Applications, Challenges, and the Future of ChatGPT* (pp. 216–225). IGI Global. DOI: 10.4018/979-8-3693-6824-4.ch012

Bhattacharya, A., Ghosal, A., Obaid, A. J., Krit, S., Shukla, V. K., Mandal, K., & Pramanik, S. (2021). Unsupervised Summarization Approach with Computational Statistics of Microblog Data. In Samanta, D., Althar, R. R., Pramanik, S., & Dutta, S. (Eds.), *Methodologies and Applications of Computational Statistics for Machine Learning* (pp. 23–37). IGI Global. DOI: 10.4018/978-1-7998-7701-1.ch002

Brown. (2018). Multi-Modal Biometric Authentication with Palm and Face Recognition. IEEE Transactions on Information Forensics and Security, 19(4).

Chandan, R. R., Soni, S., Raj, A., Veeraiah, V., Dhabliya, D., Pramanik, S., & Gupta, A. (2023). Genetic Algorithm and Machine Learning. In Advanced Bioinspiration Methods for Healthcare Standards, Policies, and Reform. IGI Global. DOI: 10.4018/978-1-6684-5656-9

Gupta, A., Verma, A., & Pramanik, S. (2022). Advanced Security System in Video Surveillance for COVID-19. In *An Interdisciplinary Approach to Modern Network Security*. CRC Press. DOI: 10.1201/9781003147176-8

Kapadiya, D., Shekhawat, C., & Sharma, P. (2023). A Study on Large Scale Applications of Big Data in Modern Era. In *International Conference on Information Management & Machine Intelligence (ICIMMI2023),* November 23–25, 2023, Jaipur, India. ACM. https://doi.org/DOI: 10.1145/3647444.364788

Kumar, S. (2017). Palm Recognition in Unconstrained Environments: Challenges and Solutions. *International Symposium on Biometrics Proceedings*, 56–64.

Li, X. (2019). Mobile Authentication with Palm Recognition: Challenges and Opportunities. Proceedings of the ACM Mobile Computing and Communications Review.

Maharajan, K., Kumar, A. V., El Emary, I. M., Sharma, P., Latip, R., Mishra, N., Dutta, A., Manjunatha Rao, L., & Sharma, M. (2023). Blockchain Methods and Data-Driven Decision Making With Autonomous Transportation. In Kumar, R., Abdul Hamid, A., & Binti Ya'akub, N. (Eds.), *Effective AI, Blockchain, and E-Governance Applications for Knowledge Discovery and Management* (pp. 176–194). IGI Global. DOI: 10.4018/978-1-6684-9151-5.ch012

Mall, P. K., Pramanik, S., Srivastava, S., Faiz, M., Sriramulu, S., & Kumar, M. N. (2023). FuzztNet-Based Modeling Smart Traffic System in Smart Cities Using Deep Learning Models. In *Data-Driven Mathematical Modeling in Smart Cities*. IGI Global. DOI: 10.4018/978-1-6684-6408-3.ch005

Mandal, A., Dutta, S., & Pramanik, S. (2021). Machine Intelligence of Pi from Geometrical Figures with Variable Parameters using SCILab. In Samanta, D., Althar, R. R., Pramanik, S., & Dutta, S. (Eds.), *Methodologies and Applications of Computational Statistics for Machine Learning* (pp. 38–63). IGI Global. DOI: 10.4018/978-1-7998-7701-1.ch003

Merlin Mancy, A., Kumar, A. V., Latip, R., Jagadamba, G., Chakrabarti, P., Sharma, P., Musirin, I. B., Sharma, M., & Kanchan, B. G. (2024). Smart Healthcare System, Digital Health and Telemedicine, Management and Emergencies: Patient Emergency Application (PES) E-Governance Applications. In Kumar, R., Abdul Hamid, A., Binti Ya'akub, N., Sharan, H., & Kumar, S. (Eds.), *Sustainable Development in AI, Blockchain, and E-Governance Applications* (pp. 124–151). IGI Global. DOI: 10.4018/979-8-3693-1722-8.ch008

Meslie, Y., Enbeyle, W., Pandey, B. K., Pramanik, S., Pandey, D., Dadeech, P., Belay, A., & Saini, A. (2021). Machine Intelligence-based Trend Analysis of COVID-19 for Total Daily Confirmed Cases in Asia and Africa. In Samanta, D., Althar, R. R., Pramanik, S., & Dutta, S. (Eds.), *Methodologies and Applications of Computational Statistics for Machine Learning* (pp. 164–185). IGI Global. DOI: 10.4018/978-1-7998-7701-1.ch009

Mondal, D., Ratnaparkhi, A., Deshpande, A., Deshpande, V., Kshirsagar, A. P., & Pramanik, S. (2023). Applications, Modern Trends and Challenges of Multiscale-Modelling in Smart Cities. In *Data-Driven Mathematical Modeling in Smart Cities*. IGI Global. DOI: 10.4018/978-1-6684-6408-3.ch001

Pandey, B. K., Pandey, D., Nassa, V. K., George, A. S., Pramanik, S., & Dadheech, P. (2023). *Applications for the Text Extraction Method of Complex Degraded Images in The Impact of Thrust Technologies on Image Processing*. Nova Publishers.

Pandey, B. K., Pandey, D., Nassa, V. K., Hameed, A. S., George, A. S., Dadheech, P., & Pramanik, S. (2023). A Review of Various Text Extraction Algorithms for Images. In *The Impact of Thrust Technologies on Image Processing*. Nova Publishers. DOI: 10.52305/ATJL4552

Patil, P., Kulkarni, K., & Sharma, P. (2024). Algorithmic Issues, Challenges, and Theoretical Concerns of ChatGPT. In Sharma, P., Jyotiyana, M., & Senthil Kumar, A. V. (Eds.), *Applications, Challenges, and the Future of ChatGPT* (pp. 56–74). IGI Global. DOI: 10.4018/979-8-3693-6824-4.ch003

Prasad, G. A., Kumar, A. V., Sharma, P., Irawati, I. D., D. V., C., Musirin, I. B., Abdullah, H. M., & Rao L, M. (2023). Artificial Intelligence in Computer Science: An Overview of Current Trends and Future Directions. In S. Rajest, B. Singh, A. Obaid, R. Regin, & K. Chinnusamy (Eds.), *Advances in Artificial and Human Intelligence in the Modern Era* (pp. 43-60). IGI Global. DOI: 10.4018/979-8-3693-1301-5.ch002

Rawat, P., Bhardwaj, A., Lamba, N., & Sharma, P. (2023). Arduino Based IoT Mini Weather Station. *SKIT Research Journal*, 13(2), 34–41. DOI: 10.47904/IJSKIT.13.2.2023.34-41

Sharma, P. (2023). *Utilizing Explainable Artificial Intelligence to Address Deep Learning in Biomedical Domain. Medical Data Analysis and Processing using Explainable Artificial Intelligence.* Taylor & Francis. DOI: 10.1201/9781003257721-2

Sharma, P., & Bhatnagar, N. (2023). Passenger Authentication and Ticket Verification at Airport Using QR Code Scanner. *SKIT Research Journal*, 13(2), 10–13. DOI: 10.47904/IJSKIT.13.1.2023.10-12

Sharma, P., & Dadheech, P. (2023). Modern-age Agriculture with Artificial Intelligence: A review emphasizing Crop Yield Prediction. *EVERGREEN Joint Journal of Novel Carbon Resource Sciences & Green Asia Strategy*, 10(4), 2570–2582. DOI: 10.5109/7160906

Sharma, P., Dadheech, P., Aneja, N., & Aneja, S. (2023). Predicting Agriculture Yields Based on Machine Learning Using Regression and Deep Learning. *IEEE Access : Practical Innovations, Open Solutions*, 11, 111255–111264. DOI: 10.1109/ACCESS.2023.3321861

Sharma, P., Dadheech, P., & Senthil Kumar Senthil, A. V. (2023). AI-Enabled Crop Recommendation System Based on Soil and Weather Patterns. In Gupta, R., Jain, A., Wang, J., Bharti, S., & Patel, S. (Eds.), *Artificial Intelligence Tools and Technologies for Smart Farming and Agriculture Practices* (pp. 184–199). IGI Global. DOI: 10.4018/978-1-6684-8516-3.ch010

Sharma, P., & Jain, M. K. (2023). Stock Market Trends Analysis using Extreme Gradient Boosting (XGBoost). *2023 International Conference on Computing, Communication, and Intelligent Systems (ICCCIS)*, 317-322. DOI: 10.1109/ICCCIS60361.2023.10425722

Sharma, P., Jyotiyana, M., & Senthil Kumar, A. V. (Eds.). (2024). *Applications, Challenges, and the Future of ChatGPT*. IGI Global. DOI: 10.4018/979-8-3693-6824-4

Sharma, P., Kapadiya, D., & Bhardwaj, A. (2023). Efficient Note Sharing Model for Collaborative Learning. *SKIT Research Journal*, 13(2), 42–46. DOI: 10.47904/IJSKIT.13.2.2023.42-46

Sharma, P., & Rathi, Y. (2016, June 5). Efficient Density-Based Clustering Using Automatic Parameter Detection. Efficient Density-Based Clustering Using Automatic Parameter Detection | SpringerLink. .DOI: 10.1007/978-981-10-0767-5_46

Sharma, P., Sharma, C., & Mathur, P. (2023). Machine Learning-based Stock Market Forecasting using Recurrent Neural Network. *2023 9th International Conference on Smart Computing and Communications (ICSCC)*, 600-605. DOI: 10.1109/ICSCC59169.2023.10335083

Tan, S. (2016). A Survey of Palmprint Recognition. *Proceedings of the International Conference on Pattern Recognition*, 120–133.

Taviti Naidu, G., & Ganesh, K. V. B. (2023). Technological Innovation Driven by Big Data. In *Advanced Bioinspiration Methods for Healthcare Standards, Policies, and Reform*. IGI Global. DOI: 10.4018/978-1-6684-5656-9

V., M. V., Kumar, A. S., Sharma, P., Kaur, S., Saleh, O. S., Chennamma, H., & Chaturvedi, A. (2023). AI-Equipped IoT Applications in High-Tech Agriculture Using Machine Learning. In A. Khang (Ed.), *Handbook of Research on AI-Equipped IoT Applications in High-Tech Agriculture* (pp. 38-64). IGI Global. .DOI: 10.4018/978-1-6684-9231-4.ch003

Xu, L. (2019). PalmPrint Recognition in Real-World Surveillance. *Journal of Surveillance and Security*, 26(4), 567–581.

KEY TERMS AND DEFINITIONS

Biometrics: The practice of employing a system or device to identify a person based on their distinctive behavioral or physical characteristics is known as biometrics, or biometric recognition. There are several uses for biometrics, including as entering a country or gaining access to computers.

Convolutional Neural Networks: One kind of Deep Learning neural network design that is often used in computer vision is the convolutional neural network (CNN). The branch of artificial intelligence known as "computer vision" gives computers the ability to comprehend and analyze images and other visual input.

Human-Computer Interaction: The interdisciplinary discipline of human-computer interaction (HCI) investigates and develops human-computer interactions and other technological systems. HCI experts take into account the user, the computer, and their mutual relationship to design user interfaces and interactions that are effective, pleasurable, and intuitive.

Image Classification: The technique of classifying and labeling groupings of pixels or vectors within an image according to predetermined criteria is known as image classification. It is possible to create the classification law using one or more textural or spectral properties.

Palm Recognition: A person's palm veins are used in the biometric security procedure known as palm recognition, or palm vein recognition. A person's veins are photographed using palm vein scanners, which then compare the picture to a database of previously gathered patterns.

Conclusion

The edited reference book *Real-Time Data Decisions With AI and ChatGPT Techniques*, curated by Priyanka Sharma, Monika Jyotiyana, and A. V. Senthil Kumar, explores the profound impact of Artificial Intelligence, particularly ChatGPT, on various sectors. The chapters presented in this book provide novel insights and in-depth analysis, underscoring the transformative potential of AI in today's society. The chapters collectively underscore the transformative potential of AI in enhancing efficiency, accuracy, and creativity in numerous fields.

Revolutionizing Customer Engagement and Content Production

A potent text-based artificial intelligence technology, ChatGPT, has the potential to revolutionize customer engagement and content production for enterprises. By automating repetitive operations, enhancing client interaction, and responding to complex search questions with efficiency and accuracy, businesses can significantly benefit from ChatGPT. Data science underpins the improved chatbot dialogues, making them more organic and engaging for users. With machine learning techniques like sentiment analysis and natural language processing, ChatGPT's chatbots can comprehend client intent, personalize responses, and foresee customer needs.

AI in Everyday Life

Artificial intelligence has permeated every aspect of our daily lives, from asking Alexa to play a song to unlocking phones using face recognition. AI extends its capabilities to writing tasks, generating code, composing emails, and even acing tests at command. However, due to its popularity, ChatGPT is frequently overloaded, making it unreliable for regular use. Nevertheless, numerous additional AI tools are available to perform these tasks, ensuring that AI continues to support and enhance everyday activities.

Addressing the Need for Comprehensive AI Research

In the modern era of artificial intelligence, there is a pressing need for an edited collection of original research. This book aims to focus on novel concepts and in-depth analysis, providing readers with a broader perspective on ChatGPT and other AI tools. By soliciting chapters that discuss both the improvement of current approaches and the creation of new methodologies, this book addresses key aspects of AI tools, techniques, development and applications.

Broad Target Audience

The target audience of this book includes professionals, policymakers, budding researchers, social science researchers, academicians, industry professionals, and other domain experts interested in artificial intelligence, machine learning, image processing, ChatGPT, and other AI tools. The book highlights how AI leads to social and community benefits, efficient use of resources, and easier life. The unique theme of this book, with few comparable resources available in the global market, makes it a valuable contribution to the field.

Impact on Society

The research presented in this book underscores the transformative impact of AI technologies on contemporary society. AI is not merely a technological advancement; it is a force reshaping industries, enhancing efficiency, and creating new opportunities. The implications of AI extend far beyond technology and business, influencing social structures, economic models, and ethical standards.

- **Enhancing Public Services:** AI-driven decision-making in public health, urban planning, and emergency response improves the quality and responsiveness of public services.
- **Revolutionizing Industries:** AI integration in engineering, healthcare, and the garment industry highlights its transformative potential, driving innovation and efficiency.
- **Empowering E-Commerce:** ChatGPT's role in E-Commerce enhances user experiences and improves customer interaction and support services.
- **Transforming Media and Communication:** AI facilitates real-time data decision-making in media communications, improving operational efficiency and accuracy.

- **Advancing Programming and Security:** ChatGPT in programming code development increases productivity and code quality while emphasizing the importance of robust security measures.

Final Thoughts

This comprehensive exploration of ChatGPT and AI technologies provides researchers, practitioners, and policymakers with a deeper understanding of AI's transformative potential. The chapters collectively illuminate AI-driven models' profound impact on reshaping traditional paradigms and fostering innovation across various domains.

The ethical considerations, potential biases, and need for robust data governance frameworks highlighted throughout this book underscore the importance of responsible AI deployment. As we navigate the evolving landscape of AI technologies, balancing innovation with ethical vigilance is crucial to ensure that AI systems are designed and utilized in ways that uphold integrity, security, and trust.

By embracing these technologies thoughtfully and responsibly, we can harness their full potential to drive progress and create a positive impact across various fields. The insights presented in this book not only reflect the current state of AI and ChatGPT but also chart a course for future research and development, emphasizing the importance of continuous learning and adaptation.

We hope this reference book serves as a valuable resource, encouraging readers to delve deeply into each chapter, to question, to innovate, and to contribute to the ongoing dialogue on the future of AI in engineering and beyond.

Compilation of References

Abbot, M. 2003, May. Standard setting for complex performance assessments: A critical examination of the analytic judgment method. Annual congress of the Canadian society for the study of education.

Abdullaev, I., Prodanova, N., & Ahmed, M. A. (2023). Leveraging metaheuristics with artificial intelligence for customer churn prediction in telecom industries. *Electronic Research Archive*, 31(8), 4443–4458. DOI:10.3934/era.2023227

Afandi, Y., Maskur, , & Arjo, T. R. (2021).. *Use of Chatbot on Online Store Website as Virtual Customer Service to Improve Sales*. Advance online publication. DOI:10.2991/aebmr.k.210717.012

Agarwal, A., Trivedi, A., Sharma, P., & Bhardwaj, A. (2024). Use Cases of ChatGPT and Other AI Tools With Security Concerns. In *Applications, Challenges, and the Future of ChatGPT* (pp. 216–225). IGI Global. DOI:10.4018/979-8-3693-6824-4.ch012

Al-Hawawreh, M., Aljuhani, A., & Jararweh, Y. (2023). Chatgpt for cybersecurity: Practical applications, challenges, and future directions. *Cluster Computing*, 26(6), 3421–3436. DOI:10.1007/s10586-023-04124-5

Ali, M. J., & Djalilian, A. (2023, March). Readership awareness series–paper 4: Chatbots and ChatGPT-ethical considerations in scientific publications. In *Seminars in Ophthalmology* (pp. 1–2). Taylor & Francis.

Alkaissi, H., & McFarlane, S. I. (2023). Artificial hallucinations in ChatGPT: Implications in scientific writing. *Cureus*, 15. DOI:10.7759/cureus.35179 PMID:36811129

AlKhuzaey, S.A systematic review of data-driven approaches to item difficulty prediction. *International Conference on Artificial Intelligence in Education*. Springer. DOI:10.1007/978-3-030-78292-4_3

AlKhuzaey, S., Grasso, F., Payne, T. R., & Tamma, V. (2023). Text-based Question Difficulty Prediction: A Systematic Review of Automatic Approaches. *International Journal of Artificial Intelligence in Education*, 1–53. DOI:10.1007/s40593-023-00362-1

Al-Mekhlal, M., Al-Buraik, M., & Al-Lubli, M. (2023). Digital transformation: AI-powered bot solutions and automation for customer services. *2023 International Conference on Digital Age & Technological Advances for Sustainable Development (ICDATA)*. DOI:10.1109/ICDATE58146.2023.10248458

Amodei, D. (2019). AI safety and reliability in engineering systems. *Proceedings of the National Academy of Sciences*.

Andoni, M., Robu, V., Flynn, D., Abram, S., Geach, D., Jenkins, D., McCallum, P., & Peacock, A. (2019). Blockchain technology in the energy sector: A systematic review of challenges and opportunities. *Renewable & Sustainable Energy Reviews*, 100, 143–174. DOI:10.1016/j.rser.2018.10.014

Anju, A., & Krishnamurthy, M. (2024). M-EOS: Modified-equilibrium optimization-based stacked CNN for insider threat detection. *Wireless Networks*, 30(4), 2819–2838. DOI:10.1007/s11276-024-03678-5

Anjum, A., Sporny, M., & Sill, A. (2017). Blockchain standards for compliance and trust. *IEEE Cloud Computing*, 4(4), 84–90. DOI:10.1109/MCC.2017.3791019

Armanious, K., Jiang, C., Abdulatif, S., Küstner, T., Gatidis, S., & Yang, B. (2019). *Unsupervised medical image translation using cycle-MedGAN.* Paper presented at the 2019 27th European signal processing conference (EUSIPCO). DOI:10.23919/EUSIPCO.2019.8902799

Arman, M., & Lamiyar, U. (2023). Exploring the Implication of ChatGPT AI for Business: Efficiency and Challenges. *International Journal of Marketing and Digital Creative*, 1(2), 64–84. DOI:10.31098/ijmadic.v1i2.1872

Aryanto, E., Mabruk, H., & Narendroputro, W. (2023). *Artificial intelligence implementation strategy to make it happen smart government Indonesia gold 2045.* International Journal of Social Science and Business. DOI:10.54783/ijsoc.v5i5.877

Bahrini, A.ChatGPT: Applications, Opportunities, and Threats. *2023 Systems and Information Engineering Design Symposium (SIEDS)*, 274-279. DOI:10.1109/SIEDS58326.2023.10137850

Baidoo, D., Tanu, L., & Kumar, P. (2023). Machine learning based heart disease prediction system. *AIP Conference Proceedings, 2963*, 020009. DOI:10.1063/5.0094875

Baidoo-Anu, D., & Owusu Ansah, L. (2023). Education in the era of generative artificial intelligence (AI): Understanding the potential benefits of ChatGPT in promoting teaching and learning.

Baidoo-Anu, D., & Owusu Ansah, L. (2023). Education in the Era of Generative Artificial Intelligence (AI): Understanding the Potential Benefits of ChatGPT in Promoting Teaching and Learning. Available at: *SSRN* 4337484. DOI:10.2139/ssrn.4337484

Basir, A., Puspitasari, E., Aristarini, C. C., Sulastri, P. D., & Ausat, A. M. A. (2023). Ethical use of ChatGPT in the context of leadership and strategic decisions. Journal of Maritime Policy. DOI:10.33395/jmp.v12i1.12693

Beatty, P. C., & Willis, G. B. (2007). Research synthesis: The practice of cognitive interviewing. *Public Opinion Quarterly*, 71(2), 287–311. DOI:10.1093/poq/nfm006

Beatty, P., Team, I., Miller, K., Wilson, B., Whitaker, K., & Kennet, J. (2002). *Cognitive interview evaluation of the blood donor history screening questionnaire. Final report of the AABB task force to redesign the blood donor screening questionnaire. Estados Unidos*. US Food and Drug Administration.

Beinborn, L., Zesch, T., & Gurevych, I. (2014). Predicting the difficulty of language proficiency tests. *Transactions of the Association for Computational Linguistics*, 2, 517–530. DOI:10.1162/tacl_a_00200

Bender, E. M., Gebru, T., McMillan-Major, A., & Shmitchell, S. (2021, March). On the dangers of stochastic parrots: Can language models be too big? In *Proceedings of the 2021 ACM conference on fairness, accountability, and transparency* (pp. 610-623). DOI:10.1145/3442188.3445922

Bhattacharya, A., Ghosal, A., Obaid, A. J., Krit, S., Shukla, V. K., Mandal, K., & Pramanik, S. (2021). Unsupervised Summarization Approach with Computational Statistics of Microblog Data. In Samanta, D., Althar, R. R., Pramanik, S., & Dutta, S. (Eds.), *Methodologies and Applications of Computational Statistics for Machine Learning* (pp. 23–37). IGI Global. DOI:10.4018/978-1-7998-7701-1.ch002

Biswas, S. (2023c). Role of ChatGPT in computer programming.: ChatGPT in computer programming. Mesopotamian J. Comput. Sci., 8–16.

Biswas, S. S. (2023). Role of ChatGPT in public health. *Annals of Biomedical Engineering*, 51(5), 868–869. DOI:10.1007/s10439-023-03172-7 PMID:36920578

Biswas, S. S. (2023a). Potential use of Chat GPT in global warming. *Annals of Biomedical Engineering*, 51(6), 1–2. DOI:10.1007/s10439-023-03171-8 PMID:36856927

Bradlow, E. T., Gangwar, M., Kopalle, P. K., & Voleti, S. (2017). The role of big data and predictive analytics in retailing. *Journal of Retailing*, 93(1), 79–95. DOI:10.1016/j.jretai.2016.12.004

Braun, V., & Clarke, V. (2012). *Thematic analysis: A practical guide*. Sage. DOI:10.1037/13620-004

Brown, T. B., Mann, B., Ryder, N., Subbiah, M., Kaplan, J., Dhariwal, P., Neelakantan, A., Shyam, P., Sastry, G., Askell, A., Agarwal, S., Herbert-Voss, A., Krueger, G., Henighan, T., Child, R., Ramesh, A., Ziegler, D. M., Wu, J., Winter, C., . . . Amodei, D. (2020). Language models are few-shot learners. arXiv preprint arXiv:2005.14165v4.

Brown. (2018). Multi-Modal Biometric Authentication with Palm and Face Recognition. IEEE Transactions on Information Forensics and Security, 19(4).

Brown, A. (2020). *AI and Media Production: Opportunities and Challenges*. Routledge.

Brown, T., Mann, B., Ryder, N., Subbiah, M., Kaplan, J. D., Dhariwal, P., & Amodei, D. (2020). Language models are few-shot learners. *Advances in Neural Information Processing Systems*, 33, 1877–1901.

Cackowski, S., Barbier, E. L., Dojat, M., & Christen, T. (2023). Imunity: A generalizable vae-gan solution for multicenter mr image harmonization. *Medical Image Analysis*, 88, 102799. DOI:10.1016/j.media.2023.102799 PMID:37245434

Cascella, M., Montomoli, J., Bellini, V., & Bignami, E. (2023). Evaluating the feasibility of ChatGPT in healthcare: An analysis of multiple clinical and research scenarios. *Journal of Medical Systems*, 47(1), 1–5. DOI:10.1007/s10916-023-01925-4 PMID:36869927

Castillo Ossa, L. F., Chamoso, P., Arango-López, J., Pinto-Santos, F., Isaza, G. A., Santa-Cruz-González, C., Ceballos-Marquez, A., Hernández, G., & Corchado, J. M. (2021). A hybrid model for COVID-19 monitoring and prediction. *Electronics (Basel)*, 10(7), 799. DOI:10.3390/electronics10070799

Castillo-González, W., Lepez, C. O., & Bonardi, M. C. (2022). ChatGPT: A promising tool for academic editing. *Data and Metadata*, 1(1), 23–23. DOI:10.56294/dm202223

Challenges. (2023). https://www.cyfirma.com/outofband/chatgpt-ai-in-security-testing-opportunities-and-challenges/

Chandan, R. R., Soni, S., Raj, A., Veeraiah, V., Dhabliya, D., Pramanik, S., & Gupta, A. (2023). Genetic Algorithm and Machine Learning. In Advanced Bio-inspiration Methods for Healthcare Standards, Policies, and Reform. IGI Global. DOI:10.4018/978-1-6684-5656-9

Chang, Y. L., Iakovou, E., & Shi, W. D. (2020). Blockchain in global supply chains and cross border trade: A critical synthesis of the state-of-the-art, challenges and opportunities. *International Journal of Production Research*, 58(7), 2082–2099. DOI:10.1080/00207543.2019.1651946

Chartsias, A., Joyce, T., Papanastasiou, G., Semple, S., Williams, M., Newby, D. E., Dharmakumar, R., & Tsaftaris, S. A. (2019). Disentangled representation learning in cardiac image analysis. *Medical Image Analysis*, 58, 101535. DOI:10.1016/j.media.2019.101535 PMID:31351230

Chen, B., Wu, Z., & Zhao, R. (2023). From fiction to fact: The growing role of generative AI in business and finance. *Journal of Chinese Economic and Business Studies*, 21(4), 471–496. DOI:10.1080/14765284.2023.2245279

Chen, Y., Yang, X.-H., Wei, Z., Heidari, A. A., Zheng, N., Li, Z., Chen, H., Hu, H., Zhou, Q., & Guan, Q. (2022). Generative adversarial networks in medical image augmentation: A review. *Computers in Biology and Medicine*, 144, 105382. DOI:10.1016/j.compbiomed.2022.105382 PMID:35276550

Chikkamath, M., Dwivedi, D., Hirekurubar, R. B., & Thimmappa, R. (2023). Benchmarking of novel convolutional neural network models for automatic butterfly identification. In Shukla, P. K., Singh, K. P., Tripathi, A. K., & Engelbrecht, A. (Eds.), *Computer Vision and Robotics. Algorithms for Intelligent Systems*. Springer. DOI:10.1007/978-981-19-7892-0_27

Choudhary, S., Kesswani, N., & Majhi, S. (2021). An ensemble intrusion detection model for internet of things network.

Choudhary, S., & Meena, G. (2022). Internet of Things: Protocols, Applications and Security Issues. *Procedia Computer Science*, 215, 274–288. DOI:10.1016/j.procs.2022.12.030

Clark, K., Vendt, B., Smith, K., Freymann, J., Kirby, J., Koppel, P., & Pringle, M. (2013). The Cancer Imaging Archive (TCIA): Maintaining and operating a public information repository. *Journal of Digital Imaging*, 26(6), 1045–1057. DOI:10.1007/s10278-013-9622-7 PMID:23884657

Coman, D., State, V., Voinea, M. C., & Cucui, G. (2023). Impacts of chatbots on the accounting service industry. *Agora International Journal of Economical Sciences*, 17(1), 1–13. Advance online publication. DOI:10.15837/aijes.v17i1.5756

Contractor, D., McDuff, D. J., Haines, J., Lee, J., Hines, C., & Hecht, B. J. (2020). Behavioral use licensing for responsible AI. arXiv. https://dblp.org/rec/journals/corr/abs-2011-03116.html

Cotton, D. R., Cotton, P. A., & Shipway, J. R. (2023). Chatting and Cheating: Ensuring Academic Integrity in the Era of ChatGPT. *Innovations in Education and Teaching International*, 1–12.

Crawford, J., Cowling, M., & Allen, K. A. (2023). Leadership is needed for ethical ChatGPT: Character, assessment, and learning using artificial intelligence (AI). *Journal of University Teaching & Learning Practice*, 20(3), 2. DOI:10.53761/1.20.3.02

Creswell, J. W., & Creswell, J. D. (2018). *Research design: Qualitative, quantitative, and mixed methods approaches* (5th ed.). Sage Publications.

Das, A., Nair, M. S., & Peter, S. D. (2020). Computer-aided histopathological image analysis techniques for automated nuclear atypia scoring of breast cancer: A review. *Journal of Digital Imaging*, 33(5), 1091–1121. DOI:10.1007/s10278-019-00295-z PMID:31989390

Deldjoo, Y. (2023). Fairness of ChatGPT and the role of explainable-guided prompts. ArXiv, abs/2307.11761.

Devlin, J., Chang, M. W., Lee, K., & Toutanova, K. (2018). Bert: Pre-training of deep bidirectional transformers for language understanding. arXiv preprint arXiv:1810.04805.

Domina, T., Lee, S.-E., & MacGillivray, M. (2012). Understanding factors affecting consumer intention to shop in a virtual world. *Journal of Retailing and Consumer Services*, 19(6), 613–620. DOI:10.1016/j.jretconser.2012.08.001

Dowling, M. M., & Lucey, B. M. (2023). ChatGPT for (Finance) Research: The Bananarama Conjecture. SSRN *Electronic Journal*. DOI:10.2139/ssrn.4322651

Duan, Y., Edwards, J. S., & Dwivedi, Y. K. (2019). Artificial intelligence for decision making in the era of Big Data–evolution, challenges and research agenda. *International Journal of Information Management*, 48, 63–71. DOI:10.1016/j.ijinfomgt.2019.01.021

Dwivedi, D. N., & Anand, A. (2021). The Text Mining of Public Policy Documents in Response to COVID-19: A Comparison of the United Arab Emirates and the Kingdom of Saudi Arabia. Public Governance / Zarządzanie Publiczne, 55(1), 8-22. DOI:10.15678/ZP.2021.55.1.02

Dwivedi, D. N., & Gupta, A. (2022). Artificial intelligence-driven power demand estimation and short-, medium-, and long-term forecasting. In Artificial Intelligence for Renewable Energy Systems (pp. 231-242). Woodhead Publishing. DOI:10.1016/B978-0-323-90396-7.00013-4

Dwivedi, D. N., Mahanty, G., & Vemareddy, A. (2023). Sentiment analysis and topic modeling for identifying key public concerns of water quality/issues. In S. Harun, I. K. Othman, & M. H. Jamal (Eds.), *Proceedings of the 5th International Conference on Water Resources (ICWR)* – Volume 1. *Lecture Notes in Civil Engineering,* vol 293. Springer. DOI:10.1007/978-981-19-5947-9_28

Dwivedi, D. N., & Anand, A. (2022). A Comparative Study of Key Themes of Scientific Research Post COVID-19 in the United Arab Emirates and WHO Using Text Mining Approach. In Tiwari, S., Trivedi, M. C., Kolhe, M. L., Mishra, K., & Singh, B. K. (Eds.), *Advances in Data and Information Sciences. Lecture Notes in Networks and Systems* (Vol. 318). Springer. DOI:10.1007/978-981-16-5689-7_30

Dwivedi, D. N., & Batra, S. (2024). Case Studies in Big Data Analysis: A Novel Computer Vision Application to Detect Insurance Fraud. In Darwish, D. (Ed.), *Big Data Analytics Techniques for Market Intelligence* (pp. 441–450). IGI Global. DOI:10.4018/979-8-3693-0413-6.ch018

Dwivedi, D. N., Batra, S., & Pathak, Y. K. (2024). Enhancing Customer Experience: Exploring Deep Learning Models for Banking Customer Journey Analysis. In Sharma, H., Chakravorty, A., Hussain, S., & Kumari, R. (Eds.), *Artificial Intelligence: Theory and Applications. AITA 2023. Lecture Notes in Networks and Systems* (Vol. 843). Springer. DOI:10.1007/978-981-99-8476-3_39

Dwivedi, D. N., & Mahanty, G. (2024). Guardians of the Algorithm: Human Oversight in the Ethical Evolution of AI and Data Analysis. In Kumar, R., Joshi, A., Sharan, H., Peng, S., & Dudhagara, C. (Eds.), *The Ethical Frontier of AI and Data Analysis* (pp. 196–210). IGI Global. DOI:10.4018/979-8-3693-2964-1.ch012

Dwivedi, D. N., & Mahanty, G. (2024). Mental health in messages: Unravelling emotional patterns through advanced text analysis. In Rai, M., & Pandey, J. (Eds.), *Using Machine Learning to Detect Emotions and Predict Human Psychology* (pp. 187–208). IGI Global. DOI:10.4018/979-8-3693-1910-9.ch009

Dwivedi, D. N., & Mahanty, G. (2024). Unmasking the Shadows: Exploring Unethical AI Implementation. In Dadwal, S., Goyal, S., Kumar, P., & Verma, R. (Eds.), *Demystifying the Dark Side of AI in Business* (pp. 185–200). IGI Global. DOI:10.4018/979-8-3693-0724-3.ch012

Dwivedi, D. N., Mahanty, G., & Dwivedi, V. N. (2024). The Role of Predictive Analytics in Personalizing Education: Tailoring Learning Paths for Individual Student Success. In Bhatia, M., & Mushtaq, M. (Eds.), *Enhancing Education With Intelligent Systems and Data-Driven Instruction* (pp. 44–59). IGI Global. DOI:10.4018/979-8-3693-2169-0.ch003

Dwivedi, D. N., Mahanty, G., & Vemareddy, A. (2022). How responsible is AI?: Identification of key public concerns using sentiment analysis and topic modeling. *International Journal of Information Retrieval Research*, 12(1), 1–14. DOI:10.4018/IJIRR.298646

Dwivedi, D. N., & Pathak, S. (2022). Sentiment Analysis for COVID Vaccinations Using Twitter: Text Clustering of Positive and Negative Sentiments. In Hassan, S. A., Mohamed, A. W., & Alnowibet, K. A. (Eds.), *Decision Sciences for COVID-19. International Series in Operations Research & Management Science* (Vol. 320). Springer. DOI:10.1007/978-3-030-87019-5_12

Dwivedi, D. N., Wójcik, K., & Vemareddyb, A. (2022). Identification of Key Concerns and Sentiments Towards Data Quality and Data Strategy Challenges Using Sentiment Analysis and Topic Modeling. In Jajuga, K., Dehnel, G., & Walesiak, M. (Eds.), *Modern Classification and Data Analysis. SKAD 2021. Studies in Classification, Data Analysis, and Knowledge Organization*. Springer. DOI:10.1007/978-3-031-10190-8_2

Dwivedi, D., & Patil, G. (2022). Lightweight Convolutional Neural Network for Land Use Image Classification. *Journal of Advanced Geospatial Science & Technology*, 2(1), 31–48. DOI:10.11113/jagst.v2n1.31

Dwivedi, D., & Vemareddy, A. (2023). Sentiment Analytics for Crypto Pre and Post Covid: Topic Modeling. In Molla, A. R., Sharma, G., Kumar, P., & Rawat, S. (Eds.), Lecture Notes in Computer Science: Vol. 13776. *Distributed Computing and Intelligent Technology. ICDCIT 2023*. Springer. DOI:10.1007/978-3-031-24848-1_21

Eaganathan, L. (2022). Intention of Consumer Perception towards Online Buying Behaviour during Pandemic Period. 2022 IEEE, 2nd *Mysore Sub Section International Conference (MysuruCon)*, 1-5. DOI:10.1109/MysuruCon55714.2022.9971806

Erickson, B. J., Korfiatis, P., Akkus, Z., & Kline, T. L. (2017). Machine learning for medical imaging. Radiographics, 37(2), 505-515.

Eshtemirov, Nazarov, Khamidov, & Dagur. (n.d.). Deep learning-based traffic congestion forecasting research, Artificial Intelligence and Information Technologies, 1-6.

Evans, K. (2014). Encyclopaedia of business and finance (3rd ed.). Thomson Gale.

Fan, L. (2021). User Study on the Usability of ChatGPT in Engineering Design Tasks. *Proceedings of the IEEE Conference on Natural Language Processing (CONLP).*

Fehrmann, M. L., Woehr, D. J., & Arthur, W.Jr. (1991). The Angoff cutoff score method: The impact of frame-of-reference rater training. *Educational and Psychological Measurement*, 51(4), 857–872. DOI:10.1177/0013164491051004006

Feng, Jiang, & Peng. (n.d.). Artificial Intelligence Leads the Innovation and Development of the Textile Industry. Modern Textile Technology, 29(3), 7.

Feng, Z., Hu, G., & Li, B. (2023). Unleashing the power of ChatGPT in finance research: Opportunities and challenges. SSRN *Electronic Journal*. DOI:10.2139/ssrn.4424979

Field, A. (2013). *Discovering statistics using IBM SPSS statistics*. Sage Publications.

Filice, R. W., Stein, A., Wu, C. C., Arteaga, V. A., Borstelmann, S., Gaddikeri, R., & Hobbs, S. B. (2020). Crowdsourcing pneumothorax annotations using machine learning annotations on the NIH chest X-ray dataset. *Journal of Digital Imaging*, 33(2), 490–496. DOI:10.1007/s10278-019-00299-9 PMID:31768897

Frid-Adar, M., Diamant, I., Klang, E., Amitai, M., Goldberger, J., & Greenspan, H. (2018). GAN-based synthetic medical image augmentation for increased CNN performance in liver lesion classification. *Neurocomputing*, 321, 321–331. DOI:10.1016/j.neucom.2018.09.013

Frieder, S., Pinchetti, L., Griffiths, R. R., Salvatori, T., Lukasiewicz, T., Petersen, P. C., Chevalier, A., & Berner, J. (2023). Mathematical Capabilities of ChatGPT. arXiv preprint: arXiv:2301.13867.

Gao, J., Galley, M., & Li, L. (2019). Neural approaches to conversational AI. *Foundations and Trends® in Information Retrieval, 13*(2-3), 127-298.

Gasperecz, E., & Gasperecz, E. (2023, June 9). Transforming banking with ChatGPT: Enhanced chat, fraud detection, personalized recommendations, and risk management - First National Bankers Bank. First National Bankers Bank - Community Banking throughout the Southeast and Midwest. https://www.bankers-bank.com/transforming-banking-with-chatgpt-enhanced-chat-fraud-detection-personalized-recommendations-and-risk-management/

Ghosh, A., & Lakshmi, D. (2023). Dual governance: The intersection of centralized regulation and crowdsourced safety mechanisms for generative AI. arXiv. https://doi.org//arXiv.2308.04448DOI:10.48550

Gill, S. S., & Kaur, R. (2023). ChatGPT: Vision and challenges. *Internet of Things and Cyber-Physical Systems*, 3, 262–271. DOI:10.1016/j.iotcps.2023.05.004

Goodfellow, I., Pouget-Abadie, J., Mirza, M., Xu, B., Warde-Farley, D., Ozair, S., & Bengio, Y. (2014). Generative adversarial nets. *Advances in Neural Information Processing Systems*, 27.

Gupta, A. (2021). Understanding Consumer Product Sentiments through Supervised Models on Cloud: Pre and Post COVID. Webology, 18(1). .DOI:10.14704/WEB/V18I1/WEB18097

Gupta, A., Dwivedi, D. N., & Shah, J. (2023a). Overview of money laundering. In Artificial Intelligence Applications in Banking and Financial Services. Future of Business and Finance. Springer. DOI:10.1007/978-981-99-2571-1_1

Gupta, A., Dwivedi, D. N., & Shah, J. (2023b). Financial crimes management and control in financial institutions. In Artificial Intelligence Applications in Banking and Financial Services. Future of Business and Finance. Springer. DOI:10.1007/978-981-99-2571-1_2

Gupta, A., Dwivedi, D. N., & Shah, J. (2023c). Overview of technology solutions. In Artificial Intelligence Applications in Banking and Financial Services. Future of Business and Finance. Springer. DOI:10.1007/978-981-99-2571-1_3

Gupta, A., Dwivedi, D. N., & Shah, J. (2023d). Data organization for an FCC unit. In Artificial Intelligence Applications in Banking and Financial Services. Future of Business and Finance. Springer. DOI:10.1007/978-981-99-2571-1_4

Gupta, A., Dwivedi, D. N., & Shah, J. (2023e). Planning for AI in financial crimes. In Artificial Intelligence Applications in Banking and Financial Services. Future of Business and Finance. Springer. DOI:10.1007/978-981-99-2571-1_5

Gupta, A., Dwivedi, D. N., & Shah, J. (2023f). Applying machine learning for effective customer risk assessment. In Artificial Intelligence Applications in Banking and Financial Services. Future of Business and Finance. Springer. DOI:10.1007/978-981-99-2571-1_6

Gupta, A., Dwivedi, D. N., & Shah, J. (2023g). Artificial intelligence-driven effective financial transaction monitoring. In Artificial Intelligence Applications in Banking and Financial Services. Future of Business and Finance. Springer. DOI:10.1007/978-981-99-2571-1_7

Gupta, A., Dwivedi, D. N., & Shah, J. (2023h). Machine learning-driven alert optimization. In Artificial Intelligence Applications in Banking and Financial Services. Future of Business and Finance. Springer. DOI:10.1007/978-981-99-2571-1_8

Gupta, A., Dwivedi, D. N., & Shah, J. (2023i). Applying artificial intelligence on investigation. In Artificial Intelligence Applications in Banking and Financial Services. Future of Business and Finance. Springer. DOI:10.1007/978-981-99-2571-1_9

Gupta, A., Dwivedi, D. N., & Shah, J. (2023j). Ethical challenges for AI-based applications. In Artificial Intelligence Applications in Banking and Financial Services. Future of Business and Finance. Springer. DOI:10.1007/978-981-99-2571-1_10

Gupta, A., Dwivedi, D. N., & Shah, J. (2023k). Setting up a best-in-class AI-driven financial crime control unit (FCCU). In Artificial Intelligence Applications in Banking and Financial Services. Future of Business and Finance. Springer. DOI:10.1007/978-981-99-2571-1_11

Gupta, A., Verma, A., & Pramanik, S. (2022). Advanced Security System in Video Surveillance for COVID-19. In *An Interdisciplinary Approach to Modern Network Security*. CRC Press. DOI:10.1201/9781003147176-8

Gupta, M., Akiri, C., Aryal, K., Parker, E., & Praharaj, L. (2023). From ChatGPT to ThreatGPT: Impact of Generative AI in Cybersecurity and Privacy. *IEEE Access : Practical Innovations, Open Solutions*, 11, 80218–80245. DOI:10.1109/ACCESS.2023.3300381

Gu, X., Gao, F., Tan, M., & Peng, P. (2020). Fashion analysis and understanding with artificial intelligence. *Information Processing & Management*, 57(5), 102276. DOI:10.1016/j.ipm.2020.102276

Haleem, A., Javaid, M., & Singh, R. P. (2023). *An Era of ChatGPT as a Significant Futuristic Support Tool: A Study on Features*. Abilities, and Challenges, BenchCouncil Transactions on Benchmarks, Standards and Evaluations.

Han, Z., Battaglia, F., Udaiyar, A., Fooks, A., & Terlecky, S. R. (2023). An explorative assessment of ChatGPT as an aid in medical education: Use it with caution. *medRxiv*. DOI:10.1101/2023.02.13.23285879

Harris, L. (2019). *Audience Analytics and AI*. Academic Press.

Hartig, M., Truran-Sacrey, D., Raptentsetsang, S., Schuff, N., & Weiner, M. (2012). Ucsf freesurfer overview and qc ratings. *ADNI: Alzheimers Disease Neuroimaging Initiative, San Francisco.*

Hill-Yardin, E. L., Hutchinson, M. R., Laycock, R., & Spencer, S. J. (2023). A chat (GPT) about the future of scientific publishing. *Brain, Behavior, and Immunity*, 110, 152–154. DOI:10.1016/j.bbi.2023.02.022 PMID:36868432

Huang, K., Zhang, F., Li, Y., Wright, S., Kidambi, V., & Manral, V. (2023). Security and Privacy Concerns in ChatGPT. In Huang, K., Wang, Y., Zhu, F., Chen, X., & Xing, C. (Eds.), *Beyond AI. Future of Business and Finance*. Springer. DOI:10.1007/978-3-031-45282-6_11

Jackson, M., & McDaniel, D. (2023). Why ChatGPT is a security concern for your organization. GitGuardian Blog.

Jahan, M. T., Rahman Laskar, C., Peng, C., & Huang, J. X. (2023). Evaluation of ChatGPT on biomedical tasks: A zero-shot comparison with fine-tuned generative transformers. *BioNLP@ACL, 1*, 326-336.

Jaimovitch-López, G., Ferri, C., Hernández-Orallo, J., Martínez-Plumed, F., & Ramírez-Quintana, M. J. (2022). Can language models automate data wrangling? *Machine Learning*, 112(6), 2053–2082. DOI:10.1007/s10994-022-06259-9

Jain, A. K. (2022). Artificial intelligence in engineering: Trends and applications. *IEEE Transactions on Engineering Management.*

Jalil, S., Rafi, S., LaToza, T. D., Moran, K., & Lam, W. (2023). Chatgpt and Software Testing Education: Promises & Perils. arXiv preprint arXiv:2302.03287. DOI:10.1109/ICSTW58534.2023.00078

Jamshed, A., Dwivedi, A. K., Mehra, P. S., & Dagur, A. (2024). Internet-of-Things-Enabled Networks: Vision Challenges and Smart Applications. *Advances in Computing Communications*, 6, 1–17. DOI:10.2174/9789815049480124060003

Jayaram, U., & Repp, R. (2002). Integrated Real-Time Calibration of Electromagnetic Tracking of User Motions for Engineering Applications in Virtual Environments. *Journal of Mechanical Design*, 124(4), 623–632. DOI:10.1115/1.1517562

Jenefa, L., Sobti, R., Kadyan, J. S., & Nasir, M. A. (2021). Impact of Consumer Intention and New Revolution Towards Online Consumer Buying Behaviour during COVI19. International Research Journal of Management Science & Technology.

Jia, D., Xu, Z., Wang, Y., Ma, R., Jiang, W., Qian, Y., Wang, Q., & Xu, W. (2023). Application of intelligent time series prediction method to dew point forecast. *Electronic Research Archive*, 31(5), 2878–2899. DOI:10.3934/era.2023145

Jiang, D., Dou, W., Vosters, L., Xu, X., Sun, Y., & Tan, T. (2018). Denoising of 3D magnetic resonance images with multi-channel residual learning of convolutional neural network. *Japanese Journal of Radiology*, 36(9), 566–574. DOI:10.1007/s11604-018-0758-8 PMID:29982919

Jiang, X., Hu, Z., Wang, S., & Zhang, Y. (2023). Deep learning for medical image-based cancer diagnosis. *Cancers (Basel)*, 15(14), 3608. DOI:10.3390/cancers15143608 PMID:37509272

Johnson, A. E., Pollard, T. J., Greenbaum, N. R., Lungren, M. P., Deng, C.-y., Peng, Y., . . . Horng, S. (2019). MIMIC-CXR-JPG, a large publicly available database of labeled chest radiographs. *arXiv preprint arXiv:1901.07042*.

Johnson, L. (2020). The Role of AI in Interactive Media Environments. *Journal of Medical Technology*, 11(2), 159–175.

Johnson, W. L. (2023). How to harness generative AI to accelerate human learning. *International Journal of Artificial Intelligence in Education*. Advance online publication. DOI:10.1007/s40593-023-00367-w

Jones, M., & Silver, L. (2022). Artificial Intelligence in Real-Time Media Operations. *Journal of Media Innovations*, 15(2), 34–50.

Jones, R. (2021). Integrating ChatGPT with Augmented Reality/Virtual Reality Systems for Collaborative Design in Engineering. *Proceedings of the International Conference on Virtual, Augmented, and Mixed Reality (VAMR)*.

Jumanov, Karshiev, & Dagur. (n.d.). Synthesis of mechanisms of increasing reliability of information on the basis of the use of redundant of different approaches. Artificial Intelligence and Information Technologies, 421-428.

Jumanov, Safarov, Djumanov, & Dagur. (n.d.). Construction of correctors for distorted image points based on neural networks for micro-object identification. Artificial Intelligence and Information Technologies, 261-266.

Jung, E., Luna, M., & Park, S. H. (2021). *Conditional GAN with an attention-based generator and a 3D discriminator for 3D medical image generation*. Paper presented at the Medical Image Computing and Computer Assisted Intervention–MICCAI 2021: 24th International Conference, Strasbourg, France, September 27–October 1, 2021, Proceedings, Part VI 24. DOI:10.1007/978-3-030-87231-1_31

Jyotiyana, M., & Kesswani, N. (2020). Deep learning and the future of biomedical image analysis. Deep Learning Techniques for Biomedical and Health Informatics, 329-345.

Jyotiyana, M., & Kesswani, N. (2021). A study on deep learning in neurodegenerative diseases and other brain disorders. In Rising Threats in Expert Applications and Solutions: Proceedings of FICR-TEAS 2020 (pp. 791-799). Springer Singapore.

Jyotiyana, M., & Kesswani, N. (2021). Introduction to Deep Learning in Health Informatics. Biomedical Data Mining for Information Retrieval: Methodologies, Techniques and Applications, 237-261.

Jyotiyana, M., Kesswani, N., & Agarwal, A. (2022, January). An improved approach for removal of salt and pepper noise in MR images. Advances in Deep Learning.

Jyotiyana, M., & Kesswani, N. (2020). Classification and prediction of Alzheimer's disease using multi-layer perceptron. *International Journal of Reasoning-based Intelligent Systems*, 12(4), 255–263. DOI:10.1504/IJRIS.2020.111785

Jyotiyana, M., Kesswani, N., & Kumar, M. (2022). A deep learning approach for classification and diagnosis of Parkinson's disease. *Soft Computing*, 26(18), 9155–9165. DOI:10.1007/s00500-022-07275-6

Kadar, T., & Kadar, M. (2020). Sustainability is not enough: Towards AI supported regenerative design. *2020 IEEE International Conference on Technology Management, Operations and Decisions (ICTMOD)*. DOI:10.1109/ICE/ITMC49519.2020.9198554

Kapadiya, D., Shekhawat, C., & Sharma, P. (2023). A study on large scale applications of big data in modern era. In *International Conference on Information Management & Machine Intelligence (ICIMMI2023)*. ACM. https://doi.org/DOI: 10.1145/3647444.364788

Kapadiya, D., Shekhawat, C., & Sharma, P. (2023). A Study on Largescale Applications of Big Data in Modern Era. *Proceedings of the 5th International Conference on Information Management & Machine Intelligence*, 1–6. DOI:10.1145/3647444.3647880

Kasban, H., & El-Bendary, M. A. M., & Salama, D. H. (2015). A comparative study of medical imaging techniques. *International Journal of Information Science and Intelligent System*, 4(2), 37–58.

Kashefi, A., & Mukerji, T. (2023). ChatGPT for Programming Numerical Methods. arXiv. preprint arXiv:2303.12093.

Kasneci, E., Sesler, K., Kuchemann, S., Bannert, M., Dementieva, D., & Fischer, F. (2023). ChatGPT for good? On opportunities and challenges of large language models for education. *Learning and Individual Differences*, 103, 102274. DOI:10.1016/j.lindif.2023.102274

Kaur, D., Uslu, S., Rittichier, K. J., & Durresi, A. (2022). Trustworthy artificial intelligence: A review. *ACM Computing Surveys*, 55(2), 1–38. DOI:10.1145/3491209

Kazeminia, S., Baur, C., Kuijper, A., van Ginneken, B., Navab, N., Albarqouni, S., & Mukhopadhyay, A. (2020). GANs for medical image analysis. *Artificial Intelligence in Medicine*, 109, 101938. DOI:10.1016/j.artmed.2020.101938 PMID:34756215

Key Challenges. (2023). https://www.makeuseof.com/openai-chatgpt-biggest-probelms/

Khan, M. K. H., Guo, W., Liu, J., Dong, F., Li, Z., Patterson, T. A., & Hong, H. (2023). Machine learning and deep learning for brain tumor MRI image segmentation. *Experimental Biology and Medicine*, 248(21), 1974–1992. DOI:10.1177/15353702231214259 PMID:38102956

Kim, M. J., Lee, C. K., & Jung, T. (2018). Exploring Consumer Behavior in Virtual Reality Tourism Using an Extended Stimulus-Organism-Response Model. *Journal of Travel Research*, 59(1), 69–89. DOI:10.1177/0047287518818915

Kim, N., & Kim, W. (2018). Do your social media lead you to make social deal purchases? Consumer-generated social referrals for sales via social commerce. *International Journal of Information Management*, 39, 38–48. DOI:10.1016/j.ijinfomgt.2017.10.006

Kirwan, A. (2023, November 24). ChatGPT and university teaching, learning and assessment: Some initial reflections on teaching academic integrity in the age of Large Language Models. *Irish Educational Studies*, 0(0), 1–18. DOI:10.1080/03323315.2023.2284901

Knorr, M., & Hissbach, J. (2014). Multiple mini-interviews: Same concept, different approaches. *Medical Education*, 48(12), 1157–1175. DOI:10.1111/medu.12535 PMID:25413910

Kong, F., Li, J., Jiang, B., Wang, H., & Song, H. (2021). Integrated generative model for industrial anomaly detection via Bidirectional LSTM and attention mechanism. *IEEE Transactions on Industrial Informatics*, 19(1), 541–550. DOI:10.1109/TII.2021.3078192

Kuhail, M. A., Mathew, S. S., Khalil, A., Berengueres, J., & Shah, S. J. H. (2024). "Will I be replaced?" Assessing ChatGPT's effect on software development and programmer perceptions of AI tools. *Science of Computer Programming*, 235, 103111. DOI:10.1016/j.scico.2024.103111

Kumar, D. A., Nagarajan, D. G., Surekha, D. M., Vijai, D. C., Mohideen, D. A. S., Dhinakaran, D. D. P., & Lakshmi, M. R. (2023). The Impact of Chat GPT on E-commerce. *Harbin Gongcheng Daxue Xuebao/Journal of Harbin Engineering University, 44*(7), Article 7.

Kumar, S. (2017). Palm Recognition in Unconstrained Environments: Challenges and Solutions. *International Symposium on Biometrics Proceedings*, 56–64.

Kumar, S. M., & Manhar, A. (2023). *Sentimental analysis of customer reviews using RPA and categorization of reviews using ChatGPT*. International Journal of Scientific Research in Computer Science, Engineering and Information Technology. DOI:10.32628/CSEIT23903101

Kumar, V., & Shah, D. (2019). AI in Finance and Healthcare: An Analysis of Challenges and Opportunities. *Journal of Business Research*, 100, 245–259.

Kuntze, R., Crudele, T. R., Reynolds, D., & Matulich, E. (2013). The rise and fall of virtual reality retailing in second life: An avatar's perspective. *Journal of Management and Marketing Research*, 13, 1.

Kushwaha, K. P., Dagur, A., & Shukla, D. (2024). HSLE: A Hybrid Ensemble Classifier for Prediction of Heart Disease. Recent Advances in Electrical & Electronic Engineering, 17, 1-12.

Lakkaraju, K., Vuruma, S. K., Pallagani, V., Muppasani, B., & Srivastava, B. (2023). Can LLMs be good financial advisors?: An initial study in personal decision making for optimized outcomes. ArXiv, abs/2307.07422.

Lee, A. (2022). Operational Efficiency in Media: The Impact of AI. *Media Management Review*, 24(1), 112–130.

Lee, K., & Nguyen, T. (2021). Enhancing Audience Engagement through AI: A Study of Algorithmic Personalization. *Media Communication Quarterly*, 18(4), 438–456.

Leong, A. (2023). *ChatGPT just created malware, and that's seriously scary.* Digital Trends.

Li, X. (2019). Mobile Authentication with Palm Recognition: Challenges and Opportunities. Proceedings of the ACM Mobile Computing and Communications Review.

Li, Y. (2020). Scaling Transformers for High-Performance Natural Language Understanding. arXiv preprint arXiv:2010.11929.

Li, B. (2021). Dynamic evaluation and system coordination degree of the integration of artificial intelligence and real economy. *Complexity*, 2021(1), 5539793. Advance online publication. DOI:10.1155/2021/5539793

Lim, J., Leinonen, T., Lipponen, L., Lee, H., DeVita, J., & Murray, D. (2023). Artificial intelligence as relational artifacts in creative learning. *Digital Creativity (Exeter)*, 0(0), 1–19. DOI:10.1080/14626268.2023.2236595

Litman, D. (2016). Natural language processing for enhancing teaching and learning. *Thirtieth AAAI Conference on Artificial Intelligence*. DOI:10.1609/aaai.v30i1.9879

Liu, X., Vatn, J., Yin, S., & Maithani, V. (2023). Performance of ChatGPT on CMRP: Potential for assisting maintenance and reliability professionals using large language models. In 2023 IEEE 49th Annual Conference of the Industrial Electronics Society (IECON). DOI:10.1109/IECON51785.2023.10311736

Liu, Y., Yang, Z., Yu, Z., Liu, Z., Liu, D., Lin, H., Li, M., Ma, S., Avdeev, M. & Shi, S. (2023). Generative artificial intelligence and its applications in materials science: Current situation and future perspectives. Journal of Materiomics.

Li, Y. (2018). Political affairs supermarket—Orientation of transformation of government management. *Proceedings of the 2018 International Conference on Contemporary Education, Social Sciences and Ecological Studies (ICCES 2018)*. DOI:10.25236/iccems.2018.13

Li, Y., Gan, Z., Shen, Y., Liu, J., Cheng, Y., Wu, Y., & Gao, J. (2019). Storygan: A sequential conditional gan for story visualization. *Proceedings of the IEEE/CVF Conference on Computer Vision and Pattern Recognition*. DOI:10.1109/CVPR.2019.00649

Li, Y., Shi, J., & Zhang, Z. (2024). An Approach for Rapid Source Code Development Based on ChatGPT and Prompt Engineering. *IEEE Access : Practical Innovations, Open Solutions*, 12, 53074–53087. DOI:10.1109/ACCESS.2024.3385682

Lohani, Dagur, Arvind, Shukla, & Dhirendra. (2024). An Efficient Approach for Diabetes Classification Using Feature Selection and Hyperparameter Tuning. Recent Advances in Electrical & Electronic Engineering, 17, 1-15.

Luckett, J. (2023). Regulating generative AI: A pathway to ethical and responsible implementation. *International Journal of Computer Informatics*, 12(5), 79–92. Advance online publication. DOI:10.5121/ijci.2023.120508

Lu, M., Gao, S., Yang, X., & Yu, H. (2023). Improving performance of decision threshold moving-based strategies by integrating density-based clustering technique. *Electronic Research Archive*, 31(5), 2501–2518. DOI:10.3934/era.2023127

Mahanty, G., Dwivedi, D. N., & Gopalakrishnan, B. N. (2021). The efficacy of fiscal vs monetary policies in the Asia-Pacific region: The St. Louis equation revisited. *Vision (Basel)*. Advance online publication. DOI:10.1177/09722629211054148

Mahapatra, D., Bozorgtabar, B., & Garnavi, R. (2019). Image super-resolution using progressive generative adversarial networks for medical image analysis. *Computerized Medical Imaging and Graphics*, 71, 30–39. DOI:10.1016/j.compmedimag.2018.10.005 PMID:30472408

Maharajan, K., Kumar, A. V., El Emary, I. M., Sharma, P., Latip, R., Mishra, N., Dutta, A., Manjunatha Rao, L., & Sharma, M. (2023). Blockchain methods and data-driven decision making with autonomous transportation. In Kumar, R., Abdul Hamid, A., & Binti Ya'akub, N. (Eds.), *Effective AI, Blockchain, and E-Governance Applications for Knowledge Discovery and Management* (pp. 176–194). IGI Global. DOI:10.4018/978-1-6684-9151-5.ch012

Makhmadiyarovich, Akbar, Asliddin, Sabharwal, & Dagur. (n.d.). Methods of applying machine learning algorithms for blockchain technologies, Artificial Intelligence and Information Technologies, 232-237

Malhotra, K. (2020). AI in the fashion industry. https://www.prescouter.com/2020/06/ai-in-thefashion-industry/

Mall, P. K., Pramanik, S., Srivastava, S., Faiz, M., Sriramulu, S., & Kumar, M. N. (2023). FuzztNet-Based Modeling Smart Traffic System in Smart Cities Using Deep Learning Models. In *Data-Driven Mathematical Modeling in Smart Cities*. IGI Global. DOI:10.4018/978-1-6684-6408-3.ch005

Manjunath, C., Dwivedi, D. N., Thimmappa, R., & Vedamurthy, K. B. (2023). Detection and categorization of diseases in pearl millet leaves using novel convolutional neural network model. In *Future Farming* (Vol. 1, p. 41). Advancing Agriculture with Artificial Intelligence. DOI:10.2174/9789815124729123010006

Maran, L. J. (2021). Data Analysis on Mobile Payment Technology with Reference to Users' Behaviour of Retail Goods in India. Proceedings of the 2021, 4th International Conference on Computing and Communications Technologies, ICCCT.

Marcus, D. S., Wang, T. H., Parker, J., Csernansky, J. G., Morris, J. C., & Buckner, R. L. (2007). Open Access Series of Imaging Studies (OASIS): Cross-sectional MRI data in young, middle aged, nondemented, and demented older adults. *Journal of Cognitive Neuroscience*, 19(9), 1498–1507. DOI:10.1162/jocn.2007.19.9.1498 PMID:17714011

Mathew, A. (2023). Is artificial intelligence a world changer? A case study of OpenAI's Chat GPT. *Recent Prog. Sci. Technol*, 5, 35–42. DOI:10.9734/bpi/rpst/v5/18240D

McCartney, G., & McCartney, A. (2020). Rise of the machines: Towards a conceptual service-robot research framework for the hospitality and tourism industry. *International Journal of Contemporary Hospitality Management*, 32(12), 3835–3851. DOI:10.1108/IJCHM-05-2020-0450

McDonnell, J. (2019). *Maine's workforce challenges in an age of artificial intelligence.* Maine Policy Review. DOI:10.53558/REUA8661

McGee, R. W. (2023b). Is Chat GPT biased against conservatives? An empirical study. *Empir.Stud.*

McGee, R. W. (2023a). Annie Chan: Three Short Stories Written with Chat GPT. Available at: *SSRN* 4359403.

Meena, G., Choudhary, S., & Choudhary, R. R. (2021). Saliency Detection in Text Documents using Policy-Driven Reinforcement Learning Methodologies. [). IOP Publishing.]. *IOP Conference Series. Materials Science and Engineering*, 1020(1), 012019. DOI:10.1088/1757-899X/1020/1/012019

Merlin Mancy, A., Kumar, A. V., Latip, R., Jagadamba, G., Chakrabarti, P., Sharma, P., Musirin, I. B., Sharma, M., & Kanchan, B. G. (2024). *Smart Healthcare System, Digital Health and Telemedicine, Management and Emergencies: Patient Emergency Application (PES)*. E-Governance Applications. DOI:10.4018/979-8-3693-1722-8.ch008

Miller, R. (2018). *Cognitive Processing in Media and Communication.* Oxford University Press.

Modran, H. A., Chamunorwa, T., Ursu iu, D., & Samoilă, C. (2023, September). Integrating Artificial Intelligence and ChatGPT into Higher Engineering Education. In *International Conference on Interactive Collaborative Learning* (pp. 499-510). Cham: Springer Nature Switzerland.

Montenegro Rueda, M., Fernández-Cerero, J., Fernández-Batanero, J., & López-Meneses, E. (2023). Impact of the implementation of ChatGPT in education: A systematic review. *Computers*, 12(8), 153. DOI:10.3390/computers12080153

Müller-Franzes, G., Niehues, J. M., Khader, F., Arasteh, S. T., Haarburger, C., Kuhl, C., & Nebelung, S. (2023). A multimodal comparison of latent denoising diffusion probabilistic models and generative adversarial networks for medical image synthesis. *Scientific Reports*, 13(1), 12098. DOI:10.1038/s41598-023-39278-0 PMID:37495660

Mundada, S. K. (2019). Optimized deep neural network based predictive model for customer attrition analysis in the banking sector. *Recent Patents on Engineering*, 13, 1–10.

Nah, F. F.-H., Zheng, R., Cai, J., Siau, K., & Chen, L. (2023). Generative AI and ChatGPT: Applications, challenges, and AI-human collaboration. *Journal of Information Technology Case and Application Research*, 25(3), 277–304. DOI:10.1080/15228053.2023.2233814

Naumova, E. N. (2023). A mistake-find exercise: A teacher's tool to engage with information innovations, ChatGPT, and their analogs. J. Publ. Health Pol. 1–6.

Neuendorf, K. A. (2017). *The content analysis guidebook*. Sage Publications. DOI:10.4135/9781071802878

Nguyen, M. (2021). Ethical Considerations in Media AI. *Ethics and Information Technology*, 23(4), 543–556.

Nie, X., Ding, H., Qi, M., Wang, Y., & Wong, E. K. (2021). Urca-gan: Upsample residual channel-wise attention generative adversarial network for image-to-image translation. *Neurocomputing*, 443, 75–84. DOI:10.1016/j.neucom.2021.02.054

Nuritdinov, Kakharov, & Dagur. (n.d.). A new algorithm for finding the Minkowski difference of some sets. Artificial Intelligence and Information Technologies, 142-147.

Oh, S., Jung, Y., Kim, S., Lee, I., & Kang, N. (2019). Deep generative design: Integration of topology optimization and generative models. *Journal of Mechanical Design*, 141(11), 111405. DOI:10.1115/1.4044229

Open, A. I. (2023). OpenAI GPT4. Retrieved from https://openai.com/research/gpt-4

Oprea, S., Martinez-Gonzalez, P., Garcia-Garcia, A., Castro-Vargas, J. A., Orts-Escolano, S., Garcia-Rodriguez, J., & Argyros, A. (2020). A review on deep learning techniques for video prediction. *IEEE Transactions on Pattern Analysis and Machine Intelligence*, 44(6), 2806–2826. DOI:10.1109/TPAMI.2020.3045007 PMID:33320810

Ordano, E., Meilich, A., Jardi, Y., & Araoz, M. (2017). Decentraland: A blockchain-based virtual world. *Journal of Virtual Worlds Research*, 2, 425–446.

Orzoł, M., & Szopik-Depczyńska, K. (2023). ChatGPT as an innovative tool for increasing sales in online stores. *Procedia Computer Science*, 225, 3450–3459. DOI:10.1016/j.procs.2023.10.340

Ouh, E. L., Siew Gan, B. K., Shim, K. J., & Wlodkowski, S. (2023). ChatGPT can you generate solutions for my coding exercises? An evaluation on its effectiveness in an undergraduate Java programming course. In *Proceedings of the 2023 Conference on Innovation and Technology in Computer Science Education* V. 1 *(ITiCSE 2023)* (pp. 54-60). ACM. DOI:10.1145/3587102.3588794

Oussous, A, Benjelloun, F, & Belfkih, S. (2018), Big Data technologies: A survey. Journal of King Saud University - Computer and Information Sciences.

Pandey, B. K., Pandey, D., Nassa, V. K., George, A. S., Pramanik, S., & Dadheech, P. (2023). *Applications for the Text Extraction Method of Complex Degraded Images in The Impact of Thrust Technologies on Image Processing*. Nova Publishers.

Pandey, B. K., Pandey, D., Nassa, V. K., Hameed, A. S., George, A. S., Dadheech, P., & Pramanik, S. (2023). A Review of Various Text Extraction Algorithms for Images. In *The Impact of Thrust Technologies on Image Processing*. Nova Publishers. DOI:10.52305/ATJL4552

Parker, J., Richard, V., & Becker, K. (2023). Flexibility & iteration: Exploring the potential of large language models in developing and refining interview protocols. *The Qualitative Report*, 28(3). Advance online publication. DOI:10.46743/2160-3715/2023.6695

Pasupuleti, R., Vadapalli, R., & Mader, C. (2023). Cyber Security Issues and Challenges Related to Generative AI and ChatGPT. *2023 Tenth International Conference on Social Networks Analysis, Management and Security (SNAMS)*, 1-5. DOI:10.1109/SNAMS60348.2023.10375472

Patil, P., Kulkarni, K., & Sharma, P. (2024). Algorithmic issues, challenges, and theoretical concerns of ChatGPT. In Sharma, P., Jyotiyana, M., & Senthil Kumar, A. V. (Eds.), *Applications, challenges, and the future of ChatGPT* (pp. 56–74). IGI Global. DOI:10.4018/979-8-3693-6824-4.ch003

Patton, M. Q. (2015). *Qualitative research & evaluation methods: Integrating theory and practice* (4th ed.). Sage Publications.

Pinaya, W. H., Graham, M. S., Kerfoot, E., Tudosiu, P.-D., Dafflon, J., Fernandez, V., . . . Patel, A. (2023). Generative ai for medical imaging: extending the monai framework. *arXiv preprint arXiv:2307.15208*.

Pozzi, F. A., & Dwivedi, D. (2023). ESG and IoT: Ensuring sustainability and social responsibility in the digital age. In Tiwari, S., Ortiz-Rodríguez, F., Mishra, S., Vakaj, E., & Kotecha, K. (Eds.), *Artificial Intelligence: Towards Sustainable Intelligence. AI4S 2023. Communications in Computer and Information Science* (Vol. 1907). Springer. DOI:10.1007/978-3-031-47997-7_2

Prasad, G. A. (2023), Artificial Intelligence in Computer Science: An Overview of Current Trends and Future Directions. In S. Rajest, B. Singh, A. Obaid, R. Regin, & K. Chinnusamy (Eds.), *Advances in Artificial and Human Intelligence in the Modern Era* (pp. 43-60),IGI Global.

Prasad, S. G., Sharmila, V. C., & Badrinarayanan, M. K. (2023). Role of artificial intelligence based chat generative pre-trained transformer (ChatGPT) in cyber security. 2023 2nd International Conference on Applied Artificial Intelligence and Computing (ICAAIC), 107-114.

Prasad, G. A., Kumar, A. V., Sharma, P., Irawati, I. D., Musirin, I. B., Abdullah, H. M., & Rao, L. M. (2023). Artificial intelligence in computer science: An overview of current trends and future directions. In Rajest, S., Singh, B., Obaid, A., Regin, R., & Chinnusamy, K. (Eds.), *Advances in Artificial and Human Intelligence in the Modern Era* (pp. 43–60). IGI Global. DOI:10.4018/979-8-3693-1301-5.ch002

Prompt engineering. (n.d.). https://help.openai.com/en/articles/6654000-best-practices-for-promptengineering-with-openai-api

Prompt, G. P. T. (n.d.). https://github.com/promptslab/Awesome-Prompt-Engineering

Radford, A., Metz, L., & Chintala, S. (2015). Unsupervised representation learning with deep convolutional generative adversarial networks. arXiv preprint arXiv:1511.06434.

Radford, A., Narasimhan, K., Salimans, T., & Sutskever, I. (2018). Improving Language Understanding by Generative Pre-training. https://s3-us-west-2.amazonaws.com/openai-assets/research-covers/language-unsupervised/language_understanding_paper.pdf

Radford, A., Wu, J., Child, R., Luan, D., Amodei, D., & Sutskever, I. (2019). Language models are unsupervised multitask learners. *OpenAI blog, 1*(8), 9.

Radford, A., Wu, J., Child, R., Luan, D., Amodei, D., & Sutskever, I. (2019). Language Models are Unsupervised Multitask Learners. OpenAI Blog. Retrieved from https://cdn.openai.com/better-language-models/language_models_are_unsupervised_multitask_learners.pdf

Rahman, M. M., & Watanobe, Y. (2023). ChatGPT for education and research: Opportunities, threats, and strategies. *Applied Sciences (Basel, Switzerland)*, 13(9), 5783. DOI:10.3390/app13095783

Ramanathan, K. (2024a). Redesigning of Marketing Mix Elements Affecting Medical Tourism Through Artificial Intelligence (AI). Reskilling the workforce for Technological Advancement, 222-240.

Ramanathan, K. (2024b). Marketing Ethics: Mediating Influences on Sales Managers' Ethical Decision-making. Proceedings of the 3rd International Conference on Reinventing Business Practices, Start-ups and Sustainability (ICRBSS 2023). Atlantis Press.

Rawat, P., Bhardwaj, A., Lamba, N., Sharma, P., Kumawat, P., & Sharma, P. (2023). Arduino Based IoT Mini Weather Station. *SKIT Research Journal*, 13(2), 34–41. DOI:10.47904/IJSKIT.13.2.2023.34-41

Ray, P. (2023). ChatGPT: A comprehensive review on background, applications, key challenges, bias, ethics, limitations and future scope. *Internet of Things and Cyber-Physical Systems*, 3, 121–154. Advance online publication. DOI:10.1016/j.iotcps.2023.04.003

Rogers, A., Gardner, M., & Augenstein, I. (2023). Qa dataset explosion: A taxonomy of nlp resources for question answering and reading comprehension. *ACM Computing Surveys*, 55(10), 1–45. DOI:10.1145/3560260

Roumeliotis, K. I., Tselikas, N. D., & Nasiopoulos, D. K. (2023). Unveiling Sustainability in Ecommerce: GPT-Powered Software for Identifying Sustainable Product Features. *Sustainability (Basel)*, 15(15), 15. Advance online publication. DOI:10.3390/su151512015

Rudolph, J., Tan, S., & Tan, S. (2023). ChatGPT: Bullshit spewer or the end of traditional assessments in higher education? *J.Appl. Learn. Teach.*, 6(1).

Russell, S., & Norvig, P. (2021). *Artificial intelligence: A modern approach* (4th ed.). Prentice Hall.

Sadiq, M. W., Akhtar, M. W., Huo, C., & Zulfiqar, S. (2024). ChatGPT-powered chatbot as a green evangelist: An innovative path toward sustainable consumerism in E-commerce. *Service Industries Journal*, 44(3–4), 173–217. DOI:10.1080/02642069.2023.2278463

Safdar, N. M., Banja, J. D., & Meltzer, C. C. (2020). Ethical considerations in artificial intelligence. *European Journal of Radiology*, 122, 108768. DOI:10.1016/j.ejrad.2019.108768 PMID:31786504

Sallam, M., Salim, N., Barakat, M., & Al-Tammemi, A. B. (2023). ChatGPT applications in medical, dental, pharmacy, and public health education: A descriptive study highlighting the advantages and limitations. *Narra J*, 3(1), e103. Advance online publication. DOI:10.52225/narra.v3i1.103 PMID:38450035

Sethi, S. S., & Sharma, P. (2023). New developments in the implementation of IoT in agriculture. *SN Computer Science*, 4(5), 503. DOI:10.1007/s42979-023-01896-w

Sethi, S. S., Sharma, P., & Kumar, A. V. (2024). ChatGPT and the moralities of large language modelling in research publications. In Bansal, R., Ngah, A., Chakir, A., & Pruthi, N. (Eds.), *Leveraging ChatGPT and artificial intelligence for effective customer engagement* (pp. 233–258). IGI Global. DOI:10.4018/979-8-3693-0815-8.ch014

Shahsavari, A., Ranjbari, S., & Khatibi, T. (2021). Proposing a novel Cascade Ensemble Super Resolution Generative Adversarial Network (CESR-GAN) method for the reconstruction of super-resolution skin lesion images. *Informatics in Medicine Unlocked*, 24, 100628. DOI:10.1016/j.imu.2021.100628

Shalabaieva, M. (2023). *The dark side of ChatGPT: Manipulation, misinformation, and malicious intent*. Artificial Intelligence in Plain English.

Sharma, P. (2023). Utilizing explainable artificial intelligence to address deep learning in biomedical domain. In *Medical Data Analysis and Processing using Explainable Artificial Intelligence* (pp. 19–38). Taylor & Francis. DOI:10.1201/9781003257721-2

Sharma, P., & Bhatnagar, N. (2023). Passenger authentication and ticket verification at airport using QR code scanner. *SKIT Research Journal*, 13(2), 10–13. DOI:10.47904/IJSKIT.13.1.2023.10-12

Sharma, P., & Dadheech, P. (2023). Modern-age agriculture with artificial intelligence: A review emphasizing crop yield prediction. *EVERGREEN Joint Journal of Novel Carbon Resource Sciences & Green Asia Strategy*, 10(4), 2570–2582. DOI:10.5109/7160906

Sharma, P., Dadheech, P., Aneja, N., & Aneja, S. (2023). Predicting agriculture yields based on machine learning using regression and deep learning. *IEEE Access : Practical Innovations, Open Solutions*, 11, 111255–111264. DOI:10.1109/ACCESS.2023.3321861

Sharma, P., Dadheech, P., & Senthil Kumar, A. V. (2023). AI-enabled crop recommendation system based on soil and weather patterns. In Gupta, R., Jain, A., Wang, J., Bharti, S., & Patel, S. (Eds.), *Artificial Intelligence Tools and Technologies for Smart Farming and Agriculture Practices* (pp. 184–199). IGI Global. DOI:10.4018/978-1-6684-8516-3.ch010

Sharma, P., & Jain, M. K. (2023). Stock market trends analysis using extreme gradient boosting (XGBoost). In *Proceedings of the 2023 International Conference on Computing, Communication, and Intelligent Systems (ICCCIS)* (pp. 317-322). IEEE. DOI:10.1109/ICCCIS60361.2023.10425722

Sharma, P., Kapadiya, D., & Bhardwaj, A. (2023). Efficient note sharing model for collaborative learning. *SKIT Research Journal*, 13(2), 42–46. DOI:10.47904/IJSKIT.13.2.2023.42-46

Sharma, P., & Rathi, Y. (2016). Efficient density-based clustering using automatic parameter detection. In *Efficient Density-Based Clustering Using Automatic Parameter Detection* (pp. 1–14). Springer. DOI:10.1007/978-981-10-0767-5_46

Sharma, P., Sharma, C., & Mathur, P. (2023). Machine learning-based stock market forecasting using recurrent neural network. In *Proceedings of the 2023 9th International Conference on Smart Computing and Communications (ICSCC)* (pp. 600-605). IEEE. DOI:10.1109/ICSCC59169.2023.10335083

Sharma, S., & Yadav, R. (2022). ChatGPT–A technological remedy or challenge for education system. *Global Journal of Enterprise Information System*, 14(4), 46–51. DOI:10.18311/gjeis/2022/30895

Sherzodjon, Fayzullo, Shaxnoza, & Dagur. (n.d.). Real estate valuation based on Feedforward neural networks. Artificial Intelligence and Information Technologies, 226-231

Shin, H.-C., Tenenholtz, N. A., Rogers, J. K., Schwarz, C. G., Senjem, M. L., Gunter, J. L., . . . Michalski, M. (2018). *Medical image synthesis for data augmentation and anonymization using generative adversarial networks.* Paper presented at the Simulation and Synthesis in Medical Imaging: Third International Workshop, SASHIMI 2018, Held in Conjunction with MICCAI 2018, Granada, Spain, September 16, 2018, Proceedings 3. DOI:10.1007/978-3-030-00536-8_1

Shneiderman, B. (2000, March). Creating creativity: User interfaces for supporting innovation. *ACM Transactions on Computer-Human Interaction*, 7(1), 114–138. DOI:10.1145/344949.345077

Silver, D., Huang, A., Maddison, C., Guez, A., Sifre, L., van den Driessche, G., Schrittwieser, J., Antonoglou, I., Panneershelvam, V., Lanctot, M., Dieleman, S., Grewe, D., Nham, J., Kalchbrenner, N., Sutskever, I., Lillicrap, T., Leach, M., Kavukcuoglu, K., Graepel, T., & Hassabis, D. (2016). Mastering the game of Go with deep neural networks and tree search. *Nature*, 529(7587), 484–489. DOI:10.1038/nature16961 PMID:26819042

Singh, D., & Taqa, A. (2023). *ChatGPT: A New Approach to Revolutionise Organisations*. Academic Press.

Singhal, Ali, Shukla, Dagur, Awasthy, & Tiwari. (n.d.). ROCK-HYRAX: An Energy Efficient Job scheduling using Cluster of Resources in Cloud Computing Environment. Cluster Computing, The Journal of Networks, Software Tools and Applications.

Singh, J., Samborowski, L., & Mentzer, K. (2023). A Human Collaboration with ChatGPT: Developing Case Studies with Generative AI. In *Proceedings of the ISCAP Conference ISSN* (Vol. 2473, p. 4901).

Smith, J. (2022). Impact of ChatGPT on Workforce Dynamics in Engineering: A Case Study. Journal of Engineering Management.

Smith, J. (2021). Digital Transformation in Media: An Overview. *Journal of Digital Media & Policy*, 12(1), 77–94.

Smith, J., & Davenport, T. (2022). ChatGPT and Real-Time Communication: Applications in Media. *Digital Media Research Journal*, 14(3), 400–416.

Sun, B. (2022). *Methodology and application of GAN algorithms.* Paper presented at the International Conference on Computer Graphics, Artificial Intelligence, and Data Processing (ICCAID 2021).

Surameery, N.M.S., & Shakor, M.Y. (2023). Use chat GPT to solve programming bugs. Int. J. Inf. Technol. Comput. Eng., 3(1), 17–22.

Susnjak, T. (2023). Beyond predictive learning analytics modelling and onto explainable artificial intelligence with prescriptive analytics and ChatGPT. *International Journal of Artificial Intelligence in Education.*

Suzuki, K. (2017). Overview of deep learning in medical imaging. *Radiological Physics and Technology*, 10(3), 257–273. DOI:10.1007/s12194-017-0406-5 PMID:28689314

Tan, S. (2016). A Survey of Palmprint Recognition. *Proceedings of the International Conference on Pattern Recognition*, 120–133.

Tanwar, A., Sharma, P., Pandey, A., & Kumar, S. (2023). Intrusion Detection System Based Ameliorated Technique of Pattern Matching. In *Proceedings of the 4th International Conference on Information Management & Machine Intelligence (ICIMMI '22).* Association for Computing Machinery.

Tanwar, P., Sharma, A., & Pandey, S., & Kumar. (2023). Intrusion detection system based ameliorated technique of pattern matching. In *Proceedings of the 4th International Conference on Information Management & Machine Intelligence (ICIMMI '22)* (Article 110, pp. 1–4). Association for Computing Machinery. DOI:10.1145/3590837.3590947

Taylor, P. (2019). Challenges in Implementing AI in Media Environments. *Technology and Media Management Journal*, 6(3), 202–218.

Taylor, P., & Francis, G. (2021). AI and Journalism: Integration, Impact and Integrity. *Journal of Digital Ethics*, 7(1), 88–104.

Thrall, J. H., Li, X., Li, Q., Cruz, C., Do, S., Dreyer, K., & Brink, J. (2018). Artificial intelligence and machine learning in radiology: Opportunities, challenges, pitfalls, and criteria for success. *Journal of the American College of Radiology*, 15(3), 504–508. DOI:10.1016/j.jacr.2017.12.026 PMID:29402533

Thrun, S., & Anderson, C. (2018). The new era of artificial intelligence in education. *AI Magazine*, 39(2), 26–40.

Tian, C., Xu, Z., Wang, L., & Liu, Y. (2023). Arc fault detection using artificial intelligence: Challenges and benefits. *Mathematical Biosciences and Engineering*, 20(7), 12404–12432. DOI:10.3934/mbe.2023552 PMID:37501448

Tlili, B., Shehata, M., Agyemang Adarkwah, A., Bozkurt, D., Hickey, T., & Huang, R. (2023). What if the devil is my guardian angel: ChatGPT as a case study of using chatbots in education. *Smart Learning Environments, 10*(1).

Tsigaris, P., & Teixeira da Silva, J. A. (2023). Can chatgpt be trusted to provide reliable estimates? *Accountability in Research*, 1–3. Advance online publication. DOI:10.1080/08989621.2023.2179919 PMID:36786391

Tug, M. A., & Basar, P. (2023). *Future of the gig economy*. Pressacademia., DOI:10.17261/Pressacademia.2023.1796

Umer, H., & Khan, M. S. (2023). ChatGPT in finance: Addressing ethical challenges. SSRN Electronic Journal. DOI:10.2139/ssrn.4433171

V., M. V., Kumar, A. S., Sharma, P., Kaur, S., Saleh, O. S., Chennamma, H., & Chaturvedi, A. (2023). AI-equipped IoT applications in high-tech agriculture using machine learning. In A. Khang (Ed.), *Handbook of Research on AI-Equipped IoT Applications in High-Tech Agriculture* (pp. 38-64). IGI Global. DOI:10.4018/978-1-6684-9231-4.ch003

Vaerst, T., Steffens, T., & Lokaiczyk, R. (2015). Concerns management, e-government and e-participation: Experiences and findings from Germany. *International Journal of E-Planning Research*, 4(4), 47–60. DOI:10.4018/ijepr.2015100103 van de Watering, G., & van der Rijt, J. (2006). Teachers' and students' perceptions of assessments: A review and a study into the ability and accuracy of estimating the difficulty levels of assessment items. *Educational Research Review*, 1(2), 133–147. DOI:10.1016/j.edurev.2006.05.001

Vaswani, A., Shazeer, N., Parmar, N., Uszkoreit, J., Jones, L., Gomez, A. N., Kaiser, Ł., & Polosukhin, I. (2017). Attention is all you need. In Advances in neural information processing systems, 30 (pp. 5998-6008).

Velásquez, J. (n.d.). ChatGPT's and Large Language Models Influence on Research, Technology, and Education: A Comprehensive Co-Word Analysis. *Technology, and Education: A Comprehensive Co-Word Analysis*.

Venket, K., Ambika, A., Freeda, A., Palla, V., Biju, J., & Shankar, Y. (2023). AI-based pandemic safe venues for effectively managing people crowds to avoid further pandemic waves. *AIP Conference Proceedings*, 2963, 020022. DOI:10.1063/5.0184379

Verbeek, P.-P. (2011). *Moralizing Technology: Understanding and Designing the Morality of Things*. University of Chicago Press. DOI:10.7208/chicago/9780226852904.001.0001

Verma, N. (2013). Open data for inclusive governance. *ACM International Conference Proceeding Series*. DOI:10.1145/2516911.2516913

Wang, W., Luo, J., Yang, X., & Lin, H. (2015). Data analysis of the lung imaging database consortium and image database resource initiative. *Academic Radiology*, 22(4), 488–495. DOI:10.1016/j.acra.2014.12.004 PMID:25601306

Wauters, K., Desmet, P., & Van Den Noortgate, W. (2010). Adaptive item-based learning environments based on the item response theory: Possibilities and challenges. *Journal of Computer Assisted Learning*, 26(6), 549–562. DOI:10.1111/j.1365-2729.2010.00368.x

Wenzlaff, K., & Spaeth, S. (2022). Smarter than humans? Validating how OpenAI's ChatGPT model explains crowdfunding, alternative finance, and community finance. SSRN Electronic Journal. DOI:10.2139/ssrn.4302443

West, A., Clifford, J., & Atkinson, D. (2018). "Alexa, build me a brand": An investigation into the impact of artificial intelligence on branding. *The Business & Management Review*, 9(3), 321–330.

Wierenga, B., & Van Bruggen, G. (2000), Marketing Management Support systems. In Springer eBooks DOI:10.1007/978-1-4615-4595-8

Wolf, T., Debut, L., Sanh, V., Chaumond, J., Delangue, C., Moi, A., & Rush, A. M. (2020, October). Transformers: State-of-the-art natural language processing. In *Proceedings of the 2020 conference on empirical methods in natural language processing: system demonstrations* (pp. 38-45).

Wollny, S., Schneider, J., Di Mitri, D., Weidlich, J., Rittberger, M., & Drachsler, H. (2021). Are we there yet? A systematic literature review on chatbots in education. *Frontiers in Artificial Intelligence*, 4, 1–18. DOI:10.3389/frai.2021.654924 PMID:34337392

Wolterink, J. M., Leiner, T., Viergever, M. A., & Išgum, I. (2017). Generative adversarial networks for noise reduction in low-dose CT. *IEEE Transactions on Medical Imaging*, 36(12), 2536–2545. DOI:10.1109/TMI.2017.2708987 PMID:28574346

Wooldridge, M. (2018). Artificial intelligence: The impact on engineering. *Communications of the ACM*, 61(10), 46–53.

Wu, Duan, & Ni. (2023). Unveiling security, privacy, and ethical concerns of ChatGPT. Journal of Information and Intelligence.

Wu, S., Irsoy, O., Lu, S., Dabravolski, V., Dredze, M., Gehrmann, S., Kambadur, P., Rosenberg, D., & Mann, G. (2023). BloombergGPT: A large language model for finance. ArXiv, abs/2303.17564.

Xiao, F., Zhao, P., Sha, H., Yang, D., & Warschauer, M. (2023). Conversational agents in language learning. *Journal of China Computer-Assisted Language Learning*. Advance online publication. DOI:10.1515/jccall-2022-0032

Xu, F., Nguyen, T., & Du, J. (2024). Augmented Reality for Maintenance Tasks with ChatGPT for Automated Text-to-Action. *Journal of Construction Engineering and Management*, 150(4), 04024015. DOI:10.1061/JCEMD4.COENG-14142

Xu, J., Zhang, X., Li, H., Yoo, C., & Pan, Y. (2023). Is everyone an artist? A study on user experience of AI-based painting system. *Applied Sciences (Basel, Switzerland)*, 13(11), 6496. DOI:10.3390/app13116496

Xu, L. (2019). PalmPrint Recognition in Real-World Surveillance. *Journal of Surveillance and Security*, 26(4), 567–581.

Yao, K., Su, Z., Huang, K., Yang, X., Sun, J., Hussain, A., & Coenen, F. (2022). A novel 3D unsupervised domain adaptation framework for cross-modality medical image segmentation. *IEEE Journal of Biomedical and Health Informatics*, 26(10), 4976–4986. DOI:10.1109/JBHI.2022.3162118 PMID:35324451

Zaremba, A., & Demir, E. (2023). ChatGPT: Unlocking the future of NLP in finance. *SSRN* 4323643.

Zhai, X. (2022). ChatGPT user experience: Implications for education. SSRN *Electronic Journal*. DOI:10.2139/ssrn.4312418

Zhang, H.-M., & Dong, B. (2020). A review on deep learning in medical image reconstruction. *Journal of the Operations Research Society of China*, 8(2), 311–340. DOI:10.1007/s40305-019-00287-4

Zhang, L., & Wallace, B. (2020). AI Applications in Editorial and News Operations. *Journal of Computational Journalism*, 5(1), 34–50.

Zhang, Y., Yin, Y., Zimmermann, R., Wang, G., Varadarajan, J., & Ng, S.-K. (2020). An enhanced gan model for automatic satellite-to-map image conversion. *IEEE Access : Practical Innovations, Open Solutions*, 8, 176704–176716. DOI:10.1109/ACCESS.2020.3025008

Zhao, J., & Lv, Y. (2023). Output-feedback robust tracking control of uncertain systems via adaptive learning. *International Journal of Control, Automation, and Systems*, 21(4), 1108–1118. DOI:10.1007/s12555-021-0882-6

Zhao, Z., Song, R., Zhang, Q., Duan, P., & Zhang, Y. (2022). JoT-GAN: A framework for jointly training GAN and person re-identification model. *ACM Transactions on Multimedia Computing Communications and Applications*, 18(1s), 1–18. DOI:10.1145/3491225

Zhou, C., Li, Q., Li, C., Yu, J., Liu, Y., Wang, G., . . . Zhang, K. (2023). A Comprehensive Survey on Pretrained Foundation Models: A History from Bert to ChatGPT. arXiv preprint arXiv:2302.09419.

Zhuo, T. Y., Huang, Y., Chen, C., & Xing, Z. (2023). Exploring AI Ethics of ChatGPT: A Diagnostic Analysis. arXiv preprint: arXiv:2301.12867.

Zielnicki, K. (2019). *Simulacra and Selection: Clothing Set Recommendation at Stitch Fix*. ACM. DOI:10.1145/3331184.3331442

About the Contributors

Priyanka Sharma is working as an Assistant Professor in the department of Computer Science & Engineering, Swami Keshvanand Institute of Technology, Management & Gramothan, Jaipur, Rajasthan, India. She has received her B.Tech. degree from Rajasthan Technical University, Kota, Rajasthan India, in 2012 in Information Technology and M.Tech. degree from Rajasthan Technical University, Kota, Rajasthan India, in 2016 in Computer Science. She is pursuing her doctorate from Rajasthan Technical University, Kota, Rajasthan India. She has 11+ years of teaching and academic experience. She has guided various M.Tech. research scholars. She is member of IEEE, ACM and various professional societies. Her Research interests are: Machine Learning, Deep learning, Data Mining.

Monika Jyotiyana received her Ph.D. and Masters's degrees from the Central University of Rajasthan in 2023 and 2012 respectively. She received her bachelor's degree from Aryan International College, affiliated to M.D.S. University, in 2010. She was UGC-JRF from July 2015–2017 and UGC-SRF from July 2017–2020 at Central University of Rajasthan. She has teaching experience at various reputed universities, including the Central University of Rajasthan, Lovely Professional University, and Manipal University Jaipur. Her research areas are machine learning, deep learning, artificial intelligence, and image processing. She has published various conference proceedings, journal publications, book chapters, and books. She is on the reviewers' board of reputed journals and various prestigious conferences.

A. V. Senthil Kumar is working as a Director & Professor in the Department of Research and PG in Computer Applications, Hindusthan College of Arts and Science, Coimbatore. He has finished is Doctor of Science during February 2023. He has more than 26 years of teaching experience and 5 years of Industry experience. He has to his credit 30 Book Chapters, 220 papers in International and National Journals, 55 papers in International and National Conferences, and 10 edited books and 2 text books. He is an Editor-in-Chief for various journals. Key Member for India, Machine Intelligence Research Lab (MIR Labs).He is Associate Editor of IEEE Access. He is the first person in South India to receive the highest degree in academic field D.Sc in Computer Science.

* * *

Anju A. received M.E. degree in Computer Science Engineering from Sathyabama University, Chennai, India. She is having immense teaching and research experience of about 14 years. Since July 2013, she has been working as an Assistant professor in KCG College of Technology, Chennai, India. Her research area is on Network Security, Cyber Security, Machine Learning and Evolutionary Algorithms.

Sridhar Devarajan is currently working as Assistant Professor in Dr. Vishwanath Karad MIT World Peace University, Pune. He has received Ph.D. from Bharathiar University in 2019 and qualified the National Eligibility Test (NET) in Computer Science and Applications in 2019. He also completed his Master of Computer Applications and Master of Philosophy in Computer Science from Bharathiar University in 2009 & 2013. He has rich blend of 14 years of teaching experience at postgraduate and undergraduate levels. His areas research includes Social Media Mining, Machine Learning and Natural Language Processing. He has published 3 Books & 23 research articles in prominent journals and presented his work in various national and international conferences. My teaching philosophy revolves around fostering critical thinking, problem-solving skills, and a curiosity-driven approach to learning, preparing students for the dynamic tech landscape.

Dwijendra Nath Dwivedi is a professional with 20+ years of subject matter expertise creating right value propositions for analytics and AI. He currently heads the EMEA+AP AI and IoT team at SAS, a worldwide frontrunner in AI technology. He is a post-Graduate in Economics from Indira Gandhi Institute of Development and Research and currently perusing PHD from crackow university of economics Poland. He has presented his research in more than 20 international conference and published several Scopus indexed paper on AI adoption in many areas. As an author he has contributed to more than 8 books and has more than 25 publications in high impact journals. He conducts AI Value seminars and workshops for the executive audience and for power users.

Adline Freeda has 18 years of teaching experience and she has received the B.E Degree and M.E in Computer Science and engineering and pursuing Ph.D. in Computer science and engineering from Hindustan Institute of Technology & Science, Tamil Nadu, India. Her current research interests include Machine learning, Software Engineering and Cloud Computing. . She is a Life Member of Computer Society of India. And published research papers in International Journals.

Vishal Jain is presently working as an Associate Professor at Department of Computer Science and Engineering, School of Engineering and Technology, Sharda University, Greater Noida, U. P. India. Before that, he has worked for several years as an Associate Professor at Bharati Vidyapeeth's Institute of Computer Applications and Management (BVICAM), New Delhi. He has more than 15 years of experience in the academics. He obtained Ph.D (CSE), M.Tech (CSE), MBA (HR), MCA, MCP and CCNA. He has authored more than 100 research papers in reputed conferences and journals, including Web of Science and Scopus. He has authored and edited more than 45 books with various reputed publishers, including Elsevier, Springer, IET, Apple Academic Press, CRC, Taylor and Francis Group, Scrivener, Wiley, Emerald, NOVA Science, IGI-Global and River Publishers. His research areas include information retrieval, semantic web, ontology engineering, data mining, ad hoc networks, and sensor networks. He received a Young Active Member Award for the year 2012–13 from the Computer Society of India, Best Faculty Award for the year 2017 and Best Researcher Award for the year 2019 from BVICAM, New Delhi.

Sujith Jayaprakash is currently the Head of NIIT in Accra, Ghana.

Leena Jenefa is working as an Associate Professor in Hindustan Institute of Technology and Science. She worked in Vel Tech Rangarajan Dr Sagunthala R&D Institute of Science and Technology, Avadi, Chennai. She is having 22 years of experience in the teaching field. Prior to joining to Vel Tech -Chennai, she worked in Tecnia Institute of Advanced Studies-Delhi, DMI- St. Eugene University-Zambia, Linton University affiliated to University of East London-Malaysia

Namita Mishra is having in depth association with education and research and projects. She completed her post graduate in Commerce from Fakir Mohan University, Odisha, MBA from MDU, Rohtak with specialization in Finance and acquired Doctorate degree from Jamia Millia Islamia University,New Delhi. She have 28 Research papers and have participated and convened various conferences/ Seminars. Professionally she engaged as teaching staff to business students in post graduate programmes in Finance and Accounting streams, also associated with School of open learning, University of Delhi as resource person . She is a life member of Indian Commerce Association and CEGR.

Archan Mitra is an Assistant Professor at School of Media Studies (SOMS) at Presidency University, Bangalore. He is the author of two book "Cases for Classroom Media and Entertainment Business" and "Multiverse and Media", he also has other several edited books to his credit. He has done his doctorate from Visva-Bharati Santiniketan, West Bengal in the field of "environmental informatics and communication for sustainability". In addition to that he is a certified Science Communicator and Journalism from Indian Science Communication Society (ISCOS), certified Corporate Trainer with Amity Institute of Training and Development, Certified Social Media Network Analyst. He has a strong interest in environmental communication. He was awarded certificate of merit by PRSI, Kolkata Chapter and Medal of Honor by Journalistic Club of Kolkata. He was working as a research assistant with the World Bank's "Environmental Capacity Building in Southeast Asia" project at IIM Kashipur. He was instrumental in launching the World Bank's Green MBA MOOC, he has also assisted in the research project on Uttarakhand disaster mitigation by ICSSR, the leading research on Uttarakhand disaster.

Sabyasachi Pramanik is a professional IEEE member. He obtained a PhD in Computer Science and Engineering from Sri Satya Sai University of Technology and Medical Sciences, Bhopal, India. Presently, he is an Associate Professor, Department of Computer Science and Engineering, Haldia Institute of Technology, India. He has many publications in various reputed international conferences, journals, and book chapters (Indexed by SCIE, Scopus, ESCI, etc). He is doing research in the fields of Artificial Intelligence, Data Privacy, Cybersecurity, Network Security, and Machine Learning. He also serves on the editorial boards of several international journals. He is a reviewer of journal articles from IEEE, Springer, Elsevier, Inderscience, IET and IGI Global. He has reviewed many conference papers, has been a keynote speaker, session chair, and technical program committee member at many international conferences. He has authored a book on Wireless Sensor Network. He has edited 8 books from IGI Global, CRC Press, Springer and Wiley Publications.

Vishnu Prasath V. is studying MBA in second year, published in Hindustan Institute of Technology and Science, Padur, Chennai, India.

Preeti Rai is an Experienced Professor with a demonstrated history of working in the education management industry. Skilled in Deep learning, Machine Learning, Teaching, Higher Education, and Education. Strong education professional with a PhD in Computer Science and Engineering focused in Computer Science from Indian Institute of Information Technology, Design and Manufacturing, Jabalpur.

Karuppasamy Ramanathan is M.Com., MBA.,M.Phil.,Ph.D.,PLME(IIM A) Dean, School of Management, Hindustan university, Chennai General Secretary, Global Society of HSE Professionals Secretary, Rotary Club of Coimbatore City (2018-19, 2019-20) Secretary, LEAD Researchers Forum Dr. Karuppasamy Ramanathan has four years of industrial experience with Cipla Ltd., Mumbai and twenty years of rich teaching experience with Thiagarajar College, Madurai and leading Business Schools in Coimbatore. He has received a Gold Medal for his academic excellence in his master degree from Ayya Nadar Janaki Ammal College (Madurai Kamaraj University). He is an alumni member of Indian Institute of Management, Ahmadabad. Dr.Samy has presented 163 research papers in various Inter-national & National Conferences, published 14 text books (including Intellectual Property Rights & Airport Management) and 65 research articles in various referred National and International Journals with impact factors. He has organized 12 Management Development Programmes (MDP's), 26 Faculty Development Programmes (FDP's), five Leadership Camps and six international level Conferences. He has also produced six Ph.D scholars and six M.Phil Scholars. He is serving as Editor in Two international Journals and also reviewer for 13 journals related to Finance and Marketing.

Gokuldev S. has more than 18+ years of academic, research and administrative experiences, served in various engineering colleges, technical Universities, Arts and Science colleges in and around Tamilnadu and Karnataka with various academic positions. Currently serving as Professor in the Department of Computer Science, Rathinam College of Arts and Science, Coimbatore and also associated with iNurture Education Solution, Bangalore as Zonal Head (South) – IT Academics. He has authored more than 25 publications in reputed International journals and more than 15 publications in National and International Conferences. He has been an active member in several professional bodies such as IEEE, CSI, IAENG, CSTA, IACSIT etc. and served as the reviewer for few reputed journals of IEEE, EAI Endorsed Journals, Springer – Publons, PLOS ONE, Inderscience Journal / IJICT, ETRI Journal etc. He has been the Session Chair and Panelist in several International Conferences.

Devaraju Sellappan received the B.Sc degree in Chemistry in 1997 from the University of Madras, Chennai, and the M.C.A. degree in Computer Applications in 2001 from the Periyar University, Salem, and the M.Phil. degree in Computer Science in 2004 from Periyar University, Salem and also received M.B.A. degree in Human Resource from Madurai Kamaraj University, Madurai in 2007. He received Ph.D degree in Computer Applications from Anna University, Chennai in 2017. Dr.S.Devaraju has 20+ years of teaching experience and 2 years industry experience. He is an Senior Assistant Professor, School of Computing Science and Engineering (SCSE), VIT Bhopal University, Sehore, Madhya Pradesh, India. Dr.S.Devaraju has published 7 patents, 8 Book Chapters and Reviewer for various reputed Journals and Conferences. He has published more than 50+ papers in international journals and conference proceedings. His area of research includes Network Security, Intrusion Detection, Soft Computing, and Wireless Communication.

Jawahar Sundaram is a passionate Assistant Professor with 13+ years of experience administering education and classroom procedures both autonomously and in collaboration with department faculty and leaders. Building foundations for the next generation of academics and workforce pioneers.

Krithikaa Venket received the bachelor's and master's degrees in Information Technology from Dr.Sivanthi Aditanar College of Engineering. She is currently a Assistant Professor of Information Technology at KCG College of Technology, Chennai. Her research interests include data mining and pattern recognition, Artificial Intelligence, machine learning and deep learning.

Index

www.ingramcontent.com/pod-product-compliance
Lightning Source LLC
LaVergne TN
LVHW061546290926
849162LV00004B/920